Autopia

Autopia Cars and Culture

Edited by Peter Wollen and Joe Kerr

REAKTION BOOKS

Published by Reaktion Books Ltd
79 Farringdon Road, London EC1M 3JU, UK

www.reaktionbooks.co.uk

First published 2002

Printed and bound in Hong Kong

British Library Cataloguing in Publication Data

Autopia: Cars and Culture
        1.Automobiles – Social Aspects 2.Culture
        I. Wollen, Peter, 1938– II. Kerr, Joe
        303.4'832

ISBN 1 86189 132 6

Contents

Introduction: Cars and Culture   10
PETER WOLLEN

Thematic Introductions
JOE KERR

CARS IN CULTURE   21

Automobiles and Art   25
PETER WOLLEN

Accidents: The Car and Literature   50
ALLEN SAMUELS

No Particular Place to Go   59
PATRICK FIELD

Crossroads: The Automobile, Rock and Roll
and Democracy   65
E. L. WIDMER

Vanishing Points   75
DAVID PASCOE

Moving Spaces   83
A. L. REES

Blood on the Nash Ambassador:
Cars in American Films   95
ERIC MOTTRAM

CARS AND CAPITAL   115

Trouble in Motor City   125
JOE KERR

Some Thoughts on Car Culture in Japan   139
DONALD RICHIE

Technik   147
DIRK LEACH

Riding the Survivors of the Soviet Union   153
MICHAEL R. LEAMAN

Our Cars in Havana   169
VIVIANA NAROTZKY

Engines of Revolution:
Car Cultures in China   177
GEREMIE R. BARMÉ

The Lada: A Cultural Icon   191
PETER HAMILTON

Automobile Metempsychoses in the
Land of Dracula   199
ADRIAN OŢOIU

The Ambassador from India   209
ZIAUDDIN SARDAR

Dangerous but Irrepressible: Cars and Driving
in Post-Apartheid South Africa   219
CATHERINE ADDISON

Automonster   227
CHRISTOPHER PINNEY

MOTOR SPACES 233

Robert Moses: The Expressway World 244
MARSHALL BERMAN

Driving the American Landscape 249
ANDREW CROSS

Erosion of Cities or Attrition of Automobiles 259
JANE JACOBS

The Asphalt Exodus 266
JANE HOLTZ KAY

L.A. Freeway: An Appreciative Essay 277
DAVID BRODSLY

Pleasure and the Motorway 281
RICHARD J. WILLIAMS

Fade to Grey: Motorways and Monotony 288
MICHAEL BRACEWELL

Roundabouts and Yellow Lines 293
MARC AUGÉ

Traffic 296
IAN PARKER

Come Together 307
SANDY McCREERY

Squealing Wheels and Flying Fists 312
JACK SARGEANT

Motopia: Cities, Cars and Architecture 315
MURRAY FRASER & JOE KERR

MYTHS AND MOTORS 327

The Birth of the Automobile 337
ILYA EHRENBURG

The New Citroën 340
ROLAND BARTHES

Sexual Ambiguity and Automotive Engineering 342
PATRICK KEILLER

America's Love Affair with the Automobile
in the Television Age 354
KARAL ANN MARLING

Men, Motors, Markets and Women 363
GRACE LEES-MAFFEI

The Downfall of the Dymaxion Car 371
MARTIN PAWLEY

References 379
Bibliography 389
Contributors 393
Acknowledgements 395
Photographic Acknowledgements 396
Index 397

Cars and Culture

PETER WOLLEN

Writing about the automobile back in 1986, J. G. Ballard posed the question: 'Autopia or Autogeddon?' On the one hand, there is an enthusiasm for the motorcar which is now more than a hundred years old, while on the other hand, there is a growing fear of the automobile's dark side – car crashes, road rage, congestion, environmental damage, oil slicks, urban sprawl, gridlock, car bombs and many other scourges. As Ballard also pointed out, the automobile is still based upon a nineteenth-century technology – the internal-combustion engine. As James J. Flink notes in his fine book *The Automobile Age*, it was a New Yorker, Stuart Perry, who first patented two-cycle versions of the internal-compulsion engine, in 1844 and 1846, followed by Etienne Lenoir, a Belgian mechanic, in 1860. Lenoir's engine was innovative in its use of a battery-powered electric spark plug to ignite the fuel mixture of aerated illuminating gas. It was also the first to succeed commercially. In 1876, in Germany, Nicolaus Otto produced a four-cycle engine, its fuel-air mixture compressed within a cylinder and with consecutive intake, compression, power and exhaust strokes. Not much has changed since then.

By 1885, one of Otto's engineers, Gottlieb Daimler, working with an assistant, Wilhelm Maybach, had developed an automobile engine that proved to be the prototype of an enduring system. Daimler and Maybach built four experimental motor vehicles between 1885 and 1889, while Carl Benz, a manufac-

turer of gas engines, built a working motor tricycle, driven in the streets of Mannheim and patented in 1886. In 1893, Maybach invented the modern carburetor, and in the same year, Benz produced a commercially successful four-wheel car, with a redesigned engine and electric ignition. Automobile manufacture quickly became a growth industry,

Carl Benz and his 1880s motor tricycle.

developing in a number of countries in Europe and in the US. This is the technology which, though improved, has not been radically reconceived since the pioneer years. The design and appearance of cars, however, have been transformed repeatedly. Designers such as Harley Earl, at General Motors, or George Walker, at Ford, transposed our image of the car from the functional into the aesthetic register, creating an eye-catching new model each year.

However, while the design and appearance of the car may have become increasingly significant, it was the car as a creature of the internal-combustion engine which has had the most wide-ranging impact, resulting from the proliferation of side effects – roads and associated construction work, parking lots and structures, rising oil prices, geopolitical rivalries, broad-ranging environmental issues, industrial manufacturing, lifestyles, marketing, population movements, congestion, the growth of suburbia, increased levels of travel and tourism, patterns of crime, the epidemiology of violence and death. It is not so much a matter of drawing up a kind of balance sheet, assessing the pros and cons of the automobile as a social and cultural force, as of trying to understand the complex ways in which the car has transformed our everyday life and the environment in which we operate – the food we eat, the music we listen to, the risks we take, the places we visit, the errands we run, the emotions we feel, the movies we watch, the money we spend, the stress we endure and the air we breathe. At the same time, we need to recognize that car culture is not simply something personal to us, but a complex global phenomenon. Cars have a different significance in rich and poor countries, rural and urban areas, and so on.

It is striking to see how easily cars can become cult objects at both ends of the automobile spectrum –

James Dean in his new Porsche 550 Spyder, 1955.

The James Dean crash site, September, 1955.

Togliattigrad and Pitjantjatjara, the aging Moskvich and the Toyota Landcruiser, Mondeo Man and Mr Toad, *Kraftwerk* and *Thelma and Louise*, Andy Warhol and T. S. Eliot, Monument Valley and The Little Chef, Marshall McLuhan and Ralph Nader, the freeway and the parking structure, the seatbelt and the flamboyant U-turn – all of which are discussed in this volume. Reading about the BMW cult of the wa-Benzi in South Africa, I was reminded of the BMW cult of the Billionaire Boys' Club in Los Angeles. Reading about styrofoam cups of takeaway coffee, I couldn't help thinking about the cascading geysers of wasted champagne with which Grand Prix drivers celebrate a victory. Reading about James Dean and Princess Diana, I couldn't help thinking about all the anonymous victims of hit-and-run drivers. The universality of automobile culture seems capable of dredging almost anything into its net, from the idyllic view of the buttes of the American West framed within a windshield to the murderous rollover of the aircraft-inspired, tail-heavy, nose-up Dymaxion car.

A word needs to be said here about parking, a sadly neglected subject. In 1916, an editorial in *Automobile* magazine noted that the 'parking problem' was becoming more and more acute with the growth of automobile traffic. Not only did city governments face 'something which was never foreseen in the planning of our towns, a thing which has come upon us so swiftly that there has been no time to grasp the immensity of the problem till we are almost overcome by it', but their preferred policy of raising taxes to build new roads, together with creating more parking facilities and introducing new regulations, simply discriminated against the poor and, specifically, against children. In 1937, the Lynds, in their classic study *Middletown in Transition*, noted that, in 1925, 'youngsters, driven from street play to the sidewalks, were protesting, "Where can I play?". But in 1935 they were retreating even from the sidewalks.' In 1961, Jane Jacobs, in *The Death and Life of Great American Cities*, documented the last stages of the disintegration of community life as streets were widened, sidewalks narrowed and communal activities funnelled out of neighbourhoods. It was the pedestrian poor of the inner city whose energies were sapped by the arrival of the car while suburbia thrived.

Detroit, of course, provided a laboratory model of this kind of social polarization and segregation, as Joe Kerr has argued. Motorization also, as James J. Flink notes in *The Automobile Age* (1988), 'profoundly changed the character of the small town'. Flink cites the example of Ogle County, Illinois, which in 1900 had 79 horse-related service facilities and no automobile-related ones. By 1930, the proportions had been completely reversed – there were 86 automobile-related businesses and only 21 horse-related ones. At the same time, shopping habits began to change as car use widened the range of choice, so that local stores began to decline. The village store and local bank are cited by Flink as particularly vulnerable. The giant mail-order houses – Sears Roebuck and Montgomery Ward – began to reduce their catalogue businesses and open stores on the outskirts of towns, in direct competition with traditional businesses. Instead of transportation systems that funnelled potential consumers into town and city centres, people were now at liberty to shop in new locations on the outskirts of towns.

Flink quotes Robert E. Wood, who had been general merchandise manager for Montgomery Ward before becoming vice president of Sears Roebuck, as explaining that, 'when the automobile reached the masses it changed this condition [the funnelling of consumers into the town centre] and made shopping mobile. In the great cities Sears located its stores well outside the main shopping districts, on cheap land, usually on arterial highways, with ample parking space.' Thus city centres came to be seen as sites of congestion, whereas the periphery was regarded as accessible and convenient. The first regional shopping mall was built in Kansas City, Missouri, in 1922, while the first shopping centre, 'planned as a unified commercial development with its stores turned away from the access street', was built in Dallas, Texas, in 1931. By the 1950s, similar shopping centres were providing parking space for several thousand cars. Meanwhile, as Flink notes, 'with the rapid proliferation of such shopping centres in the 1950s and 1960s, the downtowns of medium-sized cities came to be crime-ridden wastelands of vacated stores.' Villages no longer boasted traditional stores, instead containing petrol stations, garages, restaurants and inns, whose focus was on transients in their cars.

Moreover, the rise of the family car as a household necessity also led to destabilizing changes in family structure. In particular, teenagers now demanded access to the car, and intergenerational squabbles began to disturb family life, undermining parental authority and supervision. The Lynds pointed out that

. . . the extensive use of this new tool by the young has enormously extended their mobility and the range of alternatives before them; joining a crowd motoring over to a dance in a town twenty miles away may be a matter of a moment's decision, with no one's permission asked.

Moreover, the car itself became the site of choice for romantic interludes and sexual adventures. Small-town values were rapidly being eroded. In the end, this new and shocking state of affairs gradually became normalized. The small California town of Modesto boasts a bronze statue representing a teenage girl sitting on the hood of a car while a young man makes up to her. It was commissioned in recognition of George Lucas's success as a filmmaker – a classic example of local boy made good – a success story that began with his landmark car and cruising movie, *American Graffiti*, shot right there in his hometown.

The Cruise, a statue of two teenagers on a '57 Chevrolet in George Lucas's hometown, Modesto, California.

The soundtrack of *America Graffiti* comes straight from the car radio, a selection of music played by the radio station's charismatic disc jockey, Wolfman Jack. A similar range of contemporary music can also be found in *Easy Rider* or *Thieves Like Us*. In *A Star*

A lobby card for George Lucas's 1973 film *American Graffiti*.

Is Born, the music comes from a motel radio and in *Detour* and *Natural Born Killers* from the jukebox in a diner. The car radio and the roadside juke joint have taken over the role of the traditional symphonic score, substituting a medley of rock'n'roll songs, thereby bridging the gap between characters and spectators with familiar music, listened to simultaneously both on and off screen. Prior to *American Graffiti*, the typical road movies had always ended with death – unlike Lucas's film, which ends with its central character (a stand-in for the director himself) leaving town to go to college, another way of escaping the confinement of small-town life. Classic road movies feature a couple on the run, driving desperately across America in a crazy attempt to make it to somewhere far down the road – *You Only Live Once, They Live by Night, Gun Crazy, Pierrot Le Fou, Bonnie and Clyde, Thieves Like Us, Badlands, The Passenger, Thelma and Louise* – and end with disaster and the couple torn apart. The car is often doomed as well – spinning out of control, driven into the sea or over a cliff, crashed, shot up, the victim of a kind of ritual sacrifice.

The crashed car features not only in films but in novels. In J. G. Ballard's *Crash* (1973), for instance, there is Vaughan's last crash, the one in which he finally dies, as the out-of-control car jumps over the railings of a flyover, plunging through the roof of a bus filled with airline passengers as it drives to Heathrow. This was a crash, Ballard notes, that produced a massive tailgate. Quite unexpectedly, traffic is also invoked by Ballard in his essay 'In the Asylum of Dreams', where he remarks that 'Freud's royal road to the unconscious soon proved itself prone to delays and diversions, and by now is safely ensnarled in the traffic of rival theorists.' Freud himself, sadly, never wrote about cars, although he did have something to say about both fear of lifts and fear of trains, from which he suffered himself.

The remarkable Hungarian-born psychoanalyst Michael Balint, however, had much of relevance to say, although he too avoided mentioning cars as such. Cars were subsumed into more general topics. In his book *Thrills and Regressions* (1959), Balint wrote about the condition which he called 'Philobatism' – the enjoyment of thrills. An important category of thrills, Balint noted, are those connected with high speed, a category that explicitly includes motor racing. In more general terms, however, thrills are related to motility and the psychology of movement, a subject barely touched upon before Balint turned his mind to it. In fact, he himself remarked that he 'was surprised to find how little is known about the psychology of movement. What we know about it are its disturbances . . .' He noted, however, that Freud, in his *Three Essays on Sexuality* (1905), mentioned the excitement created by both passive and active movement – 'in the form of being rocked and swinging on the one hand, romping, wrestling, getting wild on the other'. Driving, it seems to me, might fall into either of these categories – either subordination to the movement of the automobile or speeding and reckless driving.

On the run: Ridley Scott's 1991 film *Thelma and Louise*.

Balint, however, was interested in the kind of relationship which movement – or, in this particular case, driving – might have to object-relationships and to people's relations with their environment.

Balint divided the world between ocnophiles and philobats. Ocnophiles feel uneasy at the prospect of aggression – which would include aggressive driving – and are inhibited by the trauma brought about by unusually intense movement. As a result, Balint noted, they have difficulty in acquiring the minimal skills required to enjoy the 'thrill' that driving might otherwise offer. The philobat, in contrast, is ready to acquire whatever skills are necessary 'to ride on all the machines' offered in the fairground or simply available for driving on the road. As Balint put it, '. . . his enjoyment is obvious and open' – he is a Mr Toad – 'and this hides the price he has to pay for it' – his inability to relate to others, his restriction to finding enjoyment and excitement in his own personal activities. Balint also pointed out that philobats have a particular relationship to the tools they use in pursuit of excitement and thrills. They assume complete control of equipment, in contrast to ocnophiles, whose tendency is to hold the wheel tight. The philobat is confident that he can cope with all the other drivers who intrude on the blissfully empty space in which he prefers to operate. His world is structured 'by safe distance and sight' – spatial features – rather than by physical proximity and touch or grip, as in the world of the ocnophile.

The philobat, Balint also observed, always aims to master whatever task he undertakes so completely and with such ease 'that the skill should no longer require any effort'. Thus the driver should drive almost automatically. Reality – the reality of traffic or the speedway – thus changes 'into a kind of fairyland where things happen as desired', as if automatically. Philobats aspire to a kind of 'effortless accomplishment which we admire in figure-skaters, in dancers, in actors, musicians, high-board divers, and so on', which we ourselves, in deference to our philobatic dreams, hope to achieve in our own limited sphere of, say, driving a car. The philobat becomes a kind of hero – he himself 'assesses the risks he can and dare take and devise methods of coping with them' without guidance from others. Similarly, the 'high-speed driver' relies 'much more on his own resources than the ordinary driver, although he too is also dependent on others, such as the mechanics who service his car'. The philobat inevitably 'exposes himself apparently unnecessarily to real dangers in the search for thrills', although, as Balint noted, this recklessness is likely to be diminished by the professional philobat – or driver – who earns his living by accepting serious risks.

The philobat operates in a world that is generally safe and friendly. It is only in special circumstances that danger is unavoidable – when, for instance, a driver has to avoid hazardous contacts with other drivers whose behaviour is unpredictable. As Balint noted, 'whereas the ocnophile', driving slowly and hugging the kerb, lives in 'a world structured by physical proximity and touch', the philobatic world, dependent on sight, is threatened principally by 'the sudden emergence of a hazardous object that has to be negotiated', a task that presupposes a certain level of acquired skill, even an ability to take calculated risks, which might appear reckless to others. The philobat – the daring driver – lives in the illusion that it is within his power to overcome any obstacle, that 'he can certainly cope with any situation', tending towards an undue optimism and confidence, perhaps trusting too much in his own skill. The philobat, dependent on sight, needs to watch. As Balint

observed, 'he watches for objects appearing from somewhere or nowhere', objects that are felt perhaps as uncaring, even as hostile, 'disturbing the harmony of the friendly expanses around him', watching all the time for signs of danger.

For J. G. Ballard, the driver of a car exists within a 'huge metallized dream', a communal dream predicated on 'our sense of speed, drama and aggression, the worlds of advertising and consumer goods, engineering and mass manufacture, and the shared experience of moving together through an elaborately signalled landscape'. Ballard foresees a world in which motorways will become the dominant feature of the landscape, in which our addiction to driving will lead to an ever-growing overload of traffic, counterposed to the creation of car-free zones in the centre of our towns and cities, pedestrianized enclaves in which walking replaces driving, human locomotion replaces mechanical, sauntering replaces speeding. At the same time, the culture of the car is a culture of death, a culture in which accidents and crashes become increasingly frequent, even – in a sinister and perhaps unconscious way – desired, the products of aggressivity and self-punishment compounded, the excitement of speed and the acceptance of disaster. For Ballard, there was a way out – driving would be dehumanized, cars would be electronically controlled, traffic movement determined by electronic devices, traffic flow determined by electronic signals transmitted through metal strips embedded in the road.

In his book *Sex, Drink and Fast Cars* (1986), Stephen Bayley has a slightly different vision of the driverless car. He envisages a 'zero-defect, driverless car' based upon advances in electronics, distance sensors, satellite navigation and, presumably, digital technology. A vehicle of this kind could presumably be programmed in advance by the driver, while retaining a capacity for independent decision-making in situations of unforeseen emergency. Bayley ends up with a sceptical view of the zero-defect driverless car, arguing that 'like people, cars have to be flawed to be interesting'. Erotic fantasy, he notes, is more important than technology – although, as Ballard would surely have pointed out, the two can be combined to great effect. Bayley notes that the car promises entry into a fantasy world, which can be positively erotic, as exciting as sex, and also a degree of freedom and dynamism, incompatible with digital programming or laid-back comfort. The Futurists were right, he implies, to stress speed and fantasy and even danger as crucial characteristics of a successful car. Every driver dreams of the 'perfect sweep through a difficult turn' or the 'rapid-fire tattoo' of a series of gear changes.

In this vision of a world to come, the nineteenth-century technology of the car will finally encounter the new technology of the digital age. Driving will be controlled by a computer rather than by human agency and choice. Indeed, the steering wheel itself will become obsolete, the governing feature of the car being the navigational instrument which provides for the driver 'both the greatest freedom and the greatest dangers'. The driver will become just another passenger, strapped into a fully automated vehicle, relaxed within his or her mobile cocoon. There will be no more crashes, except those caused by computer malfunction, no more ambulances weaving through the traffic, no more police officers examining the scene, no more tow-trucks scavenging the wreckage. The culture of the car has always been poised between the mechanical and the anatomical, the machine and the human subject, a complex relationship mediated and protected by speed limits, seatbelts, lane discipline, laceration-resistant windshields, stricter

enforcement of drinking-and-driving laws, better traffic-system design and so on. The end result, of course, will be to make driving safer for ocnophiles, more frustrating for philobats.

In contrast, Ballard's *Crash*, published in 1973, draws on the cult status of death-dealing celebrity car crashes – Jackson Pollock's 1950 Oldsmobile convertible, crashed in 1950; James Dean's Porsche 550 Spyder, crashed in 1955; George Lucas's Fiat Bianchina, crashed in 1962, although Lucas was lucky enough to survive. In *Concrete Island*, published the same year, Ballard describes a car crash on the very first page, the car veering across lanes, jerking the driver's hands 'like a puppet's'. Inevitably, cars are associated with death, not simply because of crashes but, in more general terms, because of the possibility of crashes, the possibility of loss of control and even loss of life. Dean and Lucas were both fascinated by car racing, and, of course, the racetrack is the most dangerous driving environment there is. In his film *The Crowd Roars*, Howard Hawks concentrates on the eerie symbiosis between drivers and spectators, the implicit contract that exists between them, a contract to risk death on the one hand and to expect it on the other. Hawks himself was obsessed with flying planes. He also founded his own motorcycle club, whose members – mostly film stars – went cruising in a pack along Mulholland Drive in Los Angeles.

The crash is irretrievably established at the centre of car culture. As long ago as 1914 the Futurist poet Mario Leone wrote his 'Fornication of Automobiles', envisaging the collision of two cars as a kind of technological sexual encounter:

> Involuntary collision,
> furious fornication
> of two automobiles – energy,

embrace of two warriors
bold of movement,
syncopation of two heart motors,
spilling of 'blood-gas'.

Decades later, in 1960, the American artist Jim Dine produced his 'Happening', *Car Crash*, which was soon followed by Andy Warhol's 'Car Crash' series, with its gruesome *Five Deaths Twice*. In 1967 came Godard's film *Week-end*, with its massive bumper-to-bumper pile-up, which was followed by Ballard's *Crash*, the basis for David Cronenberg's film.

In Henry Ford's book *My Life And Work* (1922), there is a chapter with the anxiety-provoking title 'The Terror of the Machine'. It turns out to contain Ford's thoughts on the assembly line. The 'terror' is caused not by cars themselves but by the Ford factory production line. The chapter begins with the following words:

. . . repetitive labour – the doing of one thing over and over again – is a terrifying prospect to a certain kind of mind. It is terrifying to me. I could not possibly do the same thing day in and day out, but to other minds, perhaps I might say to the majority of minds, repetitive operations hold no terrors.

Most jobs, Ford points out, are repetitive. In any case, the average worker does not want a job which demands thought. In similar vein, Ford explains that he did not expect customers to buy cars for pleasure, but for utility: 'We did not make the pleasure appeal. We never have. In its first advertising we showed that a motor car was a utility.' Plus 'the investment of an extremely moderate sum in the purchase of a perfected, high-grade efficient automobile would cut out anxiety and unpunctuality and provide a luxurious mode of travel ever at your beck and call'.

First and foremost, cars saved time, and, of course, by saving time, they also saved money. Furthermore, a car would contribute to your health. It would carry you 'jarlessly' over 'any kind of half decent roads', it would refresh your brain with 'the luxury of much "out-doorness"' and your lungs with the '"tonic of tonics", the right kind of atmosphere'. And yet, while you might like 'to linger through shady avenues', you could also 'press down on the foot-lever until all the scenery looks alike to you and you have to keep your eyes skinned to count the mile-stones as they pass' – the Mr Toad approach to motoring, so to speak. Ford began with the Model A, a car designed for use, following it up with the Model B, a four-cylinder touring car. To advertise the Model B, he entered it in races and set up attempts to break speed records. He himself drove the 'Arrow' on a straight 1-mile course over ice. The ice turned out to be 'seamed with fissures', but Ford went ahead with his time trial. 'At every fissure the car leaped into the air. I never knew how it was coming down. When I wasn't in the air, I was skidding, but somehow I stayed top side up and on the course, making a record that went all over the world.'

Many years later, the Ford roadster became the car of choice for American hot-rodders and dragsters. As Henry Flood Roberts has noted, hot-rodding began in the 1930s when groups of racers would meet in the parking lots of drive-in restaurants or rendezvous at 'some little-used section of a straight, flat road'. They would close off the road, mark off a measured stretch for racing, and risk losing their cars if they lost the race. Eventually, the dry lake beds of the Mojave Desert became the favoured location for racing, especially Lake Muroc, now the site of Edwards Airforce Base. In fact, appropriately enough, it was over Lake Muroc that Chuck Yeager broke the sound barrier in 1947. There seems to be some strange connection

Pile-up: Jean-Luc Godard's 1967 film *Week-end*.

machine that saved time for the bosses by avoiding the need for lunch breaks. Chaplin's own first car was a seven-passenger Locomobile, which he bought as soon as he saw it, much to the surprise of the salesman, who asked: 'Wouldn't you like to see the engine?' To which Chaplin replied, 'Wouldn't make any difference. I know nothing about them.' However, always the mime, he could not resist pressing a tyre with his thumb 'to show a professional touch'.

between speed and deserts, similar to that between speed and ice. As 'jets and rocket-planes were taking over the air', 'belly-tankers' and 'lakesters' were taking over the lake beds, 'little aluminum bullets' travelling at over 200 mph, with bodies made from aircraft fuel tanks, streamlined, rear-engined and with low-slung cockpits for their drivers. By 1957, there were 130 drag strips in 40 American states, with 100,000 hot rods and 2,500,000 spectators.

Hot-rodding in Los Angeles went hand in hand with customizing and decorating cars, which transformed them, not simply into stylish objects, but into artworks in their own right. There was a strange kind of synergy between the automobile and the moving picture, a meeting of two kinetic systems, machines in motion and pictures in motion. In the early days of cinema, Mack Sennett made his films of car chases, and Charlie Chaplin made *Kid Auto Races at Venice*, one of the first of his pictures for Keystone. Later, Chaplin would make *Modern Times*, a masterpiece of combined farce and social criticism set in a factory equipped with an assembly-line modelled on the Ford factory in Detroit, together with a feeding

In *Modern Times*, Chaplin satirizes and caricatures the Ford assembly line. In his fascinating book *Technik* (1986), Dirk Leach is even more devastating in his portrait of life in the Volkswagen factory, describing himself moving repeatedly through his cycle of tasks, yet somehow managing to read – Heidegger, no less – in the gap between the departure of one car down the line and the arrival of another. What struck me most about the Volkswagen factory when I went on the guided tour they offer to visitors was that the workers moved from one place to another on bicycles. Leach, in contrast, had to walk a mile from the parking lot to his place on the assembly line. In the course of his journey, however, he was passed one day by a cyclist pedalling energetically, the chain making a clicking sound as it was gripped by the turning sprocket. He found himself imagining 'steel teeth in gums of black grease, turning in a circle'. What struck me about this odd fantasy was the way in which the bicycle could be envisaged as a strange species of living creature, clicking and gripping and even masticating. The bicycle rider is like the human half of a centaur, the bicycle like its equine legs and body, galloping in response to its rider's wishes. While the car digests its driver, the bicycle is driven by its rider's power.

At this point, I should confess that I was brought up in a family that never owned a car. We cycled or used public transport or even walked. I don't think that this was because of any particular animosity towards cars. If anything, it reflected a vein of conservatism hidden away somewhere in my parents' otherwise radical view of the world. I think they still saw the car as a luxury good and recoiled against it out of a Franciscan belief in the virtue of poverty. Later, when I was a student, I would hitch-hike from Oxford down to London and back again, becoming a kind of parasite on the automobile, spending many hours standing by the roadside at Hanger Lane with my thumb pointing hopefully skywards. Looking back on those days, I am surprised that hitchhiking proved to be a viable means of travel. Partly, this was because of the generosity of drivers, an uninhibited streak of altruism that somehow surfaced at the sight of that upraised thumb. And partly, I think, it was because of the loneliness of the long-distance driver, encased within his shell, with nothing to occupy his thoughts other than the road and the traffic. The single driver felt a deep need for conversation. It was a way of passing the time, shortening the journey by human interaction, freeing oneself from the prison cell of the car.

One final confession – I now live in Los Angeles, world capital of the automobile, renowned for the scale and complexity of its freeway system, the city of valet parking and 'right on red'. Only yesterday, we drove back up the 401 freeway from San Diego, making good use of the 'diamond lane', the outside lane available only to 'carpools', which are defined as cars with a passenger load of two or more, including the driver. The purpose of the diamond lane was to reduce the overwhelming flow of traffic, clogging even a seven-lane highway, by encouraging a significant number of potential drivers to become passengers, at least for a short while. Traffic flow is everything, monitored by helicopters and reported round the clock on television. Recently, Los Angeles embarked on a rail system and a metro, but the impact on freeway traffic seems to be minimal. Moreover, the cars themselves are getting bigger, with SUV's (Sports Utility Vehicles) dominating the road, like petrol-driven dens or lounges, equipped with television screens, coffee-cup holders and satellite location systems. Our car is a Volvo stick-shift station wagon with 208,000 miles on the clock. I still prefer walking or calling Beverly Hills Cabs. Autopia? I think not.

CARS IN CULTURE

The magnificence of the world has been enriched by a new beauty,
the beauty of speed.[1]

F. T. MARINETTI

For avant-garde movements of the early twentieth century, eager to identify the correct means of expression for a new age, the rapidly evolving motorcar provided a highly seductive source of inspiration and imagery. While the realities of mechanized warfare soon provided a cautionary balance to the unbridled and uncritical enthusiasm of the Futurists (and indeed killed a good number of them), it was in the 1920s that the car became established as the essential industrial icon of the Modern movement.

In a much-reproduced spread in Le Corbusier's seminal text *Vers une architecture*, motorcars are compared to ancient Greek temples in order to demonstrate architecture's failure to reflect Modernity:

> Let us display, then, the Parthenon and the motor-car so that it may be clear that it is a question of two products of selection in different fields, one of which has reached its climax and the other is evolving. That ennobles the motor car. And what then? Well, then it remains to use the motor-car as a challenge to our houses and our great buildings. It is here that we come to a dead stop. 'Rien ne va plus.' Here we have no Parthenons.[2]

Both Marinetti and Le Corbusier wrote of a moment of enlightenment in which they came to realize the true power of the automobile, but it was the Mexican muralist Diego Rivera who articulated the car's transformative potential most vividly, when a commission to paint a mural in the Detroit Institute of Arts – America's 'Motor City' – exposed him to the sublime spectacle of car manufacturing:

Previous page: Allan Kaprow, *Yard,* 1961, environment with tyres, installation for a Happening.

I walked for miles through the immense workshops of the Ford, Chrysler, Edison, Michigan Alkali, and Parke-Davis plants. I was afire with enthusiasm. My childhood passion for mechanical toys had been transmuted to a delight in machinery for its own sake and for its meaning to man – his self-fulfilment and liberation from drudgery and poverty. That is why now I placed the collective hero, man-and-machine, higher than the old traditional heroes of art and legend. I felt that in the society of the future as already, to some extent, that of the present, man-and-machine would be as important as air, water, and the light of the sun.[3]

But however enthusiastically the car might be embraced as the epitome of Modernity, there was still the troublesome problem for artists and designers of how to represent its essential qualities of exhilarating motion and speed in a static medium. For Le Corbusier, one solution was to appropriate the car's dynamism through association: a sporty car appears in the foreground of many of his iconic designs. Other architects resorted to the crude device of applying the forms of streamlined vehicles to houses, factories and cinemas. Ultimately, though, it fell to the cinema – an exact contemporary – to explore the cultural potential of the motor vehicle. It is no coincidence that the nostalgic evocation of a golden age for both motoring and movie-going covers the same period: mid-century.

The image of the car as the embodiment of Modernity has proved as unsustainable as Modernism itself. In cultural terms, it has proved far simpler to represent the automobile in terms of its malignant effects on society. Indeed, it is the 'problem' of cars and traffic that now dominates the concerns of architects, artists and filmmakers alike. The priority for the new Autopia is to learn how to accommodate the car in our existing environments rather than to sacrifice those environments in pursuit of an outmoded ideal.

Mario Sironi, *Fiat 1900, c.* 1952, oil on canvas.

Automobiles and Art

PETER WOLLEN

The year 1893, in which both Henry Ford and Karl Benz constructed their first four-wheel cars, is also the year generally acknowledged as that in which Art Nouveau first made its appearance. (Benz had built the first single-cylinder engine in 1885, the year of Cézanne's *Mont Sainte-Victoire*). Both Leonardo da Vinci and Albrecht Dürer had envisaged proto-automobiles in the late fifteenth and early sixteenth centuries, as demonstrated by Leonardo's design for a spring-driven horseless wagon, dated *circa* 1478, and Dürer's woodblock of a triumphal car mechanically propelled by a system of hand-driven cog-wheels, dated from before 1526. These proto-automobiles do little more than establish curious precedents for the interest shown by twentieth-century artists in the charismatic charm of new machinery and technology and, more precisely, in the design and look of cars. In 1896, only three years after Benz and Ford made their breakthroughs, Toulouse-Lautrec produced his lithograph *The Automobilist*, depicting a capped and goggled figure, hands firmly clenched on a steering-wheel handle and a gear lever.

A little later, probably in 1900, Jules Chéret produced an Art Nouveau poster for 'Benzo-Moteur, Essence spéciale pour Automobiles' and, around the same time, Paul Gervais produced the lost painting *Fright* – reproduced in 1904 as the frontispiece to Filson Young's *The Complete Motorist* – showing nymphs and centaurs fleeing in terror as a car with blazing headlights approaches them along a winding coastal road. It was the Italian Futurists, however, who

Henri Toulouse-Lautrec, *The Automobilist*, 1896, lithograph.

first hailed the car as a subject for the avant-garde artist. Umberto Boccioni had painted a speeding automobilist outstripping a fox hunt as early as 1901. Then, as Futurism crystallized into a movement, Luigi painted *Dynamism of an Automobile* (1906) and Giacomo Balla produced such works as *Abstract Speed* and *Cars+Light+Sound*, a stylized geometrical representation of driving at night with shards of light cutting through the dark. Around the same time, Balla also worked on a series of sketches of moving automobiles, with superimposed wheels in forceful serpentine patterns. Marinetti himself composed images of speed and dynamism in the typographic layout of his poems, *Zang Tumb Tumb* and *Speeding Automobile*.

Above: Luigi Russolo, *Dynamism of an Automobile,* 1912/13, oil on canvas.

Left: Giacomo Balla, *Abstract Speed*, 1913, oil on canvas.

For the Futurists, the car symbolized speed, noise and power, attributes that were the foundation for an aesthetic of dynamism and modernity. The contemporary automobile, Marinetti claimed, was more beautiful than the ancient Greek *Winged Victory of Samothrace*. Thus the motor vehicle became not only a functional means of transport but an artwork in itself. The automobile engineer became an artist, and, conversely, the artist became an engineer. According to Gerald Silk, writing in the catalogue to Pontus Hulten's 1986 exhibition *Futurismo and Futurismi*, Balla painted a speeding automobile as subject in more than a hundred works. In this view of the world, cars were not so much functional objects as emblems of a new modernity, a new stage in social development, which quickly veered towards militarism and fascism. The Futurist aesthetic spread rapidly throughout Europe, eventually merging with another new trend elaborated by artists across the Continent, that of *Amerikanismus*. These artists looked to New York as the new beacon of modernity, with its skyscrapers and, of course, its automobiles. Oskar Schlemmer, working at the Bauhaus, observed that 'the artistic climate here cannot support anything that is not the latest, the most modern, up-to-the-minute, dadaism, circus, variety, jazz, hectic pace, movies, America, airplanes, the automobile.'[1]

Expatriate artists soon introduced the new European aesthetic into the New York art world. Joseph Stella, for instance, had seen the exhibition of Futurist art presented at the Bernheim-Jeune Gallery in Paris in 1912 and exhibited work clearly influenced by Futurism at the Armory Show in New York the following year. By 1915, Francis Picabia and Marcel Duchamp were both in America. Picabia, in particular, was fascinated by speeding automobiles, noting that

... almost immediately upon coming to America it flashed on me that the genius of the modern world is machinery and that through machinery art ought to find a more vivid expression ... the machine has become more than a mere adjunct of human life. It is really a part of human life – perhaps the very soul.[2]

In New York, he concentrated on his machine drawings – more specifically, his drawings of automobile parts, including his 1915 self-portrait, *Holy of Holies* (featuring cylinder, horn, valve spring and camshaft as sculptural forms), one of a set that also included the portrait of a young woman as a spark plug, presumably ready to ignite the carburettor of passion. Duchamp (who had already painted a cubist *Two People and a Car* in 1912) now produced *The Large Glass*, a work full of references to automobile technology – gasoline, magneto, motor, gears and so on. In a different vein, Henri Matisse painted *La Route de Villacablay* (1917), inspired by an automobile journey he had taken the previous year. Soon afterwards, Sonia Delaunay painted cars themselves, both a Voisin and a Talbot, with her own Simultanéist colour scheme. In retrospect, this can be seen as a crucial turning point in the relationship of art and the automobile; it is the very first example of customization (implying a personal relationship between artist and car) that I have been able to trace. Rather than being the subject of a painting which would then be looked at in a gallery or home, the car itself was transformed into an artwork, to be looked at as an art object in its own right. Moreover, Delaunay's aestheticization of the car was analogous to her aestheticization of the female body through her work

Top: Sonia Delaunay, matching clothes and car design, 1920s.
Above: Georges Lepape, front cover design for *Vogue*, 1924.

The Farmer Takes a Ride, a print from a series by Norman Rockwell commissioned by Ford as part of their 50th anniversary advertising campaign in 1953.

as a fashion designer. The car was dressed.

However, most of the representations of cars by artists in the 1920s and '30s continued to be shaped by an interest in the technological aspects of modernity. During the same period, architects had also begun to design visionary motor vehicles, such as Frank Lloyd Wright's Cantilever Car of 1920; Jeanneret and Le Corbusier's 'Voiture minimum', developed between 1928 and 1936; Adolf Loos's sketches, in 1923, of a proposed car for Lancia;

Norman Bel Geddes's streamlined cars of the early 1930s and Buckminster Fuller's 1933 Dymaxion car. Artists, like architects, were interested in the powerful geometrical forms which typified modernity – the curvilinear forms of the racetrack and of the streamlined racing car in Moholy Nagy's *Pneumatik* (1927), the oblate form of the windshield mirror in Stuart Davis's 1932 gouache with that title. Unlike the Futurists, who were obsessed with speed and power as abstract ideas, artists of the next generation, following

Picabia, Duchamp or Fernand Léger, were fascinated by mechanical parts, the anatomy of the car, stripping it down as Renaissance artists had stripped down the human body. The car was envisaged as a robotic being, both mechanical and human, as in Duchamp's *The Bride Stripped Bare by Her Bachelors, Even*.

Cars, of course, were indeed assemblages of parts, and inevitably the assembly line itself became a matter of interest to artists. The most remarkable work from the '30s was Diego Rivera's mural painting of the Ford factory in Detroit, commissioned by the Ford family, which covers all four walls of a garden court at the Detroit Institute of Arts. This interior landscape is dominated by imagery of the assembly line, the gigantic fender-stamping press and the spindle machines for reaming the valve ports of the V8 engine block. Rivera envisaged these huge machine forms as analogues to the great statue of the god Coatlicue at Tenochtitlán or the rows of pillars at the Toltec site of Tula, monuments of his native Mexico. Thus they combined, as Rivera explained, the 'tremendous plastic beauty' of the factory with the beauty of the pre-Columbian sculptures he had left behind. He saw Ford's River Rouge factory as a monument – a modern rather than an ancient monument – which demonstrated the energy and power of the Americas: 'Here it is – the might, the power, the energy, the sadness, the glory, the youthfulness of our lands.'[3]

Alfaro Siqueiros, Rivera's rival as leader of the Mexican mural movement, was also fascinated by cars. It was Siqueiros who first introduced Jackson Pollock, a student in his New York workshop, to the idea that industrial paints could and should be used

Diego Rivera, *Edsel B. Ford*, 1931, oil on canvas.

by artists. Siqueiros favoured paint-sprays and industrial paints such as Duco, a nitro-cellulose synthetic originally developed for automobiles, applied to panels rather than to traditional canvases. He believed that artworks should be viewed as industrial products, and artists as workers. Once again, there was an implied move towards customization, not in the decoration of cars as such, but in the simulating of the industrial application of paint to panel. During the 1920s, car production – and ownership – had almost tripled. Then, in 1925, the General Motors sales committee voted on a paper entitled 'Annual Models versus Constant Improvement', favouring annual models, voting for novelty rather than the status quo. Each year, there would be a new GM model looking different from the last. As Stephen Bayley has noted, 'Without quite realizing it, without the necessary vocabulary, General Motors executives had summoned up the genie of *styling*.'[4] Rather than function, style was to become pre-eminent. This shift in the aesthetics of car design was one that brought automobile production into sync with art production. Artists too needed to establish themselves as brand-names and produce constant flows of work which was both recognizably theirs and continuously innovative. The practice of the automobile industry was aligned with that of the art world.

One inevitable result of this was that automobile designers – and, to a lesser extent, company executives – began to interest themselves in art. The head of General Motors was quite clear about what he wanted. He instructed the designer Harley Earl to create 'a production automobile that was as beautiful as the custom cars of the period'.[5] Earl set up the new Art & Colour Section, through which he produced full-size models, using custom car techniques such as spraying the model with Duco to create reflection. The first of the new range, the 1927 La Salle, was based on the look of an existing luxury car, the Hispano-Suiza, the same marque for which Le Corbusier's collaborator, the Purist artist Amédée Ozenfant, had designed a model in 1912. Edsel Ford also showed a personal interest in the arts. Indeed, back in 1910, when Edsel had still been a teenager, his father had described him as 'the artist in our family', adding, as an afterthought, 'Art is something I know nothing about.'[6] Not only did Edsel Ford promote Rivera; he also enlisted the windshield and windows departments to obtain the particular glass splinters Rivera needed for his pigments. Ford would drop in at least once a week while Rivera was working to see how things were going. The engine assembled in Rivera's mural, I might add, was for the Ford V8, the engine used in the first hot rod, the first power car for middle-income youth. Artists too began to see cars in terms of a personal relationship with a stylish collectible.

The Ford company's patronage of Rivera paralleled the patronage of contemporary art by other

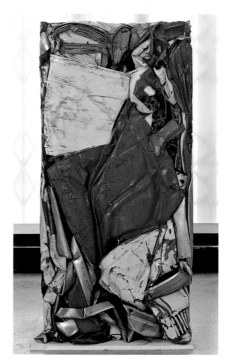

Above: Arman, *Long Term Parking*, 1982, installation at Jouy en Josas, France.
Left: César, *'Helsinki' Compression*, 1964, compressed car parts.

automobile manufacturers. Mario Sironi, for example, worked for Fiat between the early 1930s and 1954. Both Renault and BMW subsequently followed Fiat's lead as patrons of the arts. In 1967, Renault created a department of 'Recherches, Art et Industrie' under the leadership of Claude-Louis Renard. Renard, a former personnel executive, himself suggested the idea to Renault's chairman, Pierre Dreyfus, who promptly gave it the green light.

One of the first artists approached was Arman, who had already proposed a similar project to Ford in the US, one that never came to fruition. Consequently, Arman accepted Renard's proposition with enthusiasm. In fact, in the first few years he produced some hundred sculptures or reliefs from mechanical parts and sheet-metal panels, which were exhibited at his gallery, Ileana Sonnabend, and a number of major European museums. In 1973, Arman made a set of panels for the new Renault headquarters, which was then under construction. Renault also approached Victor Vasarely, whom they had previously helped to solve some technical problems. In 1972, he designed their new company logo. Around the same time, Nicolas Schoffer produced his *Scam* car sculpture, a box-like vehicle with an open tower that supported decorative tubular and disc-like elements. Renault, however, turned down a project, suggested by César, for a series of *Compressions* – crushed forms – comprising the whole Renault range of models, although they did later help him with his *Expansions*. Renault clearly showed a preference for artists from the Nouveau Réalité and Art Kinétique schools of painting, supported by the successful Denise René gallery – schools that were particularly prominent in France. Moreover, there was an implicit connection between the novelty and kinetic appeal of the chosen artworks and those of successive Renault models. Art, styling

and fashion reinforced each other.

The Renault HQ in Paris soon began to resemble an art museum, with a 150-foot frieze in its cafeteria painted by Julio Le Parc, eighteen paintings from Jean Dubuffet's *Roman Burlesque* in the executive hospitality rooms and two 'Accumulations' by Arman located in the corridors on the general-management floors. Renault justified their patronage by pointing to the role played by the creative imagination in an increasingly technological world – the search for creative new solutions and so on. Subsequently, Arman went on to create *Long Term Parking*, a work for a sculpture park at Jouy en Josas, featuring 60 automobiles embedded in concrete. He also exploded a car as an art event, thereby indicating the onset of a sharp divide between the interests of car manufacturers and the artists they patronized. Renault nonetheless continued its policy, but with a preference now for kinetic artists. In 1973, they commissioned Jesús Rafael Soto, a Venezuelan artist, to design the lobby and staff restaurant as 'environments'. At the same time, another kinetic artist, Takis, was commissioned to create moving sculptures for the space between the elevators and the cafeteria. Vasarely created an 'environment', and Arman made two further 'Accumulations' out of sawn-off engine parts. The company's collection also includes two works by Erro – *Renault Scape* and *Motorscope (Renault 5)*.

Renault eventually approached the American Pop artist Robert Rauschenberg, who suggested that he might be able to create 'a wholly transparent car built in conformity with technical standards, whose mechanical parts would all be visible, alongside silk-screened images by the artist'[7], but apparently the scheme was rejected on the grounds of cost. Subsequently, however, Rauschenberg visited the American

Motors–Renault plant in Kenosha, Wisconsin, where he took a series of photographs, some of which were used as models for four large drawings on paper, as well as two canvases – an ensemble entitled *Renault Series* (1984). Other artists involved with Renault included Jean Tinguely and even Henri Michaux, whose abstract works were justified by associating them with the concept of speed. Thus, as a Renault spokesman observed, 'the point is to go fast. Speed is the law. The titles of his texts – *Par la voie des rythmes, Mouvements, Emergences-résurgences* – allude very clearly to his insistence on a tempo.'

Wolf Vostell, *V.O.A.E.X.*, 1976, Installation at Malpartida de Cáceres, Spain.

Arman remained Renault's most visible artist, however. His obsession with dismembered car parts, however Renault may have interpreted it, seems to reflect a generally destructive impulse. The Nouveaux Réalistes, however, were not the first to destroy motor vehicles. In the early 1960s, Wolf Vostell crashed cars as part of his performance pieces, or 'dé-collages', recording the events on video. His attitude can be summed up by his dictum, 'When I see a speeding car, I also see an accident going by.'[8] Vostell, it seems, was pro-pedestrian and felt that streets should belong to people rather than motor vehicles. Car wrecks also feature prominently in Andy Warhol's silkscreen 'Car Crash' series of 1962 and '63. In general, the '60s seem to have been the decade when artists revealed an intense fascination with car culture, either adoring cars or despising them utterly. The cultural context had also changed. The Ford Thunderbird was delivered in 1954, in response to GM's Corvette, a favourite for hot-rodders and customizers. The year 1955 was the year of *Rebel With-*

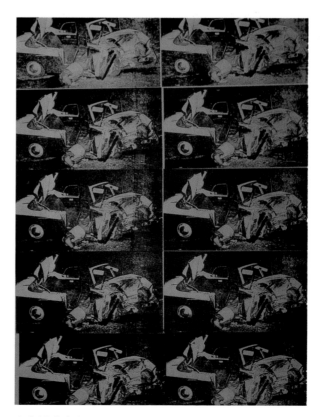

Andy Warhol, *Green Disaster*, 1963, screenprint.

James Rosenquist, *Ultra-Violet Cars*, 1966, oil on canvas.

Plymouth and Imperial adverts together with 'some General Motors material and a bit of Pontiac'. Hamilton claimed that 'the faint echo of the Winged Victory of Samothrace' evoked in this work was not intended to refer to Marinetti's dictum that a racing car was more beautiful than the *Winged Victory*, although his own generation had certainly been influenced by a renewed interest in Futurism. The new Pop artists, fascinated by American adverts and movies, wanted to integrate Futurism with the new youth culture.

After Hamilton's kick-starting of British Pop art, the focus moved across the Atlantic to the US. Rauschenberg had already produced his *Automobile Tire Print* in 1951, and in the early '60s he used a number of automobile references in the set of drawings he produced to illustrate Dante's *Inferno*. In 1960, Larry Rivers exhibited his *Buick Painting*; James Rosenquist's *I Love You With My Ford* and *Silver Skies, Ultra-Violet Fords* followed in 1962 and 1963, the latter a bumper year which also gave us Roy Lichtenstein's *In The Car* and George Segal's mixed-media environment *The Gas Station*. In 1962, Jim Dine had mounted his Happening, *Car Crash*, soon to be followed, in 1963, by John Chamberlain's sculpture *Ravyredd* (Chamberlain had found some parts from a '29 Ford at Larry Rivers's country home and realized that auto scrap from junkyards could be material for sculptures.) The year 1963 was also when Arman, his 'Renault Accumulations' now completed, produced the *Exploded MG Sports Car*, and Warhol made his 'Car Crash' series, part of the broader 'Black and White Disaster' group of works. An apocalyptic tone was creeping into artists' use of car culture.

As the Vietnam War dragged on, the car, it seems, was increasingly associated with destruction. In 1974, a year after J. G. Ballard published his novel *Crash*, the Ant Farm Collective buried a line of ten

out a Cause, followed by Kenneth Anger's *Kustom Kar Kommandos* (1965) and George Lucas's *American Graffiti* (1973).

In the years between *Rebel* and *Graffiti*, the car was correlated with a vibrant new youth culture. At the beginning of this period, Pop art took off in Britain, and for Richard Hamilton, in one critic's words, 'the motorcar became a god of sorts'. In 1955, the year of *Rebel*, Hamilton both contributed to the *Man, Machine and Motion* exhibition and designed the catalogue cover for it, which featured an image based on an Henri Lartigue photograph of a racing car, reversed to negative and blurred to intensify the image of speed. Cars appear in many of Hamilton's works from the late 1950s – as he himself recounts, he 'had been working on a group of paintings and drawings which portray the American automobile as expressed in mag-ads'.[9] The best known is probably *Hommage à Chrysler Corp.*, a collage made from

Ant Farm Collective, *Cadillac Ranch*, 1974, installation near Amarillo, Texas.

Cadillacs, their rear ends rising obliquely above the ground, in Amarillo, Texas. The following year, they drove a 1959 Cadillac (the 'Phantom Dream Car') through a wall of 42 blazing television sets, videoing the event and entitling it *Media Burn*. Indeed, other Pop or post-Pop artists actually constructed their own cars – Salvatore Scarpitta's *Ardun-Cyclone*, Don Potts's *The Master Chassis* and, eventually, Chris Burden's *B-Car*, a four-wheel vehicle built to get 100 mpg and travel at speeds up to 100 mph. Burden took the *B-Car* to Paris in 1975 and actually drove it in the streets. He described his motivation in somewhat grandiloquent terms: 'One of my most cherished fantasies has always been to manufacture a car of my own – to add the name of Burden to the list of Ford, Honda, Bugatti, Citroën, etc.'[10] In his imagination, the artist finally merged not simply with the designer, but with the manufacturer, the bearer of the permanent and lasting brand-name.

In fact, many artists were enthusiastic connoisseurs of cars. André Derain owned a Bugatti that he considered to be more beautiful than any work of art. Henry Moore's favourite was the Jaguar Mark II, which he described as 'sculpture in motion'. Max Bill drove a 1947 Bentley Mark VI and suggested that car designers inevitably drew inspiration from trends in

the art world. Gino Severini, who painted his *Speeding Automobile* in 1913, argued that the creative method used for constructing a car was very similar to that used for constructing a work of art. Frank Stella gave a number of his large abstract paintings titles that commemorated the racing drivers he admired – *Marquis de Portago* in 1960, *Polar Co-ordinates for Ronnie Peterson III* in 1980. The twenty-year span between these two works, the first a painting with metallic pigment, the second a set of screenprints and lithographs, covered a period in which cars provided a central motif for many American artists, fascinated by the fusion of human and machine in the race car, as driver and speeding vehicle formed a kind of psychophysiological unit.

The contradictory vision of cars both as engines of destruction and as aesthetic objects paved the way for the subsequent connection between cars as art objects whose creation and destruction were celebrated within the art world and custom cars created within the auto-as-art world of hot-rodders and car cultists. Both artists and car designers were slaves to obsolescence, fashionable at the beginning of a successful cycle of innovation, but prone to become unfashionable as other artists launched a new cycle that inevitably

Roy Lichstenstein, *BMW 3201*, 1977, 'Art Car'.

David Hockney painting his BMW 850CSi 'Art Car'.

A 'Von Dutch', a customized Gull-wing Mercedes from the mid-1950s.

overtook the previous generation – except for those who had achieved the status of classics, a kind of transcendence of historic time. In particular, artists could relate to the world of such popular artists as Harley Earl and his successors. In Los Angeles, others followed Earl's example, customizers like George Barris and Von Dutch, who began his career working in the Barris shop. It was Barris who 'imagineered' the hot rods for *Rebel Without A Cause*, and it was Barris who added the decorative racing stripes and the lettering 'Little Bastard' to James Dean's Porsche 550 Spyder, just three days before the mythic crash in which Dean died.

In 1975, subsequent to Renault's pioneering sponsorship of automobile-related artworks, BMW, the German automobile company, were persuaded to commission the American artist Alexander Calder to decorate a BMW car that was entered – a first for the company – in the Le Mans 24-hour race, a customizing commission for a legendary art-world figure. Calder, it should be noted, had already decorated a passenger jet for Braniff. The following year, 1976, Frank Stella emblazoned a BMW racing car with his

trademark geometrical patterns – Stella was a race-car enthusiast and welcomed the invitation immediately. In 1977, it was Lichtenstein's turn – yellow for the sun, blue for the sky, black for the road and his signature black dots, of course, as the common element. All of these cars raced at Le Mans. In 1979, Warhol was commissioned, the first artist to insist on painting the car himself – the others had all used a scaled-down model, and their artwork had then been transferred onto the full-scale car by a specialist. Warhol wanted his car to bear his personal touch: 'I tried to portray speed pictorially. If a car is moving really quickly all the lines and colours are blurred.'[11]

In 1986, it was Rauschenberg's turn, with a photo-reproduction of a Bronzino portrait on one side of the car and an Ingres odalisque on the other. Then, at the end of the 1980s, the Australian Aboriginal artist Michael Jagamara Nelson, a Walppiri painter who lived at Papunya, a centre of Aboriginal painting, was commissioned to decorate a Le Mans BMW, this time with images of kangaroos, ants and possums in the traditional shades of yellow, red, black and white. In subsequent years, BMW went on to commission artists from all over the world – Australia (Ken Done), Japan (Matazo Kayama), Austria (Ernst Fuchs), Spain (César Manrique), Germany (A. R. Penck), Italy (Sandro Chia), South Africa (the Ndebele artist Esther Mahlangu) and, in 1995, an English artist – David Hockney – albeit a resident of California. In fact, Hockney has described how he loves to drive, especially through the winding mountain roads of California, listening to classical music. Like Warhol, Hockney insisted on painting the car himself, although apparently he worked rather more slowly than Warhol!

Sylvie Fleury, *Skin Crime 3 (Givenchy 318)*, 1997,
compressed car enamel.

Hockney's LA counterpart, the legendary customizer Von Dutch, had been brought up in Compton, where as a boy he had brought broken shards of coloured tile or bottle glass to Simon Rodia, the self-taught architect of the Watts Towers. It was Von Dutch who perfected the art of pin-striping, the purpose of which, in his own words, was 'to make a vehicle look better, not to demonstrate the striper's ability. The finished appearance or personalization is what's important. Not only was I one of the original guys who was experimenting, but I was the first one to develop a distinctive and original style . . .'. In the 1940s, Von Dutch pioneered the use of flame forms and crazy landscapes and surrealistic designs. Half a century later, the Ghanaian artist Kane Kwei sculpted a coffin in the form of a Mercedes, branching out later into a range of elephants, lobsters, eagles and the like. In 1989, his work was exhibited in Paris in the global art show *Magiciens de la terre*. Then, in 1991, Kwei was approached by an American researcher, Ernie Wolfe, who admired a coffin Kwei had made in the shape of a '56 Ford pick-up. Wolfe asked Kwei about the flame forms he used, which 'could have been on any car in East LA'. In his reply, Kwei referred to the technique as 'Von Dutching'.[12]

In the 1960s, Von Dutch had been offered a

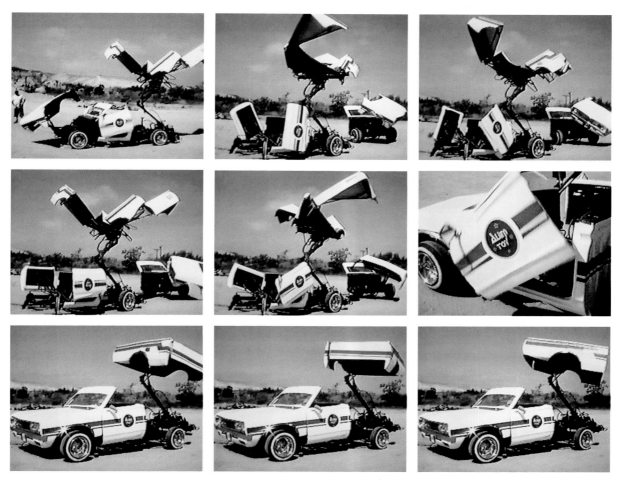

Rubén Ortiz Torres, *Alien Toy (Unindentified Cruising Object)*, 1997, video installation.

show at the Ferus Gallery, where Warhol exhibited, but he had turned it down. Nonetheless, customizers like him had a real influence on the LA art world. First, they worked with automobile paint, just as Siqueiros had done. Second, they treated cars as artworks. Robert Irwin has described how the car was central to artists' culture at the time: 'Everything was wrapped around the car. The car was your home away from home. And you put months and months into getting it just right.' Irwin recalls taking a critic to visit a garage, where he was able to show how the kid customizing his car was acting as an artist, weighing how it should look: 'Real aesthetic decisions were being made, just as they were made by a professional artist.'[13] The glossy metallic paints and smooth surfaces of customizing culture also provided inspiration for Billie Al Bengston, as well as Judy Chicago, who took spray-painting lessons from a customizer in order to compete on equal terms with her male peers.

Subsequently, Chicago created a spray-paint

Gabriel Orozco, *La DS*, 1993, sutured car.

work executed on the hood of a 1964 Corvair, later recalling how 'in *Car Hood*, which I made at autobody school, the vaginal form, penetrated by a phallic arrow was mounted on the "masculine" hood of the car'.[14] Another woman artist influenced by customizing was Sylvie Fleury, who has used body-shop flame forms in her art, as well as chroming a Chevy engine to turn it into a customized art object. She also chromed fashion items – Hermès purses and a bottle of Chanel No. 5. For her installation *The She-Devils on Wheels Headquarters*, she created an over-the-top replica of a hot-rod-girl's clubhouse, with no fewer than 55 one-off hubcaps installed on the wall. On the male side, there is Rubén Ortiz Torres's customized extravaganza *Alien Toy*, a truck that unfolds outwards and upwards on expanding hydraulic stalks, performing a strange dance of automotive parts, rising and rotating, carrying custom-car culture into yet another new dimension, a bravura theatrical happening whose central character is the automobile rather than the artist. It stands at the performance extreme of car art, at the opposite end of the spectrum from the minimal elegance of Gabriel Orozco's 1993 *La DS*, the classic Citroën sliced in three with the two outer slices sutured together to make a slender, elegant, dart-like and yet dysfunctional vehicle, far removed from the DS that Roland Barthes had once compared to a cathedral.

In recent years, as we approached and finally entered the twenty-first century, the imagery of the car in art seems to have shifted towards a much more negative attitude, exemplified, for instance, in the work of Sarah Lucas. In 1997, Lucas exhibited her installation *Car Park* at the Ludwig Museum, Cologne, in which one wall of an underground car-park was covered with 108 photographs she had taken of a similar car-park in London, titled *Concrete Void*. This provided a backdrop to a vandalized dark blue Nissan Bluebird from the 1980s, the windscreen shattered by hammer blows, the seats covered with splinters of bluish glass, a work reminscent of the Pippilotti Rist video *Ever Is Over All*, in which Rist skips and prances down a city street, smashing car windows as she sings. This was not Lucas's first car work – she had previously exhibited a Ford Capri in London, its rear end wagging – and, herself a compulsive smoker, she later showed two more cars, a Ford Sierra and a Buick Sable, burnt out, charred, decorated with hundreds of orange and white Marlboro Red cigarettes, squalid and yet visually appealing.

Finally, mention should be made of Krzystov Wodicko's many car-related projects. Wodicko's first *Vehicle* was powered by the artist himself, generating energy by walking up and down on a tilted platform, which was then transmitted by gears and cables to wheels that moved the vehicle forward, combining up-to-date technology with a medieval appearance, functional but also a throwback to the worlds of Dürer and Leonardo da Vinci.[15] Subsequently, in his *Vehicle Podium*, he used an electric motor before returning to manpower again with the *Poliscar*, a vehicle designed as living space, communications centre and means of transport for the homeless. From its fascination with racing and luxury cars, automobile art finally returned to basics, to art with a social purpose, the political presentation of the car as a kind of small-scale but high-tech mobile home for the homeless, a post-automobile coming back full circle to human-powered vehicles, a kind of anti-sports utility vehicle, an ironic footnote to the brave new world of car technology.

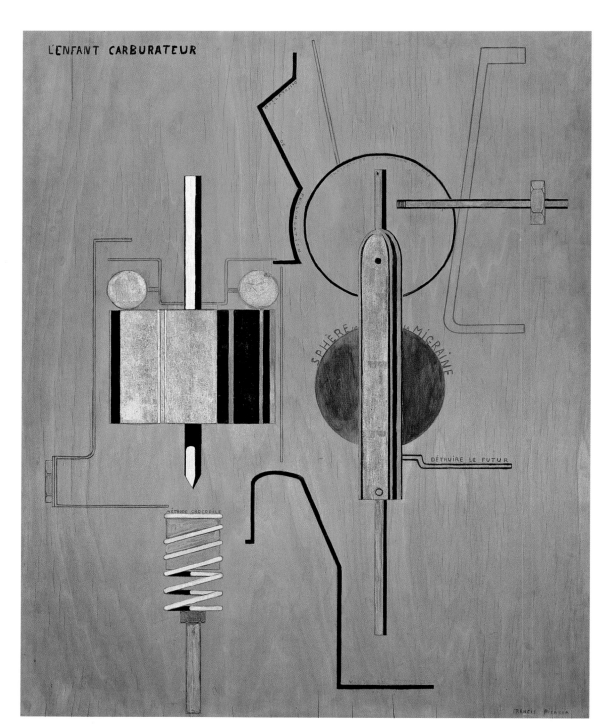

Francis Picabia, *The Child Carburetor*, 1919, oil and mixed media on wood.

Charles Sheeler, *American Landscape*, 1930, oil on canvas.

Diego Rivera, *Detroit Industry*, 1932, mural in the Detroit Institute of
Arts (South Wall).

Top: Edward Hopper, *Gas*, 1940, oil on canvas.
Above: Ed Ruscha, *Standard Station, Amarillo, Texas*, 1963, oil on canvas.

Panamarenko, *Prova Car*, 1967, mixed media.

Left: James Wines/SITE, 'The Ghost Parking Lot Project', 1978, installation in Hamden, Connecticut.

Below: Carlos Almaraz, *Beach Crash*, 1982, oil on canvas.

Robert Longo, *Love Police: Engines in Us (The Doors) with the Golden Children*, 1982–3, lacquer on cast aluminium bonding (5 panels).

Left: Edward Kienholz, *The Back Seat Dodge '38*, 1964, assemblage including a 1938 Dodge and plaster figures.

Below: Tyree Guyton, *The Heidelberg Project*, street art, Detroit, begun mid-1980s.

Accidents: The Car and Literature

ALLEN SAMUELS

Everything the traffic will allow
— Irving Berlin

REVVING UP

Henry James, marble about things, could be passionate about them even if he had fellow novelist Edith Wharton, a keen motorist, to do the actual driving. Rudyard Kipling adored them and owned several, while George Orwell disliked them; when he could, he opted for a bicycle instead. Henry Adams, with bitter reluctance, used one to search for the power of the Virgin in France. Kenneth Grahame put a poetaster-toad in at least eight of them. E. M. Forster, a fellow Edwardian, stuck three, vaguely hysterical, women in two of them. T. S. Eliot, more ambitiously, located the collapse of Western Civilization and the dissolution of a painful marriage in a 'closed one'. F. Scott Fitzgerald was magnificently obsessed by them, nearly lost his life in one driven by his near-insane wife and, as reported by a felinely malicious Ernest Hemingway, caught a nasty cold in a French one. The mechanic who looked after Gertrude Stein's provided her with a phrase – 'the lost generation' – which she then used as her own; like 'the Waste Land', in an age of bricolage, it became one of modern literature's great thefts. Evelyn Waugh, who cared to move in posh circles, had a friend who used one for housing a built-in piano. Christopher Isherwood bought one after testing his manhood on a motorbike, while Michael

Arlen wove a bittersweet romance around an expensive pair of them on a tragic race to Maidenhead. W. H. Auden, ever alert to fame and social nuance, posthumously awarded a smart one to Lord Byron because he bracketed them with the glittering prizes. Louis Macniece wrote sour poetry about them in Birmingham, whereas Virginia Woolf, as adulatory of royalty as Auden was of fame, invented a trivial-minded woman who thought she glimpsed the King's hand in one. That it was probably the Prime Minister's hand, and not the King's, made no difference. This was about the grand person in the grand car.

F. R. Leavis and F. L. Lucas, two Cambridge panjandrums who certainly did not agree about much, nevertheless concurred when they both despaired at the increasing appearance of such objects. In 1934, both made gloomy predictions about the increasing mechanization of social life, and thought any future beneficent social or cultural existence was doomed. Ilya Ehrenburg composed their first cultural analysis, part fiction, part documentary. Edmund Wilson hated their noise (associated with, as for Eliot, the gramophone), and Aldous Huxley used the name of their most famous maker as the arch-symbol of materialist deification at the same time that he satirized modern psychology, if, at first sight, for no better reason than that Ford and Freud shared the same initial letter. They sounded similar: assonance can breed strange partners in the literary imagination. J. B. Priestley at first rejected one, preferring the socialist bus, but comfort soon overcame camaraderie. F. T. Marinetti, modern and excitable, adored them. D. H. Lawrence, who loathed industrialization and anything to do with machines, nevertheless used the view from the window of one to frame and describe the destruction of the Midlands countryside.

In this litany, the 'they' are motorcars.

THE SIGN OF THE CAR

'The narratives of the world are numberless,' observed Roland Barthes, who himself joined the ranks of Franz Ferdinand, Isadora Duncan, President John Kennedy, Mary Jo Kopechne, Jackson Pollock, Albert Camus, James Dean, Jayne Mansfield, Roy Campbell, Frank O'Hara, Italo Svevo, James Dean and Princess Diana as one of the hapless celebrity victims of the combustion engine: in his case, not by the sleek, platypus-shaped, frog-eyed Citroën DS, the Goddess which he both praised and denounced in prose, comparing it, to its detriment, to the glory of the Gothic cathedral,[1] but by a humble Paris laundry van.

Of car tales, and of car authors, of the car as symbol and as narrative device, this numberlessness is unabated. Cars generate enormous, incalculable quantities of documents and written texts: licences, registrations, handbooks, MOT certificates, service manuals, insurance papers, auto magazines, car and transport histories, consumer reports, shoppers' guides, petrol receipts, poems and pop songs. The list goes on and on in Dickensian profusion, detail added to detail, stretching to infinite exhaustion. And, of course, exceeding the written word is the spoken one, for which there can be no record. Virtually from the moment of the car's invention, the public imagination was saturated with car images. Modern humans not only live in a car world, they live in the public culture of the car. And how that imagination has been created, which means not merely how we think or how we feel about cars, but the ways in which thought and feeling are intertwined – which is literature's special province – owes much to writers. Saturation has been complete for some time. Long before the copywriter invented 'Mondeo Man' as a way of identifying a social grouping, the car characterized national identity and the human type. Perhaps the most famous (if rarely remarked) instance is that great paean to wartime romance, *Casablanca* (1942), in which the nationalism of the characters is indexed by their names. Louis *Renault* is the French chief of police; the Mr Fixit character, played by a charmingly raffish Claude Rains is Sidney Greenstreet; the owner of a rival nightclub is called *Ferrari* and the small-time villain, played by Peter Lorre at his most unctuous, is called *Ugatti* (a homophone for *Bugatti*). Foreigners are given car names identifiable with their countries. The French are uneasy allies, Renault a collaborationist with the Nazis until his final declaration for the Allied cause. The Italians are Nazi collaborators; those not on the Allies' side are given Italian car names.

But, and most interesting of all, most literary writers (novelists and poets and, later, cultural critics), when they came to engage with the car, did so adversarially. In a word, they did not like it. Indeed, just about every writer who used the car, or something connected with it, as a trope or metaphor or symbol had something harsh or critical to say about it, whether directly or by implication. This is not to say that writers did not enjoy using them or indeed, when the occasion arose, driving them. Or, given their respective places in society, being driven (J. B. Priestley used a chauffeur-driven Daimler for his tour around England during the Great Depression). There were exceptions – T. S. Eliot is one whom we know disliked driving. But their works do not necessarily tell the same story as their biographies.

There were, of course, those who did praise the car, though they nearly always ended up on the political Right or as promoters of a Toad-like 'inhuman excess': Marinetti, Le Corbusier, Celine.[2]

Modern literature (in so far as 'literature' represents a single integral identity) has much to say about cars: the visual art of painting has less. This is perhaps because the dominant art forms of the car in the twentieth century were advertising and technological design, not the fine arts, and the car has figured in photography much more. Painting has not attracted anything like the interest that other visual media have. But ours is an age in which the visual image is not subject to aristocratic patronage, and thus has lost its exclusivity and 'aura'. Now it is merely subject to the frenetic impetus of commerce, in which a multinational company's advertising budget is larger than the income of a small campus, while research and development for a new model equals that of the science budgets of large universities. The car image is now freely available in the daily newspaper or in the 45-second TV advertisement. Not for nothing have Sunday supplements been described as car advertisements surrounded by casual journalism.

The car has iconic status because it is a singularly rich symbol for a host of meanings. It is a focus for a cluster of ideas. Like all epochal icons, the car does not mean one thing, but many things. In that sense, it is an 'empty sign'. It is a vacuum. We fill it with meaning. The component parts of cars have

useful symbolic power. Cars have headlights and wheels. Fire and the wheel were two primary metaphors for the ancient literary imagination: the car possesses both in deadly combination. Cars have windows and mirrors, both of which have been used frequently in literature (and art) to offer perspective, and as framing devices to capture the passing scene. And cars *en masse* produce traffic, and traffic produces accidents, which in turn impinge on all aspects of city life, from urban planning to architecture. But for the majority of writers, as opposed to the creators of advertisements, the car is nearly always an icon of disfavour because the writers of imaginative literature, of novel and poem and drama, perceive its terrible consequences, its damage, its deathliness and, above all, its potential for dehumanization. Indeed, the motorcar became *the* Icon of Disfavour of the modern age. No other icon can match the car for showing the interrelationship of human and machine which has so dominated modern technological life because no other relationship is quite so ordinary and quite so intimate.

This literary life of the car has a long and crowded history, now over a century long. It is one, though, which really belongs to the twentieth century, even if the car and the combustion engine are, technically, nineteenth-century inventions. Just about everything to be said about cars, or the way in which we fill the empty sign – death, accidents, roads, the car as aesthetic object, the car as harbinger of death, the car as sex – occurs in the early literature.

BREAKDOWN

One thing on which writers capitalized from the outset is the fact that the car involved accidents. There is not, so far as I am aware, a history of the accident.

Perhaps there should be. Literature could do with one. Accidents are real enough phenomena.[3] But for the imaginative writer, especially the novelist, the accident meant something purposeful and useful for the way he/she wrote. The motorcar offered this wonderful opportunity for making a critical moment a dramatic one. They are the entrance of the unintended. In part, novels use accidents because they allow the narrative to go forward. Like the 'turn', or *volta*, in a sonnet, they allow for the change of direction.

It is the irreducible nature of accidents that they are beyond our voluntary will. The car belongs to that realm, and the literary motorcar is always prone to revert to that primary mortifying fact. Just as in a real motor accident, metal clashes into metal or metal becomes twisted up with flesh, or stone, or tree, so in metaphor, things from different realms become intermeshed. Things interchange so that new meaning may be created. The language of metaphor is the language of transport; metaphor itself has been defined as a 'little journey'. The car is both a vehicle and a vehicle for meaning.

The accident holds the potential of what might have been. Accidents are usually perceived as unhappy, unintended events, (though they can be fortunate, in which case they are called 'luck' or 'providence'), and this is because they create a potential for situations that would otherwise never have come into being. Had Tess of the D'Urbervilles' horse not died on the road to market, she would not have been accosted by Alec, her eventual nemesis; had Anna Karenina not met Vronsky by the train, she might not have died by being run over by one. Making sense of accidents in fictions is accepting, in Eliot's phrase, that 'what might have been remains an abstract possibility'. This is not to not accept fictions for what they are not, or to assert that they can be no other, but is to be alerted to the possibilities of the many directions a narrative can take, but which an author determines it shall not. The 'turn of events', or change of direction, in a fiction may be attributable to one great event and this is likely to be called 'an accident'. The authority of the text demands our acceptance of it: to reject that authority is to rewrite the story and tell another one.

When events occur in ways that seem improbable, or the contrivance stretches credibility, it is given the name 'coincidence'. But this is only a way of saying that the potential intended narrative, the one which is hinted at, pointed to, which will never come into any realization of fullness, seems so persuasive that it appears as a real possibility, whereas the reverse is just as likely to be true. The coincidence, the accident, is the likelier possibility and the possible other a sort of poignant 'if only' and was never likely to happen at all. One of the recurrent ploys of fiction is to make us accept the unacceptable by reconciling us unsentimentally to necessity. Fate is not an accident, but we find it bearable to make it so, just as death is an inevitability.

It was equally inevitable, given the enormous power of the machine, that car inscription should be intimately tied up with accidents. Even now, so 'automanic' is our society that the word *accident* probably first conjures up thought of a traffic accident, though statistically, and more mundanely, most accidents occur in the home. Ehrenburg names the first chapter of his *Life of the Automobile* 'The Birth of the Automobile', although its opening section ends in a quick and violent death. Charles Bernard, a quiet, solitary man, is a true romantic, a reader of the aptly named *The Almanac of Nature Lovers*. He becomes a lover of screen fantasies, especially those which show exotic travel at fantastic speed. Cinema provides a more powerful stimulus than anything romantic literature can do for his imagination, and the cars on the screen inspire him to buy one and take driving lessons. A timid man, he nevertheless learns to drive, and on his first and only trip in which the car enters the countryside, the machine overcomes his will, and he ends up a fatality: 'The linnets warbled and lavender was sweet and fragrant. Car no 180-74 – iron splinters, glass shards, a lump of warm flesh – lay unstirring beneath the solemn midday sun.'

Ehrenburg's account belongs to the 1920s, but it is ironically instructive that it should begin with an accident and a death. Cars become nearly synonymous, in his documentary, with both. But, as the quote shows, other metaphorical assumptions are there as well: rural versus urban, living nature versus deathly non-human, human time versus motorized rapidity. Cinema represents speed as opposed to literature's slow meditation. Both Eliot and Lawrence had unpleasant things to say about film, and indeed this was a conjunction that occurred with frequency in the literary life of the motorcar in the '20s and '30s. It became an almost permanent feature of our ways of seeing the car. Ehrenburg described the car as a number, non-human, not sentient, a thorough act of dehumanization. Here, the romantic idealist was defeated by the cold mechanical force – an insight with which the Romantics had fed the public imagination, and which had sustained nearly all of the great nineteenth-century social critics in their animadversions on mechanization.

TOAD AND TABOO

Curiously, although cars in races (the most obvious locations for crashes and accidents) appear early on – as in James Joyce's short story 'After the Race', which uses as backdrop the winning of the Gordon Bennet

Cup by Camille Jenatzy (when, as so often later, cars signified national identity) – it was the child's tale *The Wind in the Willows* (1908) that was the ur-text for all subsequent motoring tales. Toad's adventures in motoring mayhem show Kenneth Grahame's deep rural conservatism, the Edwardian English fear of the new mechanization, and, in particular, the urban/rural divide, which the car crosses and telescopes into difference without distinction (the car, even more than the railways, can go anywhere). In this wonderfully funny, very English tale of supposedly rural bliss, what we have, through Toad's outrageous behaviour, is, in essence, a prescriptive tale of good conduct. A tale of moral conduct is, necessarily, a tale of transgressions.

Cross-dressing, prisons, gaols, female impersonation, theft, lies, the writing of bad poetry – the egocentric Toad is associated with them all. In his semi-demented pursuit of the 'real thing', he is clearly identifiable as a modern obsessive. He is, in another schema for the novel, the adolescent among the children (Mole, Rat), and this is because he is hormonally disturbed. Grahame cleverly weaves this into the car story. Take the locking up of Toad in his room for his persistent misbehaviour. Here is one of Grahame's sly jokes against the car. Early on, he recognized that cars are associated with grown-ups, and what distinguishes grown-ups from children is sexual development, which society transposes so that what legally divides childhood from adulthood in many developed societies is the licence to drive. What does Toad get up to?

When his violent paroxysms possessed him, he would arrange bedroom chairs in rude resemblance of the motor car and crouch on the foremost of them, bent forward, and staring fixedly ahead, making uncouth and ghastly noises, til

Toad discovers 'the real way to travel' – a car flashes past in E. H. Shepard's illustration for Kenneth Grahame's *The Wind in the Willows*.

the climax was reached, when turning a complete somersault, he would lie prostrate amidst the ruins of the chairs, apparently completely satisfied for the moment. As time passed, however, these painful seizures grew gradually less frequent and his friends strove to divert his mind into fresh channels. But his interest on other matters did not seem to revive, and he grew apparently languid and depressed.

No-one seems to have *quite* noticed what Toad is up to here. Or, if they have, they have drawn a discreet veil over it. But this seemingly innocent description of a childish sulk reveals a graphic parabola of sexual desire and fulfilment which implies more than playing with furniture. Withdrawal of the 'real thing' inevitably produces its own compensatory fantasy. The text describes perfectly the arc of sexual frustration and relief of the not-to-be-thwarted teenager *cum* anthropomorph.

But what Toad introduces into literature is the car accident. He has eight of them and lands in gaol because of his careless and illegal driving. Indeed, car theft and damage are never far away from Toad.

Posed against the natural (the rural, the human, the slow and meditative) was the manmade (the urban, the machine-made, the rapid). It was inevitable, certainly in English culture, that one contrast would be overlain by another. E. M. Forster, no lover of the car and what it brought, also conveys the urban/rural divide in *Howards End* (1910). Like Grahame's story, this tale of the encroaching suburb points to that collapsing distinction of town and country.

Forster, too, was a writer of car accidents. For him, the accident was the scene for heightened drama. Indeed, whenever he had recourse to accidents, the car proved useful. The first Mrs Wilcox goes to Ripon, and there is a car accident. When the second Mrs Wilcox and family go to Shropshire, there is a second car accident as a cat is run over. It is significant that whenever the upper middle classes leave the comfortable south-east of England and venture into the other England, which means Yorkshire or the Welsh border, accidents occur. Forster repeats the idea in *A Passage to India* with the accident to the Maharajah's car in the jungle. The literal journey, the plot of the narrative, comes to a halt as the characters reflect on their fate. Forster, it must be said, was a connoisseur of accidents in fiction and not merely car-induced ones. The same novel includes the Marabar Caves mystery, and boats capsizing at a Hindu festival, while in *Howards End*, when Forster comes to the death of Leonard Bast, he creates what surely must be the most overdetermined death in literature, caused by a falling bookcase, a falling sword and a heart attack. (Forster seems to have been taking no chances.) Deliberately, however, he is careful *not* to allow the car the ultimate victory of causing death directly; it is the associations of potential threat which he sets up that are a feature of such early works as *Howards End*. Nature is converted into the man-made as stables are converted into garages (nowadays, it is front gardens into off-street parking), and primary relationships are overtaken by secondary ones as the chauffeur becomes a figure of power and of menace. By the time we come to Eliot and Fitzgerald a decade or so later,

the car accident and car death are too common to be avoided.

HIS MASTER'S VOICE

T. S. Eliot, in that great hymn to modern decline and urban living, *The Waste Land* (1922), juxtaposes sex and the car in a brutal fashion, an association from which it was never to be disassociated. The bored couple wonder 'if it rains and a closed car at four' will bring any relief to the tedium of their sexually troubled marriage. The metaphor of enclosure and seclusion, too, would prove to be important.[4] Of course, this image as used for transport was not invented by the coming of the car. Most early cars were in fact 'open', or roofless, and it was not until the 1920s that they were in fact roofed, or 'closed'. Eliot was being, as so often, precise and made malice out of pedantry by using the epithet. Sweeney, his alter ego in the guise of the *homme moyen sensual*, goes to see Mrs Porter to the sounds of 'horns and motors'. At the violet hour, it is a taxi that wait and throbs 'like a human engine', thus animating the sexual energy of the seduced typist and the seducing clerk. And it is the mechanical strains of a gramophone that plays the coda to this loveless act. (Interestingly, the metaphoric conjunction of motorcar and phonograph [both mechanical] is repeated by Evelyn Waugh when the victim of a car accident on a racetrack hides her gramophone under her hospital bed.) Elsewhere in Eliot's acidulous verse, the car is there as a threat to stability and social order. Only on a desert island in his later verse drama *Sweeney Agonistes* is there peace from the cars of the rich:

> Well that's life on a crocodile isle
> There's no telephones,

> There's no gramophones,
> There's no motor cars,
> No two seaters, no six seaters,
> No Citroën, no Rolls Royce.

Meanwhile in *Choruses from the Rock* (1934) life in the suburbs is condemned for its lack of Christian devotion:

> I journeyed to the suburbs and there I was told:
> We toil for six days, on the seventh we must
>   motor,
> To Hindhead or Maidenhead.

Or its restive futility:

> But all dash to and fro in motor cars,
> Familiar with the roads and settled nowhere
> Nor does the family even move about together,
> But every son would have his motor cycle,
> And daughter ride away on casual pillions.

Remembering St Louis, where he had been brought up, Eliot recalled: 'And in my childhood before the days of the motor car people who lived in town stayed in town. So it was for nine months of the year my scenery was almost exclusively urban, and a good deal of it seedily, drearily urban at that.' It seems the perfect start for the writer of *The Waste Land*.

THE GREEN LIGHT

Vying with Grahame as *the* great car writer is F. Scott Fitzgerald in *The Great Gatsby*. As in Forster, it is 'a foul dust' that the car leaves in its wake. This early metaphor of moral pollution conveyed by atmospheric pollution became a twentieth-century cliché. Later on, chrome-plated '50s streamlined and sleek automobiles would so offend Robert Lowell, who

called them 'grease', that one of his critics – noting this denunciation – called the car 'the infection of the age' (a use Wordsworth could not have foreseen for his phrase). No other novel in English (even those ostensibly written in celebration of cars like the tales of Dornford Yates) shows such magnificent excess as *The Great Gatby*; there is hardly a page without some car reference. Cars tell you about people's sexual morés and define their characters. Jordan Baker's sexual behaviour is likened to her driving. It is an endless paradigmatic exchange. And it is the mix-up over cars, which, like sexual promiscuity, is based on exchange, that provides the necessary plot and the accident which brings about Gatsby's demise. Had the Buchanans not swapped cars with him, had Daisy not been driving but Gatsby himself, he would not have been murdered by a vengeful George, the garage owner who blamed him for Myrtle's death. The accident defers yet again to the contingent. The rich and powerful are 'careless people'. Images of hands being crushed by cars exiting from one of the Gatsbys' parties confirm this indifference.

It is a neat irony that Scott Fitzgerald, drunkenly careering around the Riviera Corniche, dollar bills stuffed down the side of a hired Rolls-Royce, or fighting with taxi drivers in Rome, should been observed in the 1930s by one of his first biographers driving over-slowly, because drunk, in the mid-afternoon. The light at the end of Gatsby's dock in the famous ending of hope and disenchantment nevertheless is green. America, and its love of the car, will not stop.

PARKING

These are but a few of countless examples of the car as trope and symbol, and of car writers. What they add up to is the view that our reactions to the car, as formulated by these writers, when not deceived by the persuasive, seductive subtleties of advertising, is a sort of persistent and anxious doubleness. Their view, and ours too, since it has become part of the literary life of the car, is always equivocal and polarized. Sometimes that polarization is between our feelings and our thoughts. Sometimes it is transposed into selfishness and altruism. On another, more abstract, plane, we are modernizers or conservatives. The car is an object of desire, because it betokens status and power. It is sometimes beautiful, a mechanical and engineering marvel, and, like no other thing, it transforms our lives. Without the car, there is no supermarket weekly shop or commute to work or particular kind of holiday or any of the other patterns of modern life in Western societies. Industrial societies are deeply connected to car production. A nation's *amour propre* is tied up with its cars and their 'branding'. Globalization is slowly eroding car names, merely repeating on a world-wide stage what has always happened under capitalism as the big swallows up the small, in the ineluctable move towards monopoly. Love and death, desire and hatred, pleasure and cost. The car literally and figuratively transports us into realms of pleasure. It is a reactionary fetishist's dream; it offers up uniformity, regularity, speed, elegant design and mechanical ease, in which form and function combine. It is, at the same time, an ecologist's nightmare, because it pollutes the atmosphere and destroys the rhythms of the human and the natural, as they are overtaken by the mechanical. It dominates the rhythms of our lives. It is always both comfort (it protects us in our carapace against the elements, against noise, against other people) and threat, whether from another driver or if we are pedestrians. It can kill and maim us.

The car is a ready measure of our selfishness; at the same time, it reminds us of other road users who may get in the way. 'Accidente' means 'Hell' in Italian, a reminder of Sartre's Existentialist conundrum that Hell is other people. All drivers at some point consider other road users as 'the other'. Traffic is always other people; other motorists are perceived as potential threats to the self. And indeed, the heavier the traffic, the greater the likelihood of an accident.

Subsequent avatars of this terrible association of car and accident (and, indeed, several of the other meanings embodied in cars) include Jean-Luc Godard's tedious *Week-end* (the seventeen-minute stationary traffic pile-up being one of the film's more dramatic points), Joseph Losey's much more interesting *Accident*, J. G. Ballard's *Crash* and Stephen King's horrific *Christine*. Yet all have learnt, consciously or otherwise, the messages the early writers gave us about narratives and accidents, though later writers emphasize the horrific and overstress the sense of catastrophe. Indeed, if there is a difference between earlier and late accidents, it is their scale, not the opportunity they offer for narrative ingenuity or moral commentary. Accidents were there from the start.

Cars, in other words, are there not only to take us on our journeys, but to help us describe, understand and reflect on culture and society. So long as there are cars and human beings, and sentient people to write about them, there will always be accidents, real and metaphoric.

No Particular Place to Go

PATRICK FIELD

All my life I've been running from something. If only I knew what it was I'd know which direction to go.
– George Jones

George Jones used to go out carousing, leaving his wife – Tammy Wynette – lonely and alone. Worried about George's honky-tonkin' ways, Tammy finally lost patience with standing by her man and decided it was time for a talk. To make Jones spend an evening in the lovely suburban home that had become her prison, she hid the keys to all of his cars. It was way too far for George to travel on foot to his favourite downtown haunts. So the self-reliant 'King of Country Music' rode into Nashville on his lawn-mower. Years later, wallowing in his hell-raising mythology, Jones recorded 'Honky Tonk Song', a jaunty ballad that takes the fabled mower ride as its subject. He explains to the stone-faced policeman who pulls him over the attractions that lured him into such a desperate journey: 'ice-cold beer', 'hardwood floor', 'smoky atmosphere' and, most of all, the urge to '. . . hear old Hank moanin' a honky-tonk song'.

Hiram 'Hank' Williams has a special place in the colourful history of self-destructive popular musicians. As a teenager, he played in school auditoriums and dancehalls around Montgomery, Alabama, developing a strong vocal style to cut across his own rhythm guitar and a small backing band. The singing-cowboy craze was at its height, and from the beginning, Hank's theme song was 'Happy Rovin' Cowboy', a vaudeville version of the horse-powered

warrior-herdsman's carefree life. Hank wore Western stage clothes, and his backing band – under his wayward management an ensemble with a notoriously fast turnover – were always billed as 'The Driftin' Cowboys'.

Hank loved to hunt and fish, but – born with a spinal deformity, frail even before he developed a taste for liquor-fuelled oblivion – his prairie idyll was an American dream that could never be realized. He always claimed aboriginal ancestry, but the nearest he got to the free, rambling life of the nomad was changing his name from Hiram – appropriately pronounced 'harm' in the antique dialect of the South – and trying to get his bones comfortable in a crowded automobile on another interminable road trip.

When 'The Lovesick Blues' – his simplified arrangement of an obscure 1922 show song – became a national hit in 1949, he wasted no time in taking over the loan on a seven-seater Packard Sedan that had already seen service with 'The Bailes Brothers', 'Curley Kinsey and the Four Deacons' and 'Curley Williams' Peach Pickers'. The car was a symbol of success, conspicuous to all those who'd been saying for years that Hank Williams was too drunk and too country to make it in the music business. It was also a commercial tool. Hank got exposure and sometimes money playing on the radio, and he made a lot of money on sales of his own records and some from pop artists covering his songs, but the mainstay of his income was cash from live performances.

Success did not satisfy him. He could stay on the straight and narrow for days or weeks, but then would get diverted and turn up too drunk to play – or not turn up at all. He got fired from network radio and was shunned by prestige venues. Back on the small-time circuit, he died on New Year's Eve 1952 while travelling from Montgomery to Canton, Ohio half a continent away. The doctor who pronounced his body dead estimated its age to be 45. In fact, Hank was 29, worn out by alcohol, 'medication' and perpetual touring. His history of turbulent marriages and squandered fortunes set the template for glorious rock-star burn-out.

Hank perished somewhere between Knoxville, Tennessee and Oak Hill, West Virginia, the place unknown, the circumstances certain: in the back of a Cadillac on the way to a show. Like Patsy Cline, Eddy Cochran, Buddy Holly, Otis Redding, Jim Reeves, Bessie Smith and many more forgotten or never known, he was using the new, cheap-energy economy to rush to a new audience, while at the same time trying to console himself with heroic consumption in a manner later adopted by Lowell George, Jimi Hendrix, Janis Joplin, Keith Moon, Jim Morrison, poor silly Sid Vicious and the undisputed king of consumption, Elvis Presley himself. By dying of accidental self-poisoning in a moving vehicle, Hank Williams successfully fused two chart-topping techniques of rock and roll martyrdom.

When the Klu Klux Klan tried to sabotage Bessie Smith's big-top performance in Concord, North Carolina, in July 1927, the indefatigable 'Empress of the Blues' chased them away single-handed – the stagehands were too scared to follow – and then continued her performance. Was the reckless courage that made her invincible boosted by the fact that her private railroad car was waiting to speed the show out of town with the next southbound train? Bessie bought her husband a brand new, limited-edition 1926 Cadillac on impulse, for cash, but at the height of her reign she had a 78-foot railroad car to accommodate her tent show. In 1937, while heading for another date in Darling, Mississippi, following a show in Memphis, Bessie was killed when her old Packard ran into the back of a slow-moving truck.

The way he liked it told, Elvis Presley wanted a bicycle for his eleventh birthday, but his mother Gladys – worried he'd get run over – could only afford a guitar. Their dialogue – which points to a random quality at the epicentre of a cultural earthquake – found its way into thousands of potted biographies from 1956 on. A different version was offered by F. L. Bobo, who ran the East Tupelo hardware store where the purchase was made. Elvis wanted a rifle, but his mother, worried he'd kill all of his playmates, steered him towards a cheap guitar. The confusion is understandable. Doubtless the sensitive boy who'd already promised to buy two Cadillacs – one for himself and one for his poor parents – dreamed of bicycles, rifles, motorcycles *and* guitars.

Bicycles and rifles both promise to increase a boy's personal power. A bicycle has wheels and enables faster travel. A gun uses chemical combustion in a confined space to propel metal forward; it can threaten those who get in its user's way. It was around this time that Elvis first began to drive the family's battered old car.

When Henry Ford put the affordable automobile on offer, his target was the farmer living outside of town; the car was not intended as a convenience for the contented but as a relief for the exile. Hank

'A fancy car for all the town to see . . .' Hank Williams drives a new, powder-blue, Cadillac convertible in his 'Homecoming' parade, Greenville, Alabama, August 1952.

Williams's pain songs follow folkloric themes, funerals and faithless lovers. Cars appear only in his happy songs, where the social possibilities of the 'hot rod' are celebrated. In 'Setting the Woods On Fire' – written by Williams's producer Fred Rose and Edward G. Nelson Snr and recorded in 1952, Hank adopts the persona of an agricultural labourer looking forward to blowing all his money on a night out with his girlfriend: 'I'll gas up my hot-rod stoker, we'll get hotter than a poker, you'll be broke but I'll be broker.' The lyric hints at uses for the jalopy that go beyond travel: 'We'll sit close to one another, up one street and down the other.' The automobile's synthesis of privacy and mobility promised a dual escape, from the frustration of rural isolation and the prying eyes of small-town morality.

Way out in Lubbock, West Texas – a town that claimed more churches per capita than any other in the US – Charles 'Buddy' Holley (later streamlined to Holly) and his friends found reception from distant AM stations better on a 12-volt car radio than the alternating current of household supply, and in a car their parents could not censor their listening. The South was strictly racially segregated, but the airwaves were free to all. Buddy liked to listen to Black music, but played country until inspired to rock by the first appearance in Lubbock of regional sensation Elvis Presley. On a subsequent visit, Elvis arrived very late, allowing Buddy and his partner, who were booked to support Elvis's trio, time to 'blow the roof off'.

During the first three months of 1955, Elvis Presley travelled 25,000 miles and played 50 shows. He bought his first 'new' car that spring, a 1951 Lincoln Cosmopolitan with only 10,000 miles on the clock. It didn't last long, written off in a high-speed collision with a hay truck. Elvis replaced it with a pink and white Cadillac which he watched burn up in June after a wheel-bearing overheated on the road to Hope, Arkansas. His third automobile was brand new, another pink and white Cadillac; he got his name painted on the side, as a race driver or a tradesman might. After a show, he would cruise the streets picking up girls. A flashy car was as important an accessory for the aspirant rockabilly as Trigger was for Roy Rodgers or Silver for the Lone Ranger.

Presley went on to buy many, many cars, motorhomes, motorcycles and aeroplanes. By the end, he was giving cars to just about anybody who'd take one. The machines of '55 were special; they motivated his ambition, they enabled his progress, and they signified his success. Perhaps the cars that carried Elvis through that frantic year came closer to reconciling the practical and fantasy functions of the automobile than any before or since.

John Lennon observed that 'before Elvis there was nothing'. Jimi Hendrix threatening to move mountains with his bare hands, the Beastie Boys declaiming their intention to fight for the right to party, the Spice Girls' affirmations of Girl Power – all youth culture, no matter how bombastic or banal, follows in the tyre tracks of Elvis's pastel-painted saloons of 1955.

Teenage Hank, presenting himself as an adult performer, drove to bookings with a rudimentary public-address system – two 12-inch speakers in a single cabinet – the beginning of an era when amplified sound would enable the personnel and equipment that one automobile could carry to replace a full dance band. Hank's first sound system lasted until November 1941, when it was smashed in a car wreck.

Young Elvis might belch at the microphone and flick his chewing gum into the audience before abandoning himself to the show, or acknowledge screaming fans with a mumbled 'Fuck you very much'. Access to automobiles allowed teenage punks – inspired by the romance of rootlessness – to hit and run with a take-it-or-leave-it confidence once reserved for stars at the peak of their careers.

The cocksure arrogance of Elvis's stage persona hid a strong suspicion that the grown-ups were right, that the craze couldn't last and he'd better cash in while he could. Awe-struck by his power to communicate emotion, Elvis believed he had been given a gift, and that, if he wasn't generous with it, the gift might be taken back at any time. The terrible anticipation of crowds of kids waiting to be sparked into ecstasy by cultural contraband intensified the traditional imperative – the show must go on – into a hedonistic battle cry. The fatalistic haste with which Elvis spread his joyful revelation became a series of auto races on a public highway.

Coincidentally, a chain of fatal racing crashes in the US and the death of more than a hundred spectators at the Le Mans 24-hour race led Senator Richard Neuberger, a Democrat from Oregon, to address Dwight D. Eisenhower, in a speech before the US Senate on 12 July 1955, as follows: 'Mr President, I think the time has come to forbid automobile racing and similar carnage in the United States.' All over the world, rules and safety procedures for car racing were reassessed. Motor-sport continued, but the pioneering era was over.

The songs that launched the Texan Buddy Holly's sixteen months of international stardom were recorded across the state line in Clovis, New Mexico.

The change in time zone allows a traveller averaging more than 90 miles per hour to arrive in Clovis before leaving Lubbock. This race against time appealed to Buddy, a reckless, optimistic young man in a hurry.

The schedule of Buddy Holly and the Crickets' 1958 tour of England was hectic. There was no time for sightseeing; the hotel rooms were under-heated; the beds were too short; everyone was homesick and full of complaints. On 10 March, they were in Birmingham to play two shows at the Town Hall, and Buddy was feverish with a cold. He still insisted on a guided tour of the British Motor Corporation's plant and showrooms at Longbridge. Buddy was a car nut, but it was already too late to enjoy racing to shows at the wheel of his own car. Cars as tools of liberation for teenagers, and the thrills – or perils – of car racing remained reliable subjects for popular songs, but the logistics of placing rock stars before the biggest audience in the least possible time was already becoming a corporate issue.

After returning from his military service, Elvis appeared in 27 fictional motion pictures. He wanted to become a serious actor, but was mostly required to be Elvis, the first of many impersonators. The stories that keep the songs apart feature good-hearted hunks with robust warrior occupations like sky pilots or rodeo riders. In three of these titles, Elvis portrays a racing driver. When he declined to attend the premier of *Tickle Me* in May 1965, they sent the next best thing: a customized gold Cadillac. When he gave up movies and returned to 'the road', his tour party numbered 75 and travelled in three chartered planes.

On abandoning Hollywood Elvis vowed that he would never again record material he didn't believe in. Back in a Memphis studio for the first time in fourteen years, he cut a song that comes close to addressing the contradictions of his life. 'Long Black Limousine' was written by Californian country singer Vern Stovall; its subject matter and brevity were in the Hank Williams tradition, but the car was no longer bound for frolics. Elvis sings in the character of a small-town boy watching a parade of grand automobiles. His former love once promised to return from the big city in a fancy car that would impress the whole town. That dream has come true, but the car is long and black, a hearse, and the heart and dreams of the singer are being carried away in it.

The dead body in the car can stand for Elvis's mother, Gladys, who had died surrounded by newly won luxury in 1958, worrying about her beloved son and wishing her family could go back to being poor. It also stands for Elvis himself and his fatal ambitions. He dreamed of fancy cars and stardom, and they became a reality that isolated him from the people he set out to impress. He dedicated his whole being to becoming somebody; then, when his ambitions had been fulfilled beyond his wildest expectations, his life lost any purpose, and success obliterated his identity. In the song, the body in the long black limousine died in a car wreck, during a race on the highway, after a party – a fate decadent enough to stand in for Elvis's own end.

On his death trip, Hank Williams was alone except for a teenage chauffeur. Hank hadn't been working enough to keep a band and reasoned that everyone knew his songs, so he'd play – without rehearsal – in front of whoever the promoter provided. This *modus operandi* was famously perfected by Chuck Berry, who – long after big-name rock tours became corporate endeavours – was turning up at show time in his own car, with his guitar, an empty briefcase to be filled with cash and maybe a pistol to safeguard the takings.

If Elvis was a White boy who remodelled the

blues, then Charles Edward Anderson 'Chuck' Berry from St Louis, Missouri, was the Black man who put a blues backbone into hillbilly pop. His innovations, as writer and performer, made him the most influential of all of the early rock stars. He had spent three years in jail before ever going near a recording studio, the result of financing a motoring tour to Kansas City with opportunist armed robbery. Perhaps it was this early education in the limits of the possible that allowed a quality of cool detachment in some of his work. 'Maybellene' – his first hit – was a car song, and the automobile is a mainstay of his repertoire. His 1964 recording 'No Particular Place to Go' begins full of lascivious promise, but twelve couplets down the road the title phrase has become a cry of frustration. In two minutes and 41 seconds, Berry's *double-entendre* novelty song distils the dilemma the twentieth century produced: no particular place to go.

The power to go anywhere we choose deprives us of motivation. Dominance of the natural world forces us to redefine our existence without our former adversary, raw nature. Without infinite untrammelled wilderness to buffer our 'cowboy' excesses, the consequences of setting the woods on fire are no longer as innocent as Hank's Saturday-night spree. To conserve the biosphere, our only living space, we have to learn – like George Jones – to stop running, to stop pretending that there is a better life just round the bend or over the hill.

'King' George's attempt to enter his capital mounted on a latter-day donkey is a poetic parable of the aching, impossible desire for unlimited mobility and party-without-end that dominated the popular culture of the twentieth century, when the notions of 'future' and 'America' ran parallel in the popular imagination. The application of Henry Ford's remedy for rural loneliness now threatens the city-dweller with the isolation and long-distance travel of suburban living.

The verse of 'No Money Down', an early Berry song, is a bombastic rap detailing the opulent and – by the standards of 1955 – increasingly surreal specification ('TV and a phone') that Chuck wants on a Cadillac he is buying on credit. In contrast, the chorus is the anxious blues of a man poor enough to include an automobile on his list of necessities: 'I'm going to get me a car and drive it on down the road, so I won't have to worry about that run down, ragged Ford.' The song reveals the desire not just to get around, but to get around in a style that proves to us and to the watching world that we are somebody – a product of insecurity and poverty, or of feelings of insecurity and poverty.

Young Elvis's idea that he could become a superstar while remaining the humble, respectful and considerate boy his mother had raised proved an impossible fantasy. The automobile's promise to take people from one place to another, leaving them, their origin and destination, and the route between unaffected by the trip while entertaining them with the thrill of operating a powerful machine and affirming their power and status, is equally unsustainable. Cars may be useful for moving people and goods from place to place; they may be enjoyable cult objects for play, display or tests of skill and nerve. Continuing with attempts to fuse these practical and aesthetic functions will only destroy the possibility that either can be satisfactorily attained. The legends of Hank, Elvis and even tragic George Jones teach us that the time for trying to live that dream has passed.

Crossroads: The Automobile, Rock and Roll and Democracy

E. L. WIDMER

It is inevitable that any twentieth-century art form should delineate cars to some extent, given their dominion over our everyday lives: what is remarkable about American popular music is the *ubiquity* of the automobile's presence. A study of the course of automobile-related music indicates not only that the car has inspired constant subject matter for aspiring minstrels but that this has remained true even as music and transportation have undergone fundamental transformations. Improved technology revolutionized both music and automobiles in the period immediately following World War II, but they remained steadfast to one another, providing an important voice for a rising generation of Americans eager to leave their impress on the national culture. Specifically, the hybrid stains of rock and roll music depended heavily on the independence offered by racy new automobiles in the early 1950s to sound a barbaric yawp over the rooftops of Benny Goodman's America.

Within a decade of the auto's appearance on American streets, Tin Pan Alley was churning out car-related hits with the speed and regularity of the auto industry itself. As early as 1899, a song entitled 'Love in an Automobile' indicated how helpful a car might prove to would-be suitors, and at least 120 similar songs were released between 1905 and 1907 alone. As might be expected, levity figured prominently in these early compositions, with titles such as 'Fifteen Kisses on a Gallon of Gas,' 'I'm Going to Park Myself in Your Arms,' and 'I'd Rather Go Walking with the Man I Love Than Ride in Your Automobile (You Cad).'[1] By far the most successful of these was the 1905 hit, 'In My Merry Oldsmobile,' which earned a free car for its two songwriters from the grateful manufacturer.

The bonanza following World War II made cars universally affordable and fostered dramatic technological improvements that pushed an already car-crazy nation to the brink of lunacy. This mania expressed itself through all the normal media: film, literature, the fine arts, and, of course, music. No genus of popular expression has celebrated the automobile with more feeling and attention to nuance than 'rock and roll.' The enormous body of music contained within this ill-defined rubric has been intimately connected with the automobile throughout its brief but mercurial history. Rock performers have not only sung the praises of the car but have traditionally dedicated every sequinned fiber of their beings to the pursuit of what we might loosely define as an 'automobile' existence, something far broader that the general itinerancy required of musicians. In the rock and roll lexicon, cars have evolved beyond simple instruments of transportation to become the very symbols of the high living and conspicuous consumption sought out by artists and savored by the public.

EASY RIDER: BLUES AND THE AUTOMOBILE

To fully gauge the extent to which this is true, it is useful to compare rock and roll, which by most accounts emerged in the early 1950s, to the simpler blues music that preceded and fostered it.

The automobile was less frequently sung about that the railroad within this musical genre, simply because it embodied a type of unlimited mobility — an *active* as opposed to a *passive* right-of-way — that many American blacks were effectively denied in the South. When it did creep into a songwriter's vocabulary, however, it clearly represented something very different from the anomie linked to train rides and hoboing. As defined in this music, cars were sexy and exciting, one might even say liberating, both for the personal privacy they permitted *and* for the social and financial emancipation they proclaimed. For several reasons, Ford was the make of choice among blues singers. Its relative affordability was appealing. Furthermore, Henry Ford had been hiring blacks in Detroit since 1914, earlier than his competitors, which lent him a certain palatability. Finally, many blacks saw in the durable, hard-working, and monochromatic Model T a crude parallel to their own underappreciated existence.[2] The allegorical songs that sprang from this perception were not only 'democratic' in their criticism of fancier models but surprisingly racy.

Most of the blues songs treating the car are shocking even today for their unabashed obsession with what Thomas Jefferson delicately phrased the 'organs of generation'.[3] In 1926, Virginia Liston lamented that her 'Rolls Royce Papa' had a bent pistol rod; a year later, Bertha Chippie Hill, in 'Sports Model Mama,' claimed to receive punctures every day; and in 1929, Cleo Gibson, in what might have proved an effective advertising slogan, belted out 'I've Got Ford Engine Movements in My Hips.'[4] Male singers were

not slow to express similar notions. At least three boasted their beds could rock 'like a Cadillac car' (Bobby Grant, Leroy Carr and Lonnie Clark), and Washboard Sam complained in 'Out with the Wrong Woman' (31 December 1936) that his woman 'was built like an automobile, but didn't have no rumble seat.'

Other songs stressed economic principles. Sleepy John Estes stated the case succinctly but powerfully: 'Well, the T model Ford I say is the poor man's friend' ('Poor Man's Friend,' 3 August 1935). Blind Lemon Jefferson announced in 'D B Blues' (August 1928) that 'a Packard is too expensive, Ford will take you where you want to go.' Ramblin' Thomas promised, 'Some of these days I am going to be like Mr Henry Ford/Going to have a car and a woman running on every road' ('Hard to Rule Woman Blues', February 1928). One singer even confused his myths as he lauded the accomplishments of 'John Henry Ford.'

Probably the most important car-related song of the period was Robert Johnson's 'Terraplane Blues' (Vocalion, 23 November 1936), the first record he released and his bestselling hit. Johnson carried the car-woman metaphor even further, if possible, announcing to his paramour, 'I'm gonna hoist your hood, mama, I'm bound to check your oil . . . / I'm gonna get down deep in this connection, keep on tangling with your wires / And when I mash down on your little starter, then your spark gonna give me fire.' Johnson's impressive know-how concerning this new make of Hudson never entered into his songs about the railroad, all of which were far less exuberant in comparison (e.g., the lonely 'Love in Vain'). Interestingly, Johnson approximated this sexual-mechanical link only in his 'Phonograph Blues' (23 November 1936), singing, 'I'm gonna wind your little phonograph, just to hear your little engine moan.' In Robert Johnson's mind, musical and automotive technologies had generated powerful possibilities for alleviating the dreariness of life in the Depression-era Delta, even if he was never to realize them during his abbreviated existence.

For post-war America, the cheapness of raw material, the scale of production, and the climate of patriotic euphoria allowed, even required, *all* classes of Americans to realistically contemplate car ownership.[5]

Coeval with these developments were rapid advances in recording technology. Just as World War I had initiated a period of intensive radio use, so World War II was followed by a dizzying sequence of technological breakthroughs. The US army discovered the Nazi invention of the magnetic-tape recorder at the end of the war. The defeat of the Japanese also meant that the shellac needed to make records could again be imported from the Pacific regions where it was cultivated, to the great relief of Americans who had been listening to the same crackly 78s for four years. Then in 1948, Columbia Records presented their new long-playing records, which greatly increased the amount of music that could be packaged by spinning at only 33 ⅓ revolutions per minute. The moribund 78 offered a mere four minutes of playing time to the LP's 25, and the latter's 'unbreakable' plastic microgroove discs were also vastly more durable. RCA Victor was quick to follow with the smaller 45-rpm record. Stereo became available in 1954 for tapes and in 1958 for records, and high fidelity was continually improved upon throughout this period. Finally, the portable transistor radio was pioneered in 1954, allowing music to be compressed and taken anywhere. It was in use in cars by 1956.[6]

These innovations soon bore fruit in an efflorescence of musical creativity and also facilitated the means by which this harvest was distributed to the eager consumer. Radio stations proliferated; between 1946 and 1948 the number of AM stations doubled, while FM stations increased from 668 to 1,005.[7] Programming methods also changed, especially as the 45 allowed stations and consumers to focus their attention on single songs that could be made and sold quite cheaply. In 1949, KWOH in Omaha was the first station to convert entirely to a pop-music format, and in 1953 the same station created the idea of a 'Top 40' countdown of popular hits.[8]

But perhaps the most important innovation for our purposes was the electrification of the guitar, which had been in the works for years but was not really perfected until the late forties, most notably by Les Paul, who pioneered the solid-body version of the instrument, inspiring the Fender Corporation to issue its famous Stratocaster in 1953. This improvement, seemingly so simple, changed the fundamental sound and rhythm of all guitar music, giving it a faster, louder, and far more voluptuous sound.

Teenagers who were spending their Saturdays fixing up hot rods were eager to absorb the strange new electric sounds coming out of their car radios, for each machine signalled a decisive rupture with older, obsolete models. Suddenly, leisure technology had become universally affordable and comprehensible; taking advantage of it, American youth seized, or rather had thrust upon itself, the cultural means of production. As Tom Wolfe has shown in his essays on the custom-car culture of southern California and stock-car racing in the rural South, the automobile allowed the postwar youth to express himself in ways that no machine had, at least in recent memory.[9] It was hardly accidental that George Barris, the Carravaggio of car customizing, opened his business in 1945, just as millions of battle-weary young Americans needed to shift their attention from the war to less serious matters. As the teenager became a potent economic force, his desires as a consumer were increasingly heeded, and it was to this enormous audience that rock and roll addressed itself, sounding at first every bit as powerful and weird as the blues had to W. C. Handy.

Seeming to suggest the forbidden mysteries of sexuality, both the new music and the new type of automobiles found easy, if not aggressive, acceptance in the concupiscent universe that was 1950s teenage America. Like jazz (and later, funk), the very words *rock and roll* provoked knowing smiles from those who understood the more organic nature of their original slang meaning. It was inevitable that the automobile, as the symbol of the economic arrival of the previously disenfranchised groups constituting the rock and roll audience, would emerge as a central motif in their new form of musical expression. Automobiles offered an easy escape route from restrictive home environments. Appropriately, many of the earliest rock and roll records were directly linked to the automotive experience.

Although there are earlier uses of the off-color phrase 'rock and roll,' it is generally conceded that the first song to mix the ingredients of modern rock was a tune called 'Rocket 88' recorded in Memphis on 5 March 1951 by Jackie Brenston and the Kings of Rhythm (featuring a very young Ike Turner).[10] A paean to the flashy new Oldsmobile model, the song celebrated little beside the joy of being seen riding around in a souped-up vehicle, but apparently this was enough, for it became a number one hit on the rhythm-and-blues charts. Significantly addressed only to women, it invited the listener to go 'sporting' with

Brenston all over town, then listed the car features (V8 motor, convertible top, smart design) that made such an invitation irresistible. The generally salacious feel of the song was heightened by the fuzzy tone of the guitar amplifier, which had fallen out of the band's car (appropriately) on the way to the session and was emitting noise like a wounded B-29 bomber.

Sam Phillips, who produced the session for Chess Records, later pinpointed this moment as the birth of rock and roll, and as the man who launched the careers of Elvis Presley, Jerry Lee Lewis, and Carl Perkins, he was in a good position to know. Little Richard acknowledged that 'Rocket 88' served as the inspiration for his 'Good Golly Miss Molly.' Perhaps even more telling is the fact that a white disc jockey in Chester, Pennsylvania, named Bill Haley liked the song so much that he covered it with his country band, the Saddlemen. This showed the crossover appeal of the song. The electricity of the simultaneous black and white influences, to say nothing of the instruments themselves, would soon allow Haley to emerge as the world's first rock and roll star, although he would not enjoy that distinction for long.[11]

The success of 'Rocket 88' launched a spate of inferior imitations, including a follow-up number by Brenston himself called 'Real Gone Rocket' (July 1951). Before long, the tiny Chess label alone had recorded Billy Love's 'Drop Top' (November 1951), Rosco Gordon's 'T-Model Boogie' (4 December 1951), Howlin' Wolf's 'Cadillac Daddy' (23 January 1952), Johnny London's 'Drivin' Slow' (8 March 1952), and Joe Hill Louis's 'Automatic Woman' (9 September 1953), which compared his girlfriend favorably to the new GM transmissions being churned out in Detroit. There seemed to be no limit to the poetic inspiration a musically inclined American youth might draw from the national love affair with the automobile.

Elvis Presley at the wheel of his 1956 Cadillac Eldorado.

The most evocative symbol of this rising generation of musical teenagers and their automotive priorities remains Elvis Presley, the self-styled 'King of Rock and Roll' (Little Richard briefly contested the title, until it grew evident he held a stronger claim to another royal moniker). Like many of the black musicians he admired and imitated, Presley had grown up desperately poor in Mississippi during the Depression, until his parents had packed all their possessions in a beat-up 1937 Plymouth and driven along Highway 78 from Tupelo to Memphis in September 1948. When he began singing, Presley was driving trucks for the Crown Electric Company, and his lifetime fascination with automobiles paralleled that of an entire underclass for whom more expensive luxuries, such as larger houses (although Presley later acquired plenty of those), were simply impossible to fantasize about. While majoring in shop at Humes High School in Memphis, Elvis announced in his yearbook that his highest ambition in life was to become a Tennessee state highway patrolman.[12]

For Presley, the supreme emblem of his liberation from poverty was a pink Cadillac; at first, just the idea of one, and late, when circumstances permitted, the reality. Although his father had scraped together 50 dollars to buy Elvis a 1942 Lincoln Zephyr coupe for his eighteenth birthday in 1953, Elvis, like most Americans, saw the Cadillac as the quintessence of the social acceptability that had thus far eluded him. In one of his earliest recording sessions (February 1955), again with the ubiquitous Sam Phillips, Elvis covered a sexy song called 'Baby, Let's Play House' by Arthur 'Hardrock' Gunter, which taunts a respectable society girl into remaining with the singer to attend to some neglected domestic chores. Elvis, however, fiddled with the words and substituted 'pink Cadillac' for a reference to her religion, and a large measure of the song's excitement derives from the singer's feeling of triumph over a girl rich enough to drive such a high-falutin vehicle.

Around the same time, Elvis bought the first in what would perhaps become the word's longest succession of fancy cars; a secondhand Cadillac financed by his manager. The night he bought it, he stayed up for hours simply looking at it from his hotel window. Although it was destroyed by fire soon thereafter, Elvis quickly bought another with the insurance money and painted it pink and black, the colors of his performance clothes. As soon as he could afford it, he bought another Cadillac that was entirely new and entirely pink, which he presented to his mother. It is still visible as part of the overwhelming armada of vehicles behind Graceland.

One vehicle especially stands out as a monument to Elvis's Veblenesque fascination with the automobile. When he turned his attention to filmmaking in the late 1950s and early 1960s, Elvis brashly declared, 'I don't want anybody in Hollywood to have a better car than mine. A Cadillac puts the world on notice that I have arrived!' Accordingly, he hired George Barris to reshape his limousine. It was inevitable that these two folk heroes, both pauper pretenders to royalty (the King of Rock and Roll and the King of Kustomizing), should meet and collaborate. Perhaps inspired by the $10,000 gold suit Elvis was wont to wear on occasion, Barris gold-plated almost every surface of the car, from the headlight rims and hubcaps to the interior accoutrements, which included a television, telephone, record player, bar, ice maker, and the obligatory electric shoe buffer.

The enormous back-seat area was called the Center Lounge, with seats arranged in a semicircle and Elvis's gold records lining the ceiling. The floor of the car, if I may call it a car, was covered with white fur, and the exterior was painted with 40 coats of a special dust made from crushed diamonds and fish scales flown in from Asia. Barris called it his 'most ambitious project,' and it garnered so much attention that RCA records sent the car itself on tour, where at one point it attracted 40,000 people to a mall in Houston. If Graceland was Elvis's Versailles, then the Gold Car was his Royal Phaeton, a hillbilly's dream come true. Indeed, the TV sitcom 'The Beverly Hillbillies' (which is nothing if not a fable of democracy) was partially inspired by this creation, now resting peacefully in the Country Music Hall of Fame in Nashville. No other material object could symbolize as vividly the values that made Elvis and America great.[13]

As Elvis grew richer, automobiles became a type of personal currency for him and purchasing them a peculiar form of economic self-expression. He bought all different types of cars; he bought many of them, and he bought them often. Like Louis XIV distributing small principalities (this metaphor is inexhaustible), the self-made Sun King offered them freely to his attendants, and these munificent bequests served as informal salaries for his otherwise underpaid minions. There are far too many stories of capricious car purchases during the reign of Elvis to repeat them all here, although my favorite is the night he bought fourteen Cadillacs from a flabbergasted Memphis dealer and offered the last of them to an elderly black woman passing by (perhaps a belated assumption of the debt he owed rhythm-and-blues artists). Throughout his life, his favorite nontoxic from of recreation was racing through the streets of Memphis with his buddies in the wee hours of the morning, and unlike most celebrities, he scoffed at the idea of chauffeurs. Driving was simply too important.[14]

Obviously, cars offered more than simple transportation to Elvis, unless the word is understood to embrace a larger meaning, a social mobility beyond the immediate physical movement they offered. Flashy automobiles did indeed transport him, away from everything that stank of the immobile, inert indigence that had ruled his Depression upbringing. Presley's immense wealth, to say nothing of his *parvenu* urge to gild everything, shocked the nation fully as much as his pelvic thrusts, and his obsession with cars reflected the collective yearnings of an entire generation of formerly underprivileged Americans. His remarkable Cadillacs threw not only sex in the face of Ward Cleaveresque America but a small dose of democracy as well.

Yet another performer who displayed this obsession with the automobile was a former car thief from St. Louis named Charles Edward Berry. Chuck Berry's first song, 'Maybellene' (recorded 21 May 1955), reworked a harmless old country tune called 'Ida Red' into a sizzling car chase/romance between the singer in his souped-up V8 Ford and an idealized woman in an elusive Cadillac (what else?). The song cleverly alternates describing the vehicle and the woman, and before long the one becomes a thinly veiled substitute for the other. It begins with the singer leisurely 'motovating' down the road in his V8 Ford, then spying Maybellene in a Cadillac Coupe de Ville up ahead of him. They engage in a furious car chase with all sorts of sexual undertones until a providential cloudburst cools down our hero's engine sufficiently that he is able to 'catch' her at the top of the hill, ending the drama and the song.

'Maybellene' is exciting not only for its original

language (neologism like motorvate) and its mixture of black and white styles (again, the hallmark of early rock and roll) but also for its openly sexual feel and the populist triumph of the Ford over the Cadillac. Both rhythmically and thematically, this is a far cry from the blues and its general association of travel with despair and escape. In his recently published autobiography, Berry explained the song 'was composed from memories of high school and trying to get girls to ride in my 1934 Ford.' Interestingly, this was the same year and make of Ford that had transported Bonnie and Clyde away from *their* stagnant southern backgrounds. The Cadillac, Berry confessed, was merely wishful thinking, a 'dream De Ville.'[15]

Later songs only strengthened the connection he saw between woman and automobiles. 'Nadine' (4 January 1964) described another allegorical chase, this time in pursuit of a girl walking toward a 'coffee-colored Cadillac.' The choice of this wonderfully evocative color could hardly be chimerical, again the car's identity seems to blend with the woman's. Despite another spirited car race and yelling like a 'southern diplomat,' he can't catch her this time, largely because she moves through traffic like both 'a wayward summer breeze' and 'a mounted cavalier.' Perhaps the most masterful statement of the car/woman conflation occurs in 'No Particular Place to Go' (26 March 1964), in which Berry actually has the girl alongside him in his car but sadly cannot undo her protective safety belt. The song is interesting also for its affirmation of Jackie Brenston's philosophy that driving – or, more specifically, 'cruising and playing the radio' – is so pleasant in and of itself that destinations have become superfluous.

Yet another Berry opus, 'No Money Down' (20 December 1955), says as much as any history book about the economic climate that allowed this expensive exploration of automotive fantasy. The song celebrates the joys of easy car financing, delineating an ideal vehicle remarkably similar to Elvis's Gold Car. Not content to wait, or even ask politely, Berry simply *demands* what he feels to be his prerogative: a yellow Caddy convertible with every option in the book. He continues, calling for power in what almost sounds like a revolutionary pamphlet: 'I want power steering and power brakes/I want a powerful motor with jet off-take.' Finally, he lists the aristocratic appurtenances that he, like Elvis, can deliciously appreciate as a true *connoisseur* (air conditioning, heat, bed in the back seat, short-wave radio, TV, telephone). Such an optimistic expression of financial and sexual confidence makes it easy to understand why 1955 was not only the year that Berry and Presley struck pay dirt but also the top-selling year for cars in American history.

Like Elvis, Berry fully lived the automotive life he projected in his 'oeuvre.' His autobiography is full of automobile references. In 1941, at the age of 14, he bought a 1934 V8 Ford for $35 ($10 down and $5 a month), the same car that inspired 'Maybellene.' As one of only two students at his school owning a car, his popularity was increased immeasurably. He went on endless joyrides with other 'car-crazy' friends, was incarcerated for car theft during one of them, and immediately bought a shiny Buick upon his release from jail. Describing another arrest in 1958, this time for violation of the Mann Act (which seems to have been tailor-made for early rock and roll stars), Berry wrote nonchalantly that the policeman 'ordered me to stand aside while he searched the cream-colored Cadillac, which I must admit was attractive.' Toward the end of his book, after discussing his children and grandchildren, Berry summarized a lifetime of achievement by saying, 'Up to then I had owned a total of 29 automobiles, most of them purchased new and most of the new ones Cadillacs, which was then the epitome of well-off.' In his recent film, *Hail, Hail, Rock and Roll*, one of the most amusing scenes shows Chuck in a garage, surrounded by old Cadillacs, trying to calculate their financial worth, as if this is the only balance sheet that can measure his importance to American culture.[16]

Following the Presley and Berry examples, legions of young rockers in the '50s and early '60s incorporated songs about cars into their repertoires. Little Richard aped car slogans by calling his 'Long Tall Sally' 'built for speed.' Bo Diddley not only adopted a rocket-shaped guitar with two fins (the Gibson Flying V) that imitated contemporaneous car styling, but claimed to be a 'Roadrunner' (1960), the 'fastest in the land.' James Brown, who also did time for car theft, surely would have disputed the claim. In 'Not Fade Away,' Buddy Holly's love was 'bigger than a Cadillac.' The Ides of March warbled 'I'm Your Vehicle, Baby,' while the Playmates sang 'Beep Beep,' about a little Nash Rambler beating a Cadillac in a race. The Beach Boys and Jan and Dean released dozen of songs that made it difficult to imagine how the state of California had ever existed before Henry Ford came along. Furthermore, many groups, ranging from the famous to the mercifully obscure, took their names from some of the more mellifluous car names floating around, including the Imperials, the Eldorados, the Continentals, the Cadillacs, and yes, even the Edsels.

Cars were so popular that even the grisly deaths they caused received thorough, almost loving attention. In 1956, Nervous Norvus scored a moderate hit with his novelty, 'Transfusion,' in which an injured driver asks for blood by saying 'shoot me some juice, Bruce' and 'pass the claret, Barrett' over dubbed-in

A promotional photo for the 1959 hit single *Kookie, Kookie, Lend Me Your Comb*.

crash sounds. Mark Dinning's 'Teen Angel' (1960), Ray Peterson's 'Tell Laura I Love Her' (1960), and Jan and Dean's 'Dead Man's Curve' (1964) all bespoke the same fascination with death and high-speed car crashes that the Italian Futurists had shown at the beginning of the century.[17] While not a rock star, James Dean immediately entered the teenage Valhalla following a fiery exit on the California desert in 1955. Eddie Cochran's death in a car crash in England in 1960 accomplished a similar deification.

Rock and roll continues to exist and seems to exert an enormous pull on the attentions of adolescents worldwide. It is one of the few art forms that we can all genuinely American in its origin, and the automobile continues to stand out as a pivotal subject, certainly more so than in other types of music. This kinship between theme and form is difficult to explain, but it seems to derive from the fact that both represented a 'liberating' principle for the individual, something that has hardly met with resistance in

American history. *Automobile*, after all, means 'self-moving' in a literal sense, and it is astonishing how many early rockers came from dirt-poor backgrounds, using the music to jack themselves up by their boot-straps. Emerson would surely appreciate this latest form of self-reliance; on a different subject, he wrote, 'All language is vehicular and transitive.'[18]

Both the automobile and popular music profited from postwar technology to offer an unprecedented amount of personal expression, and each emphasized the importance of the *solitary* performer, away from the watchful eyes of parents and neighbors. Like the automobile, the electric guitar allowed the independently inclined from all backgrounds to stand up and take charge of their own destinies, relegating the more communal forms of railroad travel and big-band music to inferior, antiquated roles in the postwar hierarchy of cultural values. Chuck Berry was one of the first popular musicians of the twentieth century to stand up and perform his own material solo before a national audience, and he remains notorious for his dislike of support bands. Elvis, Little Richard, Jerry Lee Lewis, and the other giants of fifties rock were all individual performers as well. At least in the teenage mind, which feeds on autonomy to begin with, this rebellious and discordant music has always existed in perfect harmony with the escapism afforded by the automobile. Few nations have ever needed a mood of carefree independence as America did after twenty years of Depression and war, and fewer still ever created one quite so lasting.

FROM *Roadside America: The Automobile in Design and Culture*, edited by Jan Jennings (1990)

Vanishing Points

DAVID PASCOE

'Everyone wants a piece of Kowalski . . . but they'll
have to catch him first, before he gets to the VANISHING
POINT.' So announced the publicity for Richard
Sarafian's film *Vanishing Point* (1971), the action of
which begins with the noise of earthmovers crawling
across an interstate and linking up to form an impass-
able barrier, a steel screen. Groups of civilians and
police peer down the blacktop anxiously; it is only to
be expected. Over the course of the last day and a half,
a late-model, supercharged Dodge Challenger has
rammed through every speed trap, dragnet and road-
block the Highway Patrol of four Western states have
placed before it. It has rammed a motorcycle cop in
Colorado, wiped out a Jaguar XK-E in Utah and
wrecked a squad car in Nevada. Now it has reached
the end of the road in northern California.

Kowalski (Barry Newman) – his name, perhaps,
paying homage to the nemesis of Blanche Dubois in
Tennessee Williams's *A Streetcar Named Desire* – is an
ex-Marine, ex-policeman, ex-racing driver who is
crossing the northern California desert at the wheel of
his own desired machine, a white Challenger. His car
approaches the roadblock, but then executes a U-turn
and, coming face to face with several police vehicles
following at a safe distance, swerves off the blacktop
into the desert, artfully littered with the shells of torched
cars. In the midst of this scrap heap, the Challenger

Right, from top: *Vanishing Point* (1971): Colorado, Utah, Nevada,
northern California.

stops, and Kowalski emerges to stretch his legs and survey the scene ahead. After a few moments of contemplation, he climbs back into the bucket seat and, in a spirit of contradiction, grasps the steering wheel and floors the accelerator. As he careers past the numerous glowing flares scattered across the road and heads towards the barricade, a black car streaks past in the opposite direction. The frame freezes with the timeline: 'California – Sunday – 10.02 a.m.' before cutting to another caption, 'Two days earlier' and beginning a flashback.

Forty-eight hours earlier, Kowalski had delivered a car to Denver, but, rather than staying over in the city, he had insisted on immediately taking another vehicle back to San Francisco. At the city limits, he scored some amphetamines. The dealer, a pimp, offered him a woman, but Kowalski was adamant that he had to be in California by Sunday afternoon and made off towards the desert. As the publicity for the film stated, 'Along the way he lived with speed, to get himself up . . . and get himself . . . gone.'

Though produced by a British company, Cupid, which had recently backed Jean-Luc Godard's documentary about the Rolling Stones, *One Plus One* (aka *Sympathy for the Devil*) (1968), Sarafian's *Vanishing Point* has come to be regarded as the ultimate American road movie.[1] Its title is carefully designed to suggest the instant at which some kind of consciousness or existence evaporates, but it also carries with it perspectival overtones, and indicates the point at the centre of the frame towards which everything converges before disappearing. *Vanishing Point*, then, simultaneously implies explosion and implosion, taking place along a road leading inexorably towards a darkening horizon.

America, Jean Baudrillard's singular account of a European philosopher's travels in the hyper-real spaces of the US, opens with a section entitled 'Vanishing Point'. In it, Baudrillard explains that he was searching for '*astral* America' – that is, not for a 'social and cultural' nation, but instead for that zone sharply defined by the 'empty, absolute freedom of the freeways'. Rather than the 'deep' nation of 'mores and mentalities', he sought a state characterized by its 'desert speed, motels and mineral surfaces'. His account does not take the form of a traveller's snapshots; instead, since 'the unfolding of the desert is infinitely close to the timelessness of film', it amounts to a road narrative in its own right. For Baudrillard searched out America 'in the speed of the screenplay, in the indifferent reflex of television, in the film of days and nights projected across an empty space, in the marvellously affectless succession of signs, images, faces, and ritual acts on the road'.[2]

America confirms Baudrillard's general proposition that the only post-modern truth is one that is *represented*, and so it follows that the best means to identify the culture that framed the American state of mind ought to be the road movie, whose narrative machinery reels off the miles from city to city, state to state, following a route just as simple and ineluctable as that of film through a ciné camera. The road movie, like the medium of film itself, dwells in a space of infinite possibility: the frame of a projector gate.

All along the way, *America* seeks to question the very topography of capitalism and the means by which this system organizes space around the road network. Baudrillard kicks against Route 66: 'The inhumanity of our ulterior, asocial, superficial world immediately finds its aesthetic form here, its ecstatic form. For the desert is simply that: an ecstatic critique of culture, an ecstatic form of disappearance.'[3] The vanishing it effects can only come from the 'ecstasy' of speed that produces, in motion pictures at least, such strange optical phenomena as a rotating wheel appearing stationary or even seeming to be turning backwards. But personality is affected, too, since for Baudrillard, the act of driving amounts to a spectacular form of 'amnesia' in which 'Everything is to be discovered, everything to be obliterated.'[4]

As he crosses the deserts of the Western United States, Kowalski tries to succumb to just such an amnesia, to obliterate himself. But however quickly he drives, he is unable to escape from himself. As Baudrillard explains:

This form of travel admits of no exceptions: when it runs up against a known face, a familiar landscape, or some decipherable message, the spell is broken: the amnesic, ascetic, asymptotic charm of disappearance succumbs to affect and worldly semiology.[5]

Memories – rather than coolly vanishing into the distance – pursue Kowalski furiously through his repeated glances back. His rear-view mirror becomes the screen on which are projected the repeated misfortunes that have punctuated his life: a motorcycle accident in which he was badly hurt; the end of his career as a policeman, brought about by his discovery that his partner was on the take; the drowning of his girlfriend; his heroic deeds in Vietnam in saving a

Top: *Kings of the Road* (1974): in the cab, en route.

Above: *Week-end* (1967): roadkill.

wounded comrade. As his Challenger heads towards the bulldozers, the black car is travelling in the opposite direction, and, as the camera swings to follow it, it becomes clear that it is the very same machine that Kowalski had delivered to Denver two days earlier. He seems trapped within an infinite loop.

Had Baudrillard seen *Vanishing Point*, he might have regarded such a ghostly effect as the sign of a larger cultural phenomenon:

...this spectral form of civilization which the Americans have invented, an ephemeral form so close to vanishing point, suddenly seems the best adapted to the probability – the probability only – of the life that lies in store for us. The form that dominates the American West, and doubtless all of American culture, is a seismic form: a fractal, interstitial culture, born of a rift with the Old World, a tactile, fragile, mobile, superficial culture.[6]

Applying the opposite lock in the direction of Europe's basic drives, Baudrillard identifies what is missing from the New World, that 'superficial culture' towards which the 'Old World' is now accelerating. America lacks stasis and permanence, memory and reaction; it lacks roads – Roman, lined narrowly with legions of cypress and larch, or medieval, draped around the edges of irregular fields and enclosures – with which to define *terroir* and on which to arrive where one began.

Such pronouncements may, incidentally, provide good reasons for the scarcity and the oddity of road movies in European cinema. Whenever such films have been attempted, the road is never depicted as continuous like an unrolling reel; instead, it is depicted as a medium of discontinuity and interruption, of accident and blockage. In place of the romance of the open journey and the straight line, the

Right, from top: *The Vanishing* (1988): Autoroute du Sud; Practising their French; Route Des Vins; Saskia goes to the services.

lure of speed and the danger of the chase, narratives of the European road slice up time, fragment teleology, digress endlessly. In Wim Wenders's *Kings of the Road* (1974), for instance, a pair of disaffected wanderers – one a projectionist, the other a linguist – travel around the winding back roads of provincial West Germany, never losing sight of the border with the old East along the Elbe, on a journey more about ideology than self-discovery.

Even more singular in this respect is Jean-Luc Godard's *Week-end* (1967), which describes a road trip that heads off the map and vanishes into the terrain of revolution. Its main protagonists, Roland (Jean Yanne) and Corinne (Mireille Darc), are a married couple who would happily shoot each other, but must stay together for the sake of an inheritance that *grandmaman* might soon send their way. One Saturday, the couple leave Paris and hit the road (as well as several cars parked in their neighbourhood) in a battered Facel Vega convertible, but are soon held up on a trunk road. The most famous representation of the road in European cinema then follows: a seven-minute travelling shot of a tail-back during which we follow Roland and Corinne in their car, weaving in and out of a line of traffic that appears to stretch into next week, at least. Despite the expected frustrations and occasional outbreaks of rage, people seem oddly accepting of the blockage. Certainly, drivers sound their horns, seemingly immobilized in

Left, from top: *The Vanishing* (1988): Rex's Polaroid; Lemorne's BX; The long trip; Regional news.

Jean-Luc Godard directs Jean Yanne and Mireille Darc in *Week-end* (1967).

the cacophony, but passengers toss footballs back and forth through open sunroofs, children play games by an overturned car, and couples spread board games and picnics on and around their stationary vehicles. In its pitiless approach, Godard's interminable, exasperating tracking shot eventually offers a perfect manifestation of solidarity – the patience and passivity of those held up – and also of the 'vanishing point' of individual action, since at the head of the line of trucks and cars is a multiple pile-up: the reality of the 12,000 road deaths in France in 1967, 130 killed and

800 maimed in each weekend's carnage.

It should have been sufficient for Godard to assemble the burning wreckage and bloodied corpses in what he termed this *film de ferraille*, this movie of the scrap heap. Yet as the local reaction to Roland's queue-jumping shows, the priority on this stretch of road is clear. A scratch to the bodywork to a car is a source of indignation, while the pulped bodies of passengers merit barely a glance. Roland and Corinne pay little attention to the bodies smeared across the road as they drive by, and are only concerned with how this accident will have delayed them on their way to their inheritance. Before long, as they travel deeper into the weekend, the couple will behave even more ruthlessly, robbing the corpses of accident victims and massacring the grandmother before, finally, wife eats husband. Godard's satire is lethal: the callousness of Roland and Corinne indicates a bourgeois ideology that relies on the paradox that just as they smoothly transport us to the point of vanishing, our family cars insulate us from our worst excesses.

In George Sluizer's equally disturbing road movie *The Vanishing* (1988), a young Dutch couple, Saskia (Johanna Ter Steege) and Rex Hofman (Gene Bervoets), drive through the Rhone Valley on the Autoroute du Sud, making for their destination, a *gîte* in the Gard, from which they will explore the area on cycles. Their Peugeot 404 (several of which were snarled up in the *Week-end* tailback) is solid and reliable, a throwback to the '60s. As they reel off the miles, the couple occupy themselves with word games and practice their French pronunciation, but as *autoroutes* are always dull, they take the next exit for some local colour on the 'Route des Vins'. However, their steady progress is halted when the Peugeot runs out of petrol in the middle of a quiet tunnel, and, despite Saskia's pleas not to be left alone in the dark, Rex abandons her to go to the nearest petrol station, smiling callously as he walks away without looking back. On his return with a can of petrol, she is understandably furious, but they soon make up and head for a service station back on the *autoroute* to replenish the Peugeot's tank. Saskia visits the lavatory and on her return, she makes Rex promise never to leave her again. Just before their departure, she returns to the shop for more provisions, but this time Saskia does not re-emerge. After some minutes, Rex leaves a note on their car and goes looking for her, but she is

nowhere to be found; seemingly, she has left him and vanished into thin air. The only trace she has left behind is on a Polaroid he snapped while idly waiting for her; he can just make out, in its grainy background, the bright smudge of her red hair as she walks out of the shop.

The local police can offer little assistance, and three years pass without news of the missing Saskia. Each summer, Rex returns to the Gard and puts up fresh posters of her face, a campaign that results in his receiving several taunting postcards from a resident of the ancient town of Nîmes who claims to know what happened. The letter writer is one Raymond Lemorne (Bernard-Pierre Donnadieu), a stolid chemistry teacher with a wife and two daughters. A precise and intelligent man with a round, honest face, he has just inherited his grandfather's house, in the shadow of which he spends much time sitting at the wheel of his pristine red Citroën BX, hatching his plans. Behind the solid façade of his life, Lemorne is obsessed by what he believes to be a personality defect, which first manifested itself in his childhood, when he jumped from the first-floor balcony of the family apartment in Nîmes, breaking his arm and losing two fingers in the process. It seems that he leaped in a 'spirit of contradiction' – the same mindset that drives Kowalski, perhaps – because he wanted to know whether it was a foregone conclusion that he would not jump. Now in solid middle age, Lemorne is still propelled by this 'spirit' to commit some act of motiveless malignity which might complement those earlier leaps into the unknown. Hence he is shown loitering at service stations, trying unsuccessfully to abduct foreign women in his Citroën until one July day in 1984, when, having been approached by Saskia, he manages to lure her into the passenger seat of his car and sedate her with chloroform.

Three years later, outside Rex's apartment in Amsterdam, Lemorne approaches him and offers to reveal everything. He will end the everlasting uncertainty, the not knowing, on condition that Rex accompany him on the road trip back across France, down to the Gard. During this long day's journey into night to the vanishing point, Lemorne reveals, little by little, the circumstances of Saskia's disappearance. Close to Nîmes, he stops at the same service station from which she vanished and tells Rex that the only way he can know what happened to her is for him to 'share her experience'. So, in the same 'spirit of contradiction' which drove the killer to jump from the balcony as a child (and in which Kowalski drove into the bulldozers), Rex consumes coffee he knows to be drugged with sleeping pills. A couple of hours later, he wakes in dark confinement, just as Saskia did three years earlier; Lemorne has buried Rex alive in a box in the garden of his house, next to the coffin in which Saskia must have slowly expired.

The key to *The Vanishing* is meticulousness. At every level, Sluizer dramatizes the bourgeois urge for doing things 'just so', and shares and composes the fastidious precision of his killer. He touches the simplest objects and makes them alive with fear: arm-slings and plaster casts, key-rings and thermos flasks, holiday snaps and small change. All of these things are homely, alive with dreams of freedom that only ever turn into a dead ends. The film's closing sequence consists of a travelling shot, but one not on the same scale as Godard's. Sluizer's camera warily approaches Lemorne's Citroën, now resprayed white; it peers through the tailgate window at a regional newspaper, yellowing on the rear parcel shelf, and at its banner headlines: 'MYSTÉRIEUSE ET DOUBLE DISPARITION.' Rex and Saskia, pictured smiling on the front page, are both lost for ever in the *terroir* of the Gard, but what has doubly vanished here is innocence, the human quality the road always consigns to oblivion.

Moving Spaces

A. L. REES

Cars and movies grew in tandem. Like most machines of the nineteenth century, they apply the technology of intermittent motion, as did the sewing machine, the steam train and the machine gun. The volatile element in this first machine age is signalled quite literally in two early and humorous disaster films from the Brighton School with self-descriptive titles: *How It Feels To Be Run Over* and *Explosion of a Motor Car* (both 1900). In the first, a horse-less carriage heads straight for the viewers. As it fills the screen, seeming to run them over, hand-written titles appear with a music-hall tagline that reads: 'Oh! Mother Will Be Pleased!' By 1900, in this example, the legendary terror caused by the Lumières' *Train Entering a Station* of 1895 had been converted into pleasurable laughter. In the second film, a car explodes – by stop motion – and a puzzled policeman scribbles notes while body parts – in fact, fake limbs and bundles of clothes – rain down on him.

In the earliest films, including these two by British film pioneer Cecil Hepworth, horses and cars are recorded as contemporary facts, jostling in the same space, with motor vehicles in the exotic minority. They are not yet metaphors, but they are beginning to be a threat. The dangerous and comic nature of the first motorcars is taken up later, in such period films as *The Magnificent Ambersons* (Orson Welles, 1942) and *The Wild Bunch* (Sam Peckinpah, 1968). In this genre, the car symbolizes the conflict between the old and the new, as the horse is overtaken by the machine at the turn of the century.

Two stills from Orson Welles's 1942 film *The Magnificent Ambersons*.

For Welles, the steam car and the internal-combustion engine signal the passage to a new era, just as Peckinpah's bemused last outlaws contemplate the new technologies of the aeroplane and the motor vehicle which will make them outdated. In this case, however, not without a fight, since they kill the Generalissimo who has dragged their Mexican comrade to near-death behind a car, and then use their stolen automatic weapons in a bloody showdown. Unwittingly, they invent the armoured car – a Maxim mounted on a horse-driven cart loaded with dynamite

the better. They include Norma Desmond's Isotta-Fraschini limousine in *Sunset Boulevard* (1950); Mike Hammer's Jaguar – eventually a killing machine – in *Kiss Me Deadly* (1955); the rare Aston Martin carefully picked for *The Birds* by Alfred Hitchcock (1964); another Jaguar for the heroine of *Vertigo* (1958); a Mercedes into which the drunken Cary Grant is bundled for a death-trip in *North by Northwest* (1959), anticipating the Mercedes wrecked by Ryan O'Neal for his demo-drive in Walter Hill's *Driver* (1976); the detective's unusually sinister Volkswagen in *Blood*

Three stills from Billy Wilder's 1950 film *Sunset Boulevard*.

– but the souvenir of their defeat is the dead Pyke's classic Colt, retrieved by his pursuer Bishop. A final scene over the end-titles replays the gang's last procession on horseback through the Mexican village and into the trees.

In yet another film tradition, the car is also a disturbing presence, in part because of what it can do (break down, explode or kill, for example) but also because of what it connotes. Notably, it alerts the viewer, like a danger signal, to the uncanny or 'other' nature of its owner/driver. In the US, these cars are European – the more foreign or exotic to their milieu

Simple by the Coens (1983); yet another murderous Merc in David Lynch's *Lost Highway* (1996); and the Rolls-Royce behind the Magus' locked gates in Kubrick's *Eyes Wide Shut* (2000, entirely shot in the UK, but set in New York). This tradition continues, but more demotically. The new 'Asian Diaspora' director Atsushi Funahashi, in her 2001 feature *Echoes*, has her quirky cast escape New York's urban alienation in their 'junk Volvo'.

For films set in the UK, the Rolls is a specially fated vehicle. In Antonioni's *Blowup* (1966), it stands for open-topped decadence, while *Performance* (1970)

The demo-drive in Walter Hill's 1976 film, *Driver*.

boasts no fewer than two; the lawyer's black Roller opens the film, is acid-scorched halfway through and is replaced by the gangster's white Roller in the final shot. In mainland Europe, of course, the terms are reversed or transcribed. Examples include Jean Cocteau's Rolls for the angels in *Testament d'Ophée* (1960); the Bergman-Sanders Bentley in Roberto Rossellini's *Journey to Italy* (1953); the American cars selected by Jacques Tati for his great studies of road rage and order in *Play Time* (1967). There are always exceptions, and other codes: Michelangelo Antonioni generally preferred the Alfa-Romeo, for example (as in *L'avventura*, 1960, *Cronaca di un amore*, 1955 and *L'eclisse*, 1962). But Jean-Paul Belmondo's stolen Studebaker (*Breathless*, 1959) and the proto-yuppies' English Triumph (*Week-end*, 1967) are significant examples from the aficionado and antagonist of American cinema, Jean-Luc Godard, who in some respects has gone further than anyone else in assimilating motors to movies. Since the mid-1960s, all of his cars have been colour-coded to match the constituent colours of film stock. In the long crash sequence of *Week-end*, for example, the cars and trucks in the extended tracking shot are red, blue, yellow, black or white. In this scene, of course, only the camera moves, not the vehicles.

In some, but not all, of these films, combat by car is at the heart of the plot, as it is too in *Rebel Without a Cause* (1955) and *Crash* (1997). These two particular examples show how films breed films and echo each other (in this case by design). A key moment in David Cronenberg's *Crash* re-enacts James Dean's death by Porsche, which took place two years after he starred in Nicholas Ray's film *Rebel Without a Cause*. Here, a series of myths (heroic, tragic, spectacular) produce a grand syntagm or narrative chain,

time between Howard Hawks's original version and Robert Altman's remake of *The Big Sleep*). Here, the car is both icon and index of the driver's state and status in the plot, as in reality. The Model T had a particular set of associations. Designed for farmers as a plain agrarian vehicle, but the product of a relentlessly industrialized and urban factory system, it later became a sign of bohemian revolt and disengagement. John Cage drove one around 1950s New York, and Jackson Pollock broods from the front seat of a Model T in a famous early photograph taken on the verge of

Above: Three stills from Jean-Luc Godard's 1967 film *Week-end*. Right: Combat by car: Nicholas Ray's 1955 film *Rebel Without a Cause*.

enacted on two fronts. The first links Dean as the star of *Rebel* with his replayed death in *Crash*, drawing on a second level of narrativization to seal the bargain; in both films, cars are used by the protagonists as weapons in a duel. Dean is also a frozen emblem, beyond all narrative fiction, embalmed in Cronenberg's vision of cinema as death-drive.

In the majority of cases, however, the car is a simpler and more direct icon rather than a complex narrative device, as in the farmer's black Model T (*Grapes of Wrath* to *Bonnie and Clyde*) or the detective's hard-top coupe (which flips from black to white in the

his stardom. By the time it appeared, Pollock was driving a new Buick, but the Model T stuck as an image (like Dean, and almost as emblematically, Pollock the art star was killed in a crash). As star-vehicles, the images, or rather the faces, of Humphrey Bogart, James Dean and Elliott Gould in their cars are also direct signs of cinema itself. But as with Cronenberg, these signs can multiply, although not necessarily as forms of direct storytelling.

Roman Polanski's *Chinatown* (1974), for example, is almost wholly built around filmic metaphors of vision, mirroring, reflection and glass. The passage

of the plot is traced by acts of viewing, and here the cars are part of its image bank. The detective's black coupe is wrecked in a chase through orange groves against men on foot and horses; the victim's black saloon is stolen and then abandoned by the detective; the wife's white touring car announces her death at the moment when her head falls on the horn. Here, there is a system of correspondences which resemble the architecture of the plot rather than just its process in linear time. The real villain (played by John Huston) is never seen in a car at all, and to underline the point he walks heavily with a cane (a Kane, a Cain?). But then Polanski (who appears as a 'midget' gangster, also on foot) is European, and John Huston is rather grand. The Devil don't drive, nor in this film does he ride out.

A number of these films, and others from the experimental cinema, engage with the film/car scenario in a less iconic and more structural sense. The examples are diverse and do not form a distinct pattern. They include the contrast between the stalled car and the swiftly trotting horses in *The Magnificent Ambersons* (1942), a contrast signalled in the alternating montage of the soundtrack between the cranked car and the horse bells; the montage of the hot rod and driver in Kenneth Anger's *Kustom Kar Kommandos* (1965) developed from the similar strategy in *Scorpio Rising* (1964); the precision-editing of *Play Time*'s car journeys; and Ken Russell's car-crash scenario for his section of the opera compilation *Aria* (1987). Most elaborately, if briefly, there is Len Lye's *Rhythm* (1957), made for Chrysler as a one-minute commercial, but rejected by them. His rapid 'flicker' cutting shows process at work, both on the assembly line and in the editing. The workforce is decidedly multiracial, and the soundtrack is a blues riff with African drumming – was it too much for 1957 and the start of the Civil Rights era? The political overtone was appropriate, as well as anticipating the opening title sequence of Paul Schrader's *Blue Collar* (1977), for ultimately all of these explorations of film form go back to a single model: the cream-separator sequence from Sergei Eisenstein's *The Old and the New* (1929), a classic of mechanical form meeting up with organicist vision. Here, in a ribald pun on orgasm, sceptical peasants are overcome by the shining efficiency of the new machine and its gushing cream, a promise of future prosperity, just as the progressive heroine Marfa dreams of new tractors ploughing in multiple superimposition.

As well as supplying iconic motif and narrative drive (and bad puns), the car – or, more loosely, the vehicle – is also an index of visuality. 'What goes on in the windscreen is cinema in the strict sense,' Paul Virilio has said. Anne Friedberg has echoed this idea: '. . . the private mobility of driving transforms the windscreen into a synoptic view.' In Ian Christie's summing-up, '. . . both motoring and cinema offered the satisfaction of seeing the world "whizz by" in a common sensation of speed.' But there is also an expansion of the visual theme in another grand original, Fritz Lang's *Metropolis* (1927), with its futuristic city. Above ground, the space between high-rises is filled by hovering and flying aircraft. Below ground, video links are part of the communications and command system.

Ridley Scott's *Blade Runner* (1982) deliberately echoes this urban cityscape, now rendered even more dystopic and entropic. Video and semi-digital screens fill the vehicles and guide the hero. The electronic eye acts as a link not just to the subterranean world – as in Lang's vision – but to the psychological interior (or its replicated simulacrum) of the protagonists. The same technologies appear more as farce than as tragedy in

Paul Verhoeven's post-Langian *Total Recall* (1990): the exploding auto-taxi with its puppet driver and invitation to 'have a nice day!', and the tracking devices that litter the Mars world. Late descendants of this genre include the 'Terminator' series and *The Matrix* (2000). A similar scenario of observation and surveillance is seen in full-blown sci-fi epics, especially *2001: A Space Odyssey* and *Solaris*, but here we find a final ancestor in the Freudian and cosmic fantasy *Forbidden Planet* (1956), whose Robbie the Robot was enshrined and exhibited by the Independent Group at the Institute

crossed with cars and hyper-aggressive trucks. For most of the older generation, however, driving was a personal business, while for the Pop painters it was the car as corporate sign that seized the frame. It was ambiguously celebrated as such by Richard Hamilton (as in the collage *Hommage au Chrysler Corp*) and by Colin Self in his mid-1960s 'Cars and Cinema' series. Self's graphic depictions include the stylized auto with high-rise background in *Car Drawing* (1964) and, more elaborately, his image of a back-projected car on a movie screen with 'a person with a bloody face' in

The puppet auto-taxi driver in Paul Verhoeven's 1990 film *Total Recall*.

of Contemporary Arts, London, for their seminal show *This is Tomorrow*.

The Independent Group augured the rise of Pop art, whose auto-centred flowering is notorious. Plenty of older painters had celebrated their own cars – the Futurists, Picabia, Matisse and Bonnard, for example (Picasso didn't drive). In 1956 Ben Nicholson compared painting to driving because in both cases, learnt skills become intuitive actions, 'subconsciously, instinctively, instantaneously – beyond reason'. Edward Burra was rare among English painters for his 1960s and '70s landscapes and urban scenes criss-

the foreground. For British artists, the cars were almost invariably American models (Dave Hickey is only the most recent in a long line of celebrants of the be-finned and scalloped auto-shell).

But there were dissidents as well as celebrants, desacrilizing the auto and making sacrifices on the altar of its ruined bodywork and spare parts. Andy Warhol's famous prints of 'Crashes' are the best known; other examples include John Chamberlain's and J. G. Ballard's exhibitions of crashed cars (apparantly further destroyed by participant-spectators at the New Arts Lab installation in 1969) and the horrific

Jock McFadyen, *Horse Lamenting the Invention of the Motor Car*, 1985,
oil on canvas.

racist lynching in a circle of car headlamps as constructed by Ed Kienholz (*Five Car Stud*, 1969–72). While Tony Smith was illegally riding the as-yet-unopened New Jersey Turnpike in 1966, and seeing 'things there which had not yet appeared in art' – to the disapproval of Michael Fried, who quoted this example as the shape of bad things to come – the painter Ed Ruscha was getting ready to throw a type-writer from a speeding truck and record its destruction on the always emblematic Route 66 (*Royal*, 1966). A decade earlier, such different artists as Peter Lanyon and Jasper Johns had incorporated tyre tracks in their paintings, while in the avant-garde cinema Peter Kubelka's *Mosaik in Vertrauen* (1955) and Bruce Connor's *A Movie* (1958) both included docu-mentary images of car crashes in their collage matrix. By contrast, the slow-motion cars in Stan Brakhage's landscape films, such as *Machine of Eden* (1970), or Michael Snow's 'film from the viewpoint of a tailpipe', *Seated Figures* (1989), seem almost benign.

Equally so is another unsung ancestor of contemporary art, George Brecht's *Motor Vehicle Sundown (Event)* (1960), 'for performance in and on any number of motor vehicles assembled outdoors'. The idea came to Brecht while 'standing in the woods in East Brunswick, New Jersey' waiting for his wife to come from their house: '. . . the motor running and the left-turn signal blinking, it occurred to me that a wholly "event" piece could be drawn from the situa-tion.' Suitably enough for a dissident Fluxus action, against the corporate grain, the car was an English Ford station wagon. Later, John Cage (whose Model T Ford laid the tyre tracks for Jasper Johns) was one among many who composed sound actions to be performed in a motorcar. Present-day artists have flipped back to the car as icon, an effect rather than an event, as in Graham Ellard and Steve Johnstone's

vertigo-inducing installations of car-chase clips; Georgina Starr's back-projected flying machine for a personal Hales Tour over London in her *Goodbye Baby* installation; Thomas Demand's grimly portentous tunnel-drive variations for the Tate Gallery and Sarah Lucas's cigarette-adorned motor vehicles for the 'Intelligence' show of 1999. Painter Jock McFadyen, by contrast, brings us back to the earliest days and fears of motoring in his portrait of *a Horse Lamenting the Invention of the Motor Car* (1985).

But do we take cars seriously enough? The wind-screen view of the world celebrated by Virilio and others does indeed show the world 'whizz by', and as such it is a delirious and punctuating image for Godard as for Hitchcock and Antonioni. It is Belmondo's point of view in the highway sequence of *Breathless*, shifted up to the sky for the heroine in *Vertigo* and turned back on the road for Maria Schneider's reversed viewpoint in *The Passenger*. In different ways, these shots announce the end of back-projection (a device exploited with ruthless artifice in earlier Hitchcock films such as *Psycho*) and the advent of smoother-running cars, superior roads and stable cameras in the 1960s. Cinéma vérité releases the car, at last, from the confines of the studio mock-up to offer a new and paradoxical inti-macy of the open road.

This vision was predicted by Matisse as early as 1909, with his two variations on the windscreen theme, just as Ben Nicholson toured Italy with a girl-friend in the mid-1950s, drawing the windscreen and the round steering wheel again and again (the car was a Lancia). But it took 50 years after Matisse for cinema to perfect the tracking frontal shot from a moving vehicle. Early travelogues and Hales Tours naturally turned to the literal and judderless tracks of tram and railroad for the frontal view. The track became a staple piece of technology for film locations, as it is today, used to spectacular effect from the Keystone Cops on. With odd exceptions, such as Man Ray's notably smooth windscreen shots in *Les Mystères du Château du dé* (1928), cameras rarely took the front seat. Apart from technical difficulties, front-seat shots directly implicate the spectator's point of view, unmediated by the actor, and were difficult to employ in the period of 'classic Hollywood cinema'. Like all subjective shots, they were used rarely and sparingly.

The looser and expanded film aesthetics in the counter-cinema of the late 1960s and early '70s quickly developed minimalist variations on the windscreen shot, deflating it as spectacle and celebration, restoring a sense of sight rather than speed. In *History Lessons* by Danièle Huillet and Jean-Marie Straub (1972), the journeys through Rome are undertaken by a humble Mini (but with an open sunroof). In Germany, the flat shot taken through the windscreen or from the side windows became a hallmark of radical landscape film for Birgit and Wilhelm Hein, Heinz Emigholz and Werner Nekes – the flatter the landscape, the better. Wim Wenders emerged from this structuralist genre as a Co-op filmmaker and imported its values into the wider art-house and mainstream cinema, European and American. Not for nothing is he an inventor of the appropriately named 'road movie'. A more recent example from British artist Judith Goddard reworks movie motifs in a personal mode. A 'Vegas' sequence, shot on the Strip through a car's side window, is inset within a static shot of choreographed fountains outside the Bellagio Casino, so that water seems to pour from the edges of the moving frame. In *Monument Valley*

Right: Four stills from Rossellini's 1953 film *Viaggio in Italia,* including the now classic windscreen shot.

Framed, another section from this series (2001), the camera shoots the famous Western landscape from the open roof of a moving car, to lift the standard eye-level, accompanied by music by Ennio Morricone and shown doubled and slightly phase-shifted on the screen. Many 'appropriations' of cinema by contemporary artists seem to be overawed by the Hollywood grandeur they evoke, but Goddard's videos are decidedly interventionist, restoring a personal sense of vision to the now familiar film trope of the windscreen view.

Today, the genres have blurred and their edges softened, like cars themselves. It gets harder to tell them apart, just like the cars, a predicament that is literalized in the post-post-Godardian cool world of Sophie Calle. Here, the risk of travel is yet another flattened experience, leaving only a ghostly residue in the psyche where – in spite of everything – meaning is suspected to lurk, and to lurk alone. Yet the car is a social machine; only racing cars are for soloists, the rest carry passengers. Not surprisingly, the cinema has been fascinated by its own connections with cars (sitting in a seat and facing forward) and by its differences (immobility of the body, mobility of the eye). The social issue is played out in real space as well as in the virtual image, whether sitting side by side with strangers in the cinema, watching films at home or travelling – transporting – from one to another. For city-dwelling filmgoers, 'Where shall we park?' is the next question on from 'What shall we see?' In this curious dialectic, the most poignant images are perhaps those at a tangent to the contemporary privatized experience of cinema and driving. They include the cheering truckload of football fans in *Bicycle Thieves* (1948), the jeep full of rag students in *Blowup*, and the singing soldiers in a lorry on the long road in *Lawrence of Arabia* (1962). Lawrence himself rides past

them, against their flow, in his chauffeured staff car – at which point he turns back to look at them, and the film ends.

The primal scene in which cinema meets the car is perhaps Rossellini's *Viaggio in Italia*, a 'journey to Italy' undertaken in a Bentley, that opens with the now classic shot through the windscreen. George Sanders and Ingrid Bergman drive the Bentley alternately, to and from their moderately dangerous liaisons, although it is Bergman – muttering imprecations against 'that brute', her husband – who crucially takes control in this most male of machines. But in her journeys through Naples, she is repeatedly outpowered by the pedestrians who cut across her path and block her passage, including the pregnant women, hordes of children and scuttling priests who underline her status – in the fiction of the film – as a childless woman. These unacted *vérité* documentary shots in the street enter the body of Rossellini's drama, as the bustling realism of daily life in the streets stops the forward progress of the big foreign car. As Bergman looks through the windscreen, her gaze sweeps laterally, seeing the street from the side windows – but the angle of vision is excessive, goes too far, in fact, to maintain the realism of the point-of-view shot which it enacts. Literally, the subject is split from the gaze.

In these crucial moments, Bergman's subjective gaze breaks free of her character and becomes the eye of the camera alone. Cinema's central contradiction – a mechanical eye pretending to be human – draws close to the surface of the film. In this case, that surface is the picture plane of the windscreen, suddenly disrupted. One of these excessive episodes takes place *en route* to Bergman's luminous encounter with Greco-Roman art at the Museo Archeologico, a scene in which another violent interruption occurs;

here too, the camera exceeds vision, sweeping 'too fast' across the epiphany of the sculptures to set itself at odds with the voice-over of the guide's quirky quips and the inter-cut shots of Bergman's startled stare. Bergman's look and the extent of the viewer's vision are again divided, and the repressed begins to return. 'They were so immodest,' Bergman explains to Sanders back in their flat, describing her reactions to the sculpture, an explanation never completed, since in yet another interruption their host enters to deliver a message from a friend of 'Uncle Homer', the mysterious character whose death has led to their visit.

Crossing languages (*Viaggio* was made for the international market) and cultures (the conflict of north and south), the film weaves a narrative knot, celebrates its stars (intended as the movie's selling point), mixes its media (pictorial, sculptural, dramatic, aural, cinematic) and, finally, cuts a knife-edge through its own means of representation – the gaze of the tourist's eye on a journey that is going too far. The crisis point of this representation, the excessive pan of the camera which abandons Bergman's viewpoint to assert its own seeing and which thereby sweeps us with it, takes place while a star is driving.

At the end of film, as Laura Mulvey put it in her essay 'Vesuvian Topographies', the couple and the car are completely hemmed in by the pressing crowd in a religious procession: 'Just as the film had opened with a visual play on the word "drive", so narrative closure also finds a visualisation, a graphic form . . . for the word "stop". There is an application of the brakes, a blocked passage.' But the sudden embrace of the couple in the crowd, Mulvey added, is not the end of the film, only of their story, for the camera turns from them and is seemingly carried forward by the crowd itself, in 'a renewed flow of movement, not of narration but of reality', before the final fade-out. As 'one ending halts, the other flows'. This crucial film, Modernist to its core, constructs its own powerful set of object relations, always displaced, ever realigned. Here, it is an emblem of the troubled encounter between two great machines of the last century, the motor and the camera, the bachelors and the bride, a glassy surface filled with metal and light.

Blood on the Nash Ambassador: Cars in American Films

ERIC MOTTRAM

I

Decoding the automobile in American movies is part of the study of interactions between culture and technology, between the human body, its extension in tools and machines, and their presentation in the 'multivocal and polysemous' structures of America or any society. The intervention of a new machine 'alters the sense ratios or patterns of perception' and restructures both the environment and what Claude Bernard called the *milieu intérieur*, translated by Hans Selye as 'the internal environment'.[1] Cars are used for other purposes besides transport. The large black 1920s limousines in Roger Corman's *The St Valentine's Day Massacre* (1967) register the use of vehicles for submachine-guns in the hands of gangsters; their violin cases did not protect violins (Billy Wilder had fun with this in 1959 at the beginning of *Some Like It Hot*). The car as transport is parodied, just as the mob's boardroom meetings around large polished tables parody the gangster operations of corporation directors. As Michael Corleone explains to Tom Hagan in *Godfather II* (Coppola, 1974), 'all our people are businessmen'. In Corman's film, Jason Robards' Al Capone is a Carnegie who stretches the law only a stage further than the 'legitimate' millionaire. In the interchange of cars and motorcycles, the police and the criminal share their violations within the elasticized interfaces of law and permission. In Peckinpah's *The Getaway* (1973), the car which harbours Steve McQueen and Ali McGraw parodies home as the only enclosure their love on the run is afforded, a usage which in turn parodies the usual function of the getaway car in gangster films. In these and related ways, the automobile's mobility frequently indicates the amorality and immorality of human needs in action, and the sheer adjustability of American social codes to requirements of the thrusting self – in a society which has hardly begun to consider seriously the nature of peaceful relationships between vertical personal projection and lateral community coherence. Expedient mobility evades rigid oedipal obediences as far as possible. Ever since the 1929 crash and the subsequent patching recovery, the key event of disillusionment overlaid with moral perfidy in recent American history, American films have endlessly paralleled the dramas in Stanley Milgram's *Obedience to Authority*.[2] The car has been a major instrument in the battle to establish levels of popular morality in an endlessly collapsing and recovering hegemony. Necessarily, American films have shown an insatiable appetite for this continual state of emergency.

The combined weaponry of car and gun dominates law, and thereby enables the challenge and response structure in both the elaborately timed attacks of Don Siegel's *The Killers* (1964) and Arthur

The shoot-out: Arthur Penn's 1967 film *Bonnie and Clyde*.

Penn's *Bonnie and Clyde* (1967), the classic evasory movie of the South-east Asia War and domestic Civil Rights period. Such capers invariably parody free enterprise and warfare, the main preoccupations of official America; as Edward G. Robinson says in *The Biggest Bundle of Them All* (Annakin, 1966), 'Timing, planning and, above all, daring and it's ours.' So that there are few surprises in American films, outside cutting and editing effects. Recognition patterns dominate, generating an audience with, as William Gaddis puts it, 'the unhealthy expectancy of someone who has seen a number of American moving pictures'.[3] In the history of Hollywood conventions certain 'situations are as recurrent in movies as the set themes of speeches in Seneca's plays'.[4] Even technology in science fiction films generates the unknown – a blob, a Thing, a gorilla, an ant – so that it can be dealt with in customary categories. In *Planet of the Apes*

(Schaffner, 1968), it is the apes who use minimal technology rationally, playing the Houyhnhnms to the astronauts, not the technologically superior but emotional humans. Cool Buster Keaton never actually triumphs over the machine he is caught up with: it becomes instrumental, since *he* is the ape on the planet of *The General* (Keaton and Clyde Bruckman, 1926) and *The Navigator* (Keaton and Donald Crisp, 1924), surviving the train and the liner and – in other films – the steamboat, camera, film projector, car and motorcycle. But in doing so he becomes a machine himself, hence the emotionless mask, very nearly the mask of a 'bachelor machine'[5]:

. . . each 'meet' with Machine some 'sport' with larger and more emphatically playful Gods.

The Chronological trace of his whole careering shows Buster growing smaller and – finally tiny . . . insect-like – in relation to Deus Ex Machinaes. They use him much as much as he Them. He has become a wildly flexible cog in Their destination. His is an involution sizewise back thru the whole of childhood to himself as Cosmic Hero: Tom Thumb.[6]

In comparison Jerry Lewis appears as a surreal extension of Mack Sennett's escapers in cars. In *The Family Jewels* (Lewis, 1965) he comes on as the idiot who falls out of a plane and disarms a torpedo, a fantasy comic-strip character in a world whose violence cannot violate or seriously injure. The Kid/Idiot triumphs through luck and rapid instinct rather than intelligence and understanding. Frank Sinatra's cop in *The Detective* (Douglas, 1968) uses the car to think in, and the Joad family in *The Grapes of Wrath* (Ford, 1940) escape Dust Bowl extermination in a Model T and make for the orange groves of California and a new life within the capitalist structure. The Joad trek is parodistically prefigured in the exodus of W. C. Fields and his family in *It's a Gift* (McLeod, 1934) and itself provides the model for one kind of road-movie to come. Their battered jalopy becomes the archetype of American automobile usage during the Depression and later. Survival by car is a fixed motif in American films.

But the sparagmatic dismemberment or utter demolition of the car is equally obsessive, and nowhere more so than in the Laurel and Hardy classic *Big Business* (Horne, 1929), where car demolition is paralleled by house-smashing. Brakhage takes its implication further: '. . . the subject of "war" itself . . . Xmas trees in Los Angeles – that was a start! . . . a joke perhaps – along with a house that was due to be wrecked . . . a destructable prop.'[7]

But 'war' in Laurel and Hardy's scenario is divided between the sheer fun of smashing a house and the sheer fun of competitive revenge through the vulnerability of the car's parts: a dream, in fact, of violence fulfilled within the limits of a dream movie. Cars, and any other familiar object, re-function in transformatory situations in dream and waking life alike. Hitchcock's car dream tells him a scene he can use: 'In one of my dreams I was standing on Sunset Boulevard, where the trees are, and I was waiting for a Yellow Cab to take me to lunch. But no Yellow Cab came by; all the automobiles that drove by me were of 1916 vintage. And I said to myself, "It's no good standing here waiting for a Yellow Cab because this is a 1916 dream!" So I walked to lunch instead.'[8]

The eminent practicality to Hitchcock's films demands the treatment of technology as apparatus for dream and murder. So that the sinking of the car in *Psycho* (1960) is not only Norman Bates's method of eliminating evidence against his 'mother'; the bubbling, sucking sound is the sound of traumatic experience *and* of the overcoming of any fetishistic clinging to the auto. Car-owners in the audience for *Psycho* watch the type of their beloved, paid-for, intimate object being taken over, wastefully, by nature. Two years later, in *Guns of Darkness* (Asquith, 1962), Leslie Caron and David Niven escape from a swamp in which their 1957 Ford station wagon is vanishing. Movies imitate the information processing of dreams in their semantics. The car's resurrection under the end-titles of *Psycho* adds to the perturbation, especially since it is so muddied. For those to whom the car is a partly vicious, partly lethal instrument, the scenes afford peculiar satisfaction. Ambivalently placed within the rest of the film's coding, they lead to involvement in a certain poetry:

Whereas the instruments of poetic or philosophical communication are already extremely perfected, truly form a historically complex system which has reached its maturity, those of the visual communication which is at the basis of cinematic language are altogether brute, instinctive. Indeed, gestures, the surrounding reality, as much as dreams and the mechanisms of memory, are of a virtually pre-human order, or at least at the limits of humanity – in any case pre-grammatical and even premorphological (dreams are unconscious phenomena, as are mnemonic mechanisms; the gesture is an altogether elementary sign, etc.).[9]

Hitchcock has once again involved us in the re-enaction of secret desire. The decoded scene speaks volumes about obsession with the car, the conversion of transport into libidinous impulse. The accumulation of such effects is in fact the cinema: 'Each film is not only structural but also structuring . . . The viewer is forming an equal and possibly more or less opposite "film" in her/his head, constantly anticipating, correcting, re-correcting – constantly intervening in the arena of confrontation with the given reality, i.e. the isolated chosen area of each film's work, of each film's production.'[10] Simplistic structural separations into natural and cultural, denotative image and connotative composition, primary and secondary 'levels' – as for example in the work of Christian Metz – weaken complex reception of the simultaneities in Hitchcock's vision, or indeed practically any important car images used in a film.[11] For the director who understands the film image, the sign is never, as Saussure claims, arbitrary; the object is never a metaphor; 'no symbols'.[12] Each film requires the kind of 'collective text' produced by the editors of *Cahiers du Cinéma* for Ford's *Young Mr Lincoln* (No 223, 1970), so that what Pasolini calls 'the profoundly oneiric nature of cinema, as also its absolutely and inevitably concrete nature' can be read. The oneiric and concrete consti-

tute a poetics rather than a semantics: the artist's necessity precedes the parasitism of the theorist; the society of the audience precedes the critic's journalistic need to hold his ego-column within whatever bit of the Press has afforded him a ledge. The relationship of image to reality – arbitrary terms since the reality is itself a construct – is usefully described by Umberto Eco as an 'iconic sign', which reproduces 'some of the conditions of perception, correlated with normal perceptive codes . . . we perceive the image as a message referred to a given code, but this is the normal perceptive code which presides over our every act of cognition.'[13] John Wayne big-game hunting by car in *Hatari* (Hawks, 1962) or W. C. Fields golfing from a 1930 Bantam called 'Spirit of South Brooklyn' in *The 300 Yard Drive* (Monte Brice, 1930) set up complex systems of memory and anticipation.

II

Raymond Lee's *Fit For the Chase* provides us with excellent iconic information on Hollywood's absorption of the automobile from the beginning (in fact film, car and jazz grew together as a key twentieth century triad).[14] But although cars are evident in very many movies, their use is often for purposes other than transport. Clara Bow, Joan Crawford and Jean Harlow were the first girls to have love scenes in cars, parallel to Bogart, Cagney and Robinson using cars as wheels for guns. Andy Hardy/ Mickey Rooney fell in love with a car. Miss Bow took a California football team riding in the early hours in her Kessel. Valentino raced his Isotta-Fraschini and 1925 Avion Voisin. Miss Harlow vamped it up in her black V-12 Cadillac. Jackie Coogan kept two Rolls-Royces, even if he had to maintain a kid-star image, and his father bought the first Rolls agency to Southern California. Dolores del Rio drove a Model A Ford. But then Cecil B. De Mille mounted a camera on the back seat of a car; Hoot Gibson bulldogged a steer from a car; and back in 1910 or 1913 – reports vary – Mack Sennett quoted Ezekiel x. 10 – 'As if a wheel had been in the midst of a wheel' – and the Tin Lizzie became a star: chased, caught, chasing, and choreographed. Raymond Lee's stills and snaps tell the story of the car-star-director interchange, with informative captions such as 'Adolphe Menjou tempts Constance Bennett with a 1930 Cadillac, which introduced the V-16 engine. The car, which cost over $8,000, is today considered a true classic.' (A quarter of a century later Judy Holliday will realize her dreams of wealth in *The Solid Gold Cadillac* (Quine, 1956)). Of Cagney's wound in *Each Dawn I Die* (Keighley, 1939) Lee writes: 'The blood is being spilled on a 1930 Nash Ambassador.'

The fantasizing of cars began at the birth of the movies, and since both were distributed throughout the class system, fantasy proliferated according to class need. The car has never become entirely alien, even if it is a major energy waster and environmental polluter, and was by 1960 out of date according to every rational standard. The Keystone Model T Fords were, along with the police, implements of farce and the grotesque in the national imagination. The outsize uniforms worn by Sennett's cops suited both the destroyed fetish of the automobile *and* the sense that law enforcement was acrobatics. As recently as 1963 the Model T is being fantasized – Fred MacMurray flies a 1915 version in Robert Stevenson's *Son of Flubber* (1963) – and cars are gag props in *The Great Race* (Blake Edwards, 1965), the exemplary parody of Grand Prix and road movie genres. Laurel and Hardy tore apart a 1919 Model T in *Two Tars* (Parrott, 1928), and so did Harry Langdon and W. C. Fields in *It's the Old Army Game* (Edward

Sutherland, 1926). In *Giant* (Stevens, 1956), James Dean drives a 1926 Ford pickup and is seduced by Elizabeth Taylor in a 1932 Duesenberg; the rich Texans own Rolls-Royces and Lincolns. Dean's own Porsche Spyder came later and still exists as sacred fragments in various parts of America. The Three Stooges used a Model T for fun, but in the 1930s cars began to bear the brunt of gangster action or were crashed for nemesis. The 1942 Ford Jeep came of age as a shield for Spencer Tracy in *Bad Day at Black Rock* (John Sturges, 1955) – although there had already been *Four Men in a Jeep* (Lindtberg, 1951), *Four Jills in a Jeep* (Seiter, 1944), and the Dean Martin and Jerry Lee Lewis vehicle, *At War With the Army* (Hal Walker, 1950).

Cars on fire are standard joys, especially once colour tinged the screen: the examples are too numerous to mention. But among other uses can be cited John Wayne fighting off a rhinoceros from a 1948 Chevrolet truck in *Hatari!* (Howard Hawks, 1962), John Conte caught between a 1958 Thunderbird and a 1958 Mercedes in *Ocean's Eleven* (Milestone, 1960), and probably the first car to be driven into a shop – the 1914 Model T in a 1917 Keystone comedy (this is now a cliché of course). Drunken driving for fun is established in Chaplin's *City Lights* (1931) – the car is a Rolls-Royce. W. C. Fields's driving in *The Bank Dick* (Eddie Cline, 1940) terrifies a bank bandit into a dead feint, while the gays polishing cars with swansdown puffs to the sound of the Rolling Stones's 'Satisfaction' in *Kustom Kar Kommandos* (Anger, 1965) provide other sensuous pleasures (the film was started when Anger received a Ford grant).

Taxi Driver (Scorcese, 1976) is the most recent in a long series exploiting the vulnerability and opportunities of the trade. Joan Crawford starred in *The Taxi Dancer* in 1927 and Cagney was a cabbie in *Taxi* (Roy del Ruth, 1932). 'Follow that car!' is a command convention, and so is the private eye's friendly cabbie (notably in *The Maltese Falcon* (Huston, 1941)). Scorsese's Travis Bickle investigates city life through his cab, and prepares for moralistic vengeance with fetishistic guns, becoming a national hero by rescuing an underage junkie hooker by slaughtering her pimps. His fellow taxi drivers either fantasize his sexual powers and his bravery in taking fares all over New York, or, like Wizard, grant him a sham reputation for knowledge and insight. In fact he moves out, through his cab, into an alien world of Times Square and the political upper middle-class. He works nights anywhere, as the opening scene makes clear, because he cannot sleep, the indication being that he fears masturbation and that this relates back to an experience with the Marines. His life lies between tablets and guns in a squalid bedsitter and his taxi, between an enclosed private life and a social life dominated by the exigencies of taxi driving – so that the huge opening close-up of the yellow cab and the closing shot of the same cab in the same downtown streets are appropriate. Travis is a male degenerate loose on the night streets, a soldier living a myth of violence with an ignorance appalling in its rabid self-generation. *Taxi Driver* is a war film: Travis needs to intervene in other people's lives out of inadequate knowledge and a desire to dominate – hence the Cherokee haircut. His gun-ridden invasion of the brothel and his subsequent heroism constitute an analysis of war and its glorification in a society which still refuses to understand its intervention in South-east Asia.

Between the city gangster and taxi films and the road films lies the major genre of the race movie. Examples are legion. They range from an early Christie Comedy, *Race Caper*, and the 1927 *Fast and Furious* (not Busby Berkeley's 1939 film of the same name) to Hawks's *The Crowd Roars* (1932), using an actual race track (as does *Devil on Wheels*, 1939) and Cagney as a racing driver, and Clarence Brown's *To Please a Lady* (1950), like *The Green Helmet* and *Road Racers* and *The Racers* to Corman's *The Young Racers*. In Paul Newman's *Winning* (Goldstone, 1969) the hero is a victory maniac, and the work features footage of a seventeen-car smash-up on the Indianapolis track. Stars' personal involvement in racing is well documented. James Dean's morbid desire to race probably began with the making of Nicholas Ray's *Rebel Without a Cause* in 1955, conceived as 'a pool of information gathered from police, parent and kids', The 'chickie run' scene, in which Dean drove a 1946 Ford, records a commonplace challenge structure within the corrupt morality of competitive society:

[Irving] Shulman remembered a newspaper item about a 'chickie run' at night on Pacific Palisades. A group of adolescents had assembled in stolen cars on the clifftop plateau. Drivers were to race each other towards the edge. The first to jump clear before the rim of the cliff, the drop to the sea, was a 'chickie.' On this night one of the boys failed to jump in time. The 'chickie run' on the plateau replaced the original blind run through the tunnel.[15]

(*The Blind Run* had initially been considered as a script for a film on children and adolescents; Ray chose Shulman as his scriptwriter because he had been a high-school teacher and was deeply interested in sports cars.) Dean researched his role by mixing with teenagers and gangs who modelled themselves on movies, until the film became a personal responsibility, a deliberate counteraction to Marlon Brando's *The Wild One* (Benedek, 1953). Incidentally, Brando contemplated narrating a documentary on Dean, 'maybe as a kind of expiation for some of my own sins. Like making *The Wild One*.'

Dean used cars for the risks of speed, as a philobat's need to draw near to death, first driving an MG, two Porsches, and a Ford station wagon, and then racing cars in 1955, working on his own machine, and reaching a level sufficient to be entered in the California Sports Car Club races: 'It's the only time I feel whole.'[16] He also loved bullfighting, kept a Colt .45 on the film lot, entertained Aztec fantasies, posed in a coffin, kept a model gallows in his New York hotel room, was known – according to Kenneth Anger – as 'the human ashtray' for his sexual proclivities, and used to repeat a line from Ray's *Knock On Any Door*: 'Live fast, die young, and have a good-looking corpse.'[17] He died at the wheel of his Porsche Spyder after being ticketed for driving at 65 in a 45 mph speed zone. He had driven into Ford sedan which he could not avoid. The car enabled Dean to be self-accountable, an extension of Emerson's cowboy self-reliance which remains so central to the American male. In *Giant* his cowboy hat and old car exemplify his mobility. After his death, the James Dean death club lit candles, played Wagner, and discussed their cult object. For 50 cents you could sit at the wheel of the wrecked Spyder, and bits of its metal were sold as relics. Frank O'Hara celebrated him twice as the sacrificed hubristic hero of the gods, 'racing towards your heights'. Dos Passos placed him as an age type in *Mid Century* in 1961, one of 'the Sinister Adolescents' who were 'box office'. And Dean features among both the dedicatees of Kenneth Anger's *Scorpio Rising* (1966) and the star devotees of bondage in Anger's *Hollywood Babylon*.[18]

Steve McQueen's less morbid obsession is documented in McCoy's biography.[19] After military service, he partly supported himself by racing motorcycles, but in 1960 he hung a sign on his bike reading 'The Mild One', in protest against his Hollywood

reputation, and transferred his speed addiction to cars: 'speed rivals making love'. Facial plastic surgery, broken limbs and deafness were no obstacle. By 1965 he had gained a good reputation as a racing driver and owned a glittering stable of cars. He maintained that his dedication was without 'any death wish like Jimmy Dean'. For *Bullitt* (Peter Yates, 1968), he carried out his own stunts – under licence from a generously paid city – and his role as a police lieutenant chasing criminals came second to the car smashing, reminiscent for him of 'the old Keystone Cops'. The over-rated speed sequences in *Bullitt* were followed by the dullness of *Le Mans* (Lee H. Katz, 1971) and the quieter pleasures of *The Reivers* (Mark Rydell, 1969), in which McQueen played Faulkner's Boon Hogganbeck, driving a 1905 Winston Flier. In *Junior Bonner* (Peckinpah, 1972), his old car and horse trailer take him round the dwindling rodeo circuit in an excess of nostalgia related to the car and plane killing of the last mustangs in *The Misfits* (Huston, 1961), with its receding dream of independant male life free from wage-slavery.[20]

The difficulties of creating race movies without boring duplications of car scenes are only partly overcome in John Frankenheimer's *Grand Prix* (1966), in which cars are choreographed and their engines orchestrated in pastoral and track scenes presented in split-screen images. But the aim is still to document speed in a bizarre macho drama that leads to maiming, suicide and virtual murder. The drivers are junkies of speed hurtling towards ambivalent apocalypse.

For the car chase obsessions in *The French Connection* (Friedkin, 1971), city permission was again received to clear traffic and 'use real pedestrians and traffic'.[21] The director was supplied with 'members of the New York city tactical police force to help control'

The detective attempts to save his wife: Fritz Lang's 1953 film
The Big Heat.

the streets, and maintained that 'murderous and illegal actions' in the film were justified because they were those of 'an obsessive, self-righteous, driving, driven cop'.

Disaster dominates American films as much as it governs British news bulletins on radio and television. A wrecked or flaming car evokes desire. The murder of Glenn Ford's wife in an exploding car near the beginning of Lang's *The Big Heat* (1953) is therefore ambiguously moralized as the destruction of a police family unit by a crime-business syndicate (as Emmerich remarks in Huston's *The Asphalt Jungle* (1950), 'after all, crime is only a lefthanded form of human endeavour'). To be uncertain is to be involved. Lang's skill depends on the fact – one of the reasons why Godard places him centrally in *Le Mépris* (1963). If a police or syndicate car crashed, pleasure is unalloyed. This is a mainspring of, for instance, Brian de Palma's *The Fury* (1978), in which superior scientific and occult information is hardly challenged by the old-fashioned technology of a police car. As McLuhan

once observed, in connection with 'our intensely technological and, therefore, narcotic culture,' 'at the heart of the car industry there are men who know that the car is passing.'[22] Obsolescence must be speeded up. Simultaneously the junkie needs another vein. The choreographic film crash continues the dream of inevitable casual disaster on which the renewal of the State is based: social and economic recovery is as inevitable as the Crash itself.

Films maintain the characteristic western confusion of human life with machine energy, a personal and social neurosis increasingly destructive of well-being in cultures dominated by engines and electronics. We are for ever putting on and plugging into machines and circuitry. Michel Carrouges' *Les Machines célibataires* identifies the typical networks of pleasure and pain. Men and women have always been connected to machines for torture, and *Grand Prix* is an invitation to a feast of tortured pleasure in search of heroics, money, and the deadly limits of masculinity. Its auto-erotic and automatic games are 'the nuptial celebration' of a curious but accepted alliance which produces only 'intensive quantities . . . to a point that is almost unbearable – a celibate misery and glory experienced to the fullest'.[23] By ecstatic example, *Grand Prix* increases death on the American roads by intensifying the desire to turn them into tracks of hallucinatory power whose final equilibrium is the production of stereotypical suicide and murder. The human breaking point obsesses the twentieth century, and cars in films are frequently instruments for this process of testing and climax. *Grand Prix* and the rest indicate the tolerance level for gun and car violence quite as much as the more commonly cited *Rebel Without a Cause* or *Bonnie and Clyde* (Penn, 1967), the latter with its joyful getaways in a 1930 Model A Ford, a 1931 Plymouth, a 1931 Graham, and so on. 'The observation of aggression is more likely to induce hostile behaviour than to drain off aggressive inclinations' is Leonard Berkowitz's research conclusion.[24] The range of cars and stars in Blake Edwards' *The Great Race* (1964) – a film almost devoid of brutality and suicidal climax – is the exception to the rule.

In *Bonnie and Clyde*, which combined the chase and road genres, violence results from the use of cars to challenge the status quo. The criminal pair act, in the words of Arthur Penn (perpetrator of this ambivalently focused, if not muddled, film), as 'retaliators for the people'. The 1930s cars on country roads and in fields parallel the pastoral effects in *Grand Prix* as the Barrow gang enters its own civil war, backed by the jaunty banjo-picking sounds of Earl Scruggs's 'Foggy Mountain Breakdown'. The Joads appear, as it were, in the form of a sharecropper family invited to fire at the expropriation notice the bank has placed on their old wooden house, and as Bonnie's family and the camp-site travellers who give C. W. Moss water towards the end of the trek. These are supposed to be

the 'poor folks' – Clyde's phrase – who justify robbery and murder. In fact the car wars focus this country-gangster movie, with the sheriff's posse of the Western regrouped in counter-vehicles. Certainly, Penn's car-consciousness made the film:

At the time there was no national police force: they were all state-confined police forces. When Ford made the V8, which was sufficiently powerful to out-run the local police automobiles, gangs began to spring up. And that was literally the genesis of the Clyde and Bonnie gang. What happened was that they lived in their automobile – it was not unusual for them to drive seven and eight hundred miles in a night, in one of those old automobiles. They literally spent their lives in the confines of the car. It was really where they lived. Bonnie wrote her poetry in the car, they ate ginger snaps in the car, they played checkers in the car – that was their place of abode. In American Western mythology, the automobile replaced the horse in terms of the renegade figure. This was the transformation of the Western into the gangster.[25]

But Bonnie and Clyde spoke contemporaneously, since the car remains the American's second home. This is the plot gist of scored of films, and a reason why a work as critical of car usage as Godard's *Week-end* (1968) has been virtually impossible in America. Directors concentrate on car as menace, Robert Mitchum in *Cape Fear* (J. Lee Thompson, 1961); car anxiety, classically in *Duel* (Spielberg, 1971); and the car as the centre of intense energy, *Point Blank* (Boorman, 1967), *Chinatown* (Polanski, 1974), and Barry Newman meeting death in a road block of dredger tractors in *Vanishing Point* (Richard C. Sarafian, 1971). A major part of the car's effect emerges from the common identity of cars used by gangsters, diplomats, police, millionaires and the mafia. But it is in *The Detective* (Gordon Douglas,

Left: The sacrifice of the car: Steven Spielberg's 1971 film *Duel*.
Below: The tractor road-block: Richard Sarafian's 1971 film *Vanishing Point*.

1968) that Sinatra's Joe Leland uses the car for private self-consideration. It is the only place he can be alone, think back, between the domestic apartment (the female) and the precinct building (the male job); driving in city streets is the arena of flashback; and it is only in Dreyer's accident prevention film *They Came to a Ferry* (1948) that death actually appears as a fact in driving itself, in the shape of a car driver before the victim's moment of truth; and he steers, of course, an antique car. Nor is Guido's escape in Fellini's *8 ½* (1963) American. The film begins, in absolute silence, with a shot of the back of his head as he sits in his car surrounded by traffic jammed in a low tunnel. Then the camera pans out of the darkness, over the cars, and into the over-exposed light, looking for an exit. Guido's nervous breathing breaks the silence as his car fills with steam. Other car people look dead. He pounds the window. One driver strokes a woman's breasts. Guido climbs out, *flies* from the tunnel, over the sea. Similarly, in another film by a European, Antonioni's *Zabriskie Point* (1970), Mark walks down a Los Angeles street to phone within a dense technological space, which includes cars. He escapes it in a stolen plane, rising up into clear space. Beneath him, a middle-class camper driving through Death Valley is covered with tourist labels, signs of false mobility, limited change within the urban density. Bresson's *Le Diable probablement* (1977) reverses the action: suicide takes place amid the technology of record player, phone, guns, river boats, television and cars.

III

In contrast, the car contest in *Rebel Without a Cause*, the car versus train contest in *The French Connection*, the car chase in Siegel's *The Line Up* (1958), and the cars, helicopters, motorcycles and horses entangled in the chase sequence of Arthur Marks's *Detroit 9000* (1973), all accept the perverse exhilarations of technological destiny. American directors freely manipulate audiences' possessive affection for their cars. In *Castle Keep* (Sidney Pollack, 1969), Corporal Clearboy is deeply attached to a Volkswagen, one of the most popular cars in the world. He envisages VW's populating the Earth after men have died out, and when his fellow soldiers fail to sink his car ('it's just showing off'), one of them shouts 'Jesus Christ, it's still alive!' Clearboy's response is: 'They're drowning her.' In Woody Allen's *Sleeper* (1973), a VW has survived into the future, but it has to be pushed over a cliff and into history. In Bogdanovich's *The Last Picture Show* (1971) a car is presented as a deeply felt gift between youngsters; it acts as a courting apparatus and as a major alleviator of drudgery, loneliness and isolation in rural America. Cars are courting and testing apparatus again in *American Graffiti* (1973), about which director George Lucas has said: 'That was my life. I spent four years driving around the main street of Modesto, chasing girls. It was the mating ritual of my times, before it disappeared and everybody got into psychedelia and drugs.'[26] In the film itself cars therefore function nostalgically in a vision of a barely existent, uncorrupted America before rock went political. The cars are choreographed to the 45s of the era – the age from Ike to JFK, which was the heyday of radio programmes featuring mystic disc jockeys (here it is Wolfman Jack) playing minimal unseen gurus and fixers for the kids. As in *The Last Picture Show*, this world has to be relinquished for manhood and America's wars.

Lucas's soundtrack is mainly an acoustic environment of motors and radio songs. But the car sounds are repeatedly reduced to an over-all monotone, the sound of putting on cars like clothing. Cars are homes, once again; there are no scenes inside homes, and only two buildings are entered: a drive-in restaurant with waitresses on roller skates and the college hall with a commencement dance in progress. The film's style itself is consistently mobile. Speeded up only for action against the cops (a police car's back axle is wrenched away) and a disastrous macho race at the end (much less solemnly stylised than in *Rebel Without a Cause* nearly twenty years earlier). The necessity of cars to life is as accepted here as in Michael Pressman's *Boulevard Nights* (1979), where cars are places of work and the burnt car is a personal violation. In Lucas's *THX 1138* (1970), Americans have become complete and highly technologized zombies, reminiscent of the workers in Fritz Lang's *Metropolis* (only uniformed in white, not black). God is a televised picture (based on the blown-up reproduction of a Dürer self-portrait), and the acoustic environment is as white, dehumanized and electronic as the clothing and decor. Where Curt Henderson escapes small-time American by plane in Lucas's later film, here THX reverts to a racing car to avoid total enslavement; although it is an emphatically futuristic vehicle, it images sufficient nostalgia to suggest that the automobile never entirely died. Even in *Close Encounters of the Third Kind* (Spielberg, 1977) roadside peasants react to early sightings of spacecraft with something life 'They can put rings round the moon but we sure as hell got 'em beat on the roads.'

So much attachment to the car is culturally assumed that it must hurt in Walter Hill's *The Streetfighter* (1978), not only when James Coburn's new car – a real sign of wealth in the 1930s – is smashed by a livid thug as a warning that he must pay his debts; but also when the streetfighter himself expresses his detachment from corruption by refusing a car. The sheer retentiveness of car life began controlling vocab-ulary early in the twentieth century: in *Skateboard Kings* (Horace Ové, 1977), the cult design of clothing, pads, dance routines, and the defiance of gravity by skateboarding in a desert water-pipe section are described in terms drawn largely from car and bike language – for example, movements are labelled grinder, front side-car, aerial edge, extreme tail top, and so on.

Film therefore reflects America as a nearly century-old car culture of remarkable tenacity. *Psycho*, a film dominated by women and cars, plays with the facts. A car switch enables a sensual and repentant thief from Phoenix, Arizona, with a bird's name – Marion Crane – to escape discovery. After her murder, Norman Bates sinks her getaway car to the same bubbling sounds we heard earlier in the shower as he cleaned up. Between its opening voyeuristic penetration of fugitive bedroom sex and the final retrieval of the muddied car, the film collects policemen and a car salesman, a private detective, Marion's boyfriend and Bates, like cars, to sink them. Marion is killed 'because' she acted male and trapped herself in Bates's male trap, a motel for car travellers; victory comes from the thrust of Marion's sister Lila and the woman in Bates. Back in 1932 *The Times* pointed up the ambiguities of car-obsession in *The Crowd Roars*: 'The various episodes of this romance of the American motor racing track are a least as painful as they are exciting . . . The ugly emotions of the crowd which delights in such disasters are represented with some accuracy, but it is not explained what we are to think of ourselves if we enjoy this film.' Years later Hitchcock tells Truffaut: 'The placing of the images on the screen, in terms of what you're expressing, should never be dealt with in a factual manner.' And as Lawrence Alloway observes, violence 'is still a part of general taste, embodied elsewhere in the styling of

American automobiles, which have not fundamentally altered during the same period. The annual style changes were sufficient to entertain us with a comedy of newness but not radical enough to disrupt continuity with earlier models.'[27] In his useful compilation on the 1950s, Jay Berman indicates the first climax of car culture in the United States:

Automobiles boomed in the fifties. A combination of new found leisure time and money for luxuries created a demand for more elaborate and specialised vehicles; and production facilities, swollen by the defense jobs of World War II, shifted to fulfil the demand.

The auto, formerly a mode of transportation, sought to be a total environment on wheels, rivalling home for comfort and luxury. The auto was heaped with adornment, worn as a badge of status, and admired as a piece of jewelry. It filled those empty hours with a new activity, 'motoring.'[28]

Film language using cars had likewise changed. In *The Man on the Flying Trapeze* (Bruckman, 1935), Ambrose Wolfinger's need to drive quickly to the wrestling match is interrupted and reduced to stasis by a cop, a chauffeur and a runaway tyre, but for the 1960s and 1970s such action is largely archaic. So too is the pessimism in Welles's *The Magnificent Ambersons* (1942), in which 'The Original Morgan Invincible' begins to undermine a bourgeois America founded in the horse city. But by then, as Colin McArthur shows, cars had become murder weapons in 'repeated patterns' which 'might be called the iconography of the genre . . . the means whereby primary definitions are made'.[29] Once Sergeant Bannion's car is blown up in *The Big Heat*, repetition of the same scene instills anxiety. As Christian Metz says, 'the cinema is language, *above and beyond any particular effect of montage*' (although the five bathtub images repro-

duced in Monaco's *How to Read a Film* indicate the limitations of the idea.).[30] Gangsters use city and industrial technology – guns, cars, phones – automatically (the Kojak series is dull because it repeats the genre like a doggerel of slick conservative morality, which a lollypop-sucking officer does nothing to modify). McArthur usefully quotes Andrew Sinclair, saying that the gun-cars 'created a satanic mythology of the automobile which bid fair to rival the demonism of the saloon'. But it should be added that by the 1950s the car had become the potentially lethal weapon of any 'average person', voluntary or not. The gangster film's 'symbol of . . . unbridled aggressiveness', so strong that 'characters may respond with fear to an automobile without seeing the men within it,' is repeated in general usage as much as it is in, say, the car images from *The New Centurions*, where cars are used as if they were private weapons by men committed to law-enforcement and self-enforcement in a society structured for leadership and competition.[31] The prowl car is a weapon on both sides of the law – if indeed that distinction still holds effective meaning. The Volstead Act of 1919, which declared the manufacture and sale of alcoholic drinks except for medicinal purposes illegal (hence the term 'medicine' for booze), not only gave crime its 1920s impulse, but brought death to the roads as a common daily occurrence.

Changes in the sides of law are manifest in John Carpenter's *Assault on Precinct 13* (1976). By the time the car-hunt has become commonplace – revived effectively in, for instance, *The Savages* (Lee H. Katzin, 1974), in which Andy Griffith plays a lame sadist hunting a young guide through the desert. Hunter cars are casual in American action. In Reisz's *Who'll Stop the Rain* (or *The Dog Soldiers*, 1978) cars are used as thoughtlessly as helicopters and armoured vehicles in

South-east Asian warfare, in an America given as a combat state where FBI methods are indistinguishable from those of any other terrorist order. In Carpenter's film, cars are used as vehicles of attack by urban guerrillas terrorizing a police station. Their initial prowl car parodies the police, and their siege parodies *Rio Bravo* (Hawks, 1959), pointing up changes as much as using nostalgia as technique. A small girl protests to the ice-cream man that she has the wrong flavour; she is gunned down from the prowl car. There are no innocent bystanders in America, 1976. And when Julie cries 'Why would anybody shoot at a police station?' the audience knows exactly why. The black limousine besiegers are the 1970s equivalent of gangsters or, in Hawks's terms, rustlers from out of town. Ethan Bishop, a black police lieutenant, is named after John Wayne's character in *Rio Bravo*, but it is real blood that drips – not on to a Nash Ambassador but on to a police patrol car – from the murdered telephone linesman.

In Walter Hill's *The Driver* (1978), the nature of the professional getaway driver is examined for the first time. But Hill – who wrote the script for *The Getaway* – sets Bruce Dern's obsessed cop against Ryan O'Neal getaway man. Dern's lip-smiling cop admits to no difference between police and criminal, except that he is better at his job; the scene is a game. O'Neal, a homeless, girl-less, gun-toting maniac killer, poses as a cool, sane man at play in the only game, which is also his job. Having established these contemporary facts, Hill concentrates on the sound and accelerating rapidity of the car in the hands of a maniac driver, the dream speedster inside all automobile owners. He does so with the same kind of abuse of technology that characterizes Peter Bogdanovich's *Targets* (1967). Beginning with the opening printed examples of berserk murders, Bogdanovich's film

ostensibly promotes enquiry into the uncontrolled ownership of firearms. But he lovingly shows us that the car boot also harbours the arsenal of weapons with which Bobby Thompson will pick off motorists on the highway and in a drive-in cinema. His target is the average secure American in his car home and movie seat. The film's strength is precisely this intersection of guns, cars and film at the point of maximum personal vulnerability, with Boris Karloff as the retiring horror movie actor who understands exactly what action has to be taken against a terrorist to disarm him.

The average car owner considers himself a secure citizen, as secure as the old lady nourishing herself on rape fantasies and obscene phone calls in the trailer park of Don Siegel's *Charley Varrick* (1973). But there is no privacy in the sacrificial combat state. Siegel plays variations on the city mafia extortion movie, but the genre scene is shifted to a small-change business played out in provincial trailer parks, and the action is filmed mostly in sunlit woods and fields. Like Rubber Duck and Dirty Lyle in *Convoy* (Peckinpah, 1978), Varrick is one more 'Last of the Independents' – a crop-duster and small-town bank robber. He discovers that some money he has stolen is part of an out-of-state Mafia drop. In one scene Molly, the Mafia hit-man, repossesses a car from a terrorized black family; so that Varrick's final victory over Molly is a vindication of the victimized – and it takes place in a huge used car dump, ironically re-used as a barricade against technology and terrorism. Varrick's independence, as well as his sidekick Harman's vulnerability, are exemplified by his trailer home: mobile and anonymous. This combination is neatly exploited in Howard Zieff's *Slither* (1973), where a collection of loose-moraled egoists battling for embezzled money are enclosed in a red car hauling a trailer in which

Peter Boyle's wife is permanently housed. The trailer has been converted from a quarantine tank used by astronauts returning from the moon. They are followed by two huge black, quasi-military armoured vehicles (labelled for a children's camp) whose drivers are most of the time as invisible as the aggressive truck driver in Spielberg's *Duel* (1971), the classic road movie exemplifying driving as combat between temporary psychopaths.

In Hitchcock's *North by Northwest* (1959), Roger Thornhill is hunted across an empty stubble field by a crop-duster plane flown by a faceless assassin. In Richard Matheson's screenplay for *Duel*, Franken-stein's monster had become a 1970s truck, the standard road menace for millions of American – and British – drivers. But the work is more complex than the singularity of the action suggests. The exhaust stack of the tanker (labelled or named 'Flammable') pollutes the air stream in which advertizing executive

David Mann is compelled to drive. Mann responds to the jungle demands of a male-dominated society. His car radio broadcasts part of a phone-in which includes a wife-dominated, impotent man attacking marriage. During a phone call it is clear that Mann's wife believes he failed as a man in not challenging a man who, she alleges, 'practically raped' her at a party. His sense of inferiority becomes pathologically obvious when confronted by working-class truckers in a roadside café. But it is the tanker which gives the broken-down school bus a helping push, and then, while attempting to kill Mann, wrecks an old lady's Snakerama. Mann accepts the unseen Goliath's challenge but, since he had failed to renew a damaged radiator hose, does so at the risk of burning his own car out. He ultimately sacrifices the car rather than himself, but the final shots show him whimpering and crying hysterically while tossing stones down the cliff where the two vehi-cles lie grotesquely entangled. The blazing sun seems to emphasize the futility of the whole episode.

The police are not involved as they customarily are, for example, in *Convoy*, and in *Vanishing Point* (Sarafian, 1971). The police-hunted driver in Sarafian's remarkable film is named Kowalski, ex-Marine hero with an honourable discharge after fighting in the Vietnam War, ex-police (detective) hero with a dishonourable discharge (drugs and general attitude towards the force), and ex-racing biker who now delivers cars faster than anyone else. Sarafian's hero is a man involved in America's official law and technology, who is now at large in the huge spaces of the South-west. Kowalski arrives in Denver urgently wishing to return to California; his contract entrusts him with a super-charged Dodge Challenger of exceptional performance. The ensuing chase is used to contain brief flashbacks of his life – a crash, a tender love affair, the rescue of a young girl from mauling narcotics cops, and so on – and to refer him to various people who attack or help him on the road, the latter including Super Soul (Cleavon Little), a blind black disc-jockey operation from a local Colorado station, who transmits messages between rock and country music. Hostility comes largely from small town people and from various States' police, and the man-hunt is energized by helicopter and taken up by CB radio. Police bikes and cars duel with Kowalski (no Christian name is found by the police) on the roads of Colorado, Nevada, and California; he is handed on from force to force with no explicit criminal charges except fast driving (in each crash he stops to see if the other driver is alive and walking). So that the main themes, as in *Convoy*, is official aggression on the roads. All of these films are in fact analogues of American official aggression, both imperialist and domestic. Kowalski's friends are a black biker, a white biker and his girl (who motorbikes nude around their patch of ground

in mid-Nevada), and Super Soul, who informs of police action until his station is smashed by local white thugs. In the hyped-up DJ language of Super Soul, and like the heroes of so many of these road movies, Kowalski is 'the last beautiful free soul on the planet.' Super Soul renames his station after him as it returns to the airwaves. The internal plot of *Vanishing Point* (like that of Tennessee Williams' *The Fugitive Kind*, made by Sidney Lumet in 1959) concerns not only the flight of the independent but the possibilities of salvation. The latter may take the form of a revivalist group, police law, or small-town aggression against a pair of homosexual men who fake a breakdown in their car and turn on Kowalski with a gun; or it may result from various forms of individualism: Kowalski himself, the lone snake-catcher in his broken down old car, Super Soul, and the two white hippies. Kowalski finally accepts defeat and crashes his car to explode in a police barricade of huge yellow clearage vehicles. He has used up his resources. There is no place for his courage, energy and driving skills. He takes his place with the men of *The Misfits, Convoy, Two Lane Blacktop* and *J. W. Coop.*

The road movie of the 1970s became a major vehicle for a primary and traditional American hero, translated from the West, the backwoods and the prospecting sites, and the battle fronts. Cliff Robertson's *J. W. Coop* (he starred in and directed his own script in 1971) copes with the same field as Junior Bonner but with less despair and more technique. After a ten-year sentence he resumes a rodeo career and challenges the reigning national champion, Billy Hawkins. The latter flies a Beechcraft to his rodeos, and Coop has to graduate from a 1949 Hudson to his own monoplane. Transport technology enables old-fashioned masculinity games to survive. Coop ends up broken by a huge bull, but he is still lone and independent. He is also rich and has had a love affair with an intelligent hippie, with whom he has formed a core of value against the corrupt rodeo world and the aggression of the 'silent majority,' exemplified by a middle-aged farmer driving a Ford truck and the middle-aged driver of a colossal oil tanker, both of whom identify the enemy as the unions and the 'commies'.

The three drivers and the hippie girl in Monte Hellman's *Two Lane Blacktop* (1971), are nameless, credited simply as the Driver, the Mechanic, G.T.O., and the Girl. They are also homeless. But the cars *are* named in the cast list: Chevrolet, Pontiac and so on. Human lives are dominated by the road, the characters travelling across America as if it were a plain with halts for gas, or an infinite race track. G.T.O., a dreamer and liar, a drifter and a car-proud speed-freak, meets the challenge he needs in the driver and mechanic (a certain class opposition is only identified in the cost of G.T.O.'s car). He races them to the futile end – beyond which the film itself burns out. Hellman creates a fable of expended energy in competition without end, the search for imagined and never achieved satisfactions and victories. In fact the Girl sings 'Can't get no satisfaction' – once again – while playing a pinball machine. Behind the forlorn elegance of this elegiac film lies the car door banged endlessly on Stan Laurel's bandaged foot, Jackson Pollock photographed on the running board of his old Ford, the used car dump in William Wyler's last film, *The Liberation of L. B. Jones* (1970), and scores of Westerns. *Two Lane Blacktop* is the penultimate parody of the core American movie. The ultimate is Peckinpah's effort to bring Rubber Duck and his woman through the obstacle race of *Convoy* (1978) without too much sentimentality and nose-thumbing.

The softness of Peckinpah's nostalgia can be contrasted with Spielberg's *Sugarland Express* (1973) and, more sharply, with Harvey Laidman's *Steel Cowboy* (1978). The former is based on an actual event, in 1969, when a young Texan couple hijacked a police car and forced the patrolman to drive them 300 miles to Sugarland, where the girl was to reclaim her baby, taken by the State from his foster parents. The film is one long chase by a convoy of police cars over several days. The cars talk to each other by loudspeaker, the cops trying to protect their colleague from the inevitable final bullet. The humour is more corrosive and less good-natured than in the Peckinpah, but both films are nostalgic for independence against the State. *Convoy* is nearer in spirit to Raoul Walsh's *They Drive by Night* (1940), a rig melodrama in which two truckers (Bogart and Raft) fight for their money within the competitive violence of the trucking racket. But Peckinpah is more ambitious: 'the purpose of the convoy is to keep moving' says Rubber Duck, the leading trucker. In fact this south-west road convoy is an allegorical procession, a process which deliberately collects the nation's problems of leadership, direction and law. 'Keep moving and the complaints will need no serious analysis' is the traditional motto built into the film. The status quo – combat – is maintained in a traditional 'Western' equilibrium in which Dirty Lyle Wallace, the patrolman-sheriff who claims 'I am the law,' stands against the truckers, who explicitly dramatize themselves as cowboys. Mobility within conflict is both the tradition and the very substance of American capitalism. To maintain that order, the Army is introduced to crush Rubber Duck: 'the State, its police, and its army form a gigantic enterprise of antiproduction'.[32] When, at one point, Lyle's car increases mobility and charges over an embankment, the effect is dreamlike, as if it were an invention of the unconscious.

C. W. McCall's trucking ballad is used to manipulate the cowboy-law elements into a safety jargon, but the convoy music itself is military rather than country, emphasizing combat leading to final confrontation. *Convoy* summarizes trucker and road movies right down to its repetition of the scene in John Sturges' *McQ* (1974) where John Wayne's car is crushed between two trucks. Observing Lyle's squeezing one trucker remarks: 'They're making a sandwich out of the sheriff!' But *Convoy* is as much a war film as *Who'll Stop the Rain* or *The Deerhunter* when, at the end of the film, the Army and the police blow up Duck's high explosive tanker on a bridge, the scene is duplicated and parodied from endless war movies. Ernest Borgnine's presence as Lyle ensures the stereotyping. Conflict between the trucker fraternity and the cops undermines the mutual individualist understanding between Lyle and Duck (the CB name of Martin Penwald). Pig Pen, Spider Mike, and the rest of the CB code-named truckers are finally trapped in the strict coding of American society, which they, like millions of others, believe supports independence rather than State intervention. Lyle easily obtains his bribes from the fraternity, which knows very well he will continue to demand more and that beating him up in the café makes no substantial difference. Duck faces Lyle with 'there aren't many of us left' – the Junior Bonner and J. W. Coop theme – but it is the racist issue that brings out the latent tension between law and cowboy. Smashing the jail with trucks to release black comrade Spider Mile is a minimal act of chivalrous despair in this male, police-ridden world (a world in which women have babies, are seduced by casual male glances, are eminently beddable, or themselves become forcible truckers – like the black fraternity member named Window Woman).

Peckinpah's café brawl is violent and farcical, in line with his need to make the film a victorious comedy for Duck and the fashionable photographer Melissa. The absurdity of the angry situation and its parodies of macho confrontations is not lost on the director. But the convoy still has to contain the anarchic emotions, protests and frustrations of the south-west community and, by implication, 1970s America, as it keeps moving against police, politicians, and Teamsters' union alike. Governor Haskins proposes taking Duck's protest against police harassment to Washington as a national cause, a move which will also help him politically. But Duck refuses because the immediate issue is Spider held in a Texas jail, a Black trapped in the rigidities of American racism. At this point the trucker breaks with both Melissa and some members of the trucker fraternity in order to chase 'the Devil . . . Dirty Lyle', as the ballad has it. When Melissa asks why they follow him, Duck replies: 'I'm just in front.' So the discrediting of American leaders will not be corrected by the independent loner. The politician panics when the people chose Duck as a popular hero – he is, in fact, practically manufactured by the media – but the mobility plot is easily allowed to take over: it is the civil war story, without the élitist, samurai overtones of *The Magnificent Seven*. As in *Vanishing Point*, radio communication aid the hero, although CB technology and code are devices cop and cowboy have to share. But, as in *Who'll Stop the Rain* and *The Deerhunter*, helicopters intervene, in an attempt to arrest by air the trucker's leader on the road: as Duck leads the convoy through the police cars, 'the bears in the air' extends the bear in the patrol car.

But Peckinpah's last-minute rescue of his independent is comic-strip stuff – no wonder he has Lyle laughing at Duck's escape! Once again sentimental anarchy wins in American fiction: law and army lose out to the miraculous resurrection of Duck from the final holocaust. But if the law is defied, manic law had the last laugh, as extra-legal as it was in the old Keystone movies. America remains a perpetually destructive comic society – at least in its favourite myths. Peckinpah reassembles his dismembered hero and the film ends with an old couple in an old car left in the dust of the victorious convoy, gently kissing. Spider has presumably reached his wife. Melissa has Duck. And the car and the truck have enabled Americans to evade law, the will of the people, politics and the unions. Capra rides again. Peckinpah inherits the Mr Deeds hero, the man without dogma or scripture, and asks us to accept his equation of the laughing cop and the laughing cowboy driver. Americans repeat themselves for the nth time as farce: 'Like car-stylists, film-makers have to work for the satisfaction of a half-known future audience . . . This is one source of the extraordinary quality that films have of being topical while being at the same time conservative and folk-loric. A successful film representing a mutation of a current convention will be imitated because it intro-duces vital information about previously unknown audience interests.'[33]

But a skilful director can put the sentimentality and put the realism back into a convention. Laid-man's *Steel Cowboy* modifies Walsh's 1940 simplifications while using at least some of the old myths. Clayton Pfanner's truck is called 'Outlaw', and both he and his partner K.W. ('I always wanted to be a cowboy') wear cowboy hats and speak in a south-west manner, using a language layered with exotic images and, in K.W.'s case, literary instances ('You're harder to find than Richard the Third's horse'). Clay-ton's wife, Jesse, has an unfinished university degree course to return to; she is both beautiful and intelli-gent, and finally leaves the husband she loves because his cussed independence keeps them in constant financial anxiety. The increased 1970s cost of living is explicitly the context of Clayton's outlaw sense. When K.W. says 'we're about a week away from wear-ing uniforms' – company uniforms – Clayton responds as if his manhood were at stake. He drives across a picket line of strikers, smashing through two parked cars outside the depot in order to drive through a payload.

Laidman indulges in little of Peckinpah's fantasy and is concerned continually with the practical matter of living as a trucker and with the loneliness of a trucker's wife: Jesse's response to her husband's plan for gaining an extra buck is 'And what am I?' Being steadily in debt in the 1970s is pointless; she might as well go back to college. The boss villain, Pinkie Pincus – pink shirt or, like Gatsby, pink suit, and pink custom-decorated car (with cattle horns) – offers fast money for cattle rustling by truck. K.W.'s scruples and his influence on Clayton are eliminated by Pinkie's hit men: he joins Western trucking (wears a uniform) and is blown up in one of their trucks carrying oil drums. K.W. had functioned as the male equivalent of Jesse's necessary normal perceptiveness of what the financial situation really is ('old Clint Eastwood didn't have to wait this long'). Clayton has to deny he ever had this buddy relationship in order to maintain his independ-ence, but eventually – and utterly alone – he can only assert that independence by driving his Outlaw through Pinkie's houseful of Meissen china, crystal glass, and other expensive knick-knacks: 'this is for you, K.W.!' The scene is recorded in loving and, for once, justified slow motion. Clayton hands over his truck to a driver whose own has burnt out, and fades out of the movie by thumbing a truck lift and by a long shot of reunion with his wife – a touch of sentiment which does not weaken the treatment of transport cowboy independence at all, since Jesse is the point of realism rather than rear-view mirror nostalgia.

The road saga will continue for the same reasons that America cannot solve its fuel-consumption greed: the automobile culture is coterminous with Americanism.[34] The process has been lengthy – at least from the smiling Cagney nursing a submachine-gun in his limousine in *G-Men* (William Keighley, 1935) to the two neurotic cops in *The New Centurions* (Richard Fleischer, 1972) driving a patrol car inscribed 'to protect and to serve'. The pile-up of cop cars and bikes at the end of *Scarface* (Hawks, 1932), the car advancing on you in a blind alley, the face in the windscreen wipers, the exploding car – still lovingly exploited by Coppola – have long been stereotypes. The Joads of *The Grapes of Wrath* are relegated to the margins of *Bonnie and Clyde*, a film which attempts to make fun out of murder by reverting to Keystone Kop chase methods. The Sennett system made farce out of what Ivan Illich, years later, would dub 'industrial violence such as the speed of cars'.[35] The suicidal games continue to imitate Fields's drive to the maternity hospital – his car gets stuck in a fire-engine ladder. The Princess will continue to entice Orpheus to Hell in her Rolls-Royce.

FROM *Blood on the Nash Ambassador: Investigations in American Culture* (1981).

'Like England's battles were won on the playing fields of Eton, America's were won on the assembly lines of Detroit.'

WALTER P. REUTHER, UNITED AUTO WORKERS

It is not just in a literal sense that the automobile has proved to be the driving force of the modern industrial age. The symbolic pull that the motorcar has exerted on the work of artists, architects, planners and utopian thinkers generally is well documented and widely acknowledged. But the car's cultural power is as nothing to the ideological power that it has wielded in the last century or so.

By a strange irony, when the last remaining German forces in Stalingrad surrendered to the Red Army in February 1943, this decisive event in the struggle between communism and fascism took place in the Stalingrad Tractor Factory,[1] a once magnificent automotive plant, now wrecked in the battle for the city. Ironic because this showpiece of Stalin's economic miracle was equally a manifestation of the might of American capitalist production. Erected in 1930 to produce Fordson tractors (although in the last months of its short life, it was T-34 tanks that rolled off the production line instead), the factory had been designed along strictly Fordist lines, with a conveyor belt running the length of the massive mile-long plant.[2]

So how had the moving assembly line – at once a symbol of American genius and of the enslavement of the proletariat, depending on which side of the ideological divide one was viewing it from – found its way from Detroit to Stalingrad? It was the planners of the Soviet Union's 'Great Leap Forward' who recognized that the ideas of scientific management and mass production which lay behind Henry Ford's spectacular success as a capitalist entrepreneur might equally well be applied to the building of a socialist planned economy. In 1929, a Soviet delegation to Detroit were so impressed with the automobile factories designed by Albert Kahn that they invited him to build the Stalingrad plant, and afterwards to assist in the reorganization of the entire Soviet Union along industrial lines.[3]

But the Soviet Union was not the only implacable enemy of Western capitalism to understand the powerful lessons to be learnt from its automotive industries. Henry Ford was the only American to feature in the US edition of *Mein Kampf*, and in 1933 Hitler was quoted as saying 'I regard Henry Ford as my inspiration.' In 1938, Ford was the recipient of Nazi Germany's highest honour awarded to a foreigner, and a photograph of him hung on Hitler's office wall. His assembly line has even been credited as an influence on the industrialized systems adopted in the death camps.[4]

While American manufacturers continued to dominate the world markets in the post-war era, indigenous car-making became an important ambition of numerous different cultures keen to resist the pervasive influence of Americanization. As a consequence, cars have developed a myriad of localized cultural meanings, in defiance of the realities of global production. In India, for example, the Ambassador car symbolized the industrial aspirations of a newly independent nation. In Japan, a domestic motor industry based on assiduously copied and improved Western prototypes provided the backbone for the reconstruction of its war-ravaged industrial base, while in West Germany the resurrected design for Hitler's 'people's car' provided an irresistible icon of its 'economic miracle'.

But it was the socialist economies of the Eastern bloc which proved most resistant to the example of Detroit. Following the Modernist ideal of the 'objet type' – the designed object refined to its perfect form – cars like the East German Trabant were manufactured for decades without significant modification or improvement, remaining immune to the market-oriented principles of planned obsolescence and annual model changes. Such cars proved to be among the first victims of the collapse of the Communist system after 1989, with Eastern Europe instead becoming a cheap labour pool for the car-making giants. Today, cars may be sold in ever greater numbers, but they are made by a decreasing number of multinational combines in fewer locations, meaning that it is the consumption of motorcars rather than their production that represents their most visible impact on contemporary society.

Left: Packard plant, Detroit, 1900s.
Below left: Model T 'body drop', Ford Highland Park plant, Detroit, c. 1914.
Below right: GM Poletown plant, Detroit, c. 1990.

Top: Sit-down strikers, Fisher Body Plant No. 1, Flint, Michigan, 1937.
Above: Post-war Packard assembly line, Detroit.

Detroit race riot, June 1943.

Left: Lenin's car, now in a St Petersburg museum.
Below: The Ford assembly line, Moscow, 1930.

Clockwise from bottom left:
Car lot, West Berlin, November 1989.
Leipziger-Strasse, East Berlin, on 9 November 1989, the day the Wall was opened.
Cars at Checkpoint Charlie, East Berlin, on 10 November 1989 – the day after the opening of the Wall.
Ten years on: Trabant mural on the Berlin Wall near Potsdamer Platz in the former East Berlin, 1999.

England, mid-1990s:
Top: Claremont Road, east London – heart of the resistance to the M11 link road.
Above: Twyford Down, Hants – protests against motorway 'improvements'
through a Designated Area of Outstanding Natural Beauty.

Trouble in Motor City

JOE KERR

Detroit is seven counties, 233 communities, nearly 5 million people and 300 years of history, and that's just since the Europeans arrived. On one block it looks like ground zero of the rust belt, the next, like Jay Gatsby's front lawn. Burdened by an image of grime and crime, bigger than Madrid, Miami, Saigon and Sydney, beholden to a troubled recent past, metro Detroit is a tough place to figure out.[1]

There's trouble in Motor City, but then that's nothing new. Detroit always seems to be in some kind of bother – industrial strikes, civil-rights clashes, race riots, urban depopulation and dereliction, unparalleled crime rates – and all of that in the last of its three centuries of history. To be fair, Detroit has recently looked to be on the way up again – with the city celebrating its tri-centenary in style, and with new construction promising to breathe life into its downtown for the first time in decades – but trouble there undoubtedly is, trouble of a familiar kind for the Motor City.

For the car companies are once again in deep financial gloom, signalling the latest crisis in the American economy as it lurches unsteadily from boom to bust. When Ford, the second largest of the 'Big 3' American motor manufacturers, says it will shed 5,000 jobs and cut production, then its home city starts to worry. And when General Motors, the world's largest corporation, announces a 73-per-cent drop in income for the second quarter of 2001, then the whole American economy braces itself for the onset of recession. For, as the (misquoted) saying goes

in the Motor City, 'What's good for General Motors is good for America – and vice versa.' It is with almost laughable hubris that Wall Street has tried to ignore these recent storm warnings, with one analyst claiming that 'unless the rest of the economy goes off the end of a cliff, the . . . recession in the auto business is over.'[2] But then that was in August 2001, and the following month the economy did fall over the proverbial edge.

Detroit has shrugged off the consequences of economic downturn many times in the past, and the current recession has actually arrived on the back of a long period of booming sales. But this time around, the long-term prospects are especially ominous, with foreign car companies circling like vultures over the wounded giants of the American automotive industry.

So has Motor City finally run out of road? If so, it would bring to a close the most remarkable chapter in the history of American manufacturing. For in the 106 years since the first motorized vehicle took to the streets of Detroit, the city has been at the heart of America's relentless economic expansion. We may think of New York or Los Angeles as the quintessential cities of modern America, yet Detroit could lay as good a claim to that particular honour. For despite its three centuries of White settlement, the city only assumed its role as America's powerhouse in the twentieth century, when it grew to become the greatest centre of manufacturing in the entire world. But it is precisely because Detroit was in the vanguard of America's growing economic dominance in the first half of the 1900s that its subsequent headlong decline into redundancy seems so extraordinary.

DRIVING THE WORLD ECONOMY

The enormous wealth which Detroit's car plants once generated, and which helped to build it into the third most populous city in the US, has long ceased to sustain it. Only a quarter of American cars are still made in Detroit, and those in highly automated plants, with a consequent loss of half the city's post-war population to the suburbs or beyond. The details of Detroit's slow death are complex, but the reasons for it are clear, for the Motor City and its rustbelt neighbours are the most conspicuous victims in the Western world of the relentless progress of globalization. In Detroit's case, it is the rise of the Japanese car industry, and the relocation of manufacturing and assembly facilities to cheaper and less unionized labour markets, that has done the damage. The irony of this abject decline is that the Motor City was once at the forefront of what economic historians now identify as globalization's first phase, when, in the first couple of decades of the last century, the way the world did business was utterly transformed by an unprecedented expansion in trade. A combination of surplus wealth for overseas investment, improved communications to keep track of those investments, a dramatic improvement in both the speed and the cost of transportation, and the increased mobility of labour created perfect conditions in which the twentieth century's new industries could flourish and grow.

Already a successful but modest manufacturing and trading city, Detroit provided a fertile environment for the fledgling automobile industry, replete as it was with the resources that the new industrial barons required:

Existing factories forged metal components and constructed wooden car bodies. Machine shops milled tools and parts for automobile production. Most important, Detroit's marine engine makers already knew how to make gasoline engines. Detroit was also the home of highly successful lumber, mining, and ship-building entrepreneurs. These people had capital to invest in the emerging car business.[3]

Even so, it is remarkable how rapidly car-making took root there, and how quickly Detroit grew to become not just the most important American manufacturing centre, but quite simply the largest site of industrial production in the world. The figures only hint at the extraordinary acceleration of this young industry at the turn of the century. In 1896, Charles Brady King drove Detroit's first horseless carriage down its principal thoroughfare, Woodward Avenue; in 1901, pioneer manufacturer Ransom E. Olds built 425 of his famous Curved Dash Olds, the first volume production of cars in America; and in 1913, only ten years after establishing the Ford Motor Company, Henry Ford introduced the moving assembly line at his new Highland Park factory. Within three years, he was responsible for making 50 per cent of all American cars and 40 per cent of cars around the world. By the time war broke out in Europe, Detroit was turning out 78 per cent of America's cars and had already acquired its famous and enduring sobriquet, the Motor City.

Having had the apparent good fortune to acquire the major new industry of the twentieth century, Detroit exploded at a staggering rate, expanding from 23 to 139 square miles in the first quarter of the century. Hordes of European immigrants beat a path from Ellis Island to the Motor City, part of the biggest migration in human history. In 1904, the car factories employed less than 3,000 workers, but by 1919 that number had jumped to over 75,000 in Detroit alone, without counting the thousands who flooded into the new industrial communities – Flint, Hamtramck, Highland Park and Pontiac – that now ringed the city. Even before stricter immigration controls introduced in 1924 cut off that supply of unskilled labour, agricultural workers from the Southern states of America had begun the long trek to Michigan, lured by Henry Ford's famous promise of $5 a day. As Blind Blake sang in his *Detroit Bound Blues*:

> I'm goin' to Detroit, get myself a good job
>
> Tried to stay around here with the starvation mob.
>
> I'm goin' to get me a job, up there in Mr Ford's place
>
> Stop these eatless days from starin' me in the face.[4]

Ford was one of only a handful of industrial companies who employed significant numbers of Black workers. The influx of African-Americans from the deep South may have been responsible for Detroit's unique musical culture, but the arrival of immigrants from within and without America, who were forced to settle in ghettoized communities, sowed the seeds for many of Detroit's subsequent woes.

COMETH THE HOUR

In these boom years, however, the city fathers paid scant attention to issues such as racial integration, given the pressing need to attract hands of whatever colour or creed to work the new production lines. More than 350 different makes of car were produced in the area at one time or another, but it was not long before a few select manufacturers began to outstrip their competitors, most remarkably Henry Ford.

Although Ford was not the unique innovator delineated by his many apologists, his success stemmed from the successful implementation and integration of many of the new ideas that flowed from the pioneers of the automobile industry. Ford's own contribution was to look beyond the luxury market pursued by his competitors and to concentrate his efforts on designing and producing low-cost, reliable and universally affordable vehicles. It was his single-minded ambition to push down unit costs that led to his most significant innovations, such as the moving assembly line and the standardization and simplification of parts.

It was to realize these ends that he built his revolutionary new factory at Highland Park, where his first experiments with mass production were made on the Model-T assembly lines in 1913. The benefits – to Ford at least – were instantaneous: the time needed to make a single 'Tin Lizzie' dropped from 12½ man-hours to 93 minutes, while the price plunged from about $850 for a hand-built Model T in 1908 to $298 for the same car rolling off the automated assembly line in 1922. By the time that production of the world's first mass-produced auto ceased in 1927, Ford had made over 15 million of them, and at one time it was said that every other car in the world was a Model T. The price paid for these innovations by the assembly workers themselves, and by the workers on every subsequent mass-production line, was extremely high and laid the foundations for Detroit's subsequent history of bitter labour disputes.

The Highland Park plant, Detroit, c. 1913. This publicity photograph shows a day's output.

Top: The birth of mass production: the magneto assembly line at Highland Park, 1913.
Above: 'Any color so long as it's black': Model T final assembly, Highland Park, 1923.

By the outbreak of World War II, Detroit's dominance of the market was complete, and its auto manufacturers had expanded into every corner of the globe. General Motors, which became and still is the world's largest corporation, commenced its overseas operations in Canada in 1918, established itself in Europe with a plant in Copenhagen in 1923, in Brazil in 1925, in South Africa, Japan and Australia in 1926, and in India in 1928, opening the first assembly plant there. By 1939, it was also operating in Belgium, Argentina, England, France, Spain, Germany, New Zealand, Egypt, Uruguay, Chile, Java, Mexico and Switzerland, and its overseas sales had exceeded 350,000 vehicles.[5]

'WHERE LIFE IS WORTH LIVING'[6]

In September 1937, labour activist Eli Oliver declared that 'Detroit, not Washington, is the capital of the United States today.'[7] With a war looming, Detroit could look back on an era of unprecedented growth and prosperity. Not only had it become the forge of America's new industrial empire; the city itself had taken on the guise of a great metropolis.

High-rise offices and hotels had sprouted in the downtown area, transforming the city in the manner of the classic American vision of the City Beautiful. By contrast, the enormous automotive factories ringing the city had become celebrated icons of the European Modern movement. For just as the Detroit industrial-

Picturing Modernity: the central section of *Industry*, Charles Sheeler's 1952 gelatin-silver photo triptych.

Top: The world's greatest factory: an aerial view of the Ford River Rouge plant, Detroit, c. 1957.
Above: Laid off from the line: the employment office at the River Rouge plant, 1931.

ist Henry Ford had revolutionized the means of production, so the Detroit architect Albert Kahn had pioneered a new form of architecture in which to house the new assembly lines. Most factories of the time were still being constructed on the model established by eighteenth-century British mills, but Kahn superseded the standard factory building with something quicker and cheaper to build, and infinitely more fire-proof. The system of reinforced-concrete construction he introduced at the Packard Factory in 1905, and refined at Highland Park in 1908, provided large, uninterrupted spaces between columns, essential for the new production methods, and allowed natural light to flood in from floor-to-ceiling windows.

Detroit became an essential pilgrimage destination for avant-garde artists and architects, eager to witness the miracle of mass production. Images of Kahn's Highland Park factory appeared in all of the pioneering Modernist texts, most famously Le Corbusier's *Vers une architecture* (1923).[8] The German

architect Erich Mendelsohn visited Detroit in October 1924, later recalling: 'At my first visit to the States in 1924 . . . two things stagger my imagination: Buffalo's grain elevators and Albert Kahn in Detroit.'[9] Mendelsohn would undoubtedly have seen Kahn's newest and greatest industrial structure, Ford's River Rouge plant built from 1917, which grew in ten years to become the world's largest factory. This thousand-acre complex, with its 100,000 workers, 14 miles of roadways and 92 miles of railway track, was described

'The Battle of the Overpass": UAW union organizers including Walter P. Reuther (top, third from right) beaten by Ford security staff at the River Rouge plant, May 1937.

by *Vanity Fair* in 1928 as 'the most significant monument in America'.[10] The Rouge plant, universally received as the epitome of modernity, was famously painted and photographed by such progressive artists as Charles Sheeler, Diego Rivera and Frida Kahlo.[11] But Kahn himself was no devotee of the Modern movement, and he was happy to design Detroit's grand public buildings in a variety of classical styles,

while for the great mansions of the automotive barons he turned to European domestic styles, most famously for the Edsel and Eleanor Ford House, designed as a Cotswold manor house.

But Detroit did not feel like the centre of the modern world for many of its citizens after the stock market crashed in October 1929, an event that hit the industrial state of Michigan worse than any other part of the US. Many of the smaller car-makers went under, and even in the larger plants the workers who kept their jobs faced drastic wage cuts. At the Rouge, Ford workers saw their hourly wage drop from 92 to 52 cents by 1933. Thus it was that in the 1930s, Detroit again wrote itself into American history books, this time as the centre of the struggle for union recognition and workers' rights. In 1932, a march by 3,000 Ford workers to the Rouge plant was fired on by security guards, killing five. In 1935, the United Auto Workers (UAW) union was formed, prompting a series of bitter and violent disputes which led to nation-wide speculation as to whether revolution was imminent.

THE ARSENAL OF DEMOCRACY

Detroit and America were saved from the possibility of insurrection by the outbreak of war, which returned the car plants to full production. The war was a godsend for certain previously disadvantaged sections of the labour force, in particular African-Americans and women who suddenly found themselves doing jobs that had not been open to them before, as other auto workers went off to fight. Even then, only a third of Detroit's defence plants would hire African-Americans, and in a telling portent of trouble ahead, the promotion of Black workers was a common cause of many labour

Americans at war:
Top: Rioters running from teargas, Woodward Ave, June 1943.
Above: The last peacetime Packard.

disputes during the later war years. In June 1943, racial tensions came to head with the worst race riots the nation had seen. Two nights of violence saw 34 people dead and hundreds injured before troops restored order.[12]

The attack on Pearl Harbor on 7 December 1941 may have killed demand for private cars, but this proved no bad thing for the Motor City. Far from it; it merely served to underscore Detroit's virtual monopoly on vehicle-making. With one former GM President, William Knudsen, co-ordinating national war production and another, Charlie Wilson, later serving as Secretary of Defence, it was perhaps inevitable that the city should prosper during the conflict, as its other famous nickname – the Arsenal of Democracy – suggests. But even with friends in high places, the scale of the city's contribution to the war effort was extraordinary, for it made 92 per cent of American

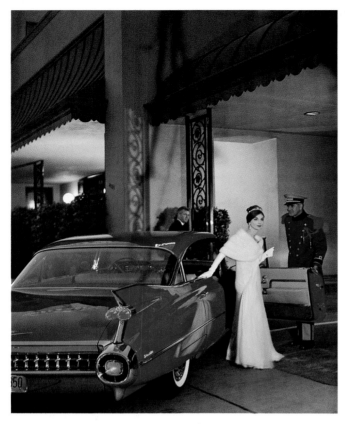

An age of plenty: the 1959 Cadillac Sedan de Ville.

for Detroit. It seemed that Charlie Wilson was right, for as America entered an unparalleled era of prosperity, increased demand for motorcars more than compensated for the cessation of wartime production. Indeed, the twenty-year period from 1945 has often been hailed as the golden age of the American auto. High wages and low oil prices fuelled demand for the increasingly extravagant products of the Motor City. Harley Earl's flamboyant designs for General Motors such as the 1955 Chevrolet Bel Air and the 1958 Cadillac Eldorado were the last word in consumer-led styling, with their towering tail fins, wraparound windshields and outlandish dashboard gadgets. These supercharged monsters proved irresistible to a generation experiencing a seemingly limitless growth in purchasing power, and in 1955 alone a staggering nine million cars rolled off Detroit's tireless production lines.

Inevitably, there was a price to be paid for this insatiable production and consumption, and it was Detroit that paid it. More cars meant more industrial facilities and more people to work in them – on the face of it, highly beneficial developments for the city. However, the new plants were built at some distance from the centre, and around them new communities sprung up with amazing rapidity, acting like magnets on existing populations and new immigrants alike. It is estimated that Detroit itself lost nearly 150,000 manufacturing jobs in the first twenty years of peace. General Motors' fabulous new Technical Center, designed by Eero Saarinen in another great act of architectural patronage, opened in the auto suburb of Warren in 1956. Warren became the fastest-growing city in the state during the 1950s and '60s as a complex web of assembly plants and supply industries developed there, along with huge tracts of new housing. The expanding expressway network facili-

military vehicles, 87 per cent of its aircraft bombs, 75 per cent of its aircraft engines and 56 per cent of its tanks. Henry Ford's Willow Run bomber factory, designed by Kahn and opened in 1941 with the world's longest production line, produced 8,000 warplanes alone, while General Motors supplied a total of $12,300,000,000 worth of war material. As Charlie Wilson actually observed at his Senate confirmation hearings in 1952, 'For years, I thought what was good for our country was good for General Motors – and vice versa.'

THE CARS THAT ATE DETROIT

By the war's end in August 1945, Michigan's industries had supplied 12 per cent of all war materials produced in the US, far outstripping any other area. But VJ Day did not mark the end of the good years

From Motor City to Motor Suburb.

tated the relentless migration from downtown to the suburbs. The first of these, the Detroit Industrial Expressway, was built during the war to carry 20,000 workers a day from metropolitan Detroit to the new bomber plant at Willow Run. By the mid-1950s, 17,000 Detroiters had been displaced by motorways, and many previously flourishing inner-city neighbourhoods had been bisected by them, precipitating rapid social decline.

In 1954, America's first 'cluster' mall, the Northland Shopping Center, opened in the outer suburbs, developed by Detroit's famous downtown department store, Hudson's, and planned by the king of the post-war shopping mall, Victor Gruen. It was followed by the Eastland and Westland centers, forming a noose to throttle the life out of downtown. Ever

greater numbers of Detroit's population now drove their new cars along new roads, carrying them from new houses to new factories and shopping malls. The city, like a tree, was dying in the middle as fresh growth sprouted on the outside.

'MOTOR CITY IS BURNING'[13]

The phenomenon of 'White flight' was not unique to Detroit, although few other cities have experienced such a dramatic collapse in their inner-city populations. Between 1955 and 1960 alone, Detroit lost as much as 25 per cent of its population of two million, as those who could headed for cheap housing and low taxes in the suburbs, leaving the inner city with fewer tax dollars and a residual population that was

Top: Civil Rights: picketting General Motors, 1964.
Above: Civil riots: fear and loathing in Detroit, spreadeagled on a '64 T-bird, July 1967.

unique Black musical culture, it is perhaps less known outside the US as a hotbed of the civil rights movement. When in June 1963, Martin Luther King Jr first declared 'I have a dream,' he was speaking not on the steps of the Lincoln Memorial in Washington, DC, but in Cobo Hall in downtown Detroit, after leading a 125,000-strong civil-rights march up Woodward Avenue, the largest in America up to that time. And while it is a well-publicized part of Detroit folklore that Motown founder Berry Gordy once worked on the Ford production line, composing songs to alleviate the tedium of assembly work, guidebooks to the city generally neglect to mention that at the same time Ford was also employing the future Nation of Islam leader, Malcolm X.

It can have come as no surprise to anyone when inner-city Detroit finally boiled over in July 1967, after a police raid on an illegal speakeasy sparked off a week of rioting that left 43 dead and 467 injured, the worst civil unrest in twentieth-century American history up until that time. The physical damage was immense, with about $50 million of property destroyed, including hundreds of homes and thousands of shops looted or burnt, leaving whole city blocks in ruins. But it was the social damage that inflicted the biggest wounds on Detroit. Although segregation was already a fact of life there, the riots left an enduring legacy of extreme polarization that further contributed to the community's social collapse. By the 1970s, Detroit had acquired the thoroughly deserved nickname of Murder City. Its 1974

predominantly poor and Black. It may have been well-paid jobs that had drawn African-Americans to the Motor City in the first instance, but it was poor race relations that subsequently alienated them, in the process lighting a powder keg under the city's social fabric.

For while Detroit is justly famous for nurturing a

Detroit in decay: the ruins of Kahn's Packard plant of 1905.

research and technical facilities – increased rationalization and automation, and the relocation of production facilities to cheaper-wage economies, massively reduced their dependence on local labour. Added to this was the steady loss of consumer confidence in American-designed and -built automobiles.

In this respect, the Motor City was once again the victim of its own earlier success. The outrageous excesses of its annual model updates had so successfully stimulated consumer desires that the manufacturers had devoted themselves more to innovations in styling than in technology. The disastrous consequences of this policy were exposed in 1965, when Ralph Nader's *Unsafe at Any Speed* slammed Detroit for designing and selling cars that were known to be dangerous, allegedly causing untold injuries and deaths on America's roads. The Ford Mustang and General Motors' Corvair were singled out for particular criticism, with the result that sales of GM's fabled 'muscle' car fell by 93 per cent. The American public were waking up to the fact that what was good for General Motors wasn't necessarily good for them after all.

Over-confident from decades of total domination of American markets, the car-makers were still building their unwieldy and antiquated products when the oil crisis hit in 1973. With petrol suddenly expensive and scarce, American buyers shied away from Detroit's lumbering 'gas guzzlers' in favour of smaller, more fuel-efficient Japanese imports – particularly as growing concerns over environmental pollution increased the attractiveness of less ostentatious private vehicles. Throughout the 1950s, American cars had accounted for 95 per cent of the American market, but by the late 1970s imports had risen to as much as 25 per cent of total sales. However, even that diminished market share seems like a strong performance given the parlous state of the industry

record of 714 homicides was the worst in the nation, a feat it matched in several other years in the following decade.

THE END OF THE LINE?

Detroit's social plight was reinforced by the steady decline and displacement of the auto industry. Many famous car-makers had ceased production or been taken over, eventually leaving just the Big Three: General Motors, Ford and Chrysler. While they continued to maintain a considerable presence – including the world's greatest concentration of

Detroit destroyed: Woodward Ave, looking towards downtown.

today. For, as the *Detroit News* revealed on the fateful morning of 11 September 2001:

The once Big Three . . . have seen their collective share of the U.S. car and light truck market shrink from the 73 percent they enjoyed in 1993 at the start of the unprecedented sales boom to nearly 14 percentage points lower last month . . . Their share has sunk below 60 percent for the first time since 1920.[14]

It remains entirely possible that one day soon, cars will finally cease rolling off the production lines of the Motor City. Chrysler continues to lose money and market share, despite having merged with German car giant Daimler-Benz, and is in real danger of being displaced from the Big Three by Toyota. Even mighty General Motors, the only one of the three to turn in a profit this year, has seen its market share slip continually, from 60 per cent in the 1950s to 28 per cent today. One can only hope for America's sake that its destiny is no longer so closely tied to the GM Corporation.

But where does that leave the Motor City? As one drives past its derelict towers and shattered neighbourhoods, it might seem that God has deserted

Centre: Drive-in: the auditorium of the Michigan Theater, Detroit.
Above: A distressed landscape: inner city Detroit.

Detroit, but the automotive industry certainly hasn't yet done so. The city that witnessed the birth of the mass-produced automobile a century ago is still home to the giants of American car production. General Motors, Ford and Chrysler all maintain headquarters in the area.[15] The very names of the city's streets and buildings read like an almanac of America's most famous car-makers: Edsel Ford, Walter P. Chrysler, Packard, Studebaker, Fisher.

Unfortunately, speeding past downtown Detroit, as opposed to wandering through it, is exactly what most people are keen to do, intent on avoiding unimaginable dangers on the rutted streets of this ruptured urban landscape. Although new buildings are once again rising in the city centre, they are overshadowed by the empty shells of elaborate skyscrapers, including such once-famous hotels as the Cadillac, the Madison and the Statler, whose only remaining function is to support microwave aerials for the new information technologies. The fabled department store Hudson's has been put out of business by its suburban progeny and was recently dynamited. Many of Detroit's theatres are destroyed or abandoned, while the grand auditorium of the Michigan Theater has been converted into a multi-level parking garage. 'The Fabulous Ruins of Detroit' is a website that charts the wreckage of the Motor City. With wry native humour, it compares Detroit to ancient Rome; the comparison seems all too plausible as one surveys the jagged skyline of this decaying metropolis.

Moving away from downtown, the ring of inner-city suburbs that once housed the Motor City's workers have largely disappeared, creating one of the most distressed urban landscapes in the Western world. Between the deep fissures dug for the urban expressways, and the mountainous hulks of the

Top: The General Motors building, downtown Detroit.
Above: Chrysler Headquarters, Auburn Hill, Michigan.

Rural splendour: Nature returns to Detroit.

deserted car plants, run streets almost wholly devoid of the buildings that once lined them. The charred remains of timber-frame houses in various stages of collapse are interspersed with plots of grass, flowers and trees; the last surviving dwellings sit in semi-rural splendour, with some intrepid inhabitants even starting to cultivate the redundant acres around them. A 1989 survey by reporters of the *Detroit Free Press* counted '15,215 vacant structures, including 9,017 single-family homes, 225 apartment buildings and 3,404 vacant businesses. The city estimated then that up to 200 structures a month were being abandoned in Detroit.'[16]

Detroit's official motto, *Speramus meliora; resurget cineribus* – 'We hope for better days; it shall rise from the ashes' – was penned after a disastrous nineteenth-century fire. But as the industry that once drove twentieth-century American expansion contin-ues its inexorable decline, it is difficult to imagine how Detroit can ever rise from its present ruination. While the Motor City will always hold a unique position in the history of America, it now seems less and less likely that it will play a significant part in its future. Given that prospect, Henry Ford's famous dictum, delivered at a time of unbridled optimism in his adopted city, now sounds suspiciously like a verdict on its demise: 'History is more or less bunk. It's tradi-tion. We don't want tradition. We want to live in the present, and the only history that is worth a tinker's damn is the history we make today.'[17]

Some Thoughts on Car Culture in Japan

DONALD RICHIE

The Japanese may not have invented the wheel, but they certainly went on to perfect it. Just look around. Japanese wheels abound. There is not, I think, a single country of the world, emerged or emerging, that does not have its quota. The names of Honda, Toyota, Nissan, Isuzu, Suzuki – all are known everywhere: cars from Japan.

The history of the vehicular wheel in this archipelago is long. First references (*c.* fifth century AD) are to be found in the *Nihonshoki*, that politically correct Japanese history, and in the later *Manyoshu* poetry collection. Both, fittingly, refer to methods of transportation – probably the two-wheeled ox-cart, early Chinese models having perhaps been adapted by the Japanese. But, and here we see early prowess, using a much more efficient double-shaft yoke.

It was also the Japanese (say the Japanese) who invented the later and more efficient jinrikisha, that vehicle which came into general use around the middle of the nineteenth century. This improved model boasted a real Japanese internal-combustion engine – that is, it was a real Japanese who pulled it.

As is indicated in the name. Jinriki means 'man-power', and sha means 'vehicle'. The method was said to have been inspired by the horse-drawn carriage, which had just been introduced from abroad. Japan did not have many horses, but it had lots of people, and the rickshaw (as it is still called in other countries) was, after governmental permission was received in 1870, produced in quantity.

One of the reasons for its popularity was the means of public transportation that it had replaced. This was the *kago*, a palanquin born on the shoulders of two or four men, depending on the weight inside. No wheels were involved, the runners bodily carried it, and the journey was expensive to the passenger and exhausting for everyone. The rickshaw, being comfortable and cheap, was shortly so popular that it was exported to Shanghai, Hong Kong and other south Asian cities. There, it so took such root that even now many think it a Chinese invention.

In the land of its birth, however, it did not last so long. After the Tokyo earthquake of 1923, the rickshaw completely disappeared – taken over by the automobile. It made a reappearance after the defeat of 1945, however, in the form of the *rintaku*, a bike-drawn cab, all of which are long gone. It is now seen in its original form only at tourist sites (Kamakura, the Asakusa Kannon Temple in Tokyo, Arashiyama in Kyoto), where one is pulled about at considerable expense by young part-time workers.

The first steam automobiles were imported from the US in 1897. By 1902, two business partners, Yoshida Shintaro and Uchiyama Komanosuke, had produced a trial car with a two-cylinder, 12-hp American engine. In 1904, one Yamaha Torao was manufacturing the first two-cylinder steam auto in Okayama, to be followed in 1907 by Tokyo Jodosha Seisakusho's first domestic petrol-fuelled car. In 1912, Kaishinsha, a company established by Hashimoto

Masujiro, produced one called the Dattogo.

These, however, were all trial models – as was the Otomogo, created in 1920 by the Hakuyosha plant. By 1923, some 250 of this model had been created, the largest total production of any make in Japan during these years. This was also the year of the Tokyo earthquake, an event that hit all industries hard. Not only was production curtailed, but imported cars, almost entirely from the US, soon flooded what market existed. This process was encouraged by the government, which purchased a number of Model-T Fords – the auto of choice since Ford had moved into the Japanese market as early as 1903. These were remodelled into minibuses (the popular Entaro bus), which provided the only means of public transportation within the devastated city.

Scenting a market, both Ford and General Motors had established subsidiary companies in Japan by 1925. Five years later, some 16,000 new American cars annually were running around the islands. It was not until 1933 that the native industry could even boast 1,000 sold locally.

That the Japanese automobile industry was so swiftly left behind by foreign competition is to be attributed to the backwardness of the country's industrial technology, particularly that involving machine-tooling. The few companies which existed were, despite commendable early activity, all considered bad risks, and few of the established financial and industrial combines (such as Mitsui and Mitsubishi) wanted to make any commitments. The Japanese military authorities were, on the other hand, pressing for a locally made car. Actually, it was trucks they wanted, and though the large combines resisted the pressure, new small companies (Nissan, Toyota, later Isuzu) were being licensed by 1935.

After the beginning of World War II, the govern-ment and the now more enthusiastic combines closed ranks, and Mitsubishi Heavy Industries Ltd, did their share in producing the necessary trucks, as well as planes and their weaponry. This continued even after the war was lost, encouraged by the Allied Occupation authorities, who had a vested interest in getting the company back on its feet, or at least on its wheels.

After the war, production was almost entirely of trucks. People either walked, took streetcars or buses, or hired the fume-emitting charcoal-fuelled taxis which were to be seen on all streets until the late 1940s. By this time, however, another war was loom-ing (the Korean conflict), which was good economic news for everyone (except the Koreans). Japan, taking advantage of the military-procurements boom, began to manufacture passenger cars.

This was around 1952 and shortly after the government began its own policy of support/protec-tion of the domestic auto industry. The Ministry of International Trade and Industry (MITI) provided no money, but it did ensure favourable allocations of foreign currency and began to restrict vehicle imports. It still does.

As a result, by 1960 the domestic production of passenger cars had increased. More companies – Fuji Heavy Industries (makers of the Subaru and the Prince), Toyo Kogyo (the Mazda) and Honda (which also made motorcycles) – climbed on board. Strategic models (Crown, Cedric, Corona, Bluebird) were designed for high-volume production, and by 1965 the auto industry was here to stay.

The rate of production was enormous. In 1955, only 20,000 cars were made and a mere two were exported. Twenty-five years later in 1980, seven million were made and nearly four million exported. This steep success continued on and on until over-extended Japan's economic collapse in the 1990s.

To keep up with the number of new automobiles being sold, new methods of accommodation were sought. Roads were built, often to nowhere and over unnecessary bridges, simply to have somewhere to drive to. Parking space diminished to the point where prime land found its most advantageous market as car-park property. 'My Car' was pushed as a theme, and it soon seemed that every man, woman and child on the archipelago owned one.

It would probably be unfair to blame the automobile industry alone for the massive despoiling of the country during the latter decades of the past century (and coming years of this one). There were other factors such as governmental pork-barrelling, a destructive alliance between construction companies and local governments, and unbridled 'development', which saw even national parkland pressed into service. At the same time, however, as in many other countries, it was the coming of the automobile that heralded a wholesale destruction of the environment such as Japan had seen hitherto only in such natural disasters as earthquakes and such unnatural ones as wars.

The government attempted to cope. The horrendous traffic conditions in Tokyo (plus a level of industrial pollution so high that it is said nylon stockings ran on women's legs) was brought under control. New trains and subways took the pedestrian flow, and a system of elevated highways siphoned off much of the car glut. By 1964 (the year of the Olympic Games in Tokyo), auto flow (which had often, as in Bangkok, stopped cold) was again possible. Later, despite a runaway economy (first running straight up, then running straight down), there were some attempts made to temper the depredations of the auto. A recall system to improve safety has been established. Laws now deal, in a way, with pollution. There is an emphasis on fuel-saving in the small energy-saving cars

A solution to the parking problem: double parking, Tokyo suburbs, 2001.

presently being pushed – partly through a steep petrol law. The brightest hope of the nation is the darkest fear of the industry. Car business is nothing like it was in the so-called 'bubble era'. People cannot now afford the product. Shimakawa Koichi, to whom I have turned for some information in these pages, maintains that 'the industry will now have to make a transition from a period of simple quantitative growth to a period of qualitative improvement'. And so it must. If it can.

The car has truly changed Japan's culture just as it has that of many countries. There are, however, a few differences. Family outings may be more frequent than they were, but drive-ins never caught on. Nor did the phenomenon of lovers' lanes packed with parked autos – since Japan is already equipped for this purpose with the ubiquitous 'love hotel'. Shopping, however, is much facilitated – at least in the suburbs. In the city itself, parking is usually thought too much of a problem.

The car-packed metropoli of Japan have yet to designate 'carless' days; the always unpopular alternate-driving-day plan was never suggested, much less implemented. And there are no non-driving zones. Any street wide enough to take a car is already full of them.

At the same time, there are some tokens that at least the problem is seen as a problem. Many large-city thoroughfares now have carless Sundays (10:00 a.m. to 6:00 p.m.). Despite some complaints from the police (the rerouting problems are considerable) and also from merchants (until they discovered that more patrons than usual took advantage of the weekly Pedestrian Paradise), the custom continues and offers a few hours of respite.

Most inventions are intended to create advantages for those inventing them. Man-made fire cooks meat, etc. An invention such as the wheel is an attempt to mould space and time into shapes more conducive to human comfort. Few have ever argued against these inventions which so change our environment, and yet the wholesale dispensation of space and time has both advantages and disadvantages. We take the former for granted and sometimes complain (though never seriously) about the latter. The automobile is too convenient for anyone to seriously doubt its virtues. It gets, say, the child to the hospital in time to save its life. If we still had to rely on the doctor and his buggy, the tyke would be dead in its bed by the time he got there. About the adverse results of mass automobilization, however, we have less to say.

Indeed, so completely have cars created our environment that we have, with scarcely a thought, shaped how and where we live according to its demands. We live in the suburbs, we drive in to work, the kids are bussed to schools, the parents shop at the mall. Without the car, this suburban life would not be possible. It might not even have been necessary, since the flight to the suburbs was both the cause and the effect of collapsing city centres.

Since everyone has a car, no-one rides public transport, and it consequently becomes too expensive to maintain. In a city like Los Angeles, if you do not have wheels, you might as well have no feet. For people with no automobiles, spaces stretches impossibly vast, and the time taken to get anywhere is endless. At the same time, for those with wheels it is common (in Texas, I hear) to take an hour and drive 100 miles simply to eat at a particular restaurant.

The car has created its own space. We are all, everywhere, used to (and grateful for) the ingenious highway systems which cut through forests, cross mountains, span bays. Thruways slice up our cities. yet so few complain when the needs of the auto destroy and create hardship.

I am thinking of Seoul, where the needs of the motorcar have destroyed all of the old sections of the city and where the carless must, at every city-centre crossing, clamber down stairs to a tunnel and, on the other side, climb up from it.

At the same time, in Japanese cities the carless are forced to climb high bridges which span busy highways and then descend. The more elderly call

Human and motor traffic, Nippon-Bashi, Osaka, 2001.

these 'heart-attack machines'. Down, up – up, down. This is a true disadvantage, and yet none complain. Or if they do, they are in such a minority – as mere pedestrians – that their voices are not heard.

Yet, though the bane of car culture is omnipresent, the forms it takes are various. A country like Japan experiences the automobile in a manner different from some Western countries. Let us count the ways.

Though the car is ubiquitous in this archipelago, there is the difference that distances are not great. No question of driving an hour to dine. Great four-lane motorways do run up and down the main islands, but sheer geographical length is broken up, and thus that temporal quality, sheer speed, is limited. In addition, there are the tollbooths. Japanese motorways are designed to be expensive. In most countries, once the road is paid for, it becomes free. Not here. Motorways are perpetual money machines. The results are said to go into 'upkeep'.

Another difference is that in Japan, the automobile has not cancelled out public transportation. Indeed, Japan has one of the best public-transportation systems in the world – the famous bullet-trains, all sorts of inter-city 'interurbans', the finest of

Traffic congestion on the Kan-nana ring road, Tokyo, 2001.

subways and inner-city train systems, and an admirable bus system.

A major reason for this is that there are too many people for all of them to be driving at once. The equivalent of half the population of the US is crammed into an area a little smaller than California. If everyone took to the road (as everyone does in, say, the US), terminal gridlock would be nationwide.

Another reason for the excellence of Japan's public-transportation system is that it is widely used. It is not given over to the poor and otherwise underprivileged whose small numbers would eventually

force it into bankruptcy. It is used because having a car can actually be an inconvenience. Car-parks costs as much as hotels, police routinely tow away street parkers, insurance is high and car taxes are higher. Consequently, 'My Car' is not used as much as its Western equivalent. At the two times that it is, the effect is immediately apparent. This is at New Year's and during the midsummer vacation week, when all city dwellers return to the country, the *furusato*, the hometown. Since they drive (the whole family goes, the car is a lot cheaper than train or bus), all of Japan appears on the highway at these times.

The result is a national traffic jam of Bangkokian proportions. 'Delays' up to half a day or longer are common, the whole family crammed into 'My Car', fretting and bickering through their holidays. And no sooner do they finally, eventually, arrive at their rural destination than it is time to drive back, the dreaded 'U-turn' of which the press bi-annually speaks, where getting back into the city is even more traumatic than getting out of it was.

Except for these two periods of automotive excess, however, Japan is relatively free of the damage which the private car has elsewhere inflicted on public transportation. At the same time, the ubiquitous auto has introduced values which have done much to degrade traditional Japanese attitudes and, I think, virtues.

Let me explain. Ideas of space and time inform every culture. Japanese traditional culture was noted for the way in which these ideas were used. The haiku, for example, depicts the crux between the two. To use a common example, here is a famous lyric of Basho:

An old pond: a frog jumps in – the sound of water.

Here, in Hiroaki Sato's single-line translation, we have the conjunction. First, the spatial setting, then the temporal event. We contrast the two and appreciate – splash – their coincidence. For us to do so, we must conceive them, momentarily, as opposites brought miraculously together by their correspondence.

To make this occur, we must have, perhaps like Basho himself, been sitting by a pond for some time, since frogs are not continually jumping into them. Our assumption is that the moment is privileged. We have been sitting quietly in one place (space is empty), and suddenly the equally vacant flux in which we live (time is empty) is stamped, signed, sealed, by the extraordinary occurrence of a single sound which makes us aware for an instant of our true spatial and temporal position.

To explain in such a manner is, of course, to destroy the poem. It is about sudden apprehension, not laborious interpretation. But it does help us understand that it would not have occurred at all had Basho been in 'My Car'. Even if he had driven to a lake and hung around for a while, it would not have been the same thing. In all likelihood, the only frog he would have seen would have been road-kill.

This is because the point of the poem is that the conjunction was not searched for. Basho was not going anyplace at the time. He was not thinking about his destination. Indeed, during the whole trip along the narrow road to the deep north, getting anywhere was not the point. The journey, which came out shaped something like a circle, not the destination, was the point.

I suppose it is possible to drive aimlessly, going nowhere. There are such things as outings in the family car and adolescent joyrides in the hot rod. I do not, however, believe that these are considered major employments of the automobile. They certainly aren't in Japan.

A result is that what happened regularly to Basho and his contemporaries now happens to very few. One cannot completely blame the automotive industry for this – there have been too many other changes. At the same time, however, the automobile has played its part in the redefinition of time and space which has not only filled in most old ponds but has also made their contemplation unlikely.

An illustrative parallel. For most of its existence, Japan has been a poor country. It was overpopulated early on, and there are few natural resources. While there have been a wealthy few, the majority were what we would now describe as financially challenged. Indeed, so general was this situation that an entire culture rose which was, it could be argued, based on want.

There was, however, lots of mud and so, with help from Korea, extraordinary pottery. There was also lots of space, but no furniture, and so the concept of *ma* – space itself as not an absence but a presence. And an aesthetic vocabulary that stressed *l'art pauvre*. *Sabi* can mean not only the rusted but also the lovingly worn, the patina given by use. *Wabi* can mean the elegant loneliness of the common, the singularity of the aesthetically quotidian. The mysterious and beautiful *yugen* can arise when the everyday meets, in some time-worn way, the eternal.

This state of affairs continued from around the sixth century to approximately the 1960s. Then, Japan began to become wealthy, not just the privileged few but the common many. The era now termed 'bubble' (a structure bound by definition to burst) found Japan buying everything in sight, including the Rockefeller Center and the more famous golf-courses. In a decade, the country at large became nouveau riche, and all those centuries of maigre beauty became beside the point.

Among signs of new affluence was the automobile. The rise of the mighty industry coincided with this extraordinary enriching of the citizenry. Considerations of space, time, beauty and life itself would never be the same.

One can offer no solutions, since the situation itself cannot encompass one. And of course, many in Japan itself would not believe that one is required. Certainly, any proposed solution would have to be impracticably radical. A radical solution would have to wait until the time machine is available (a mere matter of time) and then return and murder Henry Ford in his crib. This is unlikely, and impractical in that no such Japanese Luddites exist.

One way, then, as Basho might have said, is to adjust to things as they are. Few ponds, fewer frogs, but getting there faster, on time, efficiently, economically. At the same time, one might also reflect on the fact that the triumph of the wheel is a mixed achievement for its users.

Technik

DIRK LEACH

A siren went off and the line began to move. In the trunk of every car I placed a wheel cover and carpet and under each hood I set the hoses in place for hydraulic oil and radiator water. My work-cycle ran so: I lay a carpet in a trunk, turned, and looked down upon the exposed engine of the car following. I stepped down to the right from the stamped plate between the two rails of the moving line and onto the drain grate, reached under the hood of the new car and unscrewed the wing nut on the cover to the hydraulic oil cup, placed the nut and cover on the air filter, turned, and walked forward downstream to the engine of the first car. There I flipped the vacuum switch that released the nozzle to the hose of radiator-water and set the nozzle in its bucket on the pump, which slid on a track suspended from the girders overhead. I put the radiator cap on the radiator spout, removed the mouth of the oil hose, put it in its bucket on the pump, and screwed the oil cover back in place. Then I pushed the pump and both hoses along the track up the line to the different colored sedan I'd just left and set the hoses, first water, then oil, over their respective holes. I completed the cycle I repeated all day by walking to the two supply-baskets nearby, getting another cover for the spare tire and another carpet and laying them, first cover and then carpet, in the trunk of the new car. Every two or three cars I had to wait a few moments for the next one to come within reach of my hoses.

I read in the spaces between cars for the first three hours – a sentence or two at a time before I had to look up a word in the dictionary. This was usually interrupted while I did the work on two or three passing cars. Heidegger wrote to Jünger about the present time and called it the time of consummated nihilism, *vollendeten Nihilismus*, when the entire world was mobilized in the effort to dominate the earth with technology. We live, he said, in the border-zone between historical ages, on the line separating an only partially nihilistic past civilization from a future which, being beyond the present of complete

nihilism, was either utter annihilation, the destruction of the planet, or a basic and presently unimaginable change in the direction of history. Jünger had written of crossing the line. Heidegger proposed examining the line itself, referring to it as a zone of indefinite temporal duration, perhaps centuries wide, the zone of active nihilism. He spoke of the difficulty a thinker faced in attempting even to

imitate the machines. I let them push me along in the reading and when I stopped reading I took photographs for a half an hour or so, trying my best to do so casually and to talk to anyone who became interested. Most asked me if I were a spy. I told them that no, I was studying technology, showed them Heidegger's book, and told them that he and Jünger called technology 'nihilism'. No one objected to this characterization.

___

As my days at the factory wore on, I began to notice a sort of experience that exemplified what Heidegger, in contrast to the 'positive nothing' that nihilism stove to nullify, called the 'negative nothing' that nihilism promoted. The negative nothing was a plenitude. I found it everywhere at the factory and described it several times. The box of gas caps supplying me was as big as a medicine ball and stacked with five others between the tire covers and trunk mats. I was tempted to say its poetic significance was 'work' and call myself lazy for feeling repulsed by the sight of it. But I could not quite accept that laziness controlled my perception. It was what the work *meant* that repulsed

define nihilism and complimented Jünger for his likening this attempt to the search for the cause of cancer. The words I read seemed to fuse into an ever-increasing distress. 'Nihilism' weighed with a dreadful, apt utterness, its meaning unclear but promising to prove appropriate.

In between cars I read this philosophical letter about the bleakness of the world-situation, or I waited. To stand still while the machines I operated 'quickly' did their jobs, to wait to remove them from under the hood of one car and replace them under the hood of the next, was strangely hard to endure. I listened to the ventilator overhead. It groaned without gasping, never pausing for breath. It labored but was tireless. When I waited I heard uninterrupted and lifeless power at work. It was dead but active. I compared it to my living activity and found it stronger. I paused, I stopped to think, to adjust my stance and grip, to breathe.

The best method of working seemed to be to

me. It meant too much of the same thing – so much the same as to be the same as nothing. This was the negative nothing, the nothing at all that lurked in pallets of parts on the assembly line. Working with the caps, handling each one singly, taught the sense of this nothing.

For a critic faced with world-wide nihilism such words as 'world', 'nothing', and 'being' found for him a discourse that is *mehrdeutig*, an awkward journey into the unsaid. This is an 'unsaid' called to be spoken by the historical age in which we live, a speaking-thinking that is subject to a hidden law, one poetic and not merely logical.

At the factory it was difficult to admit that there was a nature to nothing. It came to me as I read at the job. I could not settle down and think for myself, take the time to compose statements of any adequate length, but I did have my small recorder and when I became tired of reading I put it in the bib-pocket of my overalls and carried it with me as I worked on the cars.

I made observations. They were incomplete, disconnected bits and pieces, all of them lacking the conclusive closure that makes prose. They usually concerned the twisting subtleties of the routine I performed, subtleties gigantic in their structure but so minuscule in their relevance to anything anyone else was concerned with that they seemed submicroscopic. This was a poverty for which I knew no remedy and I did my best to spite the sense of futility it aroused. I made futility a recurrent question, itself an aspect of the job to be observed and described whenever it presented itself from a new angle.

If anyone had tried to interest me in the idea of the 'different aspects of futility' before I had come to think about it as I had, I would have told him the theme was a circle of hopeless and depressed reflection best ignored. 'Futility', 'absurdity', 'nihilism' – these words robbed a person of words, made it impossible to think. But they were the right words. They were dangerous and strange, but proper.

About the empty plenitude that I found surrounding me as I worked – the crates of parts and the complicated logic of petty jobs – Heidegger had much to say. He identified this plenitude as nothing less than the essence of technology. As a self-augmenting growth, technology has one supreme command for mankind the world over: to store up replacements, to collect and alter the material of nature into stores of homogeneous supplies.

I didn't write much in the off-hours now. Whenever I did, a motor somewhere always seemed too loud. Work at the factory had become a duller, more massive, and less eventful experience. It seemed to consist of nothing so much as getting especially close to the noise one heard everywhere all the time. After work, the work of others dominated the air. An urgent drone was the basis of the sound and internal combustion engines or sputtering power tools usually clattered in the foreground. When I tried to write, more and more often I became distracted and wondered at the noise. It was fast and regular. It went

on. It approximated constancy with a blattering push punctuated by the shortest of pauses. I knew that a long time at the factory would eventually destroy my ability to write altogether – and that my being aware of this would not even survive to witness the end. Heidegger's first words in his essay 'What are Poets For?' identified this situation as a dying of the critical capacity. The destitution of the technological age increased, he said, as the ability to recognize this destitution faded.

My new interest in poetry seemed to set me up for abrasive surprises that hastened this fading. Whenever I tried to fasten on the character of my surroundings at the *Werk* I was quickly overcome with plenitude. The mile I walked from the parking lot to building 38 had become a worn-out experience, smooth and meaningless, and I tried one morning to describe it into my recorder. I took the shortest possible route now and met few people along the way, which passed a chain-link fence and ran alongside a railroad track for half its distance. Great, dark, block-shaped buildings stood sleeping like strange, intentional mountains to my right. It was dark and quiet, like a city's edge, periodically lit by street lights. There was nothing to listen to but the subdued drone of motors. Every building hummed, leaking light and vibration from each great door. I heard a bird. Then a man on a bicycle caught me up, passed, and I heard a long-familiar sound. I called it the click of the spokes, then the click of ball bearings, and then admitted I'd never known its source. I listened to the recorder recording my footsteps as I thought and then I saw: steel teeth, a turning sprocket slapped by the links of a slack chain. I thought of lines of falling dominoes.

I remembered the recorder and turned it off. My mind had run ahead and left it behind recording only the sound of my footsteps. I had been imagining steel teeth in gums of black grease, turning in a circle. I looked up.

A vision overwhelmed me. I had come upon the parking lot of finished automobiles outside building 38. So big, with so much in it – a magnified and reinterpreted reflection of my tiny discovery. It was lit by too-white street lights, sprigs of regularity in a field of chrome cobbles, like pert dead daisies in a vast meadow of machines. I felt perplexed, as if I had looked too hard and been punished with a shock. I had hunted down a secret, discovered a seductive, spinning multiplicity, looked up, and seen a plain of parked cars: the same thing, but no secret, nothing to be curious about.

Inside my building, as I climbed the stairs to *Band Acht*, the work-lights leapt on. I saw the worn front edges of the metal stairs before me suddenly wink awake together in a stack of silver lines.

I felt surrounded by metaphors of multitude. To think about nihilism on the job was asking for trouble. Placing a cover in the trunk of the first car, a matador among slow bulls, I turned and was pierced by a ghostly hole: a rear-mirror reflecting the chrome and glass of an empty window. My eye raked over the regular, oily ridges in the plastic sheath of the oil hose. It was better to forget it.

For weeks I had been giving great amounts of

energy to the sharpshooting of transitory moments. Why? It was saddening to watch the finished Mercedes automobiles slide by under the inspection lights. The absurdity of the pretence of being one of the leading automobile manufacturers in the world of gasoline-powered transportation, a rank achieved through the appeal of the luxury car, was a pompous parade before me which no statement could stop. This parade of wasted resources which we tended all day was pushed forward by a struggle for survival, a race. We were all driven to work at the speed of the belts in the factories. It had been calculated, estimated, how fast we had to work to keep up. The military economy set the pace for our 40 hour week. We needed the money to pay for the guns, soldiers, and bombs – to defend ourselves from the 'Great Enemy,' and to exploit the populations of poor neighbour-nations. Building Mercedes Benzes was one of the most lucrative of the different enterprises constituting the war

effort: these automobiles were a powerful weapon in the fight for more power, power to fulfil ideas and realize projects. And power, as far as technology understood it, was fuel. Fuel was the life in a dead machine. We were mobilized by machines, fighting each other for the power to animate the dead products of our technological skill. They would all stand useless without fuel. And if we understood this we were challenged to overcome the voracious system we had created as our slave. It was our own incomprehension of strength made metallic and automotive.

FROM *Technik* (1986)

Pobeda outside a registry office.

component of wedding celebrations, which usually last about a week. The groom's family celebrate the wedding in their village and the bride's family in another village, but in between they pile into lorries and cars and visit each other's villages with gifts, singing and dancing until the early hours.

Then on to Primorskii Boulevard, a long and

Moskvich and Lada near Vorontzov Palace.

elegant tree-lined street looking down over the port and the Black Sea where Odessites linger at night in the summer heat. A Lada is parked in front of a hoarding advertising an exhibition of live snakes. We pass benches lined with *Spaziergänger* and chattering people of all ages on the way to the Vorontzov Palace with Arabic inscriptions on its façade, now a school. From the end of the promenade, one can look down on the port and lorries belching along a flyover.

The car only begins to feel in its element as one approaches the suburbs and the monotonous housing projects of the '40s and '50s. The vast apartment blocks are spread out in rows and show some neglect. On the edge of the centre is Moldevanka, famous for its courtyards where once people would eat, sleep and play in the open air. It seems one is back in Isaac Babel's time – this is the haunt of everyday people but also of alcoholics, prostitutes and drug addicts. A few cars, old Volgas and Moskvichs, are parked on the streets, some battered. Then, in a courtyard, an expensive car with Dutch number plates. What can this mean? Traversing the outskirts of the city near the bus station, we have some trouble in flagging down a car. We walk down a side street to catch a ride in an old vehicle driven by a wiry man in his 60s. The driver takes off, is obviously surprised and amused to have some passengers, and hands out biscuits as we drive to the sounds of early Beatles music. On the way, we speed past a car completely filled with melons.

Odessa is well known in the Russian-speaking world for its beaches. Arcadia is the fanciest and at the same time the most popular one. The Odessan beaches are crowded with white-skinned bodies (many from more northerly parts of the ex-Soviet Union), spread out on sun chairs placed inches away from each other. Some beaches are private, and paid

Lada in Primorskii Boulevard.

Exterior of Vorontzov Palace.

entry includes both a sun chair and waitress service with drinks from the bar. In Arcadia, fantasy runs wild; every other building is a beach disco or restaurant with shimmering artificial waterfalls under neon lights. Away from the beach, small traditional dachas are flanked by the apartment buildings of ex-Communist party workers and the huge houses of the new rich – a mafia boss, an author from Moscow, whoever has plenty of new money. To get back from Arcadia to the centre of the city, it is advisable to walk at least five minutes first of all. If, when you wave down a private car, you start from Arcadia, the price will be fifteen Hrivna; as you walk round the corner, it goes down to seven and, further still, to five.

Leaving Odessa and entering Ukraine (it feels like another country), we head for Uman, a town with a landscaped park nearby called Sofiyivka and built by a Polish count, Felix Pototsky, in 1796 for his wife Sofia, a former Turkish slave whom he purchased for 2,000,000 Zloty. Three police checkpoints. They don't wave down every car, just the ones which take their fancy. We are stopped by a friendly-looking Ukrainian-speaking policeman. Our Russian-speaking driver explains that he has to pay three Hrivna (it costs ten Hrivna if the driver wants a receipt) because the car had driven over a white line in the middle of the road. Travellers in the Ukraine always budget for at least two or three fines like this on a longish journey. No doubt the money supplements the policeman's meagre income. Of course, if there is a real contravention, like speeding, the fine is more severe.

As an example of the black economy, this is fairly typical, symptomatic of the Ukrainian economic malaise whereby various shady interest groups have accumulated wealth by granting political favours while poverty and wage arrears are widespread. The

Volga in Moldevanka.

Battered Moskvich in Moldevanka.

average wage in Ukraine is something like $50 per month; such economic indicators would normally put the country on a par with some of the poorest in the world. However, the huge size of the black economy tells a different story. One of the biggest unofficial businesses in Ukraine concerns the gas and petrol industry, whose income is recorded as much lower than is feasible.

Petrol is a monopoly, but by the time it gets to individual stations, much illegal money has been made on its transport. Ukrainian drivers are choosy about where they buy their petrol: some stations are reputed to mix their petrol with water.

Ukrainian motorways are rather lumpy. Bus stops appear at intervals, covered in colourful mosaics, some in good condition, others looking like incomplete jigsaw puzzles. The earliest are from the 1960s, but many date from the '70s and '80s. Along the roads, peasants sell farm produce: cucumbers, apples, tomatoes, garlic, honey. Here, the prices are cheaper than in the markets, as there are no middlemen. Most Ukrainian farms are still collectives, but many peasants have their own patches of land which allow them to sell produce on the side. The motorway is hardly bisected by any side roads the whole distance between Odessa and Uman (approximately 280 kilometres). Peasants and farmers are expected to walk to their fields from the road. Russian- or Ukrainian-built cars are more numerous in the countryside. We pass a Lada with a rusty fridge strapped to its roof (later, I realize that my apartment bedside table in Odessa is just such an fridge) and a Zaporozhets stuffed with boxes of produce.

The Zaporozhets was the only mass-produced Ukrainian car and became the most popular post-war small car in the Soviet Union, as it was the first car within the reach of average wage earners. The

Above: Mosaic-decorated bus stops in the Ukranian countryside.

Zaporozhets (manufactured in the town of Zaporozhets, Ukraine, from the 1960s on) was soon known punningly as (Zhapa)rozhets ('arse-face'). It was the only Soviet car obtainable without being placed on a waiting list because the production standards were so abysmal. People from all over Russia would travel to Ukraine to get hold of one. In the later '90s, Daewoo collaborated with ZAZ to produce cars supported by a decree from the Ukrainian government to ban importation of all foreign cars over five years old, but production has recently trickled to a few hundred cars a month. The Zaporozhets is the most basic car in the somewhat limited hierarchy of Russian cars. Its nearest rivals, the Moskvich and Lada, look down on it.

On revisiting Odessa a second time, almost nothing had changed. It was early morning. Melon sellers had locked up their melons in wire cages on the street corners. The Vorontzov Palace was still crumbling. The same Moskvich was parked at exactly the

same angle in front of a dwelling. In the harbour, a cargo ship was being loaded for Istanbul. The heat was oppressive, but made somewhat bearable by the tree-lined boulevards of the city centre and the open-air cafés selling cold drinks. Where the sun sifted through the trees, there was jagged, piercing light. A car was flagged down to take us to an Arcadian dacha. It was a Mercedes estate car, maybe fifteen years old. The driver was a lady well into her 70s with horn-rimmed spectacles. She drove vigorously as she talked and gesticulated.

THE MOSCOW RACETRACK

In Odessa, cars weave their incongruous way through the streets of the nineteenth-century inner city, whose basic thoroughfares have hardly changed since horses and carriages rode over them. In contrast (as Svetlana Boym wrote in her chapter 'Moscow, the Third Rome' in *The Future of Nostalgia*), by the 1990s Moscow was no longer a city for pedestrian experiences: 'To appreciate the Moscow miracle one had to be either high up enjoying the panoramic views or moving in a high speed BMW.' The years between 1995 and 1998 were a period of planned and frenzied reconstruction; the largest shopping mall in Europe was constructed (the Manezh Shopping Mall), as well as amusement parks and casinos, and Moscow became a more cosmopolitan (or less Russian) city with the influx of lowly paid workers from other ex-Soviet states (including Chechens) and of highly paid expatriate workers and technocrats with their own networks of cafés, bars, restaurants, clubs and housing.

Only in a car can one experience Moscows's recent post-modernity. The bewildering juxtaposition of architectures, the vistas which appear and reappear through the angles of the windscreen: the majesty of the Bolshoi, the Stalinist skyscrapers or the domes of the cathedrals or the kitschy malls and casinos of New Arbat. As we drive down Tverskaya Ulitsa, the open-air cafés are full. Security guards are everywhere. Pedestrians spill out of the metro stations into the road and onto the squares. Russian and Western cars fight it out on the broad boulevard and are part of the cinematic confusion which exhilarates the spectator.

Drivers throughout the world like to claim that driving in their city is civilized and reasonably safe compared to some other place they have imagined or maybe even experienced. And so it is in Moscow, where drivers are consistent in their driving and in one sense predictable. Moscow driving is uniformly aggressive. Lane discipline is almost non-existent. Drivers weave in and out of lanes on either side with just inches of clearance, cars will overtake in either lane, while at the same time quite flamboyant and breathtaking U-turns are undertaken and contribute to the mysterious anarchism of traffic snarl-ups. Large Western cars seem to enjoy terrorizing smaller Russian-made cars by speeding up to them at high speed and slamming on the brakes at the last moment or by recklessly overtaking them. Seatbelts are not much used – many cars do not seem to have them. I saw one accident every other day in Moscow in the course of a seven-day stay, two of which seemed serious (I was reminded of Tehran in the '70s). Fast or reckless driving is thought by many to be 'manly', and the notorious traffic police seem uninterested in stopping many of the main offenders – those with expensive Western cars. Eighty kilometres per hour is the official speed limit on the radial motorways such as Leningradsky or Kutuzovsky that cross the city. Speeding, drunkenness or undisciplined driving are, unsurprisingly, the official main causes of accidents.

The Moscow racetrack.

(On the Russian 'Interceptor' TV programme, as reported on Western TV, contestants steal real cars and have to evade capture by the police – if they are caught, they go to jail.) At certain hours of the day, the seemingly chaotic traffic coagulates as no further space can be found for speeding. Then there is time to meditate upon how this all came about . . .

No doubt in the rush to embrace capitalism, the city's fabric was remoulded to accommodate capitalism's vehicles, but, interestingly, until the 1930s only trains, waterways, rivers and animal-driven vehicles appeared in paintings and photographs of Moscow. After the Battle of Borodino and Napoleon's retreat, which saw most of Moscow devastated by fire, the city's medieval circular-cell structure was expanded by the addition of ring roads. The Boulevard Ring and Garden Ring roads were created, lined with trees and made into elegant boulevards. Under Stalin and Kaganovich (the Politburo man fascinated by architecture), Moscow was further transformed into a model city based on the radical urban plans that created the superb Moscow metro as well as such huge roads as Tverskaya, ulitsa Gorkogo and Teatralny Proyezd. Churches and old buildings were demolished and Italianate mansion blocks erected. The Garden Ring was cleared of trees and made wide enough for planes to land on it. The road-clearing and rebuilding were also partly ceremonial in intent, meant to pave the way for parades and celebrations to compete with those of ancient Rome. Later, the outer Moscow ring road was constructed. (A third connecting ring road is now being built.)

In many ways, then, the rapid increase in gigantic road projects in Moscow far preceded and exceeded the needs of cars in Communist society. In the '40s and '50s, the production of private cars in the whole of the Soviet Union rose from 20,175 per year

(in 1948) to 107,806 (1955). By 1970, production had risen to 344,248, and by 1974 it had more than tripled to 1,119, 422. It was the huge change of policy under Khrushchev and the vastly increased production during those years which made the difference. Previously, the assumption had been that most citizens would have to use taxis or public transport. Priority in the early years of the Communist state had been given to lorries and military vehicles – Lenin set the scene in his 1913 speech, which urged the production of automobiles as a replacement for working animals. Nationalization followed between 1918 and 1919. As the statistics show, production was slow. One of the earliest factories (started in 1923) was the Likhachov car factory in south-east Moscow, which became the Stalin factory in 1933, producing Zis cars (in 1958 renamed Zil after the factory director Ivan Likchacev). This factory was integrated architecturally into the (partly surviving) buildings of the ancient Simonov Monastery to provide a Constructivist complex of workers' housing, schools, bathhouses and metro station. Zils became the cars for Russian leaders.

One of the few paintings from the Soviet period to show the new pleasures of driving on the broad boulevards is Yuri Pimenov's *New Moscow* (1937). The driver, a young woman, is heading down from the Lubianka towards Red Square with the State Duma on the right and the asymmetrically fashioned Hotel Moskva (both new buildings at the time) on the left. The modernity of the scene is enhanced by the sparkling effect of a recent rain shower, but it should be remembered that private driving was a new experience in the 1930s and the privilege of a very few.

In Moscow today, almost 50 per cent of all cars are foreign, the rest being mainly Ladas, Volgas or Moskvich's, a large proportion of which are ageing. The Moskvich dates from the 1940s and is of 'pure'

Yuri Pimenov, *New Moscow*, 1937, oil on canvas.

Lada in Moscow.

Soviet construction, the first original model dating from 1956. The Moskvich 402 was a small family saloon that looked modern for its time. By 1967, over a million had been built. By the second half of the 1990s, production was well under a 100,000 per annum. Today, most of the production is for the city authorities who own most of the company shares, and the factory often runs out of parts to complete them, so that uncompleted cars start rusting before they leave the factory floors. Moskvich's were sold to countries like Iceland and the UK in the 1970s. The Icelandic story is symptomatic. Exchanged for fish and raw materials, the somewhat sturdy cars soon found a home in the island's rugged conditions. Ten years later, all the Moskvich cars in Iceland were

repurchased by Russian ship's captains and taken back on Russian vessels. Once back in the Soviet Union, they were cannibalized for spare parts.

By contrast, the Lada's future seems secure, with 1999 production at over 800,000 cars. The Lada, a joint venture with Fiat, was produced in the Togliatti plant (named after the leader of the Italian Communist Party) on the River Volga. The first model, a slightly redesigned Fiat 124, was developed and adapted to suit Soviet conditions. Metal 30-per-cent thicker than the Italian version was manufactured; the suspension, steering, gearbox and rear axle were all strengthened and adapted to make it into a rugged car suitable for bumpy Russian roads. Today, there are many Lada models with a wide range of prices, which

Inside the grounds of the Kremlin.

Moscow roads at night.

Cadillac parked among Russian cousins.

may be a reason for the cars' adaptability and success in the Russian market.

The Volga is the product of the important factory at Gorky (Nizhny Novgorod) which was the result of the Ford Motor Company's decision to enter the Russian market. The earlier models had massive frames and were built as luxury limousines right up to the 1980s, when directors and lower Party functionaries would drive around in Gaz-3102s. By the 1990s, only one car remained: the Model 24, which became the middle-range family car within the budget of the average citizen. Volgas continue to be built despite their unreliability and gas-guzzling properties, and some continue to be used by the government. One can see them lined up on the grounds of the Kremlin.

The Stalinist master plan of the '30s re-established Moscow's ancient skyline of a few towering buildings (the domes of the great cathedrals) dominating over the rest of the city. The eight high-rise buildings, all centrally located except for the colossus of Moscow State University, compete to this day with the cathedrals' golden domes and green turrets and create dramatic effects as one drives round Moscow's racetrack highways or across the bridges over the River Moskva. Modelled in a Neo-classical or sometimes Palladian style, with spires reminiscent of seventeenth-century Russian architecture but also imbued with the residues of a Constructivist aesthetic, these colossi peer down on the myriad of architectural styles – eighteenth- and nineteenth-century modes and the new Russian post-modernism to be found throughout this vast city. If you travel for about an hour by car from city centre, you at last reach the outer ring, where cars and lorries thunder past modern factory developments and the vast housing estates constructed in the twentieth century. Beyond the newer suburbs lie areas of open land and forest, satellite industrial towns and more suburban settlements.

Russian cars in some ways reflect Moscow's architectural fantasies and failures from the '30s on. The first cars like the Zil or Gaz were objects of fear and power, as they were used by functionaries of the State. Only recently have the special VIP car lanes in the middle of the main roads been phased out. Stories abound of how Beria, the KGB boss, for example, would drive around in his black limousine peering from behind white curtains, looking for women to abduct for his bed (he had syphilis at the time of his arrest by the Kruskchov faction). As motoring became a somewhat more egalitarian pursuit, Russian-manufactured cars, essentially based on foreign prototypes, developed their indigenous Soviet aura as they became caught up in the politics of central planning. This meant that they did not develop along purely commercial lines as their equivalents did in Italy and the US. However, each main marque of Russian car underwent many changes, and many different models were introduced. On the whole, they represent an ageing population, reminders of the past in a changing city. As vehicles and moving faces of a discredited system, they display all the virtues, disadvantages and dilemmas of the ex-Soviet state: they are inefficient yet strive to be modern, egalitarian yet usually beyond the means of lower-paid workers. Now they drive side by side with their flashy distant relatives, harbingers of a new materialist spirit.

Our Cars in Havana

VIVIANA NAROTZKY

It is early summer 1957. A brand new white and gold Plymouth Belvedere V-8 Sports Coupé is carefully lowered into a time capsule on the south-east corner of the Tulsa County Courthouse lawn. The car has been chosen as a symbol of American industrial ingenuity to be admired by future generations, an object, say officials, 'with the kind of lasting appeal that will still be in style 50 years from now'.

How right they were to be confident. Those tail-finned stunners of the mid-twentieth century have indeed retained their brazen beauty, becoming the gleaming paradigm of a golden era's zeitgeist, the very flesh and chrome of its material culture. When the '57 Plymouth is unearthed in the early twenty-first century, it will find itself surrounded by compact Japanese cars, towering sports utility vehicles and bulky, boring people carriers. It will probably wish it could travel back in time to that June day in Tulsa.

While time travel may still be a dream in the Western world, it is easy in Cuba, and reassuringly low-tech: nothing more sophisticated, in fact, than what challenged US car mechanics *circa* 1950. The eerie feeling of time suspended that is inescapable in Cuba is nowhere stronger than in Havana, its most striking visual metaphor being those oversized, 50-year-old American cars that rattle down potholed streets and along the seaside Malecón.

It is Cuba's misfortune to be a fruitful land, a rich source of fragrant tobacco and sweet sugar: for

Driving along the Malecón, Cuba, 2001.

A 1953 Chevrolet Bel-Air. Vintage body, modern hub-caps.

Procter & Gamble, Colgate-Palmolive, Goodyear and Firestone, Standard Oil, Shell Oil, Texaco. Although US ownership of the island's sugar mills had decreased since the 1930s, it was still very substantial, and 60 per cent of the total sugar production was exported to the US under extremely favourable quota arrangements. In his monumental study of Cuba, Hugh Thomas describes the sugar industry as 'a foreign enterprise, a great international exhibition set up on Cuban soil, with foreign capital, foreign machinery and sometimes . . . even foreign workers'.

In reciprocity for the sugar quota, import duties on US consumer goods were cut or frozen, neutralizing the efforts of local industry and binding Cuba to

centuries, it was the perfect colony. In 1898, Spain lost the island to the US, who, a couple of years later, graciously handed the territory back to the Cubans. Not before Congress had passed the Platt Amendment, giving Washington 'the right of intervention for the preservation of Cuban independence and the maintenance of stable government'. A string of brutal, corrupt and inefficient local governments mediated US power on the island. From 1953, Cuba's President was General Fulgencio Batista, an unscrupulous and charismatic *mulato* who had been at the forefront of the country's agitated political scheming from the mid-1930s.

Around the time when the Plymouth Belvedere was being buried in Tulsa County, Cuba was therefore an independent republic effectively owned by the US, as well as its favourite playground. The list of US subsidiaries read like a rollcall of American corporate power: Coca-Cola, Pepsi-Cola,

The make-do economy: any colour so long as it's blue.

A street-scape in Centro Habana, Cuba, 2001.

the consumption of American commodities. Thus the 'great international exhibition' extended into Cuban middle-class homes, into the country clubs and yacht clubs, the fashionable hotels. It was at its most spectacular on the capital's streets, where Chevrolets, Buicks, Fords and Pontiacs were as ubiquitous as in any North American suburb: Havana in 1954 is said to have bought more Cadillacs than any other city in the world. The Catalan writer Josep Pla complained that the traffic had left him 'trepidating and exhausted', and recalled that he had seen 'in the city's streets over 70,000 magnificent automobiles, all of them American', driving past at dizzying speeds. America of the 1950s turned Havana into a city with suburbs; with over 800,000 inhabitants, it was the largest metropolitan area in the Caribbean, and its extensive local middle class fraternized with the American community. These Cubans got their cars, their refrigerators, their cocktail dresses and, if they were well bred, often

their husbands from the US. Such was the Cuban bourgeoisie's fascination with all things American that, in the words of the poet Pablo Armando Fernandez, even its bad taste was imported.

Feeding the tourist gaze: paintings on sale in a Havana street market.

All this changed on 1 January 1959, the day Castro, Che Guevara and the Fidelistas overturned the Batista regime. The success of the revolution signalled the end of US involvement in Cuba, and the beginning of the trade embargo: 1959 was the last year in which American consumer goods – or spare parts – entered the island. It was also the beginning of the Cuban freeze-frame, making ordinary objects and revolutionary events more than half-a-century-old vividly central to Cuban daily life.

Buying a new car in post-revolutionary Cuba was no mean feat. The right to a boxy Lada was a privilege reserved for doctors and other valued professionals, or conferred on fellow workers by voting committees of their peers. Some of the few cars imported were US makes such as Ford and Chevrolet manufactured in Argentina, but they were for the most part Peugeots, Fiats and Soviet Ladas. From 1959 on, oil became an expensive commodity as well, coming all the way from the USSR, and often rationed.

A 1954 Buick Super in Baracoa, 1999.

In the early '90s, the oil supply disappeared with the Soviet Union. Having once been home to the most vibrant automobile culture in the Caribbean, Cuba had to rely on Chinese bicycles.

Although they became ever harder to maintain and run, the cars that were once the pride of American ex-pats and the Cuban middle class seeped deep into the local structures of everyday life. They were slowly integrated into a profoundly transformed Cuban automobility, becoming valued sources of personal income as taxis and generating (from 1976) a legal network of small, privately owned garages that would work miracles to keep them going. In the 1980s, the government realized that it had a potential goldmine in those old machines. It somewhat forcibly bought many of them in exchange for a Lada, selling them abroad to auction houses and collectionists for a hefty profit.

By the mid-'90s, its economy seriously affected by the disappearance of the Soviet

The carcass of a Pontiac in a Havana back street, 1999.

The Malecón, Havana, 2001.

Union and gasping under the increased pressure of the US trade embargo, Communist Cuba fought for survival by playing the tourist card. Suicide by tourism, some have called it. It is certainly hard not to have mixed feelings about the double-decked economy that has sprung out of the tourist dollar. In any case, the island has more than its share of attractions, and every right to use them to scrape a living: tropical beaches, salsa, friendly locals, wonderful colonial architecture, dreamy landscapes and lots of rum. But beyond the glossy-brochure aspect of its offerings, there is something else that makes Cuba most perversely appropriate as a tourist destination: its quality as an *authentic* theme park. The iconic images of Cuba engraved in our collective memory – Korda's picture of Che Guevara, or those 1950s Cadillacs – are the real thing, there for Cubans, not for tourists.

Nevertheless, with the rise of tourism, ordinary Cubans have become more clearly aware of the market value of those icons. Now one can be taxied around Old Havana in a lovingly restored cream and burgundy '55 Chevrolet, all shining fenders and sticky fake leather, with a liveried chauffeur at the wheel. The old cars are there to be consumed by tourists in many different incarnations: in the photographs they bring back home, as luxury taxis that compete with the latest air-conditioned Japanese models, as small papier-mâché reproductions and in Edward Hopper-inspired paintings found on countless street markets. The way we interact with those objects in the streets of Havana is as multi-layered as our own cultural myth about them, as self-conscious as our aestheticizing gaze.

Beyond the extremely thin veneer of this newly manufactured commodity, however, one finds the real place these cars occupy in Cuban life. They are the Cuban workhorse, cheaper to buy than a 1970s Fiat,

A 1956 Dodge Coronet in Centro Habana, 2000.

and considerably more unreliable. They have passed from one owner to the next in a never-ending river that has been flowing for the last six decades.

There are still well over 5,000 registered Chevrolets on the island, and many are falling to pieces, rusty old bangers that often wear what's left of their first factory-issued coat of paint. The American *cacharros* require endless tinkering, are held together with chicken wire and mechanical ingenuity. These monumental objects never die in Cuba: they become part of an endless life cycle, a vortex of use, re-use, transformation, appropriation and reconstruction. This process does leave behind some haunting carcasses. They lie on back streets and behind garden fences, eyeless, wheels gone, no fenders left. But they are still, to all effects, very much alive: a vital quarry of spare parts and engineering bits, a constant source of inspiration. When they have truly given up the ghost, they are re-sold to the government, which then disassembles them piece by piece and puts them back into circulation. What comes out of this *ronde* are fascinating hybrids. There is nothing further from the Cuban experience of restoration than the Western concept of

purity or historical truth. A '58 Dodge may have a Cadillac front grille, a Skoda radiator, a Plymouth fender and a Honda wheel cover. The brake fluid will be 50 per cent shampoo. None of the push-buttons will work. These cars are an ode to colourful and messy mechanical syncretism, as powerful as that of the *santería*. The *orishas* Changó and Elegguá watch over them, invoked by beaded necklaces hanging from rear-view mirrors.

Once the white knights of planned obsolescence, Harley Earl's dream machines have found an undignified eternal youth in the streets of Havana. For all the tender loving care lavished on them, they are meant above all to stay on the road. There is nothing precious about the way they are treated. With enormous respect, of course but never with foppish fastidiousness. What gets these cars taken care of might not be anything like the purism of the classic-cars market, but neither is it the post-modern irony that has rescued old Trabants from the ex-Soviet industrial dumps. The late '90s craze that turned them into a cult car was fuelled by an ironic, post-political kitsch charm that has helped the Trabi rise from its East German ashes as the cherished Phoenix of a lost socialist youth. One magic ingredient is similar in both cases. Trabis are simple machines, easy to customize, dismantle and repair, a perfect DIY job. Part of their regained success is the strong appeal that mucking around with a spanner holds for disaffected young men. As hot-rodding did for suburban youths in 1940s America, so the Trabis and Chevys now spawn their own web of male mechanical know-how; they are at the heart of social networks of support, making-do and hidden economies. They enable their users to display their mechanical prowess, to tell their tales of how to beat the system, their secret tricks. Like all similar networks, from bikers to hacker culture, this one thrives on technicalities and loves a challenge.

The allure of these rocket-cars, needless to say, defies their function. Who could be immune to their poetry? Their raw power of seduction is still very much in play, although sometimes hidden among so many other layers that it is hard to tell them apart. Is it the many hours spent on them, the sheer joy of mechanical craftsmanship? The glint of faded chrome? The familiarity of a door that will only respond to its master's voice? The nostalgia? Many have remained in the hands of their original owners or are family heirlooms, gleaming cars lovingly cared for and stashed under a piece of canvas behind a rubber tree, to be used on special outings. The pleasure in these cases speaks of festive

use: holidays, parties, girlfriends. In the 1940s, the Habaneros would drive up and down the Prado and the Malecón, a practice that encapsulated, for Alejo Carpentier, the 'clearest manifestation of our provincial spirit', an 'endless, monotonous and gyrating' occupation that 'reduced cars to the category of merry-go-rounds'. True to their origins, the *cacharros* will still be driven up and down the Malecón, half a dozen young men sitting inside them, cruising.

Unlike newer cars, which can only be sold back to the government, old American cars dating from before the revolution have *traspasos*, and can therefore be traded freely amongst individual buyers. They can cost anything from a couple of hundred dollars to a few thousand. Once the epitome of a clear hierarchy of consumption through product differenciation, these cars generated in Cuba a new set of social and cultural meanings that repositioned them in terms of both their economic worth and their visual connotations. Their prices transcend easy concepts of social

Wedding-day Cadillac.

A lovingly maintained 1950 Chevrolet Styleline.

prestige and have often lost all relationship to the original scale of values they were carefully tailored to create. With functionality, reliability and ease of maintenance clear priorities, Cubans will pay a premium for a Fiat 127, leaving decrepit old Cadillac Eldorados to the less well off. Within the misty realm of pre-revolutionary American cars, however, and notwithstanding basic mechanical soundness, the old hierarchies still apply.

With the island now opening up again to tourism, this network is once more realigning itself, and a new automobile hierarchy is being created. The *guajiro* musician Eliades Ochoa bought his first car, a '54 Chevy, in the early '70s, moving on to a '54 Dodge, a Peugeot 504, then a Lada 2105. Now that the Buena Vista Social Club has turned him into one of the island's hottest exports, he drives a 4x4 Mitsubishi. The way he sees it, 'The best car is a new car.' A

younger member of his orchestra, however, prefers to drive a 40-year-old Detroit machine, the one that gets foreigners dreaming.

It would be hard to find a time and place where more strata have sedimented around a particular object. One year after the 1962 Cuban Missile Crisis took the world to the brink of nuclear war, John F. Kennedy was shot in one of these cars, and the American Dream was shattered. Their paradigmatic position in the history of design, their role as the exuberant symbol of post-war American industrial power and cultural pre-eminence, makes their enduring presence in twenty-first-century Communist Cuba all the more fascinating.

Engines of Revolution:
Car Cultures in China

GEREMIE R. BARMÉ

One of the opening scenes of the 1964 film *Sentries under the Neon* shows the public fanfare surrounding the People's Liberation Army's occupation of Shanghai in May 1949. Serried ranks of troops take up defensive positions on the main thoroughfares of the coastal megalopolis, until that moment China's bourgeois heartland.[1] One company of stalwart peasant soldiers is shown patrolling Nanjing Road, the bustling shopping street that abuts the Bund, where they encounter a mass street demonstration against the continued foreign presence in the city. As the marchers surge forward, a swank convertible comes careering down the street, driven by a brash American (or, rather, a lanky Chinese actor with a plasticine nose imitating a brash Yank). Forced to halt by the soldiers after threatening to drive through the crowd, the foreign interloper is confounded by the pedestrians' militant anger, given a stern lecture and sent packing. This is a paradigmatic moment, for it encapsulates much of the public attitude towards both the car and things foreign in China throughout the twentieth century.

From dynastic times on, those in China 'with a vehicle' were regarded as a class apart, and from the early years of the twentieth century a widespread prejudice aimed at mobility was translated into popular unease towards those who travelled around the burgeoning urban centres like Shanghai in imported motorized vehicles. Lu Xun, the scarifying literary giant of the 1920s and '30s, would habitually use the expression 'the car-owning class' (*youche jieji*) to lambast both the new rich and bureaucrats (of the Left and the Right) whom he encountered. To this day, in Chinese culture the motorcar is as readily associated with corruption and untoward influence as it is with individual wealth and merited luxury.

Lu Xun had good reason to treat the car with a measure of suspicion; one of the most notorious literary figures who flaunted his gas-guzzling freedom was Shao Xunmei (1906–1968), the Francophile publisher, poet and celebrity of Shanghai's belle époque who made a mockery in both his writings and his lifestyle of all that committed litterateurs like Lu Xun held dear. With flare and insouciance, Shao motored between his mansion in Jiaozhou Road and such cultural salons as the Xinya Teahouse in Sichuan Road, or dropped in to see fellow authors and translators who frequented cafés like the Balkan Milk House or who gathered at the home of Zeng Pu in the Rue Massenet. Indeed, either driven by a chauffeur or 'dressed in his purple tweed suit, Shao could be seen dashing around town in one of the family's two automobiles: a brown Nash or a sporty red roadster'.[2]

The first roadworthy vehicle had taken to the old cart streets of Shanghai in 1901, having reportedly been shipped in at great expense by a wealthy foreign doctor. (It was in that same year, coincidentally, that the political pamphleteer Kang Youwei had published his famous utopian manifesto, 'The Great Harmony'; that his former cohort Liang Qichao had advocated the new concept of 'nationalism' in the media; that the first

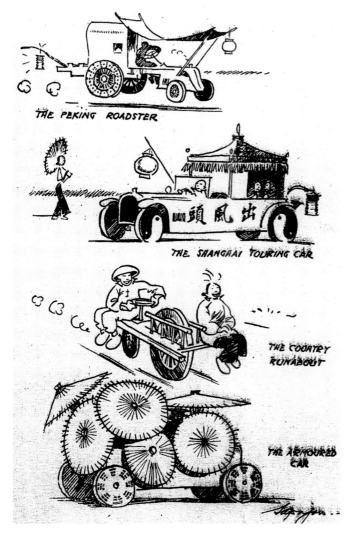

THE PEKING ROADSTER

THE SHANGHAI TOURING CAR

THE COUNTRY RUNABOUT

THE ARMOURED CAR

'The importance of China in the motor market has naturally stimulated designers' imaginations.' Cartoon by Sapajon, *North China Daily News*, 1925.

personal ad had appeared in a Chinese newspaper; and that a modern police system had been established). Due to its initial paucity, motorized traffic was governed by regulations devised for horse-drawn vehicles. But that soon changed and, by 1912, there were some 1,400 motorized vehicles in the city, and, with the introduction of car insurance the following year, the old proscriptions covering buggies were withdrawn.

In late 1903, a rather grand automobile – a German Benz, in fact – had been presented to the Empress Dowager Cixi in the imperial capital of Beijing with the aim of making her frequent trips to the Summer Palace situated north-west of the walled city more commodious. There are no reports of her ever availing herself of the vehicle, as she is said to have remarked that it was unconscionable that the driver (or 'cart handler' – *che bashi* – as she called him) would be seated in front of the august presence, with his back to her.[3] Eventually, the becalmed vehicle was sequestered in its own ornate pavilion at the Summer Palace, where it remains to this day. Even if Cixi was reluctant to put speed before dignity, the prestige of motorcars was soon recognized by the populace at large. By the 1910s, the first to-scale paper funeral cars were being built for posthumous immolation: in the nether regions, the deceased could now enjoy the opulence of modern transportation even if they had no access to it in life.

Later rulers, too, were more alert to the potential of the modern vehicle for ostentation. Following the abdication of the Qing dynasty in 1911, Yuan Shikai, the General-turned-President and putative Emperor, created the Avenue of Eternal Peace (now Chang'an dajie) as the new east–west axis of Beijing, to be used for both military parades and his own passage by limousine into the city. It was along that avenue, and in the square that was created in front of Tiananmen Gate, that later leaders would take to vehicles of various descriptions to display the power of the state, whether reviewing troops in the 1950s, inspecting the army of Red Guards that flourished in the mid-1960s or celebrating the victories of economic reform variously in 1984 and 1999.

Under the aegis of the People's Republic of China, founded with a triumphant spectacle that featured army jeeps bristling with guns and mechanized military hardware in Tiananmen Square on 1 October 1949, Beijing itself was transformed into a highway city

Funeral procession, early Republic (1910s or 20s).

Army leaders in convertible Red Flags reviewing People's Liberation
Army troops in Tiananmen Square, National Day (1 October), 1959.

that for years remained eerily car-free. The Avenue of Eternal Peace was widened and extended, while gradually the old city walls were razed and replaced by encircling surface highways, and underground by a mass-transit system. The concentric configuration of old Beijing has meant that, unlike the highways of newer cities that criss-cross the landscape or strike out with Promethean energy to other cities over the horizon, those of the Chinese capital radiate (as in the case of its Moscow model) in ever-larger rings and feed into the congested centre of the city itself. Even Shanghai, whose arterial topography was redesigned in the 1990s, is now encircled by an elevated ring road.

In the early 1970s, Simon Leys observed of the macadamizing transformation of the old Chinese capital that:

the disappearance of the [city] gates has permitted the widening and straightening of the streets; muleteers and bicyclists do not have to waste two or three minutes going around those majestic sentries; now they can dash in a straight line across a desert. In Europe one is, alas, used to seeing the beauty of historic cities destroyed to make room for cars. In Peking, it is more original; the city has been destroyed not under the pressure of existing traffic, but in pre-vision of traffic yet to come.[4]

The vision of just such a modern, car-oriented metropolis was first essayed in the Chinese urban landscape, not by the Communists but by the Japanese imperial authorities who occupied the country's north-east in the 1930s and set up the client state of Manchukuo. In 1934, the seat of government for the new country, quite literally a concrete expression of Japanese pan-Asian expansionism, was established at Changchun in what was formerly Jilin province. Named Xinjing (Shinkyō), the 'New Capital', it took as its blueprint the plans for another visionary city, the highway-garden capital designed by the Americans Walter Burley Griffin and Marion Mahony for Canberra, the federal capital of Australia.[5] With its broad avenues and massive rotaries built for the traffic of the future, Xinjing also became the base for China's nascent automotive industry. When the Communists took over the city, it was a centre for socialist car production, and in the 1950s the Number One Automobile Plant eventually gave birth to the Red Flag limousine, a lugubrious vehicle that would become the pride of the national car industry during the Mao era.

SOCIALIST ECONOMIES

Although the vast avenues and square of Beijing, inspired as they were by Moscow's Red Square, were emulated by cities throughout China, the exigencies of socialist politics meant that the actual number of vehicles navigating the sweeping empty spaces fell off dramatically, the private car being one of the first victims of the stringent wartime rationing of gasoline introduced from the late 1940s.[6] In tandem and inverse relationship with this, however, was the fact that bureaucratic access to public largesse increased dramatically. Indeed, from the early 1950s on, the allocation of a particular make of vehicle, with attendant mod cons, was carefully calibrated to accord with the position a cadre enjoyed in the political hierarchy. Only the highest-level cadres in the party, army and state bureaucracy could travel by the new Chinese-made limousine, the Red Flag, for example. The Soviet 'Gim' was reserved for ministers and provincial leaders, the 'Volga' was assigned to bureau chiefs and divisional commanders, and the Polish 'Warsaw' was left for the common riff-raff, known derisively as 'cigarette, oil, sugar and bean' cadres.[7]

The origins of the Communist Party as a war-fit organization that came to power through force of arms, however, meant that its leaders had an abiding soft spot for the jeep. During the happier days of Sino-Soviet co-operation, leaders like Mao, Liu Shaoqi, Zhou Enlai, Deng Xiaoping and the marshals of the army each had their own 'Gaz 69'. After 1965, following the collapse of the international socialist fraternity, these were replaced with locally manufactured 'Beijing 212' jeeps. Thereafter, at the height of 1960s military fashion, political figures like Marshal Lin Biao (Mao's one-time hand-picked successor and 'close comrade-in-arms') and Wang Hongwen (the rebel leader from Shanghai, subsequently a member of the Gang of Four), made a point of travelling by jeep, their favoured expression of proletarian egalitarianism.

Top: Official vehicles massed outside the Workers' Stadium in Beijing for the first All-China Athletics meet, 1959.
Above: Mao Zedong (standing with fist raised in first jeep) acknowledging the crowds of Red Guards in a motorized review, 1966.

The revolution, a process that readily inspired modernist mechanical metaphors of engines, factories and skyscrapers, also bestowed on the motor vehicle a powerful charisma used to convey messages to the proletariat about the significance of their contribution to the state. The renowned champion of do-gooder socialist docility in China was the soldier Lei Feng, an army martyr used as a model of Communist morality since his apotheosis in 1964, and a figure still regularly touted by the country's social engineers. For nearly four decades, the nation has been exhorted to emulate his example of unwavering loyalty to the party, as well as to study his numerous bons mots, one of the most noteworthy being: 'Just as a motor vehicle does

whatever the driver wants, so people obey the directions of the party.' This particular quotation is often illustrated with an image of Lei Feng in the cabin of his army truck studying a copy of *The Selected Works of Chairman Mao* propped up against the steering wheel.

The hapless Lei Feng was martyred while attempting, unsuccessfully it goes without saying, to direct a reversing truck: the vehicle hit an electricity pole, which felled the 'good student of Mao Zedong Thought'. The irony surrounding his demise and his legendary devotion to the automobile has made him

Lei Feng addressing a 'suffering speaking rally', comparing the sweetness of the new society to the horrors of the old.

the butt of jokes in China ever since. Waggish humour has never been limited to lesser Communist saints, however, and one 1964 child's rhyme from Beijing reflects the comedic pride that people took in both the stature and means of locomotion – the Red Flag limo – of the great leader Chairman Mao himself (while including a swipe at American imperialism for good measure):

Little car, beep-beep-beep,
Chairman Mao has taken his seat,
And in his Red Flag drives away.
US imperialist JFK,
Furious does an anxious reel,
Turns and slips on watermelon peel.
Falls on face, mud in mouth goes,
And right there in Dallas turns up his toes.[8]

While the chairman and his comrades coursed through the newly created boulevards of the capital in their tank-like limousines, for the private motorist socialism continued to have a sombre impact. On the eve of the

Cultural Revolution in 1966, there were only eleven privately owned – that is, non-state-allocated – cars in use in Beijing. At the height of the initial Red Guard violence aimed at 'destroying the old world' that year, during what became known as 'Red August', the rebels took to stopping and harassing all vehicles, however, both private and public. Anyone travelling by car was immediately suspected of being a foreign spy, a member of the bourgeoisie or a party member taking the 'capitalist road'. Even the sedans of members of the Central Cultural Revolution Directorate, the party group nominally in charge of the movement, were frequently detained at Red Guard pickets and their occupants interrogated. Vehicles belonging to the Soviet embassy, the much-excoriated Soviet Revisionists, became the object of particular ire, and one car featured in a Soviet documentary detailing the fanaticism of Maoist China is shown covered with Red Guard denunciations and slogans.

The initial radical egalitarianism of the Cultural Revolution saw the physical vestiges of both the feudal and the bourgeois past destroyed, or at least momentarily displaced. However, such outward expressions of iconoclasm did little to disguise the deep-seated hierarchies of power, privilege and locomotion within the society as a whole, and even among the zealous rebels. As one Red Guard from the wrong side of the Avenue of Eternal Peace (that is, south Beijing, traditionally the impoverished part of the city) remarked in the 1990s:

Society's never fair. Even in the chaos of the Cultural Revolution the Red Guards were divided into different classes. Look at the kids in 'United Action.' They were from 1st August High School, all privileged kids; they wore real army uniforms; they had black leather shoes, all shining, that's if they weren't wearing snow white sandshoes. They all sped around on brand new 'Forever' brand pushbikes, too. When a pack of them went riding past it was like the Praetorian Guard. They really were in your face. They were all from high-level cadre families, or army brats. How could alley-scum like me compete with that? In the Cultural Revolution they were still the ruling class. Our rebellion was a joke; sure it felt good, but we were only the shit-kickers for those people. You've got to face the facts . . .

Of course, I didn't understand all of that at the time. But I reckon I still would have got into it even if I had. Look at me now. I started out with nothing and, fuck, here I am – a small capitalist, you might say. I've got myself a car and everything. And I reckon I'm shit-hot, too. But what about those people from 'United Action'? Man, they've been driving around in Mercedes-Benzes for years, and it has to be the right model and the right year, and they have to have a chauffeur! My hat's off to them, man. The country belongs to them.[9]

As is evident from these remarks, when bourgeois-generating change did eventually come to China via the economic reforms initiated in 1978, it led to a consumer individualism that, since 1992,[10] has increasingly promoted one of the most visible and status-laden vehicles for cultural and social expression: the car. From the late 1970s on, Chinese viewers caught their first glimpses of the outside capitalist world on television and cinema screens when the party leader Deng Xiaoping travelled to Japan and then to the US; there, of course, limousines, highways and urban traffic were part of the landscape. Taiwan and Hong Kong films introduced to the mainland at around that time also featured gangsters in flash sports cars, vertiginous car chases and, surprisingly, the wanton destruction of vehicles for the sake of high drama. To possess a car, and to enjoy the cocooned freedom that it promised, became emblematic of the spirit of enterprise encouraged by the economic reforms. It was still years from the moment when aspiring members of the middle class would regard the right to a vehicle as more important than other civil liberties, but the foundations were being laid for a major shift in cultural perceptions. As street advertising was once again allowed in the capital in 1982, one of the first slogans – for the Toyota corporation – was to become an ubiquitous quotation that gave voice to popular aspirations: 'When the car reaches the mountains it will find a way, for where there are roads there are always Toyotas.'[11]

THE MARKED MOBILE

Despite the new-found primacy of the sedan in post-socialist China, as we have noted earlier, much of the history of the motorized vehicle in China has been one marked by scorn, rejection and opprobrium. If the slick, latest-model cars of the 1980s and '90s were mobile advertisements for the branding of international capitalism, throughout Chinese modern history the car has equally been a moving target for popular discontent, protest and defacement.

Early suspicions of the motor vehicle were far from restricted to issues of courtly protocol. In June 1907, when the first Beijing–Paris car marathon was held, the Chinese press speculated that what lay behind such a seemingly innocuous sporting event was a canny Western plot to survey the geography of inland China so as to gauge popular sentiment and facilitate the building of communications and trade routes into the nation's heartland.

Such suspicions and concerns (many of which were well founded) continued throughout the century. The sense of aggrieved nationalism that flourished at the time of the economic opening up of the 1980s (and that fed into the incipient patriotism of the '90s and beyond) found particular expression in the highly popular television documentary 'River Elegy', made in 1988. One of the authors of that programme, Su Xiaokang, later a prominent dissident-in-exile, gave voice to the widespread disquiet in the following way:

Over the past century we have continually been losers. First we lost to England, then to the eight powers during the Boxer Rebellion, then to the Japanese. Having finally got rid of the Japanese, New China enjoyed a short period of pride and achievement. Who was to guess that when we woke up from the thirty-odd years of internal turmoil we had created, we found ourselves in the company of nations like Tanzania and Zambia. Even South Korea and Singapore were ahead of us. And as for the Japanese, they were the ones laughing now that they were back with their Toshibas, Hitachis, Toyotas, Crowns, Yamahas and Cassios.[12]

This sense of frustration, reflecting as it did a consumerist imperative that was both fuelled and enraged by the lure of foreign goods, had only a few years earlier sparked an outbreak of violence aimed against the motor vehicle. On 19 May 1985, a soccer riot had broken out in Beijing after the local team had been trounced by visitors from Hong Kong. Gangs of angry young men roamed the streets outside the stadium after the game, detaining every passing taxi to shout and jeer at the drivers. One particularly vociferous rioter screamed: 'Fuck it, while I spend my hard-earned money to go to some lousy game, these guys are sitting in their cars pulling in a coupla hundred bucks a night. Get the bastards!' The mob soon set to spitting on windows, kicking doors and beating bonnets.

Foreign journalists who observed the mayhem drew parallels between the brutish anti-foreignism and the Boxer rebels of 1900 whose xenophobia led to the occupation of Beijing by the colonial powers. But Liu Xinwu, a novelist who wrote a 'reportage' account of the 1985 riot, 'Zooming in on May 19', remarked that the Boxers had sworn an oath beginning with the words 'Heavenly spirits, earthly wraiths / We beg all masters to answer our call' and ending with a plea for the spirits of traditional China 'to lead a hundred thousand heavenly troops' to support their anti-foreign cause. The rioters of 1985, however, were far from being so fanatical. 'If they were to have a chant,' Liu observed, 'it would probably go like this:

Heavenly spirits, earthly wraiths
We all want to have a good time,
Let's evoke Xi Xiulan, Zhang Mingmin,
Wang Mingquan, Xu Xiaoming;[13]
Let's watch [the TV series] 'Huo Yuanjia'
and 'Love Ties Together the Rivers and Mountains'
We want jeans,

We want discos and Washi Cosmetics,
We want Sharp, Toshiba and Hitachi electrical appliances,
We want Suzuki, Yamaha, plus Seiko and Citizen . . .
They are the most ardent consumers of popular Hong Kong culture and Japanese products. The real reason they targeted foreigners and Hong Kong people during the incident was that they dislike the way these people enjoy special privileges in Beijing and flaunt their superiority. What the mob was expressing was a long-repressed resentment and jealousy.

The rioters eventually managed to overturn a vehicle or two, and numerous arrests and police action finally quelled the disturbance.[14]

TAXI > *DIKSEE* > *DI*

It was not surprising that taxis attracted such ire, for they provided the first privileged private spaces in reformist China, for drivers and passengers alike. Long before the car-owning driver appeared in the 1990s, taxi drivers were a class apart: they were mobile, free from the fetters of their original work units, and their wages were based on kilometres travelled rather than on the old, rigid socialist pay scale.

Initially, taxi drivers were recruited from among former government chauffeurs or lorry drivers, but as the urban economic reforms took hold during the 1980s, many men and women quit their state jobs to drive taxis, attracted by the promise of better pay and relative freedom. Soon, the taxi driver, a kind of entrepreneur with state backing, became one of the most liminal figures in the urban landscape. Not only did these drivers transport more traditional fares around the city; they also ferried prostitutes (members of another newly visible class of entrepreneur) from hotel to hotel and provided the covert environment for illicit contacts of all descriptions. Taxi drivers also

constituted one of the most garrulous and outspoken social groups: they could declaim on issues of the moment with little thought of being caught out or penalized as they coursed their way around the streets, spreading gossip and generating innuendo as they went. For foreign journalists working in the restrictive media environment of Deng Xiaoping's China, the taxi driver was a boon companion, providing many of the *vox populi* quotes that peppered international news reports from Beijing.

Those early taxis had very particular interiors. Prior to the advent of car-washing stations in the early 1990s (including 'digital and computerized' car cleaning), a feather-duster for the daily removal of urban grime was a feature of the rear window of virtually every taxi (now they are generally relegated to the boot), and the drivers would don grubby white gloves to carry out this operation. Day-Glo-coloured and sickly-sweet air freshener would feature on the front dashboard, and a large jar (a '*cha gangzi*' – usually an old Nescafé instant-coffee jar) of thickly brewed Chinese tea would ride shotgun near the handbrake by the driver. The passenger windows were often cloaked with green or brown gauze shades, while the back seats were covered in tan cloth with fussy antimacassars or woven-mat seat coverings – often still a feature – making the taxi a miniaturized version of the official audience hall or meeting room, always open for a new session the minute a fare got in. These appointments presaged the busy interiors of the future: deodorizers, rear-view mirror adornments, frilly tissue boxes and head-wagging dogs.

Since 1989, however, the taxi has also been dragooned into more direct service to the state. Starting with the preparations for the 1991 Asian Games in Beijing, taxi drivers began to be used regularly as hospitality representatives and

Advertisement for the re-branded 'Audi-Chrysler-Red-Flag', 1998.

propagandists for official campaigns aimed at international visitors and foreign residents. For years now, taxi companies have been required to festoon their vehicles with public-service announcements (or, to use the language of the past, 'propaganda slogans'). In the more quotidian realm, the taxi has also given birth to its own vocabulary. The Cantonese sinification of the word taxi, *diksee*, has been in common use in the former colony of Hong Kong for many decades. When the cultural influence of south China began to expand northwards in the 1980s, the standard Chinese pronunciation of the term, *dishi*, as opposed to the official term for taxi, *chuzuche* (a vehicle available for renting), became fashionable. In Beijing slang, a language renowned for abbreviations and humorous word play, this was simply reduced to *di*. Thus 'to hail a taxi' or 'take a cab' became *da di* (literally, 'travel by taxi'). Soon *di* was being used to describe a range of locomotive possibilities unrelated to its Hong Kong-Cantonese origins: *tui'rdi*, or 'leg taxi' meant 'to walk'; *rendi*, or 'human taxi', was a new word for 'pedicab'. *Juedi*, or 'crippled taxi' indicated a motorized wheelchair,[15] while *miandi*, or 'bread taxi', indicated a mini-bus taxi (the shape of the vehicle being likened to a loaf of bread). *Qiongdi*, 'pauper's taxi', was another name for Xiali taxis, the cheapest kind of taxi in Beijing

from the late 1990s. Last but not least, there is the *boyindi*, or 'Boeing taxi', a slang expression for 'airplane'.

From 1991 until the mid-1990s, a new taxi and car craze hit China when laminated portraits of Mao Zedong started to appear hanging in the windscreens or set up on the dashboards of vehicles throughout the country. The fad reportedly originated in Guangdong province after a person or people miraculously avoided injury in a traffic accident because, it was said, their automobile had been protected by a portrait of Mao on the dash. Like the door gods and lucky talismans traditionally used in homes to ward off malign influences, the Mao portrait was suddenly recognized as a way to ensure safety and good fortune in the fast-paced urban environment of highway and car.

The laminated Mao mobiles were simply called *guawu*, literally 'hangings'. During the height of the fad, they were sold all over the country and by a range of outlets: from street-side stalls and temple stores to the Mao Mausoleum in the heart of Tiananmen Square itself. They varied widely in design. The more austere simply featured a picture of Mao, the most popular representations being of 'the young Mao' – that is, the retouched picture of Mao in a Red Army uniform taken by Edgar Snow in the 1930s – or the official portrait of

Toy car packaging, 1980s.

the aged Mao, although Mao in a PLA uniform dating from the early Cultural Revolution was also common. More elaborate hangings had the Mao picture framed in mock-Chinese temples, or with gold ingots hanging from the picture with more traditional benedictions like 'May the winds fill you sails' (*yifan fengshun*) or 'May you make a fortune' (*gongxi facai*) on the reverse.

But luck can also be a matter of numbers. Although cars might not legitimately require the ministrations of feng-shui specialists, the wrong number plate (with too many 4s–*si*, a homophone for 'death', for instance) can be challenging. That is why plates with the digit 8 (*fa* or *fat* in Cantonese, 'prosper'/'thrive') sell for such a premium at auctions, not only in the Chinese cultural world, but internationally.

The melding of hoary traditions, old socialist icons and new commercial practices became possible in this environment of economic boom and retro fashion. By employing the tropes of nostalgia typified by the 1990s Mao cult or the numerological fixation on number plates, state enterprises increasingly

attempted to cast themselves as the representatives of both national and consumer interests. An egregious example of this style of agitprop appeared in early 1997, when the aforementioned Number One Automobile Plant in Changchun, now a joint venture invested with a new lease on life (suitably renamed 'The Number One Automobile Production Consortium of China'), launched a national competition for an advertising slogan to launch the remodelled Maoist-era Red Flag, re-branded as the 'Audi-Chrysler-Red Flag'. The advertisement took up nearly half a page in the weekend edition of *Beijing Youth News* in early 1997:

All Chinese celebrated the birth of the original 'Red Flag' limousine. All Chinese have been proud of the brilliant glories of the 'Red Flag.'

Today, we are appealing to every Chinese to take up their pens and celebrate the great leap of a new generation of 'Red Flag' cars . . .

Beijing street scenes, 2000.

In 1958, designers at the Number One Plant combined their extraordinary talents to create the first generation of Chinese luxury limousine, the 'Red Flag'. They wrote the first page in the history of China's automotive industry.

As the paramount make of Chinese vehicle, the 'Red Flag' is not merely a legend in motoring history. She crystallises the ceaseless faith, the tireless struggles, and the fiery emotion of the whole country over a period of dozens of years and a number of generations. She symbolises the eternal glories of the wisdom and the spirit of the Chinese nation.

The 'Red Flag' is a National Car of the latest international standard . . .

We are determined to create a new slogan for the 'Red Flag' that will resonate everywhere. We want to raise high the bright red banner of Chinese-manufactured cars, the banner of our national industry. We need a slogan from every warm-blooded Chinese. If you want to make your contribution to the resurgence of the national automotive industry then pick up your pen and participate in our advertising slogan campaign!!![16]

The retooling of the lumbering limos of high socialism was not restricted to the Red Flag. In 2001, General Motors in Shanghai was producing a Buick GLX, for, as the journalist Lynne O'Donnell remarked, 'the cadre who knows what he wants in luxury road travel.'[17] The sedan, designed for specifically Chinese road and bureaucratic conditions to be a 'rear-passenger-oriented' luxury vehicle, was targeted at chauffeur-driven officials and executives. The legroom for the back seat was extended, a head-rest was added, pockets were put on the backs of the front seats, and the panel between the latter had controls for air conditioning and heating as well as the radio; a fancy ashtray was thrown in for good measure. In keeping with this adjustment to China's cadre culture, Volkswagen went to work on the Audi A6 (manufactured, like the Red Flag, in Changchun), adding 9 centimetres of legroom for the lounging comfort of the back-seat passengers.[18]

ON THE ROAD

We bleed and sweat, earning millions for the factory.
They go buy a tortoiseshell [sedan], and sit like tortoises
[bastards] inside.

No matter how small the village, the head gets a Bluebird;

Regardless of their rank, they all take to Audis.
Even when the business is broke, the bosses flaunt their
Hondas;

The workers might get zilch, but they still buy Santanas.

– popular rhymes on official corruption on the cusp of the
millennium.[19]

In the mid-1990s, there were 30 million car-licence
holders in China; in mid-2001, that number was
approaching 75 million. With over 60 million motor
vehicles on the country's roads, and with an increase
of some 18 per cent annually, there was speculation
that by the end of the first decade of the new century
one in three urban families would be motorized. Not
surprisingly, driving schools are a growth industry,
and they attract customers of all ages with such
advertising hooks as 'I might not have a car yet, but I
do have a licence' and 'Wanquan Driving School will
set you on the road to the future.'[20] Even the
precipitous increase in road fatalities has done little
to detract from the car boom. There were some
94,000 deaths in 2000, nearly a 10 per cent increase
over 1999. If nothing else, this is a boon for car
security and safety specialists, and airbags and
seatbelts are only some of the features in cars that are
more often than not becalmed in the traffic snarls
that choke the country's urban roads. On-board
domestic luxuries – TV's, digital links, elaborate
sound systems, DVD players, game platforms and the
like – are just around the next bend.

Finally, the vast boulevards envisaged as
futuristic highways for socialist modernity since the
avowal of socialism in all but name have been filling up
with the joint-venture vehicles of international

Planting at the edges of the newly built expressway in Shanghai reassures drivers used to more traditional roads.

are cutting a swathe through cities and wending their way through the countryside to link urban hubs with townships and provincial centres. As the private car has promised personal space and freedom only to be frustrated by the economies of scale that sometimes make the outmoded form of bicycle travel seem relatively convenient and fast, it is the dream of free movement as made possible in the living room or cramped study by broad-band links to the web that assuages the frustrated desire for a real-time Chinese autopia. Download time may still be slow, but a republic of rapid-exchange information within the Sinophone world has existed for some years.[21] It might be no more of a reality than the netopia (or cyberia) proffered in other cultures, but the modernist dream of such a *deus ex machina* dovetails neatly with the abiding socialist imaginary of the People's Republic. Reduced today to a more postmodernist formula that celebrates the ecstasy of instant communication regardless of cost and content, it is only a matter of time before the onboard cyberlink makes the car the ultimate vehicle for Chinese-style modernity.

capitalism. In Canton and Shanghai, the narrow streets and old suburbs have been giving way to a new urban architecture of the flyover, the bypass and the tunnel, in which there is sparse room for the bikes that were once a trademark of mainland Chinese life. And everywhere there are traffic jams and road rage. If nothing else, this has all been a boost for radio programmes targeted at frustrated motorists who can ring up talk-back shows on their mobiles and participate in the imagined community of migratory white-collar workers.

Paradoxically, access to the internet, the vaunted information superhighway, has proliferated in near-direct inverse proportion to the choked highways that

The Lada: A Cultural Icon

PETER HAMILTON

Q: What's the best way of doubling the value of a Lada?
A: Fill it up with petrol.

Q: What do you call your Lada?
A: Skip.

For a good many years before and after the Velvet Revolution, cars made in the Soviet zone of production (what used to be known as Comecon) were the perennial butt of playground jokes. The marque-name – Lada, Moskvich, Yugo, Dacia, Polski, Skoda, Wartburg etc. – was almost interchangeable in the first line of any joke. Interchangeable, that is, with the one outstanding representative of the breed: the Lada. Other makes came and went as the acme of motoring naff, but Lada stayed put, until it too imploded and disappeared, perhaps forever, as a well-loved but at least equally well-loathed feature of the UK's car universe.

It was always, despite the multiplicitous models and sub-variants, *just* a Lada. Perhaps the problem was the word itself, with its English overtones of '40s austerity (larders being places supposed to hold food, but in which it was difficult to locate anything remotely edible). The awful drabness of 'Lada' held the psyche in so tenacious a grip that the merits of an individual variant – such as the remarkably effective four-wheel-drive Niva – could never escape the black-hole of Lada-ness in general. Undistinguished by reference to any of its particular models – as Ford could be with its Escorts, Cortinas, Sierras or

Mondeos – Lada came to represent the definitive backstop of the motoring hierarchy.

The Russian Lada, as it came to be known throughout Europe, started life in another country. Private cars were not originally thought to be a necessary element of Soviet existence (though Lenin, of course, owned a superb Rolls-Royce). The revolutionary proletariat would have little need for such capitalist luxury. But the Soviet Union was an enormous state, and motorized transport became increasingly essential in vast swathes of the country, despite, or rather because of, a chronic lack of roads. Utility vehicles – trucks, lorries, small buses and vans – were therefore produced in large numbers, and many did double duty as military transport. There were few private cars apart from those supplied to the upper echelons of the Party – usually vast limousines based on the most sybaritic of American examples such as Packards or Cadillacs. A few attempts to create 'people's cars' along the lines of VW were made in the 1930s, but it was not until after 1945 and the fortuitous acquisition (i.e. plunder) of the entire Opel Kadett factory from Germany, that significant production of the Moscow-built Moskvich 400 (a sovietized Kadett) could begin.

By the 1950s, however, the need to compete

more directly with the West and to show that the Soviet way could also supply workers with the good things in life encouraged the large-scale production of smaller cars. Moskvich cars evolved slowly, but were clearly well below Western standards, and the decision was taken to import capitalist technology. A deal was hatched in 1966 with Fiat, brokered by Palmiero Togliatti to create an entirely new factory 600 miles south-east of Moscow. Along with the car factory – state of the art as it then was – a new town would also be built and Togliatti honoured by having it named after him. By comparison with the simple Ukrainian Zaporozhets and the Moscow-built Moskvich, the new Vaz Zhiguli, as it was named, would bring the best of Western design standards together with Soviet engineering prowess to create a car built for the steppes rather than the *stradi*.

The Russians soon realized that the version of the Fiat they would have to build in Togliatti (and very large numbers were projected) would need to be greatly modified for local use. Climatic conditions in the Soviet Union were extreme: -60°C in winter and a potential 50°C in summer. Only main roads were paved, and in some areas they didn't exist, even in dirt form. The Zhiguli's steel body panels were made 30 per cent thicker than on the Fiat model. Its suspension was redesigned to give a higher road clearance, and the engine, transmission, brakes and rear axle were beefed up to stave off the worst effects of Soviet driving conditions.

Vaz made the Zhiguli into a solid vehicle, but one that was far less sophisticated even than its Fiat cousin, a car that was hardly at the forefront of motoring technology even during its brief heyday in the mid-1960s. Yet it was exactly this 'reverse engineering' that gave the Zhiguli its distinctive qualities and helped it to survive for so long. The great need of the

Soviet Union for foreign currency to stave off economic collapse during the 1970s and '80s led to export sales becoming a high priority. For export, the car was known as the Lada (derived from the name for a Russian version of a Viking long ship, and symbolized by the car's badge). It proved a remarkable success, partly because it was sold at prices far below the market rate and partly because it was rugged enough to withstand severe climates and poor roads. Nearly every country in the world (with the exception of the US) imported Ladas, and they are still to be seen in those where the marque did not suffer a credibility collapse of horrendous proportions. Even Cuba, that last bastion of socialist society, has far more Ladas on its roads than of the ageing Americana so beloved of the tourist brochures. Germany, widely considered to be the home of quality car production, always had a thriving market for Ladas, and the latest model continues to do well there.

Britain's love-hate affair with the Lada is a strange quirk of automotive cultural history. With a design that (even when it was first produced in 1969) resembled a garden shed on wheels, borrowed (but not improved) from the Fiat 124 saloon of the early 1960s, the Lada came to represent automotive poverty. Yet its early days were rosier. When the Zhiguli was first imported as the Lada 1200 in 1973, 2,500 cars were sold. At that point, it was a vehicle not too far out of line with the offerings of mainstream manufacturers, a car not so dissimilar to the Ford Cortina or Morris Marina. Russian cars looked to be good value in general, and even did well in motorsport! Post-1970 and amid the general decline of the UK economy through oil shocks, miners' strikes and three-day weeks, someone came up with the bright idea that the British Saloon Car Championship should be run for production-based cars divided up into cate-

ISSUE NUMBER 4
SUMMER 1987

LADA CARE

* LADA IN
IRELAND
* NEW
MODELS

* MOTOR SPORT
IN THE SOVIET UNION

Front cover of an issue of *Lada Care* magazine, 1987.

gories determined by list price. The overall winner would be the car with the most points across the board. The Moskvich 412 was as cheap as a Mini, but more powerful than anything in its class, and could be persuaded to corner relatively quickly. It cleaned up the championship against far more exotic machinery such as BMW's until the potentially embarrassing rules were hurriedly changed.

But Moskvich could advertise that its cars were 'Marathon-bred . . . Rally-tested . . . and now Race-proven too!' A new company, Satra Motors, was set up to market them, installing a new import centre

at Carnaby (near Bridlington on the Yorkshire coast and close to the port of Hull, where the cars arrived from Russia). Satra took over several fields worth of unsold and rusted Moskvichs from the previous importer, resprayed them and did very well with the franchise until a damning report by *Which?* magazine suggested that they were less than safe. Since the Moskvich sported interior fittings apparently designed to fatally injure driver and passengers in the event of a crash, there was some justification to the *Which?* report. The net effect was that Moskvich sales nose-dived. The more 'modern' Lada looked to be

Rebuilding 'new' Ladas for the UK market, Carnaby, near Bridlington, 1993.

Satra's best option to maintain the budget-car market, and from modest beginnings in 1973–4, the car gradually conquered an increasing share of the new car market, running at about 10,000 cars per annum. And then, in the mid-1980s, sales began to soar. By 1986, and with the help of newer models such as the four-wheel-drive Niva and Estate versions, 20,000 Ladas were sold in the UK. This rose to over 30,000 in 1988.

Many people in Britain, too many in fact, were sold these cars by an organization apparently without scruples as to whether they could afford them, using advertising designed to look, appropriately enough, like it was selling garden sheds off the back page of the *People's Friend*, and calculated to confuse the *lumpen*-purchaser into parting with their hard-earned wedge. For in Britain, at least, the rise and fall of Lada coin-

cided neatly with Thatcherism. If there was 'no such thing as society', wasn't everybody entitled to be a citizen-consumer, the owner of a shiny new motor? The Lada was a car that looked amazingly cheap to buy, and it was bought in embarassingly large numbers by the newly consumerized ex-working classes, heady with the equity that came from council-house sales and the promise of the ready credit that property ownership could guarantee. For the first (and probably last) time in their lives, such people could own a 'new' car.

In a brief blaze of glory, the UK importer managed to lever the marque into tenth place in the bestseller charts in 1989 – the high point of the Thatcherite boom. This was not entirely because the car represented amazing value for money. As a design that was, even then, about 30 years old, it offered less in most areas than the majority of the competition. Sales were accomplished by means of the clever marketing of 'cheap' finance deals which were, in fact, anything but. At the end of the 1980s, you could put a Lada Riva 1300 on the road for £3,999 cash. To many of those trooping into Lada dealerships, it seemed much better to opt for £99 down – and a fortune in repayments. The standing joke in the motor trade (not a haven for those over-possessed of the milk of human kindness) was that the typical Lada buyer was 'welded into' the four-year finance deals that made the repayments look low – at least on paper. The interest was high, the trader's commission fantastic. More could be made on hire-purchase kickbacks than on the dealer's margin. But the car had a resale value

worth less than the outstanding loan after a mere twelve months (when the guarantee also ran out), so it could only be traded in at a loss. Running costs were considerable, because these were cars that weighed a lot due to their rugged construction and that used a thirsty carburettor designed to run on the cheapest and worst fuel in the world, but which drank four-star like it was going out of fashion.

Garages were few and far between in the Soviet Union, so the Lada was designed to be serviced by its owners. All it required was simple but regular maintenance. This, however, was something the typical UK buyer was unlikely to supply once the warranty period had expired. Parts either dropped off or failed. Lack of preventive maintenance caused damage to major

Pages from 1980s issues of *Lada Care* magazine.

The Niva four-wheel-drive model.

components. (The standard joke in the franchise was that a used Lada was more reliable than a new one, because it had been back to the dealer so many times to replace the bits that did not work).

The paradox of Lada's success as a brand was that it became a familiar vehicle on the streets of Britain, and therein lay the seeds of disillusionment. Cheap to purchase, but expensive to run, the Lada began to acquire a negative perception as soon as it was sold in large numbers. This may have had something to do with the owner profile: most Lada buyers were male, and in late middle age or retired. They came predominantly from the manual working classes and poorer sections of society. These were not the aspiring, socially mobile yuppies most car makers yearned to have competing for their products, and their street cred was zero as a result. This did not deter the small core of Lada enthusiasts, who delighted in the quirks and foibles of the Soviet cars. One of the objects of their desires, the Niva four-wheel-drive model, was an outstanding vehicle that regularly beat the cream of the Western and Japanese off-roaders in competition. Yet its exceptionally noisy transmission and lack of creature comforts could not hold a candle to the other vehicles in this burgeoning

marketplace, increasingly dominated by middle-class mothers ferrying their kids to school and taking their Range Rovers or Pajeros to the shopping mall. They would not be seen dead in a Lada Niva – or, as one very sporty young teacher said in a group discussion, 'I'd love a small off-roader like that, but the kids at my school would never stop teasing me about the fact it was a Lada.'

The introduction of a modern, Porsche-designed model, with bodywork suggestive of a late 1970s French car, with front-wheel drive and a hatch-back, gave a brief fillip to the Lada brand image in the late 1980s. But the Samara, as it was known, suffered from zero recognition and simply replicated the build quality and reliability problems of its better-known predecessor. Despite extensive pre-sale preparation and general naffing-up for the UK market at the lavishly appointed Carnaby works, Ladas suffered from outmoded design, were appallingly poorly made, and were consequently wretchedly unreliable. The net result was that few owners or cars made it beyond the first couple of years. The demise of the Soviet Union did not help, of course: the Togliatti factory closed on several occasions when it was starved of resources. But perhaps the UK economy was more to blame: after all, the recession of the late 1980s started just as Lada's fortunes began to peak. As unemployment rose inexorably, Lada sales went in the opposite direction. Perhaps that was why the cars came to symbolize the motoring equivalent of negative equity, languishing to this day as rusting hulks on sink estates. When we asked why so many were sold in the valleys of South Wales in the aftermath of the miners' strike and coal privatization, the local dealer had a ready answer: 'They're the only new, or for that matter used, car you can buy round here that won't be stolen.'

For a heady couple of years back in the early 1990s, I spent a lot of time with Lada and its products, working on advertising research designed to boost sales in the recession. It was like pushing water uphill, but full of lighter moments, including the bright idea somebody had of fitting Riva saloons with 'whippet-and flat-cap racks' instead of parcel shelves. I was given six cars to drive during this time and made extensive use of them. They were all, without exception, ghastly to drive, uncomfortable and unreliable. Yet I became fond of them. The enthusiasts had a point. They stood for another world, an alternative universe of motoring. You could imagine yourself a Soviet person, experiencing all of the ersatz things that pass for the Russian versions of Western products. Strangely brittle plastic, lumpy foam and clingingly uncomfortable fabric, hideously inadequate

The Lada Riva Estate

Some of the creature comforts of the Lada Riva.

fittings, parts that came off in your hand when using them – such as handbrakes. Erratic gauges, either wildly optimistic or non-functioning. Keys that broke in the locks. Seats that listed drunkenly. Paint work whose surface recalled the bark of a tree rather than the peel of an orange.

And this was not always how they left the Russian republic or whatever it was during that confused

post-Soviet era. To be honest, not all of the Ladas made in the Fiat-built Vaz factory got to the West: for a start, a lot of the car fell off or was stolen along the way. The importer paid only £750 for each one (and a bit more for the 'modern' Samara that came out in 1987), then painstakingly rebuilt them near Bridlington in a parody of hand-made construction *à la* Rolls-Royce. The labour-intensive modifications and 'adaptations' made to Ladas at the Carnaby factory, designed to make the vehicle legal and resemble the worst of its competitors down at the economy end of the market, deserve a book to themselves.

There was even a special-projects department at Carnaby. I recall that we spent a long time trying to promote a Lada Samara 'Flyte'. It had a ridiculous body-kit that made it look like a 'Coronation Street' version of a concept car, and was named to evoke Lada's sponsorship of darts tournaments (a contract signed just at the moment when the sport lost TV coverage). The Flyte was all show and absolutely no go; if it had, the result would have been terrifying, the Samara's brakes not being its best feature.

Despite the happy band of workers at Carnaby, there was sadly little point to their efforts. It was easier to make a decent cheap car from Japanese parts in Malaysia, India or whatever. Once VW got hold of Skoda (which had, after all, made good cars), the game was up. And even a ten-year-old Ford was a better car than a new Lada. In the end, it was emission-control regulations that got them. Vaz could not find anybody to sell (or, more exactly, 'give') them a fuel-injection system to meet EC standards. And, cheap as they were, nobody really wanted to buy them anymore. Carnaby closed in 1997. The franchise died. More recently, entrepreneurs have been snapping up the survivors – for £750 or less – and shipping them back to Mother Russia, where they fetch a tidy premium. Older Ladas have even taken on a cult status as classic cars. And Vaz is still making cars, including the Fiat-styled one we called the Riva. Its latest model is a bulbous device of uncertain stylistic parentage. Some are sold in Europe, where its marque image never fell so desperately low as here. But the UK may never return to the fold.

There is an argument that if the Lada had not existed, somebody would have had to invent it. If the peerless German brands that rule the roost at the top of the market are to hold their sway, there must be something awful, a sort of automotive Other, against which they can be judged. A car is, after all, something you can be seen in. At one stage, we were asked whether the Lada had any future in the company-car market. To which the answer, rather surprisingly, was 'Yes – but not for the right reasons.' One City firm had so tired of its executives' habits of carelessly damaging their Mercedes, BMW's and Audis that it had instituted a new policy. Three prangs in a year and their car was replaced with a Lada Riva. Apparently, it worked (as a policy, not as a car).

Automobile Metempsychoses in the Land of Dracula

ADRIAN OŢOIU

'Reincarnation is possible!' Loudspeakers began blaring this announcement all over Romania at the end of March 2001. Lest anyone should entertain vain hopes, it was toned down by a disheartening coda, roared in the same deep persuasive voice, '. . . but only in April!'

Yet at the end of April, the same voice announced that the reincarnation programme had been 'exceptionally extended at customers' request'. The success of this spring sale of metempsychosis led to its continuation in June and July. In August, as I wrote these lines, the voice offered a renewed reprieve for mortality, reassuring me: 'Reincarnation is still possible! Only in August.'

The creators of this commercial for the newly introduced buy-back schemes – you know, one of those you-bring-us-your-old-jalopy-and-we-offer-you-a-brand-new-car-for-10-per-cent-less schemes – are right in ways they haven't thought of. When a Western citizen – say, Giovanni from Italy or Geert from the Netherlands – gets rid of his old car; when, after a couple of second-, third-, or fourth-hand sales, the car reaches the dead end of a junkyard; well, then the candid Giovanni (or Geert) thinks that this is the end of it, that there is no afterlife for ten-year-old wrecks.

Well, he is wrong. Had he had the curiosity to inquire further (maybe by bugging his old car and satellite-tracking her movements beyond the junkyard gates), he would have been surprised to see her metamorphoses, nay, her *metempsychoses*.

One month ago, she was just a pathetic jalopy, whose old-fashioned curves made him feel ashamed; whose whimsical engine, inappropriate windscreen slant, missing right-hand airbag, minor scratches on the wing, wrong shape of headlights, infelicitous dashboard texture and indecorous bumper line made him feel miserable. One week ago, she seemed to have taken the one-way road to nothingness, the compacter and, eventually, the foundry.

Now, instead of rusting in some limbo of dead car limbs or being melted down at the foundry, she is returned to life! She has a new master and can procure for him the same joys she once offered Giovanni – oh, he remembers it so well! – ten years ago.

Romanians would far rather buy a Western, preferably German, car than a homegrown brand.

She is the apple of her new master's eye, let's call him Petre. Petre is not an avatar of St Peter, even though he opened the gates of a new existence for this car. He washes her every couple of days; strokes her body with circular motions, waxing sponge in hand; buys her new wheel caps, new seat covers, an almost new radio. (To those of you who have recoiled at the gender bias of this story of male-chauvinistic seduction, I can only confirm it: yes, this is a politically incorrect description, as is this whole Romance country, where most women make use of their driving licences on very rare occasions, such as when hauling their husbands back home after they've boozed it up at some party.)

Yes, indeed, the commercial is right. Reincarnation is possible, no matter how old the car. Afterlife exists, even for hopeless cars. But where is this magic land of automotive afterlife? Let's go to the rear of the car and see what its national sticker says. Oops, surprise! It hasn't changed. It still reads 'I' for Italy, or 'NL' for the Netherlands. But the language in which her master caresses the car is neither Italian nor Dutch, nor is the landscape.

Let's keep monitoring the movements of this automobile spectre. One day, a traffic cop pulls her over and argues about the sticker. It has to be removed and replaced with the sticker of the country you're in. 'It's the law!' argues the law enforcer. Petre, her new master, sighs and replaces the sticker. The new one reads 'RO'.

'RO' for Romania! Instead of Western blood, the land of Dracula sucks Western cars, in an endless draught. No matter how old (even if the law bars the importation of cars more than eight years old, there are, as always, many ingenious ways to circumvent this hindrance), no matter how rusted, Western-made cars get a chance of a new life and a new master.

Visiting certain towns in the heart of Romania might serve to plunge you into tear-jerking bouts of nostalgia. All of your youth is there, revived in its full, if somewhat spectral, splendour; the streets swarm with Ford Sierras, Renault Fuegos, Opel Kadetts, Fiat Regatas, VW Sciroccos and even Talbots or Simcas. You feel you have entered some twilight zone inhabited by automobile zombies brought back to life by some sort of black magic. In a wholly post-modern mixture, these remainders of the '70s or '80s mingle in hectic traffic with the state-of-the-art Ford Focus, Toyota Yaris or the ever more popular Renault Mégane.

Romanian-made cars prevail, however, in various stages of dilapidation, and many autochthonous Dacias flaunt the chrome symbols of more prestigious makes, such as Renault's lozenge, Audi's Olympic circles or even Mercedes's star. National pride might remain high in opinion polls, but is very low when it comes to car makes.

We shouldn't be amazed about such travesties in a country where campaigns promoting Romanian products (such as the one proudly entitled 'Made in Romania') inevitably fail, since customers will always prefer the most obscure brands, provided that they are produced anywhere beyond the former Iron Curtain. This is not a result of cosmopolitanism, but of experience. Brand-name counterfeiters thrive in Romania, and virtually every Romanian wears or uses some sort of ersatz. 'Clujana' – a manufacturer of stout and virtually indestructible shoes – has gone bankrupt because everyone prefers to wear trainers that are perfect replicas of Nike or Puma in every detail except flexibility, comfort and durability; even respectable and copyright-abiding manufacturers set out to produce sport shoes that are deceptively branded 'Adiddas' (who cares about the number of

The Dacia: the ubiquitous Romanian family car.

'd's anyway?) or Recbok (the 'c' passing easily for an extra 'e'). Of course, at least some customers realize the difference, but they hope that others won't. If one judges by the labels, every Romanian drinks exquisite Napoleon Cognac and Chivas Regal whisky, uses state-of-the-art Compaq computers, high-end stereos, genuine brand-name French perfumes and cosmetics. In a country where, two centuries ago, popular lore had word-of-mouth circulation, one should not be surprised that only 10 per cent of the software produced is legally licensed, that most music CD's and cassettes are pirated and that international bestsellers are immediately translated in total disregard of copyright laws.

In this world of Baudrillardian simulacra, it is no wonder that most car owners prefer to entertain their own illusions. Were it not for vigilant traffic cops, stickers indicating country of origin would never be replaced, nor would many car plates, which make their owners daydream about Vienna or Naples or Barcelona. Second-hand vans brought from France will go on advertising some exquisite winery in Burgundy even if their present

A Dacia chassis takes a ride to one more metempsychoses.

owners use them to carry manure. All the buses in my town were brought from Germany, and their flanks bear exotic, if incomprehensible, adverts for Saxon tabloids and lotteries. One should not scrape them off; this glint of prestige, which feeds passengers' reveries of rides across some Teutonic burg, would be lost, and they would wake up to the harsh reality of potholed roads 'made in Romania'.

And yet, one should not look down on Romanians' infatuation with simulacra. The scars of recent history are, alas, too present. Until 1989, Romanians were 'blessed' with the 'benefits' of a nationalist type of Communism, which meant turning one's back on the Big Brother from the East and haughtily rejecting 'the interventions of Western imperialism'. Apart from extreme isolation, omnipresent secret police and the censoring of all public expression, there was only one advantage to this system: Romania resisted the pressure of Comecon treaties which caused some sort of mischievous 'division of labour' among Soviet satellite states (thus Hungary produced buses, the GDR locomotives, Poland ships and Czechoslovakia aircraft). Defying this crippling specialization, Dictator Ceauşescu insisted that Romania should develop every industrial branch and become self-sufficient. Thus the country's autarchic economy produced buses, train carriages and locomotives, ships, airplanes (from light ones to jets) and even helicopters, often in several competing plants.

Thus automobiles were assembled in several facilities. A pre-war factory in Brasov (rebaptized 'Red Star' and, later, in a bout of patriotism, 'Roman') produced trucks, later to be hybridized with the German MAN. The nearby Câmpulung-Muscel plant manufactured four-wheel drives entirely designed in Romania and quite uninspiredly called ARO. In the late '70s, Romania started a joint-venture with

Renault, which produced the ubiquitous Dacias. One decade later, a similar agreement with Citroën led to the opening of a plant in Craiova that created better-looking but less reliable Oltcit (rebaptized 'Oltena' when the French broke the deal). The last-born (or rather aborted) offspring of Romanian original engineering was the short-lived Lăstun, made in Timişoara.

Automotive onomastics in the Ceauşescu era were highly nationalistic. 'Dacia' was the name of the ancient province that the Roman Emperor Trajan conquered in AD 101, which later became 'the cradle of Romanian civilization'; 'Oltcit' was a portmanteau word, reminiscent of both 'Citroën' and the River Olt, or Oltenia, Ceauşescu's native province; the national four-wheel-drive ARO claims to be the epitome of 'automobilul românesc' (The Romanian Automobile), as does the national truck 'RoMan' (in whose deceptive name the participation of MAN Diesel, the German patent holder, is effaced in a subaltern position); by some accident, only the tiny Lăstun was devoid of patriotism, as its name meant just 'house martin', the bird whose celerity ironically contrasts with this car's famed sluggishness.

None of the neighbouring Communist countries had such a profusion of car makes, the official propaganda boasted. Yet quantity is not always a synonym for quality, and the unpatriotic, ungrateful Romanians had much to complain about with their national car makes. 'Made in Romania' was a suspect label.

The Dacia, showcased as the truly national family car, was modelled on the Renault 12. This car, with its lozenge-shaped body, was sold in huge numbers, as it could be purchased in instalments. However, because Renault had withdrawn from the deal in the meantime, no major change of mechanics or design could be initiated. This once avant-garde car began to look more and more obsolete as the decades passed. The manufacturer kept trying to cosmetically improve its body, but the changes were slow and always lagged behind international design trends. The Dacia shifted to rectangular headlights when every other make featured round ones, displayed black ornaments when others were rediscovering polished metal, and adopted an angular body shape when everyone else got those round, feminine curves which are so 'cool' today. The same base model was used to develop a station-wagon variant, a small pick-up (endearingly called 'Papuc', meaning 'slipper'), an abortive two-door sportscar . . . Though the list includes neither a truck nor a bus, I am sure that there were plans for those too.

With these slight variations, the Dacia, manufactured in the millions, became ubiquitous. The limited choice of seven or eight colours only added to the dullness of Romanian cityscapes. Car owners did their best to escape this monotony. They added fancy wheel caps, rear wind spoilers, tinted windscreens; some hung dozens of decorative dolls in their windscreens; others, dreaming of some other unattainable car make, replaced the Dacia logo (written in contorted medieval letters copied from Moldavian Orthodox monasteries) with chrome signs plucked from foreign cars; fuelled by wishful thinking, this operation, alas, failed to change Dacias into BMW's, Mercedes or Volvos.

Owning a Dacia is still the surest thing in Romania, as spare parts abound, and any repairman is knowledgeable in its ways. Dacias are reputed to be easy to mend, which encourages many Romanians to try their hand at more or less successful bricolage. 45 per cent of Romanians never use specialized car-service workshops, preferring to do their own repairs, tinkering about their cars in parking lots, in children's

An Oltcit encounters a gypsy cart in the Bicaz Gorge, not far from the Borgo Pass mentioned in Bram Stoker's *Dracula*.

playgrounds or on the pavement. Such open-air workshops have the picturesque look of a witches' coven, with cauldrons (e)sc(h)atologically simmering the tar needed for insulation, among skeletal chassis and rusted Dacia bodies heavily patched with home-made plaster and mastic.

In the back country, one can come across strange apparitions: Dacias carrying rakes and spades on their roofs, Dacias hardly visible under huge haystacks or towing makeshift trailers loaded with piglets. The Dacia remains an example of longevity. Its history spans over four decades and doesn't seem to be getting close to an end. The Dacia plant in Pitesti has recently made the leap to a new generation of Dacia Novas, fully equipped with EURO-2 norm-complying catalytic converters.

For a while, the closest competitor to the Dacia

seemed to be the better-looking, roundish Oltcit, freely modelled on the Citroën Axel. Yet once the deal with the French had been broken, the Romanians insisted on 'assimilating' most of the car parts, and many subcontractors produced parts that were unreliable if not downright dangerous. Besides, the car was never supported by a good service network. For many, it soon became an anthology of breakdowns. I used to drive one, and all I can say in its defence is that it has a lot of imagination: one can hardly run 300 miles without something breaking down, but the intricate time scheduling of such mechanical failures is ruled by an algorithm whose mysteries are yet to be fathomed. This car was the salt and pepper of my existence for many years: I was never able to second-guess it. The brake pump crumbled like cheese, the gas ducts popped up like pods, the rear-view mirror dropped off the windscreen, the front door fell off its hinges; obviously, my car was plagiarizing Mr Bean's Mini. Oil seeped out of the engine, and no mechanic was ever able to tell where it came from; sometimes, I thought that it was trying to deliver me some mysterious and yet to be deciphered message; 'Stop now!' shrieked the brakes when unexpectedly clutching the iron to incandescence; 'No more curves!' rattled a pin under the steering wheel, blocking it suddenly. Maybe this is why the Oltcit earned the title of 'a car for a lifetime'. If you think this sounds like praise, let me decode it for you: 'a car for a lifetime, because once you have bought it, you will never be able to sell it!'

Yet the most surrealistic car of the late '80s is the suavely named Lăstun. This was supposed to be the true urban car: compact, manoeuvrable, economical. What resulted was a conceptless concept car, a fibreglass dwarf that looked like an idiot boy's oversized toy. A colleague of mine came in every week with yet another Chaplinesque story of automotive striptease:

she was either shedding her windscreen on warm, sunny days or dropping her bumper. 'It's so easy to drive,' my colleague argued, and, after some thought, added, 'except when I have to use the gear shift; it's a bit too stiff, so I have to use both hands to budge it.'

If you think this car never sold, you are wrong. In the days when gasoline was rationed (the Party allotted every car a trifle of 15 litres per month), some people bought the cheap Lăstun as a second car, just in order to get an extra portion of gasoline.

Apart from Romanian-made cars, there was a limited choice of other makes imported from the Eastern bloc: the Lada (a Russian-engineered Fiat mutant), the reliable but bland Czech Skoda, the box-shaped three-stroke Wartburg. And of course, the popular tiny Trabant, which, as the joke goes, is similar to a satchel in two particulars: it is made of cardboard and has belts to fix it on your back. This joke hardly makes me smile: the car of my childhood was a Trabant 600 Combi; now, after 40 years of service, the brave red and white Trabi has outlived all other cars in our neighbourhood and is still used by my parents at their cottage.

After the fall of Communism, the Romanian automotive landscape diversified dramatically. The production of Oltcit was discontinued, ARO underwent a face-lift and was marketed in France as the Spartane. Daewoo took over the Oltcit facilities in Craiova and started to assemble its models: Cielo (Nexia), the luxury sedan Nubira, the monovolume Matiz ('the small giant'), the Tico, a fridge-shaped compact car, and a minivan called Damas. Cielo and Tico are nowadays the favourite cars of the scarcely visible Romanian middle class, while Nubira and Espero are executive cars, patriotically adopted by government officials.

Despite this diversity, 51 per cent of Romanians

Still running: a 40-year-old Trabant 600 is used at a country cottage.

When the only station wagon in the village is a second-hand Opel Kadett, even a red hearse will do.

would buy a foreign car rather than a Romanian one. The conditional 'would buy' measures the distance between desire and possibility. While their monthly salary barely averages $100, many Romanians can only daydream about buying a brand-new car. Statistics show that only 25.9 per cent of urban households intend to buy a car in the future (in rural areas, this figure might well be lower than 5 per cent). Of these,

53.6 per cent would purchase a brand new car, most likely a $3,500 Dacia or $4,700 Tico. Of the 43.3 per cent that would buy a second-hand car, a vast majority would opt for a foreign make, preferably German.

Some people prefer to buy their cars directly from the source, and there are many travel agencies that offer special one-way trips to the Netherlands; no sightseeing is included, for these trips go straight to

Holland's greatest attractions: junkyards and used-car dealers. However, such trips are taken mostly by professionals smart enough to circumvent customs barriers. Before such cars are put on sale, they usually need major rehab, performed in one of the numerous semi-clandestine car-repair shops that have mushroomed all over the country.

Some of these cars were stolen, in which case the mechanic must become a prodigy in combinatory arts, able to assemble a car from many sources, to erase ID numbers and repaint in different colours. Apparently, Romania has become a hub in the trade of smuggling stolen cars from EU countries into the former Soviet Union. Car thieves can be very fast. I learned this when I was a witness for the parliamentary elections at the local police prison. Having noticed a yuppie-like inmate who stood out among the freshly arrested small fry, I was surprised to find out that he was a famous car thief. The police officer pointed to a limo parked in the yard of the police station. 'This is his latest exploit,' he explained. 'We caught him yesterday and phoned the car owners at once. An old couple in Italy. When we asked them if they knew where their car was, they answered in all innocence: "In our garage, of course"!'

No matter how it is acquired, 'a car is just another member of the family.' This is what most Romanians think. If one has to baptize one's newborn baby, why shouldn't one call the priest to bless one's new car? It was a weird ceremony I once attended at Neamt Monastery in Moldova; the Orthodox priest, clad in black and gold vestments, swayed the censer over the bonnet, sprinkled holy water on the bumper and chanted a blessing to protect against head-on collision, traffic radar or breathalyzers.

One amazing fact is that, for all their scanty wages, many urban Romanians parade about in almost new luxury cars, ranging from the latest Mercedes to the Jeep Grand Cherokee. How can they afford such cars when customs tax reaches 30 per cent for American and Japanese cars? Well, few of them bother to pay such taxes. One in ten Romanians proudly drives one of the Western-made cars offered as fringe benefits by many joint ventures operating in Romania.

As for the few who own such cars, they exploit tax loopholes intelligently. One way to avoid paying customs tax was to describe the car as a 'vehicle for the use of a relief organization'; phoney charities mushroomed all over the country, like that village in northern Moldova, which boasted as many as 200 registered charities (one on every farm!) whose only *raison d'être* was to smuggle tax-exempt cars across the border.

Any foreign citizen who becomes a resident of Romania has the right to bring in two cars which are tax-exempt. Now, with its shaky economy, Romania is not exactly a country of immigration. And yet, every year several dozen thousand cars are brought to Romania as new residents' property. This mass fraud (amounting to some $19,000,000 yearly) indicates the easy way in which the citizens of the Republic of Moldavia may become legal residents of Romania. Smugglers pay about $200 to penniless Moldavian farmers who 'lend' them their passports; a similar amount is paid to poor Romanian pensioners, who in turn declare that they have rented their flats to the new 'immigrants'. This is sufficient for the police to stamp 'resident' in the passports of those old chaps who will probably never see Romania. Then the smuggler is free to advertise the sale of a 'repatriated car' in the classifieds. Oddly, the car make is never specified; it is the buyer who will indicate his preferences. The transaction makes a lot of people happy: the buyer can have a luxury car and pay a mere $5,000 in taxes instead of $20,000; the smuggler makes a $4,000 net profit, and the poor pensioners earn the equivalent of six months' pension for doing nothing!

Such cars will never be seen in the countryside. Powerful Jeeps will only shine their freshly polished bodies on the streets of Bucharest or Timisoara. The back country, with its primitive roads, scares them. Driving on those unlit roads with gaping potholes and missing traffic signs is a real challenge. Weird encounters might occur at any time; at dusk, the cattle bucolically returning from pastures feel it is their right to take over the road; on weekends, wedding parties merrily sprawl onto the road, as does cement, sand or mortar wherever a new roadside house is being built; funeral processions force you to drag along for miles with your headlights duly dipped in sign of reverence. In springtime, interminable herds of sheep occupy the road for hours on their way to alpine meadows; in the autumn, the flow of transhumance is reversed. No-one would ever dare to reproach the shepherds; after all, Romania's great ballad and national myth, *Miorita,* is all about shepherds; one does not tamper with national myths.

If *Miorita* is for domestic consumption alone, then Dracula – the country's most enduring and, to many, infuriating myth – is a global bestseller. All roads seem to lead to Dracula. And they will do so even more in the near future: the Ministry of Tourism has just laid the cornerstone of DraculaLand, the horror variant of Disneyland, a tourist trap to be built near Vlad Dracul's fortress in Sighişoara. The sado-masochist will have plenty to rejoice in: trips on horse-drawn hearses, plunges into horror chambers, seances at the Institute of Vampirology and dinners in a restaurant offering such mouth-watering delicacies as Impaled Beefsteaks and Dread Jelly with Gory

Custard. There is only one S&M pleasure omitted from the official line-up: driving on a typical Romanian road, preferably at night. This is the quickest way to become an Enduro race driver (doesn't the 'RO' in 'EnduRO' stand for Romania?). Potholes cave in after every shower, roads are in chronic disrepair and in want of traffic signs. Every cat's-eye has been plucked from the asphalt and riveted onto farmers' wagons or bicycles. A recent news item announced that several thousand miles of road in Bacau County were stripped of their milestones; those metal prisms could be easily made into great chimney flues. The country's only motorway, a stretch of merely 80 miles, needs repair every couple of years. In my town, at the end of each autumn, psychotic gas workers dig unfathomable trenches; poor souls, they have a pathological need to check how the pipes are doing down there.

At night, the dangers multiply. This is the favorite time for ox-drawn wagons to carry huge haystacks; hay, as everyone knows, is highly flammable, so no wonder none of these wagon drivers ever uses the cressets or torches required by the law. This is the time when bicycle riders turn off their headlights, in order to better contemplate the moon. This is the time when the pubs spit out their last customers, who may choose either to zigzag about the road or take a nap on warm asphalt. No matter what the statistics tell you, believe me, this is 'deep Romania'. And it is a country that was never conquered by the sophisticated newborns of Western technology. The 1,400 brand-new Fiats or 6,000 Renaults imported yearly stay away from these roads. These battered country roads remain the realm of the same old Dacias and of the many cars that find a haven for their final reincarnations in Romania.

The Ambassador from India

ZIAUDDIN SARDAR

It is all some years ago now, but I have never quite recovered from my first arrival in Delhi. My family originally came to India in the baggage train of conquerors. I had no intention of repeating the impertinence. I, a Pakistani-born British Muslim, conceived of myself as an ambassador of amity. My visit had a dual purpose: I was to reacquaint myself with a world sundered from me, but ever part of who I am; I would establish the possibilities of collaboration across false divisions. The conception was impeccable; the execution turned into a cruel parody – a comic-relief scene taken from some old Indian film with me in the standard Johnnie Walker role. The actor, screen name indeed taken from a whiskey bottle, always played the seeming idiot; his inept antics were laughable; only slowly did they reveal that he had the surest grasp of what was actually happening.

I put the blame for the debacle that became my arrival squarely on the Ambassador, India's most venerable and loved car. Based on the Morris Oxford, the Amby, as it is affectionately known, is inescapable: it is the first and most distinctive mode of transport any visitor to India has encountered since Independence. It is still the first landmark you meet as you come out of the Delhi airport. You track down the taxi booth, purchase your chitty to ride, and exit the building to be greeted by the awaiting swarm of Ambassador taxis: liveried in black and yellow, smugly

lining the road, rounded, plump, instantly demanding to be personified.

It was from this point that the high-blown sentiment of my imagination and the actual scene began to diverge. A small, spindly young man approached me with dispatch. He grabbed the proffered chitty fluttering hopefully in my hand and motioned me to my chariot. I picked up my hand luggage and turned round. Chariot? Ambassador? No, an aged, moth-eaten rust-bucket, a demented, rabid bee in visible terminal decline greeted my eyes. When the driver opened the boot to stow my suitcase, I glimpsed the road through numerous holes in the floor. As if sensitive to my gaze, the driver shooed me towards the rear door, opened it gingerly on creaking hinges, and I was motioned to take my seat.

Even a near-death Ambassador is a surprise to the uninitiated. It stands high on its wheel base and has plenty of headroom. One does not collapse in the middle, semi-squat and then contort at a perilous angle to inveigle oneself sideways into an Ambassador. One addresses the vehicle directly, making a subtle bow as if to say 'namaste' and, having suitably greeted one's conveyance, one steps forward in this mildly stooped position. The seat is a generous space, amply provided with legroom. One settles back in an Ambassador, even if the upholstery is threadbare and rancid, scourged with who knows what disease. One sits in an Ambassador regally. One is ensconced, like some plenipotentiary potentate, not a ten-a-penny tourist.

An Ambassador in New Delhi.

One has a vantage point, a position, one must cast one's gaze upon the surrounding scene.

I anticipated my arrival in the fabled city of my dreams – Delhi! The driver rather sheepishly took his position at the wheel. There was a momentary pause, no doubt for silent prayer. Then, with greater determination than his frail frame promised, he turned the ignition key. Nothing! Ensconced potentates of plenipotentiary nature do not panic. The key turned once more. Nothing! Several further turns of the key, followed by equal amounts of nothing, accompanied by various sighs of sundry order, and the driver turned to look at me. He shrugged. I raised my eyebrows. He made calming movements with his hand and leapt out of the vehicle. I saw him disappear beneath the bonnet.

A small crowd of potential sage advice and mechanical expertise clustered around him. I realized

that my arrival was becoming a spectacle. The driver returned to the steering wheel for another determined turn of the key. Nothing! I thought it would be proper to show some concern for his plight. I extended my hand to the door handle and froze, caught in his vicious, malevolent glare. Clearly, my function was to remain exactly where I was: the fact that the taxi was not going anywhere was not my concern. With a disdainful motion to me to stay still, the driver half exited and began to push the car. He was joined in his exertions by the gaggle of advisors. We moved six inches; it is amazing how heavy a rust-bucket can be.

It suddenly struck me that everything was happening in silence, with implicit understanding. There was no shouting, cursing or general rhubarb of disconsolate banter. Everyone had an appointed role, in an appointed order of things to be done, and

Ambassador taxis, Calcutta, 1992.

everyone got on with their tasks. More people arrived, a swift backward glance assured me that half of the assembled company of drivers were on the case. All the doors of the taxi were now open, heavers and pushers strategically positioned at each; some gave me looks of acknowledgement and seemed to sigh in consolation. There was a general quickening in the assembled mass and definite motion ensued. The motion was forward, but neither determined nor sufficient to engage any mechanical response.

The company stood, gazed at each other. There was a collective shaking of heads. Someone motioned for the remaining drivers to assemble; the situation was serious, all hands were needed. I looked behind me to see three long lines of eager bodies ready to push, others positioned themselves at the open doors, perhaps to prevent my escape. They looked at me, with

discernible interest and a touch of pity. There was a general murmur: 'Ek, do, teen' ('One, two, three'). And we began to move. We lurched and seemed to attain wheel revolution in an instant; after a modicum of momentum was attained, we continued to move; we were hurtling over the immense, flat expanse; huffs and puffs were becoming audible; some feet were half jogging to keep pace with our volition. The engine clicked and came to life. Lithely, the driver jumped into the moving vehicle, and we were off.

We overtook a cart pulled by oxen. I was delighted, overjoyed even. I could hear a clucking sound. No, not the engine, I assured myself. We described a sweeping bend and were about to meet a larger way, the main motorway into the city. Instead of slowing down, we seemed to be accelerating. The clucking sound accompanied the driver's vigorous

Ambassadors through a window, Hawai Mahal, Jaipur, 1988.

attempts to brake, except there were no brakes. I took a long, anxious breath; what traffic there was parted to clear our path. I held my breath as we progressed. I cast eager looks ahead, searching for glimpses of the city of my dreams. Thinking of the monuments to come, I exhaled slowly. And so did the Ambassador. Winding down from fever pitch to a stately trundle, it spluttered onto the side of the road and ground to a point of finality in the nothingness where all things end.

The driver slumped forward over the wheel. What words could there be? A long moment later, he simply got out of the car and stood by the side of the motorway casting longing looks back towards the airport. We were alone. Afternoon shadows were lengthening into dusk. Time passed us by, though nothing else did. An hour later, the phut-phut of an

auto-rickshaw broke the silence. The driver ran into the middle of the road and bodily insisted that the rickshaw stop. A simple conversation between the drivers, then I was ushered from my Ambassador. The chitty now fluttered like Chamberlain's paper of appeasement as it was handed on to the rickshaw driver. Clinging desperately to my luggage, I made my incongruous, decidedly humble entry into Delhi. I consoled myself with the thought that I was definitely not arriving as my ancestors had.

The Ambassador is as Indian as Gandhi – the Mahatma, that is. Its image, like that of the Tata truck, has come to symbolize Indian independence and modernity. Manufactured by Hindustan Motors at their Calcutta factory since 1942, it enjoyed a virtual monopoly of Indian potholes and overcrowded roads for much of the Cold-War period. It has proved to be enduring, sturdy, long suffering and resilient. It wears its capabilities lightly and therefore is ever ready to surprise. It can be adapted for endless uses, and yet always carries itself with a certain grace, even in the most unfortunate of circumstances. It is robust, having much to endure and surmount, yet it always appears ample and compliant rather than muscular. Strength the Ambassador has in abundance, but it is not hard-bodied, making a peacock display of its powerful attributes for idle curiosity or self-aggrandisement.

But the Ambassador is not just an Indian icon; for me, it is India itself. To begin with, it is ubiquitous. Wherever I went, the Ambassador was there too. No segment of India can be India without the presence of the Amby and its diesel-infested fumes. It is more than a cherished part of the national imagination. Since every mechanic of any ilk, every taxi driver, can take it apart and put it together again blindfolded, it is integral to the Indian subconscious. The Ambassador is also a metaphor for India in a much deeper sense.

An Ambassador on display at a trade exhibition at the West Bengal Pavilion, Prasati Maidan, Delhi, 1992.

Like India, the Ambassador is tradition – self-confident and self-assured tradition. It is tempting to read tradition merely in its look and feel of a motor vehicle of a bygone era, a most mistaken thought. The Amby has undergone several 'modernizations'. Its traditional authenticity is in remaining timeless and therefore able to show the folly of time as mere surface change for the sake of change. The vehicle has no need to court fashion, merely to increase replication to meet, most adequately as it does, practical need. As a ubiquitous mode of transport, the Ambassador is tradition in another sense: it is autochthonous, home grown, built out of the landed resources and enterprise of India. In its conception, the Ambassador is stately, staid, defying categories, a classless conveyance for all and sundry – yet effortlessly able to denote subtle distinctions of rank, privilege and pedigree. One reads status in an Ambassador and its occupants as surely as one judges, with a practiced eye, the status of any person one meets for the tell-tale signs of who they are and where they belong in the pecking order.

In rural areas, for example, the white Amby stands for officialdom. All varieties of local bureaucrats – from magistrates to tax collectors and members of the internal security service – have regulation white Ambassadors, in the way the Army has khaki jeeps. Even today, in large parts of the Indian countryside, the 'authority' of a white car with a flashing red light evokes curiosity and eagerness among villagers to catch a glimpse of the 'Burra Sahib' inside. Different cities have embraced different incarnations of the Ambassador. In Calcutta, no other car can be a taxi. Widespread, affordable, they are part of the everyday life of Calcuttans. The social dynamics of the city itself are reflected in the Ambassador. In the '60s, the taxi drivers in Calcutta tended to be Sikhs who spoke Bengali. They had internalized the city's etiquette of decorum in public behaviour. They engaged in conversation with their passengers and expected to be treated with civility in return. By the '90s, other ethnic groups had entered the trade; there was no longer any guarantee of finding a Bengali speaker driving one's taxi. The new generation was younger and brasher, their driving skills were less polished, and their attitudes to their passengers tended towards disinterested insolence. Calcuttans read this as both a decline in the moral fibre of their city and disrespect for the legacy of the Ambassador.

When the Ambassador is not epitomizing the driver or the passenger, it is the occasion. The roominess of the Ambassador makes it an ideal car for ceremonies. Almost every wedding is graced by its presence. After the wedding ceremony, the bride often leaves her parents' house in an Ambassador. The car is bedecked in wedding finery, like the bride herself. The other traffic will give way to the cortege with indulgence, while people crane their necks to catch a glimpse of the bride. For that day, with its garlands and tinsel, the Ambassador is more than just a car: as the replacement of the old palanquins, it is the bearer of tradition.

The Ambassador is not simply 'out there' in the real world, but also 'up there' on the silver screen. Indian filmmakers have readily embraced the known characteristics of the Ambassador to structure and turn their plot lines. In his famous Calcutta trilogy (*Pratidwandi, Simabaddha* and *Jana Aranya*), Satyajit Ray used the interior of the Ambassador to make social comment, as well as to observe the lives of the rich

segment of the city. Ray presented the Ambassador as a symbol of wealth, respectability and comfort: its occupants were always affluent industrialists and officers of private companies. But in populist Bollywood films, as opposed to art-house movies, the person sitting in the rear of an Ambassador is likely to be a corrupt politician. Jeeps are reserved solely for the police; the villains drive flashy foreign cars; where else would you expect to encounter a corrupt politician except in his white Ambassador? In the 1992 film *Roja*, for example, there is a famous scene where a top-ranking Minister meets with the heroine Roja. It ends with the Minister driving off in his white Ambassador. Implicitly, the car conveys an obvious meaning: his promise to help Roja is going to be betrayed.

The film I remember most, because it so intrigued me, is Ritwik Ghatak's *Ajantrik* ('Lifeless'). The protagonist of this 1957 Bengali film, Bimal, is a ne'er-do-well tribal taxi driver besotted with his battered taxi, an ancient Chevrolet he calls 'Jaggadal' (literally 'burden'). Bimal sees Jaggadal as a living person: he talks to her constantly, asks if she is thirsty and dresses up as a bridegroom to have his picture taken with her. He is surrounded by more enterprising taxi drivers, all with Ambassadors, personified by the Sikh who always teases him about his 'old pile of scrap'. Bimal is touchy about criticism of Jaggadal and refuses to trade her for a new Ambassador. He has confidence both in his abilities as a master mechanic and, above all, in the car never letting him down. Three notions of technology are pitted against each other in this film: imported outmoded technology, domestic technology, and greedy capitalism and rampant development in the shape of bulldozers. We see technology-driven change – in the arrival of electric telegraph wires and trains – sowing discord among the people of Bimal's tribe. As he struggles with Jaggadal, the other taxi

An Ambassador and threshing machines outside the home of a rich farmer.

drivers with their Ambassadors are always in the background counter-pointing the dependent nature of his relationship with his old Chevrolet. When Bimal finds himself attracted to a woman, Jaggadal throws jealous tantrums and nearly kills the human object of Bimal's love. In the end, Bimal sells the car for scrap to a rich merchant and watches as it is dismantled and carted away.

For me, an imported Chevrolet remains a powerful symbol of the primrose path to the global dilemma of inappropriate technology, as opposed to the indigenous inhabitant, the Ambassador. Yet to foreign eyes, the Ambassador as India's answer to modernity may appear both quaint and exotic. There is nothing quaint about a vehicle that is so eminently

practical, so suited and fitted for service under almost any circumstance. How can something so mundane, so common, be exotic? Like all attempts to apply these false ideas to India, the Ambassador shows the paucity of imagination the labels 'quaint' and 'exotic' betray. The words feed the misunderstanding of those who cannot live without a fabled India, finding the real one far too competent, capable and unconcerned with the approval of foreigners.

An Ambassador, like India, is fitted for its own existence according to its own perceptions and gets on with the work. The Ambassador takes to the road and jostles with bullock cart, rickshaw, bicycle, scooter, bus and foul-fume-belching lorry or camel-drawn truck. It is never out of place and does not displace any other form of transport it encounters.

My visit led me to confront various foreign ideas about India, just as my progress around the country encountered the effects of colonial imposition. In Cochin, I visited the grave of Vasco da Gama, to ensure that he was really dead and buried. Consulting a map revealed that I could trace the footprints of European arrival by following the major trunk road along the Western Ghats. From da Gama's end in Cochin to Calicut (now reverted to its original name of Khazikhode), where he first landed, then on to Goa, the administrative centre of the Portuguese Empire of India he helped to establish. So I took to the open road, hiring my own Ambassador with a driver. This time, I requested an inspection and a test drive before confirming my travel arrangements.

Early the following morning, we set off. This was an immediate mistake. It was morning rush hour in Cochin, and we had to negotiate the town centre before hitting the open road. I began to apprehend how people come up with words like 'quaint' and 'exotic'. This derives from not understanding the order of events in an endless sea of movement, not grasping the basic principles behind what looks for all the world like chaos and disorder. Every form of conveyance was on the road, every road user a rajah disdainful of all other travellers. 'Jostle' does not do justice, 'cheek by jowl' is too distant from the reality. And all on roads bent and twisted with age, pockmarked and wrinkled by years under sun, rain and heat.

My seat was up front beside the driver, the better to converse and learn more about where I was going. Before I could utter my first question, I was struck dumb by pure fright! To enjoy the morning air, and to take in my full ration of various belching exhaust fumes, I had the window rolled down with my arm half out of the vehicle. As we overtook a cumbersome,

heavy-laden cart operating under push power, we pitched into a major crater in the road. Gyrating left and right with engine gunning and exuding power, we lurched sideways to meet a lorry making its own determined path directly towards us. The merest hint of a touch on the steering wheel was all the acknowledgement this confrontation warranted. We breezed past each other, an infinitesimal distance between carrying my body and severed arm on different trajectories. Nothing stirred, nothing was said, all was under control.

Only I felt the need to turn, first in disbelief to the driver, a centre of complete calm, then in angry wonderment to glower at the retreating lorry. On all the lorries one sees in India, the high board behind the drivers cab is vividly painted. St Sebastian martyred by numerous arrows is very popular, as are basic Crucifixion scenes. I well remember one depicting the Garden of Gethsemane, where Jesus prayed for the cup, symbol of his forthcoming trials, to pass from him. One often saw Durga, the awesome goddess who rides on the back of a tiger, or Lakshmi, goddess of good fortune who is wisdom-bestowing, the entrance to transcendental life. Was I hallucinating, or did the lorry that had so nearly dismembered me portray a crescent moon and minaret dominated by the horse that bore the Prophet Muhammad on his miraj, his night journey up to heaven? If not, why is that particular image still burned into my mind's eye?

I closed my eyes. When I looked again, it was with enlightenment; everything made perfect sense. Three days we were on the road to Goa, largely a single-lane motorway, as contorted as the streets of Cochin. It was now evident, with startling clarity, that I was being borne along within the very essence of Indian modernity.

The Ambassador personifies India, this much I had already apprehended. Enlightened understanding revealed that roads, travel, connection and their appropriate conveyance have always been timeless in India. But time comes in different phases. The Ambassador was consciously designed to serve modern, independent India. Its purpose was to fare forward. Time itself is accumulation, the medium in which accretions are added to what is. The effect is contemporaneous coexistence of everything. All stages and ages are represented, colonial as well as ancient. Yet subtly, all is reworked; everything is represented, but not everything survives, for there is subtraction as well as accretion. The process of time is accommodation, not always easy or felicitous, to the particular character of India itself. What results is living tradition that always fares forward. The most common sign on the roads of India is 'Horn please' – it appears on the rear of every lorry, every bus, every mode of public transport. Living tradition, like every motorist in India, does not need to look behind; the rear-view mirror is a redundant piece of equipment. The past, what is behind, is also ever-present; when it needs attention, it can speak for itself. A polite honk of the horn, or any other variety of utterance a horn is capable of, is sufficient to alert any driver to the presence and needs of another road user.

Living tradition is not static; it fares forward in a specific way. For long periods, the road to Goa was devoid of traffic. But whenever a dot appeared on the horizon, the driver would shuffle in his seat, bestir the Ambassador, and together they would go hell for leather at maximum speed to catch up with whatever vehicle dared to be ahead of us. Tradition contains the competitive instinct, a self-conscious drive to prove its virility and potency. It is not a simple race for sheer delight in the chase. All other vehicles exist to be overtaken. Confidence coupled with competitiveness breeds the conviction of boundless invincibility. Only this can account for the invariable tendency to wait until one has reached a blind corner to overtake. Faring forward requires neither looking back or beyond; living tradition is everywhere; whatever the circumstances, there can only be the appointed destination.

Living tradition can fare forward exuberantly, even recklessly, because it operates within visible, prudential restraints. On every road, Indians amble, stand or sit sedately, the mobilized traffic-calmers. Where craters, potholes and cracks are challenges, obstructions to progress, hazards to normal usage, mobilized traffic-calmers are constraints that keep living tradition channelled and mindful of itself. What are mobilized traffic-calmers? The cow, mother of India, she who cannot be collided with, who has total freedom while all else must accommodate her pleasure in the operation of their existence. This universally accepted principle of restraint determines how India fares forward. It provides perspective on the various incarnations of technology. Over time, this ever-present system of constraint reveals the inner character of technology, its fitness to serve, permitting the selection process, the addition and subtraction, to shape and mould them into domesticated form. You can see how this operated in history; the bullock cart is supremely adapted ancient technology. Modernity was much more of a challenge, coming after the dislocation of colonial disruption, increasing the pace and scale of technological impact. It found its answer in the Ambassador, not chic, not flashy, not the most efficient of vehicles, but home-made, sustainable and enduring, cheap and available: domesticable, domesticated and domiciled in India. The Ambassador is testimony that prudential restraints work. Confidence in the efficacy of the system obviously explains why, although ideally every car in India has brakes, no driver ever feels the need to employ them.

Borne by modern Indian identity, my trusty Ambassador, I arrived in Old Goa. There stand three magnificent, majestic churches, a selection of cloisters and other imposing European buildings all clustered around a square dwarfed by an enormous outspreading boa tree. The buildings are alive only with tourists. It is not that nothing else remains of any phase of colonialism, here or elsewhere in India. Colonial accretions, fitting, unfitting and yet to be resolved, are everywhere. Indian modernity has evolved to transcend colonialism. Like its self-sufficient incarnation, the Ambassador, it is a mode of transportation, a means of faring forward. Among the vestiges of foreign power, the cows roam freely. As I contemplated this pleasing scene, there was a general hubbub as a Maruti made a high-speed dash that caused everyone, including the cows, to scuttle to the side of the road.

For 40 years, Indian modernity underpinned political independence and the national love affair with the Ambassador flourished. In 1983, the Maruti arrived, more modern-looking, the product of a partnership between the Indian government and the Suzuki corporation of Japan. Maruti cars proved an instant hit with the burgeoning middle class; they have become the vehicles of choice for yuppies. Statistics, however, are deceptive. Today, the Amby commands only 5 per cent of India's car market, compared to Maruti's 80-per-cent share. But Ambassadors continue to be more visible, and more common on the roads, because vast numbers remain in existence and operation. They continue to give resilient service long after more expensive and younger breeds have gone to the eternal scrap yard, defeated by the adventure that is

A Karma Kab Ambassador taxi in London, 2001.

the roads of India. So long as the Ambassador remains on the road, technology will be subject to Indian modernity rather than driven who knows where by rampant technological imperatives.

Dangerous but Irrepressible: Cars and Driving in Post-Apartheid South Africa

CATHERINE ADDISON

In South Africa, cars are inextricably connected with crime. Even within my own limited acquaintance, I know almost no-one who has not had a car stolen at one time or another. If not whole cars, at least parts of cars – hubcaps, batteries, wheels – are purloined, as are contents of parked cars, such as sound systems, clothes, guns, money, even a cake just baked for the old people's home from my mother's car. A terrible old radio, repaired with dental floss, was once taken from a rusty Golf of ours; the thief broke the side window to get it. It must have been worth about 50 cents.

Of course, theft from unoccupied cars is considered relatively good luck. The great fear of all motorists is hijacking, so common in some parts of cities, Johannesburg in particular, that they have become no-go areas for ordinary people. Many drivers will not stop near the line at a traffic light, but drift nervously to a halt a car's length before it, in order to give themselves space to manoeuvre. On an intersection busy with pedestrians, you can feel the tension as drivers grip their wheels, waiting interminably for green and imagining the worst: demonic figures, armed and balaclava'd, appearing out of nowhere and demanding not their soul, but their keys.

As car crime escalates, both petty and organized, so anti-crime measures become more and more ingenious – and demonic. Now that car alarms, engine immobilizers, satellite tracking devices and gear-stick- and steering-wheel locks have proven ineffective – over and over again – people are taking to more sadistic methods of property protection. The most famous of these is a device called the 'Blaster', invented by Charl Fourie in 1998, which is basically a flame-thrower controlled by the driver's foot that produces a sizeable fireball at each side of the car. Costing approximately £300, it uses liquefied gas from a small tank in the car's boot, which is squirted past an ignition spark when the device is activated. Although the gas jet can be

Charl Fourie and Michelle Wong's in-car flame-thrower, the 'Blaster'.

adjusted, it cannot be limited to one side of the car, so innocent passers-by can easily be incinerated along with potential hijackers. Fourie claims that the 'Blaster' is unlikely to kill anyone, but believes that it has the potential to blind a person for life.

The 'Blaster' has received a great deal of publicity – not to mention notoriety – both in South Africa and abroad, and it has inspired many variations by bloodthirsty amateurs. A local air-conditioner technician of our acquaintance has a device that electrocutes anyone who tampers with his 'bakkie' (a small truck, considered a symbol of masculinity). He nearly killed a young man with it. The youth was found unconscious from repeated high-voltage shocks and had to be hospitalized. The local police were delighted, though I suppose they would have had to open a murder docket on the inventor if the device had put out half an amp more current.

A sergeant of the Johannesburg Flying Squad ordering suspects out of a suspected stolen car.

The morality of car crime is nowadays more clear-cut than it was during the struggle years of apartheid. Comrades would then sometimes steal cars as part of strategies of terror or sabotage. At times of political unrest, 'young lions' would drop bricks or cement blocks off highway overpasses onto cars below. (In Somerset West, a town separated from Cape Town by a notorious stretch of motorway, there was at one time a good market for iron grids that

A Khulame Springbok patrol hijacked in Soweto.

An attempted car theft in downtown Johannesburg.

The remains of a burnt-out car, a symbol of violence in the townships during the Apartheid years.

fitted over windscreens like cages.) Stoning and setting vehicles alight used to be among the commonest forms of protest in some areas. All of these activities were regarded as acts of war – by those who took part in them, anyway. Many of the freedom fighters of those days are now irreproachable members of the new government, their earlier acts not so much forgiven as glorified by the great cause in which they laboured.

But some ex-comrades in the new government have turned out not to be absolutely above reproach. And in South Africa, the bribe that proves least resistible is a set of fancy wheels. The latest scandal of the month has involved Tony Yengeni, erstwhile Chief Whip of the ruling party. He was observed driving around in that most desirable of vehicles, a Mercedes Benz 4x4, bright green and brand new. A local newspaper did some snooping and discovered that this was a 'donation' – unacknowledged by its new owner – from a company involved in the sale of arms to South Africa. So Tony, party stalwart and veteran soldier of liberty, is a political has-been – and all for a tarted-up Jeep that he had no intention

of taking off the road at any time. How the mighty are fallen, as the saying goes.

This tragic little tale demonstrates the exaggerated value placed on cars as status symbols in the strangely mixed-up first-world, third-world country that is South Africa. Although vehicle one-upmanship has always been apparent among Whites, it is perhaps more noticeable nowadays among the new Black élite. In city slang, these are named 'wa-Benzi', after the defining feature of social arrival, the Mercedes Benz. A 'Be My Wife' is a BMW in the same slang. So desirable are German luxury cars that they can frequently be seen parked in squatter camps and in other scenes of abject poverty. The juxtaposition of expensive car and squalid environment is not always a consequence of a criminal connection; it is often just a sign of priorities. Before a decent roof over his head or any other outward sign of prosperity, a man on the rise will often acquire a car costing at least double the price of a modest house. (This is not equally true of women, I am glad to say, though it may be because women are almost never targeted by car advertisements, despite the fact that a very large number of drivers and car owners in South Africa are female.)

South Africans' veneration of the German luxury car makes a gift given to Nelson Mandela on his inauguration as President all the more touching. Mercedes Benz factory workers did overtime for many weeks in order to be able to give him a car. Fire-engine red like the Communist Party flag, it was a symbol of worker solidarity, and also a true gift of love, personalized and yet collective.

But most South Africans do not drive this sort of

Nelson Mandela receives a Mercedes built as a gift by workers at the Mdantsane plant. Each employee worked a few hours unpaid overtime and the car rolled off the line in four days rather than the usual 38.

vehicle except in their dreams. Cars are expensive. For the middle classes, they are in the same price range as houses and in the old apartheid zones where accommodation is cheap, they cost far, far more than houses. The cheapest house in a historically White suburb may sell for around R100,000; the cheapest new car costs approximately R60,000. Second-hand cars are not much less, unless you happen to 'know someone in the business'.

The options are widening a little at the moment, but during the late decades of the apartheid government, there was very little choice among car makes unless you could afford to import your own. British cars were the norm in my family when I was growing up. We had a Morris Cowley in 1957, a Ford Zephyr and a Morris Mini in the early '60s, then a Vauxhall, a Ford Zodiac, an Austin Apache, two different Rovers and a Ford Taunus station wagon. When he had finally achieved what he considered to be success, my dad bought himself a second-hand Jaguar. But after the boycott against South Africa started to take effect in the late '70s, British cars gradually disappeared, as did Italian, French and American makes. German and Japanese were just about the only choices, Volkswagen and Toyota competing furiously for the small-car market – as they still do, with Toyota firmly in the lead. (Of course, just about all of the cars on the road are actually made in South Africa itself, so car nationality is a subtle matter.)

One of the cheapest cars available is a Volkswagen model known as the Citigolf. This is the same – in shape and appearance, at least – as the first small Golf that appeared in the '70 s, known in America as the Rabbit. This car was so popular in South Africa that it was never discontinued. I suppose that this is a sign that Volkswagen regard us as a third-world country. The Citigolf is still made in vast numbers in the Eastern Cape and sells very well among the unadventurous, such as myself. My husband and I have owned several, the most recent in a nondescript white (for the heat) and with a 1600 rather than the smaller 1300 engine, because we insist on an air conditioner in this subtropical region (the Zululand coast). We gain no status from our car whatever, since it is identical to thousands of vehicles owned by the police, the post office and the national electricity company.

But new cars of any make or description are luxuries never even imagined in the majority of South African households. Thanks to lax licensing and road-worthy regulations, widespread ignorance, poor policing, a mild climate, poverty and a host of other factors, many of the vehicles on South Africa's roads

Top: The N1 motorway from Pretoria to Johannesburg.
Above: A car crash at a crossroads in Johannesburg. (The 1999–2000 year-end holiday death toll neared 900 people.)

are in unspeakably bad condition. In rural Zululand, truly finished cars, decayed so far that their ability to move at all is quite astonishing, are an everyday sight. Relics of the past, giant old American tanks like the Chevy Impala, Volkswagen Variants, Fiats and Citroëns, and British cars like the Austin Apache and the Ford Taunus that bring back my childhood surreally, are all to be seen crawling lopsidedly along dirt and tar roads, traversing the lush countryside of sugarcane and banana palms, natural bush and timber plantations. Most days, I drive the 20 kilometres to work on a winding, potholed country road that

allows overtaking in only a few places. I do this in order to avoid paying a toll, as has become the norm on all major roads. I regularly get stuck for kilometres behind these ancient cars that creep along at a fraction of the speed limit, pouring out smoke-screens of foul-smelling exhaust. Their shattered or non-existent windows, rust holes, skew alignment, smooth tyres and other noticeable deficiencies do not discourage great numbers of passengers from entrusting their lives to them. Driving the route at night is like Russian roulette because every second vehicle has no lights, or only some lights. These conveyances are not maintained at all; their owners, like them, are often not licensed, and when you are involved in a collision with one of them – as frequently happens, for obvious reasons – there is no point in trying to pursue reparations.

Accidents, however, are not caused principally by poor vehicle maintenance. The main cause of our extremely high road-death rate is clearly aggression. Although our speed limits are high – 120 kph on highways – no-one keeps to them. Even the worst old jalopies will be seen wobbling up to 140 on the longer down-hills, and the rest of us just cruise as fast as our engines will allow, sneering as we whiz past people in lesser cars and giving the finger to anyone who pulls in front of us or tries to prevent us from overtaking. Road rage is not an isolated event; it is the permanent condition of most motorists as soon as they get behind the wheel. Some psychologists put the aggression down to our apartheid past, but this does not wash with me, since the rage is so widespread and indiscriminate.

Only one habit, catching tourists by surprise, suggests that there may be another side to us. When a slow car or truck pulls over to let us pass – which does in fact happen now and then – we have a custom of thanking it by turning on our hazard lights for a few seconds as we speed away. This courtly gesture is often followed by an answering single flash from the slow vehicle, and so a polite conversation of lights – presuming these to be functional in the two vehicles in question – may continue, in contradiction of our usual behaviour.

Perhaps our habit of warning each other about speed traps and traffic police is also symptomatic of an underlying camaraderie. It is certainly part of the general lawlessness on the roads. That cops are the

Top: Moving house, Johannesburg style.

enemies of freedom and should be outsmarted is the unspoken belief of nearly all drivers, even those who imagine themselves to be model citizens. Though we ourselves do not directly benefit, we warn oncoming cars of speed traps and police roadblocks that we have recently passed. Perhaps this is the closest we ever come to a sense of civic duty: we have ourselves benefited from the warning flash and will benefit again, and so we pass the goodwill on – often to drivers who quite clearly deserve to be jailed. I suppose we are at least not self-righteous. 'There but for the grace of God go I' is what we truly feel as we watch a fellow-motorist being booked for an offence.

No discussion of cars in South Africa would be complete without mention of the taxi industry. A South African taxi is not a taxi at all, but a combi or a large van operating as an unofficial bus. Taxis have definite routes for which rival outfits compete mercilessly – 'taxi wars' regularly claim more lives than many revolutions. And yet the taxi industry is proud to be one of the great Black success stories of the Apartheid years. Against the laws and against the

A taxi rank in central Johannesburg.

odds, taxi operators built up a giant moneymaking concern that gave to the poor a system of affordable transport whose networks extended to the most remote kraals of the 'homelands', to the corrugated iron doors of the urban shanties. Minibus taxis are still the transportation mode of most people's choice, though few Whites ever use them.

Whatever their attractions for the cash-strapped commuter, however, to the motorist, taxis are a curse and an affliction. Notorious for doing highway speeds in built-up areas, stopping dead in the middle of the road at sight of a fare, driving in bus lanes, on pavements, through red traffic lights and down one-way streets in the wrong direction, their drivers habitually intimidate other road users with lurid threats in assorted languages – threats that are worth heeding, since they are often carried out.

Most of the taxi passengers one meets swear that they look for the slowest and most law-abiding drivers and are terrified of the cowboy-like tactics for which so many of them are famous. But urban legend claims that the drivers who streak through Johannesburg streets in the evening rush hour are loudly encouraged by cries of 'Make the Bold!' from the female passengers jammed like sardines into the back. 'The Bold and the Beautiful' is the most popular soap opera in Soweto, aired at 17:30 on one of the local TV stations. A law-abiding driver could never get his passengers home in time to watch it.

The government has plans to regulate the taxi

industry and phase out the present fifteen-seat minibus and replace it with a larger eighteen-seater that is safer and more comfortable for passengers. But I am not alone in having doubts as to their ability to do anything about this utterly South African invention, the privately owned minibus taxi. Incredibly annoying, dangerous, dirty, stuck about with vulgar slogans and religious platitudes, taxis are probably the best symbol of our freedom and our personality. They may not be a pretty sight, but at least there is something irrepressible about them.

Automonster

CHRISTOPHER PINNEY

ek kar, do kar, tin kar: sab bekar!
('One car, two cars, three cars: all useless!')
– Raj Kapoor, in the Hindi film *Shri 420* (1955)

What options does the history of our relationship with objects – such as cars – bequeath us? Recent investigations of 'promiscuous'[1] objects which stress their tendency to appear differently according to cultural context, while couched as a radical critique of earlier concerns about the fixed identities of objects, might be seen as the paradoxical fitting into place of the last humanist fragment of an anthropocentric 'man'-besotted puzzle. 'Things' were the final frontier – the last recalcitrant domain of the unmanly, now fully incorporated into our empire of subjection. Denied a presence of their own, they are fully crowned as objects mirroring our infinite power.

A recent insightful ethnographic exploration of the 'humanity' of the car evinced Pitjantjatjara Australian Aboriginal driving-related practices as proof of the automobile's propensity to 'resist alienation'. Pitjantjatjara use Toyota Land Cruisers to visit sacred sites and to screen secret ceremonies from the intrusive eyes of outsiders. In other words, the car facilitates 'a phenomenological and cosmological relationship to the land'.[2] The implied conclusion here is that all cars are perhaps capable of participating in such a relationship. Cars themselves, it is reasonably claimed, have no essential qualities; they are ciphers for cultural 'entailments'. As the editor of the volume containing this study concluded, the car's culturaliza-tion 'problematize[s] any assumptions that we know what the car is, except by developing a greater sense of what it has become'.[3]

The alibi acquired by the car through Pitjantjat-jara uses of it might be seen as similar to the proposition in the National Rifle Association bumper-sticker slogan that 'Guns don't kill people, people do.'[4] However, to demonstrate an exception does not undermine the validity of claims about the performa-tively dominant relationship between objects and humans which the bulk of historical and cross-cultural data show to be true. The discovery that somewhere a kindly person dusts and admires a collection of decommissioned guns demonstrates that a totalizing claim that 'all guns are dangerous' is untenable. It does nothing, however, to destabilize the proposition that a world without guns would be a better place.

Much academic literature has convinced itself that if 'they' consume, what is consumed must be good. In the 1980s, cars were the agent of a neo-liberal privatization of the soul dividing those that speed from those left behind to breathe the fumes. Freedom became the freedom to get away, To Go. Then somehow – who can disentangle the process which made this possible [5] – that neo-liberal evil became the mark of active citizens, apparently embracing neo-liberalism's bribes, but (we convinced ourselves) all the while coolly, slyly, extracting what 'we' (oh heroic man!) wanted without buying into the whole seductive lie. To Go, but not only where (or how) the capitalists told us to. A thousand articles and books were produced chanting a similar self-glorification: man is finally the master of his own destiny, free to consume as the transcendent agent of his own utility.

The desire to reveal the car's 'humanity' (also evident in this book) is a symptom of a very powerful consensus – the new orthodoxy – which cuts across several disciplines including anthropology, cultural studies and media studies. This consensus assumes that everything can be explained through 'culture'. Culture has taken on the role of heroic biography in Victorian narratives. It is no longer fashionable to rely on explanations that invoke the actions and intentions of individuals; many elements of this earlier individualistic paradigm have been collectivized under the new rubric of culture. The chief problem with the invocation of individual actions was that it failed (as Bruno Latour has noted) to recognize that humans are 'no longer *by themselves*'.[6] The corresponding problem with the concept of culture is that there is no longer a 'nature' against which it can be brought into being.

The anthropological/cultural-studies celebration of cultural agency is paradoxical, because it emerges from an explicit desire to supersede either technological or social determinism through an exploration of the network of reciprocal determination. But the triumph of the cultural is perhaps inevitable given the tenacious attachment to a concept of culture which is an intimate product of the binary being attacked. Any project concerned with car *cultures* will inevitably conclude in favour of the cultural at the expense of the material. This is the point made by

Heidegger in his account of the foundational, we might say mythic, separation of nature and culture:

. . . the more extensively and the more effectually the world stands at man's disposal as conquered, and the more objectively the object appears, all the more subjectively, i.e., the more importunately, does the *subiectum* rise up, and all the more impetuously, too, do observation of and teaching about the world change into a doctrine of man, into anthropology.[7]

To start by stressing the 'humanity' of the car is to re-inscribe the very problem which we should be attacking: our concept of what it is to be 'human', and what it is to have 'culture'.

In contemplating the car as an artefact, we have two fundamental options. We may choose to remain locked within a notion of conventional subjects and objects (the NRA model or, conversely, the Adornoite attribution of essential qualities to the car[8]). Or we may opt for an understanding that collapses these familiar points of identification and searches instead for some comprehension of the fused, 'hybrid' domain of the car.

This latter option has been most fully explored by Latour in a post-disciplinary space that he terms 'Science Studies'. Latour's radical starting point is that since there is no such thing as 'nature', there is no such thing as 'culture', and hence there are no cultures.[9] Instead, there are 'natures-cultures', zones inhabited by hybrids in which humans and non-humans are 'folded into each other'.[10] This is rather startling news (especially, perhaps, if you happen to be an anthropologist), but becomes more plausible when we consider some of Latour's examples such as an ozone hole. It ceases to make sense to ask whether an ozone hole is 'natural' or 'cultural': it is the product of a folding of the two into a new 'hybrid'. The world is increasingly

Buried Machinery in Barn Lot, Dallas, South Dakota, 13 May 1936.

configured by such complex entities, Latour has argued.

The expansion of the car into a wider space can also help us to confront the problem of naming. The banal slipperiness of 'car' fails to measure up to the hugeness of its power. Cars have first to be made linguistically more weighty, more difficult to bear, so that in their omniscience they cease to be able to pass through the micro-capillaries of our perception. But renaming must also respond adequately to the expanded frame of reference. The hybrid is monstrous (transcending a human/non-human dichotomy); thus the car-hybrid will become the 'automonster'. This term will be used here to describe not only the metal artefact on wheels (which is the unit of comparison in most writing on the 'car'), but the entire network or complex in which that metal artefact is embedded, the entire field of inputs and outputs that cohere around that hybrid network or automonster: the geopolitical order structured to facilitate the easy flow of oil to industrialized nations, metal, rubber, tarmac, speed, vehicle emissions, ozone holes, melting polar ice, the decreasing options of the world's poor. All of these are elements in the complex hybrid that is the automonster.

The dimensions of the hybrid automonster can perhaps more easily be grasped through an exploration of a similar argument advanced by Roland Barthes concerning the differences between contrasting kinds of stories about objects. In his essay 'The Metaphor of the Eye' (1963), he suggests that Georges Bataille's *Story of the Eye* (1928) 'really is the story of an object', implying that some narratives about objects are not really concerned with those objects.[11] Objects can feature in stories in which they are 'pass[ed] from hand to hand', as in *The History of My Pipe* or *Memories of an Armchair*.[12] Barthes descibes these as 'tame fanc[ies]'; they mirror the strategy of anthropological engagements with the car which, as it passes from culture to culture (rather than hand to hand), becomes (ultimately) immaterial. Hence in the case of Car Cultures, the conclusion is the tautological one that the culture of the car is only what different cultures inscribe it as. The object that is ostensibly the focus of the narrative becomes merely a manner of foregrounding different cultures (and hence Man). As narratives of the social lives of things, they reaffirm the agency of those humans between whom they pass.

The object in *Story of the Eye*, by contrast, traverses a fluid trans-substantiation across a common network of objects triangulated by a saucer of milk, a human eye, a skinned bull's testicle and the moon. Barthes terms this a 'spherical metaphoricity':

The Eye's substitutes are declined in every sense of the term: recited like flexional forms of one word; revealed like states of the one identity; offered like propositions none of which can hold more meaning that another; filled out like successive moments in the one story.[13]

This declensional, 'wavy' form of story comprised of a series of avatars follows a pathway on which 'its essential form subsists through the movement of a nomenclature'[14] and which emerges as a series of settings for the further unfolding of the complex identity of the central object.[15] In the case of *Story of the Eye*, the story takes us to a park at night merely in order that the moon can shine on a stain on Marcelle's sheet, Madrid is visited only so that a bullfight might occur and the eye transmute into a bull's testicle, and so on. The narrative itself is a mere *mise-en-scène* for the appearance of various avatars of the central eye/testicle/moon object. This is in many ways the inverse of the story of Car Cultures, in which narrative (the staging of distinct cultural settings) inevitably (see Heidegger) fragments the continuity of the central car-object. Similarly, the possibility of an 'Autopia', proposed by this volume, can only be achieved through a blindness to the hybrid complexity of the automonster. Wavy meaning, conversely, allows a different kind of narrative, one that brings out the complexity of the car-network.

Bataille's story is a literary experiment, but everyday life in the Age of Oil bears a striking similarity to its conceit, for our narratives are 'simply a kind of flow of matter enshrining the precious metaphorical substance'[16] of the automonster. The world has settled itself around the central shape of this narrative.

How, then, might we decline the automonster, explore its flexional forms, the different, intimately connected, aspects, of the same story? What might be the automobile equivalent of the mutating eye/testicle/moon path of wavy meaning? The convulsive economy of the automonster suggests a seething wavy meaning in which worlds are created through its agency: motorways are built, ocean levels rise, US-supported despotisms become the framework for the new world order. If this 'general contagion of qualities and actions'[17] once had a causal hierarchy and rationale, it is now lost, as car-events in the car-network are transacted simultaneously and indeterminately without clear causal motivations: America's foreign policies need the Age of Oil as their justification just as much as cars need the oil that these foreign policies attempt to secure.

Lacking the space to elaborate a story of the complexity of that of Bataille's Eye, I can only enumerate points within the car-circle, drawing attention to some of the mutations within this network in which 'each of its terms is always the significant of another term'.[18] These are all transformations of the car-hybrid, all essential parts of the story of the car as automonster, points traversing an arc of fused meaning.

Part of this arc takes us through a series of interconnected aesthetic dimensions. If, as Lewis Mumford once suggested, the Age of Iron and Coal was founded on an aesthetic of blackness ('the black boots, the black stove-pipe hat, the black coat or carriage, the black iron frame of the hearth, the black cooking pots and pans and stoves. Was it mourning? Was it protective colouration?'),[19] what is the aesthetic of the Age of Oil? Perhaps the grey of a concrete kerb abutting withered grass, or the luminous red of a Little Chef sign, the charcoaled bodies of Iraqi conscripts on the Basra road, or the spaghetti tangles of a motorway intersection embodying a completely new ergonomics.

Or perhaps Leadvilles, the non-places that slither around automobiles. The poet Alan Brownjohn describes in *For a Journey* the 'heavy, whittled-down simplicity' of rural place names. Names such as 'Top Field' or 'Oak Field' inscribe locations and pathways – 'Where has yielded best, or the way they walked from home' – and testify to the fusion of memory and place:

You can travel safely over land so named –
Where there is nowhere that could not somewhere
Be found in a memory which knows and loves.
So watch then, all the more carefully, for
The point where the pattern ends . . .[20]

The spaces where the pattern ends, Brownjohn observes, have 'the air of not needing ever to be spoken about'. The terrain of the automonster is increasingly unknown. Endless Leadvilles, each with their main drag. Philip Larkin captured these perfectly: '. . . the next town, new and nondescript . . . with acres of dismantled cars'.[21]

'Not needing ever to be spoken of' – the non-space of modernity: the paradoxical result of the routinized bourgeois cult of travel which has as its aim the homogenization of space. *Vitruvius Britannicus* has been replaced by *Boring Postcards*, the photographer Martin Parr's catalogue of dismal roadside cafes, outer ring roads and desolate motels, all situated in the purgatorial antechamber which is not quite on the main drag (to be viewed with a mirthful, only barely ironic, chuckle at our own enslavement). And this unspeakability is a measure not simply of the absence of the conventionalized poetic trappings that can hang so easily on archaic places but also a product of the non-place's refusal of poetic adhesion, its surfaces hostile to the tropical complexity of metaphor.

Another part of the arc traces the automonster's climatological consequences. Some of these are already apparent, such as melting polar-ice caps and the 30-per-cent increase in the amount of carbon dioxide in the atmosphere over pre-industrial levels, to which vehicle emissions have been a major contributor. Others are forecast. The cracked surface of dry lakes along the route of the Silk Road suggesting that temperatures are likely to rise 5°c by the end of the century. Uzbekistan, Tajikistan, Afghanistan and Iran facing perpetual drought and consequent famine.[22] The burning sun defining not clouds but the hexagonal, basalt-like formations of croaking riverbeds into whose tumults shepherds once threw sticks, dreaming of speed. The probable parameters of other more dramatic consequences are outlined in the various 'Intergovernmental Panel on Climate Change' scenarios. These suggest global temperature rises of between 1.4 and 5.8 °c by the year 2100, which, if the higher figures hold true, will produce a 3-foot rise in sea levels and the inundation of densely populated regions such as Bangladesh and the Nile Delta. Longer-term futures factor in the cataclysmic release of methane from thawing permafrost and worst-case scenarios detail 30-foot ocean rises.[23]

Other points of the arc reveal the new world order as a transubstantiation of the car. The geopolitical order is to the car as Bataille's moon is to the eye. The US and its European allies have engineered the collapse (or artificial sustenance) of political regimes in order to guarantee the density, the delirious congested frenzy, of happy citizens on its freeways and interstates. The Age of Oil's new world order is as much a part of the car as skid marks on the road, or a puddle of sump fluid.

Finally, the arc conjures distance. Cars invoke speed; the automonster invokes distance. Paul Virilio's diagnosis of speed[24] needs to be superseded by an analysis of distance. Until the mid-nineteenth century, Sven Lindqvist has shown, unreliable and inaccurate European weapons were often outperformed by indigenous soldiers with the result that colonial wars were 'lengthy and expensive'.[25] In 1853, Enfield rifles with a 500-yard range precipitated an increasing imbalance. The development of nitro-glycerin after 1885 meant that marksmen could remain invisible when they fired,

for they ceased to emit explosions of smoke and ash, and the Maxim gun permitted the delivery of eleven bullets per second without smoke. The battle at Omdurman, on 2 September 1898, was a theatre for the first systematic demonstration of what Carlo Ginzburg has termed the 'moral implications of distance'. Gunboats, automatic weapons, repeater rifles and dumdum bullets were all deployed against a 'numerically superior and very determined enemy'. Over 9,000 of the Caliph's men were mown down, and not one got within 300 yards of the British positions. Lindqvist takes as an epitaph a naval bombardment survivor's testimony in Joseph Conrad's *An Outcast of the Islands*: 'First they came, the invisible whites, and dealt death from afar.'[26] That might also serve as the epitaph for those regions most immediately imperilled by climate change, those who will be the first to be flooded, to suffer crop failures and famines. The distance at Omdurman prevented any ethical revelation of a common humanity, as well as any need for Maxim-wielding soldiers to assume responsibility, just as the distance between a Californian sports utility vehicle and a peasant's hut in the Brahmaputra delta provides an alibi for those who know 'analytically' what the consequences of their actions are, but who can't 'feel' their implications: 'they' remain metaphorically and politically faceless.

These are just some manifestations of the automonster 'in the manner of a vibration that always gives the same sound'.[27] My aim has been not to attempt to fully complete the automonster's flexional circle, but to give some taste of its 'wavy' presence and its difference from the more familiar object-narrative of the car as a thing 'passed from hand to hand'. The car is dead. Let us now slay the automonster.

MOTOR SPACES

The modern motor car represents an astonishing feat of human ingenuity.
Consider the number of them out on the roads and the extraordinarily few
accidents due to any fault in the vehicle itself. If we were one half as clever in the
matters that lie far outside machinery as we are about machinery itself, what
people we should be and what a world we should leave our children. If life were
only an internal combustion engine![1]

J. B. PRIESTLEY

We have lived with the motorcar for more than a century, yet we remain ambivalent in our attitudes towards it. For while the car itself has become an irreplaceable fact of modern life, we maintain an uneasy relationship with the landscapes it has helped to shape. When Priestley wrote his eulogy to the car in the early 1930s, the environments that had grown up to accommodate it were still unfamiliar. In common with most intellectual fellow travellers, he was disconcerted by the 'England of arterial and bypass roads, of filling stations, and factories that look like exhibition buildings, of giant cinemas and dance-halls and cafés, bungalows with tiny garages, cocktail bars, Woolworths, motor coaches, wireless, hiking' and all the other evidence of what he took to be the increasing Americanization of English culture. While conceding that this new England was probably more democratic than the old one, Priestley resented its cheapness and monotony, and would probably have agreed with the sentiments expressed by a contemporary critic:

> Visualise please a modern, post-war arterial road . . . in a year or two
> bungalows (cheap and nasty perhaps); allotments; muddy chicken runs;
> pig styes; filling stations; advertisement hoardings; news bills; flagrant
> stores . . . a modern highway cursed by . . . ribbon development − or 'go
> as you please' − It is offensive, objectionable, unnecessary and
> wasteful.[2]

Those were voices from a different age, but every subsequent generation has thrown up its own criticisms of the spaces of motoring: in 1970, for instance, John Kenneth Galbraith called the petrol station 'the most repellent piece of architecture of the past two thousand years'.[3] Today, it is no longer arterial roads and their attendant houses, pubs and factories that are the objects of derision, but shopping malls, retail parks, distribution warehouses and the parking lots surrounding them, which attract the ire of urban commentators.

This rejection of contemporary reality has increasingly been called into question, however. *Learning from Las Vegas*, published in 1972, played a key role in promoting acceptance of the developing landscapes of car culture by exposing the essential illogicality of resisting 'the automobile-oriented commercial architecture of urban sprawl':

> Learning from the existing landscape is a way of being revolutionary for an architect . . . Architects are out of the habit of looking nonjudgmentally at the environment, because orthodox Modern architecture is progressive, if not revolutionary, utopian, and puristic; it is *dissatisfied* with existing conditions. Modern architecture has been anything but permissive: Architects have preferred to change the existing environment rather than enhance what is there.[4]

For the majority of people, this new landscape requires neither eulogizing nor mythologizing; it is simply there to be consumed, appropriated and enjoyed. Across America, and now across much of the rest of the developed world, the spaces of work, leisure and home are exclusively linked and accessed by the car. The car-based future championed by the Modernist avant-garde may not have come to pass exactly as they envisioned, but it has happened all the same.

Standard Oil gas station, USA, 1927.

The Chinese garage, Beckenham, Kent, built *c.* 1928.
The Duke of Bedford's garage, Store Street, London, built in 1929.

A SuperAmerica gas pump.

Roadside pump, Valetta, Malta, 2000.

Avia petrol station, Enschede, Netherlands, 1997.

Top: The 'Big Tire' by the side of Interstate 94, near Dearborn, Michigan.
Above: Pennsylvania Turnpike, 13 September 2001.
Left: Oil crisis, USA, 1973.

Top: Motorway bridge, Nevada.
Above: Motel, Illinois.

Left: Diner on the old Route 66, near Flagstaff, Arizona.
Right: Dustin Shuler, *Spindle*, 1989, Berwyn, Illinois (the so-called 'Car Kabob').

Above: Pile-up in Michigan.
Right: Second-hand car-lots,
Livernois Avenue, Detroit,
1958.

Drive-in movie theater, Lynchburg, Virginia, in the 1950s.

Robert Moses:
The Expressway World

MARSHALL BERMAN

Among the many images and symbols that New York has contributed to modern culture, one of the most striking in recent years has been an image of modern ruin and devastation. The Bronx, where I grew up, has even become an international code word for our epoch's accumulated urban nightmares: drugs, gangs, arson, murder, terror, thousand of buildings abandoned, neighborhoods transformed into garbage- and brick-strewn wilderness. The Bronx's dreadful fate is experienced, though probably not understood, by hundreds of thousands of motorists every day, as they negotiate the Cross-Bronx Expressway, which cuts through the borough's center. This road, although jammed with heavy traffic day and night, is fast, deadly fast; speed limits are routinely transgressed, even at the dangerously curved and graded entrance and exit ramps; constant convoys of huge trucks, with grimly aggressive drivers, dominate the sight lines; cars weave wildly in and out among the trucks: it is as if everyone on this road is seized with a desperate, uncontrollable urge to get out of the Bronx as fast as wheels can take him. A glance at the cityscape to the north and south – it is hard to get more than quick glances, because much of the road is below ground level and bounded by brick walls ten feet high – will suggest why: hundreds of boarded-up abandoned buildings and charred and burnt-out hulks of buildings; dozens of blocks covered with nothing at all but shattered bricks and waste.

Ten minutes on this road, an ordeal for anyone, is especially dreadful for people who remember the Bronx as it used to be: who remember these neighborhoods as they once lived and thrived, until this road itself cut through their heart and made the Bronx, above all, a place to get out of. For children of the Bronx like myself, this road bears a load of special irony: as we race through our childhood world, rushing to get out, relieved to see the end in sight, we are not merely spectators but active participants in the process of destruction that tears our hearts. We fight back the tears, and step on the gas.

Robert Moses is the man who made all this possible. When I heard Allen Ginsberg ask at the end of the 1950s, 'Who was that sphinx of cement and aluminum,' I felt sure at once that, even if the poet didn't know it, Moses was his man. Like Ginsberg's 'Moloch, who entered my soul early,' Robert Moses and his public works had come into my life just before my Bar Mitzvah, and helped bring my childhood to an end. He had been present all along, in a vague subliminal way. Everything big that got built in or around New York seemed somehow to be his work: the Triborough Bridge, the West Side Highway, dozens of parkways in Westchester and Long Island, Jones and Orchard beaches, innumerable parks, housing developments, Idlewild (now Kennedy) Airport, a network of enormous dams and power plants near Niagara Falls; the list seemed to go on forever. He had generated an event that had special magic for me: the 1939–40 World's Fair, which I had

A westbound Cross-Bronx Expressway from Grand Concourse.

attended in my mother's womb, and whose elegant logo, the trylon and perisphere, adorned our apartment in many forms – programs, banners, postcards, ashtrays – and symbolized human adventure, progress, faith in the future, all the heroic ideals of the age into which I was born.

But then, in the spring and fall of 1953, Moses began to loom over my life in a new way: he proclaimed that he was about to ram an immense expressway, unprecedented in scale, expense and difficulty of construction, through our neighborhood's heart. At first we couldn't believe it; it seemed to come from another world. First of all, hardly any of us owned cars: the neighborhood itself, and the subways leading downtown, defined the flow of our lives. Besides, even if the city needed the road – or was it the state that needed the road? (in Moses's operations, the location of power and authority was never clear, except for Moses himself) – they surely couldn't mean what the stories seemed to say: that the road would be blasted directly through a dozen solid, settled, densely populated neighborhoods like our own; that some-

thing like 60,000 working- and lower-middle-class people, mostly Jews, but with many Italians, Irish and Blacks thrown in, would be thrown out of their homes. The Jews of the Bronx were nonplussed: could a fellow-Jew really want to do this to us? (We had little idea of what kind of Jew he was, or of how much we were all an obstruction in his path.) And even if he did want to do it, we were sure it couldn't happen here, not in America. We were still basking in the afterglow of the New Deal: the government was *our* government, and it would come through to protect us in the end. And yet, before we knew it, steam shovels and bulldozers were there, and people were getting notice that they had better clear out fast. They looked numbly at the wreckers, at the disappearing streets, at each other, and they went. Moses was coming through, and no temporal or spiritual power could block his way.

For ten years, through the late 1950s and early 1960s, the center of the Bronx was pounded and blasted and smashed. My friends and I would stand on the parapet of the Grand Concourse; where 174th Street had been, and survey the work's progress – the immense steam shovels and bulldozers and timber and steel beams, the hundreds of workers in their variously colored hard hats, the giant cranes reaching far above the Bronx's tallest roofs, the dynamite blasts and tremors, the wild, jagged crags of rock newly torn, the vistas of devastation stretching for miles to the east and west as far as the eye could see – and marvel to see our ordinary nice neighborhood transformed into sublime, spectacular ruins.

In college, when I discovered Piranesi, I felt instantly at home. Or I would return from the Columbia library to the construction site and feel myself in the midst of the last act of Goethe's *Faust*. (You had to hand it to Moses: his works gave you ideas.) Only there was no humanistic triumph here to offset the destruction. Indeed, when the destruction was done, the real ruin of the Bronx had just begun. Miles of streets alongside the road were choked with dust and fumes and deafening noise – most strikingly, the roar of trucks of a size and power that the Bronx had never seen, hauling heavy cargoes through the city, bound for Long Island or New England, for New Jersey and all points south, all through the day and night. Apartment houses that had been settled and stable for twenty years emptied out, often virtually overnight; large and impoverished Black and Hispanic families, fleeing even worse slums, were moved in wholesale, often under the auspices of the Welfare Department, which even paid inflated rents, spreading panic and accelerating flight. At the same time, the construction had destroyed many commercial blocks, cut others off from most of their customers and left the storekeepers not only close to bankruptcy but, in their enforced isolation, increasingly vulnerable to crime. The borough's great open market, along Bathgate Avenue, still flourishing in the late 1950s, was decimated: a year after the road

A newly completed viaduct of the Cross-Bronx Expressway in the late 1950s.

came through, what was left went up in smoke. Thus depopulated, economically depleted, emotionally shattered – as bad as the physical damage had been the inner wounds were worse – the Bronx was ripe for all the dreaded spirals of urban blight.

Moses seemed to glory in the devastation. When he was asked, shortly after the Cross-Bronx road's completion, if urban expressways like this didn't pose special human problems, he replied impatiently that 'there's very little hardship in the thing. There's a little discomfort and even that is exaggerated.' Compared with his earlier, rural and suburban highways, the only difference here was that 'There are more houses in the way . . . more people in the way – that's all.' He boasted that 'When you operate in an overbuilt metropolis, you have to hack your way with a meat ax.'[1] The subconscious equation here – animals' corpses to be chopped up and eaten, and 'people in the way' – is enough to take one's breath away. Had Allen Ginsberg put such metaphors into his Moloch's mouth, he would have never been allowed to get away with it: it would have seemed, simply, too much. Moses' flair for extravagant cruelty, along with his visionary brilliance, obsessive energy and megalomaniac ambition, enabled him to build, over the years, a quasi-mythological reputation. He appeared as the latest in a long line of titanic builders and destroyers, in history and in cultural mythology: Louis XIV, Peter the Great, Baron Haussmann, Joseph Stalin (although fanatically anti-communist, Moses loved to quote the Stalinist maxim 'You can't make an omelette without breaking eggs'), 'Kingfish' Huey Long, Marlowe's Tamburlaine, Goethe's Faust, Captain Ahab, Mr Kurtz, Citizen Kane. Moses did his best to raise himself to gigantic stature, and even came to enjoy his increasing reputation as a monster, which he believed would intimidate the public and keep potential opponents out of the way.

In the end, however – after 40 years – the legend he cultivated helped to do him in: it brought him thousands of personal enemies, some eventually as resolute and resourceful as Moses himself, obsessed with him, passionately dedicated to bringing the man and his machines to a stop. In the late 1960s they finally succeeded, and he was stopped and deprived of his power to build. But his works still surround us, and his spirit continues to haunt our public and private lives.

It is easy to dwell endlessly on Moses's personal power and style. But this emphasis tends to obscure one of the primary sources of his vast authority: his ability to convince a mass public that he was the vehicle of impersonal world-historical forces, the moving spirit of modernity. For 40 years, he was able to pre-empt the vision of the modern. To oppose his bridges, tunnels, expressways, housing developments, power dams, stadia, cultural centers, was – or so it seemed – to oppose history, progress, modernity itself. And few people, especially in New York, were prepared to do that. 'There are people who like things as they are. I can't hold out any hope to them. They have to keep moving further away. This is a great big state, and there are other states. Let them go to the Rockies.'[2] Moses struck a chord that for more than a century has been vital to the sensibility of New Yorkers: our identification with progress, with renewal and reform, with the perpetual transformation of our world and ourselves – Harold Rosenberg called it 'the tradition of the New.' How many of the Jews of the Bronx, hotbed of every form of radicalism, were willing to fight for the sanctity of 'things as they are'? Moses was destroying our world, yet he seemed to be working in the name of values that we ourselves embraced.

I can remember standing above the construction site for the Cross-Bronx Expressway, weeping for my neighborhood (whose fate I foresaw with nightmarish precision), vowing remembrance and revenge, but also wrestling with some of the troubling ambiguities and contradictions that Moses' work expressed. The Grand Concourse, from whose heights I watched and thought, was our borough's closest thing to a Parisian boulevard. Among its most striking features were rows of large, splendid 1930s apartment houses: simple and clear in their architectural forms, whether geometrically sharp or biomorphically curved; brightly colored in contrasting brick, offset with chrome, beautifully interplayed with large areas of glass; open to light and air, as if to proclaim a good life that was open not just to the elite residents but to us all. The style of these buildings, known as Art Deco today, was called 'modern' in their prime. For my parents, who described our family proudly as a 'modern' family, the Concourse buildings represented a pinnacle of modernity. We couldn't afford to live in them – though we did live in a small, modest, but still proudly 'modern' building, far down the hill – but they could be admired for free, like the rows of glamorous ocean liners in port downtown. (The buildings look like shell-shocked battleships in drydock today, while the ocean liners themselves are all but extinct.)

As I saw one of the loveliest of these buildings being wrecked for the road, I felt a grief that, I can see now, is endemic to modern life. So often the price of ongoing and expanding modernity is the destruction not merely of 'traditional' and 'pre-modern' institutions and environments but – and here is the real tragedy – of everything most vital and beautiful in the modern world itself. Here in the Bronx, thanks to Robert Moses, the modernity of the urban boulevard was being condemned as obsolete, and blown to pieces, by the modernity of the interstate highway. *Sic transit!* To be modern turned out to be far more problematical, and more perilous, than I had been taught.

FROM *All That Is Solid Melts Into Air: The Experience of Modernity* (1982)

Driving the American Landscape

ANDREW CROSS

Delve into a contemporary account of the American landscape and you can be certain that driving along a road will be close to its heart. Whether in song or in print, the merest suggestion of a journey made by automobile triggers in the mind whole swathes of imaged possibilities stretching out across the North American continent. Of course, it is because the mythology of the road journey is so well established in American music, literature and film that it is so easy to imagine oneself being out on the road. But it is also because travelling by car is something we all experience in some way or another. As an immediate point of access to an essential part of contemporary American culture, the long-distance journey – a journey measured in days rather than hours – has particular resonance. This is also true for many Europeans, particularly those who are not only eager to engage with American 'culture' on its home turf, but who are also all too conscious that their own national borders, in any direction, may only be a couple of hours away.

To those Europeans who, like myself, seek an expansive landscape, few things will better the experience of driving in America. Just to think about it is so appealing, it is like a seductive drug – the tacit freedom of the long, open road, and the vast, vaulting skies stretching over and ahead of you towards a seemingly endless horizon. As Jean Baudrillard observes in his book *America*, it is a sky that can expand the mind:

Clouds spoil our European Skies. Compared with the immense skies of America and their thick clouds, our fleecy skies and little fleecy clouds resemble our fleecy thoughts, which are never thoughts of wide open spaces . . . Europe has never been a continent. You can see that by its skies. A soon as you set foot in America you feel the presence of an entire continent – space there is the very form of thought.

It's not that Europe, and the greater Eurasian continent to which Europe is attached, isn't physically big. It's just that somehow the landscape isn't the right scale; the *idea* of the landscape isn't big enough. In Europe during one day's travel, you can pass through six countries and as many languages. This is not bigness; this is a number of little-nesses bunched together. In America, one knows with certainty that it is possible to drive from the Atlantic to the Pacific with relative ease, unlike, for example, driving from Spain to China. Travelling any great distance across Europe or Asia is to revisit the great political upheavals of recent times. The pan-European motorcar journey has always been curtailed by war, hot or cold. As a unifying entity across the us, the romantic partnership between road and automobile has remained peacefully unchecked for a century.

Except for a few concentrated urban areas, the actual manner of driving in America is quantifiably different from that in Europe. Traffic is significantly less dense, and the pace is seemingly much more leisurely – most people drive at fairly similar and

consistent speeds averaging 60 mph. If a destination is, say, 75 miles away, you know with some confidence that the journey will take you, well, 75 minutes. The relatively stress-free driving conditions are, however, only part of the attraction. It is the whole dreamscape of America that will condition your anticipation and satisfy your every need when you are on the road. It is where the expansive existential abstracts can be encapsulated by a mug of coffee set on a Formica counter. These are the scenes set in wayside diners and motel nowheresvilles that provide the indelible romantic tone to the American road trip that is so singularly lacking on the European motorway.

The mythology of life 'on the road' is not only a draw to European tourists. For the generations of Americans who came of age during the second half of the twentieth century, the road trip has been held as a sacred dream – even an essential right – if not a frequent reality. First embodied in Jack Kerouac's *On the Road* (1957), the story of the misfit heading out to meet his or her future was reinforced by subsequent novelists and film directors.

What is that feeling when you're driving away from people and they recede on the plain till you see their specks dispersing? – it's the too huge world vaulting us, and it's good-bye. But we lean forward to the next crazy venture beneath the skies . . .

More often than not, though, these narratives generated from 'the road' evolve around encounters between people. They are usually less about actually

driving than about the consequences of the drive, bringing the narrator or lead character to a particular place at what usually transpires to be a crucial time. The reality is more likely to be a road trip spent meeting few people and encountering situations that are in fact rather mundane. Whether travelling alone or with companions, there is little reason to communicate with others outside the car, only the occasional exchange when filling up with petrol and buying a coffee and donut. Even in a diner, one need only order food. One will check in to a motel on the outskirts of a city and, instead of going out, watch TV eating food from a drive-through restaurant. Indeed, it is likely that much of the journey will be spent away from the railroad-influenced centres of old towns. The co-ordinates of a cross-country road trip are now the

out-of-town intersections of interstate highways. It is at these intersections that motels, petrol stations, food outlets, distribution warehouses and giant truck-stops now cluster. More often than not, if your journey is about getting from A to B, it will be spent driving along major interstates, not mysterious back roads.

Supplanting the various older and mythologized Route 66's, and constructed from the 1950s through to the '70s, the interstates are the great multi-lane transcontinental motorways that reach across America from east to west and north to south. The network of thick red lines on the road atlas. These roads, like the 10, the 40, the 80 and the 90 running east–west, or the 5, 15 and 95 running north–south, are now the main routes along which Americans make their transcon-

tinental migrations by road. There is something satisfyingly prosaic in the way American roads are numbered. Nothing like the aspirations or the bureaucracy of an A1, M6 or E40. Just a number, and the 10 is simply the 10 whether it be in San Bernardino, California, or Mobile, Alabama. As the ideal province of cruise control, interstates possess their own personalities, which can range from the exhilarating to the stupefyingly dull. As you glide at a steady 65 or 75 mph across the continent, interstates will fly you over houses and train yards in suburban Chicago or Houston; grace you with wide, immaculately manicured verges and meridian as you gently roll through rural Indiana or Pennsylvania; or offer spectacular views as you sharply descend off an escarpment on to a desert plain – as the 15 does near the Utah/Nevada border. It

is not always so stimulating, of course, or even restful. For example, the 5 as it passes down the Central Valley of California is not only – as far as I can tell –the longest dead-straight stretch of interstate in the US; it is eternally boring to drive.

Not that driving in itself is meant to be that interesting. While the mythologized charm of a wayside halt can nearly always be guaranteed, such stops cannot be made at every junction or town. Many hours can be spent floating in relative tedium. Whether on interstates or older highways, a lot of time is spent travelling roads that change only imperceptibly. Yet these sometimes tiresomely long bouts of driving are somehow effortless. And it is while floating through the slow vastness of the landscape that you can exercise your deepest thoughts and most

wonderous adventures. In the words of Bad
Company:

So I'm burning up the freeway,
ain't nothing in sight
You know it takes a lotta loving,
To keep me driving all night . . .

As it is inside the car that most of one's journey
is spent, the idiosyncrasies of this interior world
become an essential vocabulary of references that
articulate the big abstracts beyond it: the interior
smell of a brand-new rental car, take-away coffee in
styrofoam cups, over-sweet donuts, the countless local
FM radio stations: 'KKRW 93.7FM "The Arrow" –
Houston's only classic rock station'.

The point about FM radio is that whatever your
choice – rock, pop or country – the same music will be
played all day every day, so whenever you hop in your
car you can tune in knowing what you will hear. It
doesn't matter how unsophisticated or how unfashionable the music might be. While you may be inside
a car in the middle of Nebraska, the music gurus have
no idea what you are up to. To a large extent, classic
rock stations play British rock music from the 1970s –
whether it is Bad Company and Led Zeppelin – the
kind of music that no self-respecting British radio
station would ever play. But much of this music wasn't
necessarily produced for British ears. More than
anything, it was written to accompany the expanding
monotony of the American highway.

The incidentals generated inside the car

become the all-important accompaniment to the vast landscape passing slowly by, a landscape seemingly with no particular beginning or end. Narrated by one's own musings and conversations, the comparison is unavoidable: it's like being in your very own movie. As Don DeLillo puts it in *Underworld* (1997):

And once we were in Yankton, South Dakota, early on that summer, and the movie theatre was just letting out, the Dakota it was called, with a bright tile façade and Audie Murphy on the marquee, and the young people of Yankton got in their cars and drove up and down the main drag and we drove with them, nearly falling asleep, and we went to drive-in movies and talked about life and we rode across the prairies and talked about movies and we drove through car

washes and read poetry aloud, one of us to the other, and soapy water slid down the windows.

Henry James suggested that America was too large for any human convenience, too diverse in geography to form a single unit. This is perhaps why the landscape of the US is best experienced through a frame. Indeed, the history of modern America, or rather the myths of the country's past, could be told as a history of frames. First, there was the frame of the railroad-carriage window, strips of field, forest and factories passing at right angles to the tracks in regular rhythm. Completion of the trans-continental line in 1869 was effectively the beginning of the end of frontier America, as the landscape seen subsequently through the carriage window increasingly became a

function of the American economy. The frontier did not die out totally, however, but was re-invented in the frame of the silver screen, on which the heroics of cowboys were enacted against the dramatic landscape of the West.

The frontier of the Western film was in turn dismantled by the hyper-reality of TV, and it was through a third frame, the car windscreen (or windshield), that pioneering adventures would be relived. During the 1950s and '60s, many Americans re-engaged with their landscape by taking lengthy road trips as families or – encouraged by Jack Kerouac – as high-spirited beatniks and hippies. Even after the nation took *en masse* to the air from the late 1960s, driving the interstate highway remained the only way Americans could know that there was a landscape

beyond the nearest airport. Today, there is no landscape if it is not seen through the windscreen, only a series of places, postcard snapshots separated by time and space. It is only within the frame of the windscreen that places co-exist, that they become animated along the continuous narrative of the landscape through which you drive.

Indeed, to drive in America – to have America driven in – is to make the American landscape incarnate. All significant moments in the American landscape are by necessity driven to. In some cases, the landscape is more appropriately viewed from a car, something the designers of the federally sponsored highways built during the 1920s and '30s (including Benton MacKaye and Norman Bel Geddes) were very mindful of. Monument Valley is best seen when driving

towards it or indeed away from it, as the 'valley' area is home to buttes equal in their beauty to the group made famous by John Ford in the classic Western *Stagecoach* (1939). Like great sentinels, these geological formations line the only road that leads to the Monument Valley site. And if you do arrive there, don't leave the car. Keep the buttes framed within the windscreen. To leave the car is to remove the frame, the animation of movement and the significance given it by Hollywood. In fact, it is on the screen that the buttes are best seen. Viewed for real in the open air, these otherwise highly aesthetically and culturally charged rocks lose any dimension, like discarded props.

For many people, their relationship with the American landscape is conditioned less by Hollywood than by their view of it through the window of an airplane at a height of more than 30,00 feet. To fly coast to coast is to experience every school geography lesson unfold beneath you. Pilots proudly announce national monuments that are being passed over and often dip the aircraft's wings so that a better view can be had of the Grand Canyon. But as with the movies, this is a distanced hyper-reality whose connection to down-to-earth reality occurs at the airport hire-car office. For most ordinary people – apart from long-distance lorry drivers – driving in America is a very localized experience (although this may still mean journeys of a few hours). This is why, as in so many works of fiction, the road trip is still charged with a sense of connecting people to a kind of more innocent reality of landscape, lost but yet somehow still obtainable. To quote J. B. Jackson,

You think of your past, think about your work, think about your destination and about those you have left. The dashboard display shows how fast you are driving, tells you the hour and how many miles you still have to go. The sameness of the American landscape overwhelms and liberates you from any sense of place. Familiarity makes you feel everywhere at home.

My own early acquaintance with the American landscape was developed as a small boy growing up in the English countryside. It came through the filtering of Hollywood movies and TV programmes. ('The Virginian', though mostly shot on a sound stage, somehow had the ability to project the feeling of wide-open spaces.) When I was a teenager during the 1970s, it was the sound of American rock music – Neil Young,

the Allman Bros – that became the trigger for imagining what America was like: the soundtrack to lazy afternoons daydreaming over *The Times World Atlas.* Scratchy black lines linking dots named Kansas, Bakersfield or Barstow.

Then my viewpoint was not particular but more general, possibly seen from the air as much as from the ground, an amalgam of received and imagined images. Today, I photograph American trains, but in many respects the photographs I make have everything to do with driving. They are the end point of nights spent in motels, meals taken in diners and many hours of driving. These are journeys made across deserts, across plains, over mountains and through industrial suburbs. Like most things in the US, the only way to reach the places where the trains are is by car.

I first visited America as a student in New York in 1982; I soon began to explore other parts of the country, although I would not get far until much later. After a few years, I had driven a fair bit of both the East and the West coasts, but increasingly it was the vast bit in the middle that attracted me. Yet it was not until 1995 that my first coast-to-coast trip would be made, in the company of my girlfriend, Jack.

While the road trip has changed since Kerouac's day, the idea retains much of the same romantic spirit. Driving is about being by oneself, alone in a vast landscape but alone with ease. For this is now a landscape that is facilitated by the credit-card economy of motels, rental cars and fast food. This underlying presence of corporate America supports that perfect romantic sensation of anonymity, the kind of anonymity that only seems possible after many hours and miles spent travelling. As it was for Kerouac's hero Sal Paradise, the coast-to-coast trip is a kind of rite of passage to be taken at any age, on your own or with someone special. Three thousand miles all joined up in one relatively straight line. The subject of much personal mythology. I know some-one who claims that he drove from Seattle to New York on his own in three days and two nights without stopping to sleep. That's an average of over 80 mph. Most people spend weeks. Jack and I did it in ten days. Just prior to our trip, American friends were eager to suggest landmarks for us to visit en route. 'What route are you taking?' they would ask. 'The "northern" or the "southern" one?' 'Across the middle,' we would answer.

Erosion of Cities or Attrition of Automobiles

JANE JACOBS

Today everyone who values cities is disturbed by automobiles.

Traffic arteries, along with parking lots, filling stations, and drive-in movies, are powerful and insistent instruments of city destruction. To accommodate them, city streets are broken down into loose sprawls, incoherent and vacuous for anyone afoot. Downtowns and other neighbourhoods that are marvels of close-grained intricacy and compact mutual support are casually disembowelled. Landmarks are crumbled or are so sundered from their contexts in city life as to become irrelevant trivialities. City character is blurred until every place becomes more like every other place, all adding up to Noplace. And in the areas most defeated, uses that cannot stand functionally alone – shopping malls, or residences, or places of public assembly, or centres of work – are severed from one another.

But we blame automobiles for too much.

Suppose automobiles had never been invented, or that they had been neglected and we travelled instead in efficient, convenient, speedy, comfortable, mechanized mass transit. Undoubtedly we would save immense sums which might be put to better use. But they might not.

For suppose we had also been rebuilding, expanding, and reorganizing cities according to the project image and the other anti-city ideals of conventional planning.

We would have essentially the same results as I blamed on automobiles a few paragraphs back. These results can be repeated word for word: the city streets would be broken down into loose sprawls, incoherent and vacuous for anyone afoot. Downtowns and other neighbourhoods that are marvels of close-grained intricacy and compact mutual support would be casually disembowelled. Landmarks would be crumbled or so sundered from their context in city life as to become irrelevant trivialities. City character would be blurred until every place became more like every other place, all adding up to Noplace. And in the areas most defeated, etc.

And then the automobile would have to be invented or would have to be rescued from neglect. For people to live or work in such inconvenient cities, automobiles would be necessary to spare them from vacuity, danger, and utter institutionalization.

It is questionable how much of the destruction wrought by automobiles on cities is really a response to transportation and traffic needs, and how much of it is owing to sheer disrespect for other city needs, uses, and functions. Like city rebuilders who face a blank when they try to think of what to do instead of renewal projects, because they know of no other respectable principles for city organization, just so, highway-men, traffic engineers, and city rebuilders, again, face a blank when they try to think what they can realistically do, day by day, except try to overcome traffic kinks as they occur and apply what foresight they can towards moving and storing more cars in the future. It is impossible for responsible and practical men to discard unfit tactics – even when the results of their own work cause them misgivings – if the alternative is to be left with confusion as to what to try instead and why.

Good transport and communication are not only among the most difficult things to achieve; they are also basic necessities. The point of cities is multiplicity of choice. It is impossible to take advantage of multiplicity of choice without being able to get around easily. Nor will multiplicity of choice even exist if it cannot be stimulated by cross-use. Furthermore, the economic foundation of cities is trade. Even manufacturing occurs in cities mainly because of attached advantages involving trade, not because it is easier to manufacture things in cities. Trade in ideas, services, skills, and personnel, and certainly in goods, demands efficient, fluid transport and communication.

But multiplicity of choice and intensive city trading depend also on immense concentrations of people, and on intricate minglings of uses and complex interweaving of paths.

How to accommodate city transport without destroying the related intricate and concentrated land use? – this is the question. Or, going at it the other way, how to accommodate intricate and concentrated city land use without destroying the related transport?

Nowadays there is a myth that city streets, so patently inadequate for floods of automobiles, are antiquated vestiges of horse-and-buggy conditions, suitable to the traffic of their time, but . . .

Nothing could be less true. To be sure, the streets of eighteenth- and nineteenth-century cities were usually well adapted, as streets, to the uses of people afoot and to the mutual support of the mingled uses bordering them. But they were miserably adapted, as streets, to horse traffic, and this in turn made them poorly adapted in many ways to foot traffic too. Victor Gruen, who devised a plan for an automobile-free downtown for Fort Worth, Texas (about which I shall say more later) prepared a series of slides to explain his scheme. After a view of a street with a familiar-looking automobile jam, he showed a surprise: just about as bad a jam of horses and vehicles in an old photograph of Fort Worth.

———

Le Corbusier, when he designed his Radiant City of the 1920s, as a park, skyscraper, and automobile freeway version of Howard's small-town Garden City, flattered himself that he was designing for a new age and, along with it, for a new system of traffic. He was not. So far as the new age was concerned, he was merely adapting in a shallow fashion reforms that had been a response to nostalgic yearnings for a bygone simple life, and a response also to the nineteenth-century city of the horse (and the epidemic). So far as the new system of traffic was concerned, he was equally shallow. He embroidered (I think that is a fair word for his approach) freeways and traffic on to his Radiant City scheme in quantities that apparently satisfied his sense of design, but that bore no relationship whatsoever to the hugely greater quantities of automobiles, amounts of roadway, and extent of parking and servicing which would actually be necessary for his repetitive vertical concentrations of people, separated by vacuities. His vision of skyscrapers in the park degenerates in real life into skyscrapers in parking lots. And there can never be enough parking.

The present relationship between cities and automobiles represents, in short, one of those jokes that history sometimes plays on progress. The interval of the automobile's development as everyday transport has corresponded precisely with the interval during which the ideal of the suburbanized anti-city was developed architecturally, sociologically, legislatively, and financially.

But automobiles are hardly inherent destroyers of cities. If we would stop telling ourselves fairy tales about the suitability and charm of nineteenth-century streets for horse-and-buggy traffic, we would see that the internal combustion engine, as it came on the scene, was potentially an excellent instrument for abetting city intensity, and at the same time for liberating cities from one of their noxious liabilities.

Not only are automotive engines quieter and cleaner than horses but, even more important, fewer engines than horses can do a given amount of work. The power of mechanized vehicles, and their greater speed than horses, can make it easier to reconcile great concentrations of people with efficient movement of people and goods. At the turn of the century, railroads had already long demonstrated that iron horses are fine instruments for reconciling concentration and movement. Automobiles, including trucks, offered, for places railroads could not go, and for jobs railroads could not do, another means of cutting down the immemorial vehicular congestion of cities.

We went awry by replacing, in effect, each horse on the crowded city streets with half a dozen or so mechanized vehicles, instead of using each mechanized vehicle to replace half a dozen or so horses. The mechanical vehicles, in their overabundance, work slothfully and idle much. As one consequence of such low efficiency, the powerful and speedy vehicles, choked by their own redundancy, don't move much faster than horses.

Trucks, by and large, do accomplish much of what might have been hoped for from mechanical vehicles in cities. They do the work of much greater numbers of horse-drawn vehicles or of burden-laden men. But because passenger vehicles do not, this congestion, in turn, greatly cuts down the efficiency of the trucks.

Today, those in despair at the war between those potential allies, automobiles and cities, are apt to depict the impasse as a war between automobiles and pedestrians.

It is fashionable to suppose that the solution lies in designating certain places for pedestrians, and certain other places for vehicles. We may be able to make such separations eventually, if we find we really want to. But such schemes are only practical, in any case, if they *presuppose* a spectacular decline in the absolute numbers of automobiles using a city. Otherwise, the necessary parking, garaging, and access arteries around the pedestrian preserves reach such unwieldy and deadening proportions that they become arrangements capable only of city disintegration, not of city saving.

The most famous of pedestrians schemes is the Gruen plan for the downtown of Fort Worth. The firm of Victor Gruen Associates, architects and planners, proposed that an area of roughly a square mile be circled with a ring road feeding into six huge, oblong garages, holding 10,000 cars each, which would each penetrate from the ring-road perimeter deep into the downtown area. The rest of the area would be kept free of automobiles and would be intensively developed as a downtown of mixed uses. The scheme has run into political opposition in Fort Worth, but imitative plans have been proposed for more than 90 cities and have been tried in a few. Unfortunately, the imitators ignore the salient fact that the scheme treated the entire part of Fort Worth which could be described as city-like in the form of one interlocked, uninterrupted whole, and in these terms it made sense; to this extent, it was an instrument of concentration rather than separation; to this extent, it fostered greater complexity rather than greater simplicity. In the imitations, the idea is almost invariably perverted into dinky and timid designs for isolating a few shopping streets in the fashion of suburban shopping malls, and surrounding them with dead borders of parking and access.

This is about all that can be done – and indeed it is all that could have been planned for Fort Worth – unless a problem much more difficult that shrub-planting and bench-installing is faced. This problem is how to cut down drastically the absolute numbers of vehicles using a city.

In the case of the Gruen plan for Fort Worth, Gruen had to presuppose such a decrease, even though the city is relatively small and simple in comparison with our great cities, and even though the arrangements for cars were enormous and elaborate. Part of Gruen's scheme included arrangements for express bus services tying the downtown into the whole city and its suburbs, and absorbing a far higher ratio of downtown users than is now served by public transport. Without such an arrangement and such a presupposition, the ring-road scheme would have been unrealistic embroidery in the Le Corbusier tradition of wishful frivolity, or else – the difficulties faced realistically – it would have meant converting virtually the entire downtown to garages and rendering the ring road inadequate for access. To be sure, a greatly enlarged perimeter might have served; with the garages disposed far out, but then the practicality of a concentrated, intense district, readily used on foot, would have been defeated. The plan would have no point.

Some varieties of traffic separation, conceived for heavily congested downtown streets, envisage not a horizontal separation as in the Gruen scheme, but a vertical separation with either the pedestrians put above the automobiles on an upper street level, or the automobiles put above the pedestrians. But removing pedestrians gives very little more room to cars. To provide roadbeds of the dimensions needed for the cars that bring in the pedestrians – which is the cause of the congestion and the reason for the separation – means stretching the dimensions of the corresponding pedestrian levels to the point of self-cancellation of pedestrian convenience. These schemes too, to be practical either for cars or for the pedestrians, must presuppose a drastic reduction in absolute numbers of automobiles, and much greater dependence on public transportation instead.

And there is another difficulty behind pedestrian schemes. Most city enterprises which are a response to pedestrian street use, and which, reciprocally, generate more pedestrian street use, themselves need convenient access to vehicles for services, supplies, or transport of their own products.

If vehicular and pedestrian traffic are completely separated, one of two alternatives must be accepted.

The first alternative is that the preserves for the pedestrians must be streets which do not contain such enterprises. This is automatically an absurdity. These absurdities can be found, in real life, and just as might be expected, the preserves are empty. The pedestrians are in the vehicular streets, where the enterprises are. This type of built-in contradiction afflicts much grandiose 'city of tomorrow' planning.

The other alternative is that it is necessary to devise schemes of vehicular servicing, separated from the pedestrian preserves.

Gruen's scheme for Fort Worth handled the servicing problem with a system of underground tunnels for trucks and for taxi service to hotels, with access through basement-level loading.

Except in the most intensively used central downtown areas, it hardly seems that the service complications accompanying thoroughgoing separation of pedestrians and vehicles are justified.

I am doubtful as to whether the advantages of thoroughgoing separation are, in any case, very great. The conflicts between pedestrians and vehicles on city streets arise mainly from overwhelming numbers of vehicles, to which all but the most minimum pedestrian needs are gradually and steadily sacrificed. The problem of vehicular dominance, beyond toleration, is not exclusively a problem involving automobiles. Obviously, excessive numbers of horses produced similar conflicts; people who have experienced an Amsterdam or New Delhi rush hour report that bicycles in massive numbers become an appalling mixture with pedestrians.

Where opportunity affords, I have been watching how people use pedestrian streets. They do not sally out in the middle and glory in being kings of the road at last. They stay to the sides. In Boston, which has experimented with closing two of its downtown shopping streets (the deliveries were the knotty problem, of course), it was quite a sight to see the almost empty roadbeds and the very crowded, very narrow sidewalks. On the other side of the continent, the same phenomenon occurs in the model Main Street of Disneyland. The only vehicles on the Disneyland town's roadbed are a trolley which comes

by at rather long intervals, for kicks, and once in a while a horse and buggy. Nevertheless, visitors there use the sidewalks in preference to walking down the middle of the street; the only times I saw them choose the street instead were, perversely, when one of the vehicles or a parade went by. Then they went out to *join* what was in the street.

A certain amount of such inhibition in Boston or in Disneyland may be caused by the fact that we have all been so conditioned to respect the kerbs. Paving

Built for horse-and-buggy traffic: Greenwich Village, New York.

which merged roadbed and sidewalk would probably induce more pedestrian use of roadbed space; certainly, where sidewalks are wide (even in Boston) people do not bunch themselves up to the laughable degree that they do in Disneyland or on the narrow downtown Boston sidewalks.

However, that is apparently only part of the answer. In suburban shopping centres where 'streets' are wide but thoroughly pedestrian and without kerbs, people stay to the sides also except where something interesting to see has been deliberately placed out in the 'street'. It takes tremendous numbers of pedestrians to populate the whole width of a roadbed, even in scatterings. The only times pedestrians seem to use, or want to use, a street roadbed in this fashion are in cases of extraordinary floods of pedestrians, as in the Wall Street district or the Boston financial area when the offices let out, or during the Easter parade on Fifth Avenue. In more ordinary circumstances, people are attracted to the sides, I think, because that is where it is most interesting. As they walk, they occupy themselves with seeing – seeing in windows, seeing buildings, seeing each other.

In one respect, however, people on the pedestrian streets of Boston, of Disneyland, or of shopping centres do behave differently from people on ordinary city streets heavily used by vehicles. The exception is significant. People cross over from one side to the other freely, and in using this freedom they do not seem to be inhibited by the kerbs. These observations, coupled with the way people are forever sneaking across streets at forbidden places if they can get away with it – even at risk to their lives – and coupled with the palpable impatience people so often exhibit at crossings, lead me to believe that the main virtue of pedestrian streets is not that they completely lack cars, but rather that they are not overwhelmed and dominated by floods of cars, and that they are easy to cross.

Even for children the point may be less to segregate the cars than to reduce the domination by cars and combat the erosion of sidewalk play space by cars. It would, of course, be ideal to dispose of cars entirely on city streets where children play; but worse troubles still are harvested if this means disposing of the other utilitarian purposes of sidewalks, and along with them, supervision. Sometimes such schemes, too, are automatically self-cancelling. A housing project in Cincinnati affords an illustration. The houses in this project front on pedestrian precincts of lawns and sidewalks, and they back up on service alleys for cars and deliveries. All the casual coming and going occurs

The motorized city: downtown Dallas.

between the houses and the alleys and therefore, functionally, the backs of the houses have become the fronts and vice versa. Of course the alleys are where the children all are too.

Life attracts life. Where pedestrian separation is undertaken as some sort of abstract nicety and too many forms of life and activity go unaccommodated or are suppressed to make the nicety work, the arrangement goes unappreciated.

To think of city traffic problems in over-

simplified terms of pedestrians versus cars, and to fix
on the segregation of each as a principal goal, is to go at
the problem from the wrong end. Consideration for
pedestrians in cities is inseparable from consideration
for city diversity, vitality, and concentration of use. In
the absence of city diversity, people in large
settlements are probably better off in cars than on foot.
Unmanageable city vacuums are by no means
preferable to unmanageable city traffic.

FROM *The Death and Life of Great American Cities* (1961)

The Asphalt Exodus

JANE HOLTZ KAY

World War II did what no Depression could accomplish: it stalled the American motorist. As the nation mobilized its armed forces, highway construction ground to a halt and civilian car making all but ceased. The most motorized war in history throttled car production, lowered mileage, and braked the automobile culture. Motor vehicle manufacturers became munitions makers, and car sales plummeted by 3 million in the first year of war. To secure oil, tires, and batteries for the 'arsenal of democracy's' trucks, tanks, airplanes and jeeps, Washington encouraged conservation. 'Victory Speed 35 miles per hour,' said the signs urging Americans to slow down in order to save rubber. Boy Scouts collected tons of tires, while other home front patriots heaved scrap into piles labeled 'aluminum for defense fund.' Though pioneering expressways like Davison and Willow Run heading to 'Bomber City' Detroit opened during World War II, road building lapsed.

A nation of car owners tinkered with rebuilt engines, retreaded their tires, scraped together gas rationing coupons for two gallons a week – and took to their feet. 'Citizens learned to walk again,' historian Doris Kearns Goodwin writes. 'Car pools multiplied, milk deliveries were cut from twice a day, and auto deaths fell dramatically.' Desperate to move workers to new jobs, planners began to think in terms of human mobility as well as automobility. Government posters sloganeered life by rail and foot power, not horsepower, admonishing citizens to car pool, to 'conserve everything you have, to walk and carry packages.' 'When you ride ALONE you ride with Hitler!' one poster admonished. 'Join a car-sharing Club TODAY!'

World War II would mark the last time that catering to the car and using it to disperse the population did not constitute the nation's manifest destiny. Instead, public transportation moved the masses.

A 1943 poster for the US government's Office of Price Administration.

Throughout the nation the war engine ran at double time as it raced to stop Hitler's army advancing across Europe. Heroes in an emergency, us automobile leaders gained the wealth and credibility lost in the Depression, and the forerunner of the military-industrial complex was born. In what historian John Morton Blume called 'the hardening pattern of bigness,' government grew bigger and bigger businesses got the bucks. Among them the biggest of all was the automobile industry. Washington handed out two-thirds of its $175 billion in contracts to the nation's top 100 corporations, 8 per cent to General Motors alone. 'The hand that signs the war contract is the hand that shaped the future,' a Senate committee summed it. Some of these 'hands' belonged to GM's William Knudsen and to home lender Jesse Jones, chief of the Reconstruction Finance Corporation. These directors of the War Production Board would indeed shape the future. As they attended their private luncheons, they lobbied for the post-war highway leading to the single-family home. From this place of privilege, such corporate chefs would become the fathers of the 1950s Road Gang in the post-war world.

COMING HOME

The end of war was the beginning of building America anew. 'So nice to come home to,' said a Buick ad. 'You're a swell looking guy in civvies, too!' said the classic Rosie the Riveter as she welcomed homecoming vets in a *Time* magazine insurance ad in 1946. Other pages featured advertisements to coax post-war Americans to buy tires, fly self-propelled planes, or drive a shiny Nash. The Nash family sedan was more than an automobile, said the advertisement. It was a 'Prophecy – on Wheels.' It was 'so big and roomy that the front seat was *sofa* size – and the back seat can be stretched out into a double bed at night.' Spread out. Expand. In the decade after 1947, Americans would buy 30 million cars to help them do so. Forget austerity. Conservation was over, consumption was in. Christian Dior's 'New Look' featured lavish swirls of fabric. The new look in mobility was equally expansive.

The pages of *Automotive Industries* predicted a glowing future. The car, helpmate to housing and partner with Cold War defense industries, would power the boom. Forget 'freedom from want' and the New Deal dole. New mind the 'commodious . . . crowdhaulers,' those Chicago trains pulling voters to whistle-stop speeches by the newly elected President Harry S. Truman in 1949. Within eight years, rail trackage was half of its 1916 peak. Airplane travel was the way to go, plus those newly engineered highways. In the first five post-war years, dealers and buyers jump-started the automobile culture with an average of three million car sales a year. Consciousness II, the auto as icon, had returned full-blown. 'There's a Ford in your future,' the carmakers had advertised midwar. The postwar nation bought it.

Americans took their pent-up dreams and drove to their green horizons. The states financed big city Detroit, New York and Chicago expressways. Toll roads were built. In a decade, Americans had doubled their 25 million automobiles. The car and road consumed four times the road and land space of a bus and twenty of rail. Appetites reined in by the Great Depression and war controls were unleashed at every level. In urban America, though, dwellings were crammed to capacity. Ten million veterans added to the vast numbers of Americans in shacks, garages, Quonset huts, and decayed housing stock. The postwar housing crisis made the need for new homes severe.

Just before the war, John T. Howard, a planner at the Massachusetts Institute of Technology, had divided America into the 'gone' and 'going' neighborhoods of the city and the 'coming' ones of the suburbs. Then he uttered a caution. 'The bottleneck in city planning is people,' he wrote. 'The bottleneck can be broken. But not by splashing superhighways across the newspapers, or dreaming visions of the ideal City of 1970 . . . Good neighborhoods – good 'old' neighborhoods – are the blocks with which we must build.' He went unheeded. The old was ignored. At one million and then two million housing starts a year the new rose, and soon yet one more federal subsidy helped tear down the old blocks.

The Housing Act of 1949, designed by Congress to remedy city housing ills, initiated what would be called 'urban renewal.' Descended from New Deal legislation to replace slums with housing through private enterprise and create 'a decent home and a suitable living environment,' the act set the wheels in motion to clear the land. With money to level working-class housing – termed 'slums' – but not put up public housing, with funds to builders and business districts – but not to owners – the act worked in the opposite direction: it shuffled the poor and flattened downtowns. In *The Federal Bulldozer*, a decade and a half later, Martin Anderson would describe how the federal legislation sacrificed working-class communities on the altar of development, aggravated racial and class differences, and obliterated neighborhoods.

The search to tab a neighborhood 'blighted' and hence fundable, to find, as Robert Moses had it, 'the blight that's right,' now took precedence. Moses and his allies were back in action, coupling stump clearance and highway construction, ransacking the city for suitable sites and reducing them to rubble. Solid, if frayed, neighborhoods, two-thirds of them minority, and historic, if worn, buildings became multilane highways and public housing towers. 'You can draw any kind of picture you like on a clean slate and indulge your every whim in the wilderness and lay out a New Delhi, Canberra or Brasilia, but when you operate in an overbuilt metropolis you have to hack your way with a meat cleaver,' Moses declared. The modern automotive city was under construction. Hearings on Moses's Lower Manhattan Expressway and the rebuilding of the West Side Highway incited opposition and inspired him to declare the political credo of the highway age – 'Nothing I have ever done has been tinged with legality' – and its supplement – 'If the end doesn't justify the means, what does?' His notorious Cross Bronx Expressway, which smashed through 113 streets and 159 buildings, taking the homes of 5,000 people, was the means.

The ballyhoo for 'modern expressways right through and not merely around and by-passing cities [and] offstreet parking facilities of all kinds' traveled through the nation. Toll roads had carved through the country in Illinois, New Jersey, and Virginia. They soon spliced Oklahoma, Colorado, Texas, and Kentucky. In 1953, Philadelphia, Detroit, and Pittsburgh built their first freeways direct to the suburbs from downtown. Mimicking Moses elsewhere, the Baltimores, new Orleanses, Bostons, and Philadelphias of America would pluck the meat from the federal bone to aid highways and recast neighborhoods. Reaching their peak in the mid-1950s with 12,000 miles executed or en route, the new local roads presaged the interstate.

For cities the combination of building highways and taking homes was a disaster; for if urban renewal sounded fine in theory, it was mayhem in practice.

The Edens Expressway, Illinois, in the 1950s.

'Negro removal' was the epithet of opponents. Beset by road building, plus the continuing arrival of the rural poor from the South and from Caribbean nations and the exodus of the rich, cities flared into that expletive 'inner cities.' Costing more than $10 billion, the urban renewal program would level 300,000 more homes than it raised in the next quarter century. Combined with the magnet of single-family housing policies – FHA and VA postwar programs that excluded urban and minority populations and income tax deductions for property taxes and mortgage interest – the 1949 act had monumental consequences. The outward drift seemed like an act of nature. Its hurricane force would sweep through urban centers and blow the brick house down.

THE SPANNING OF AMERICA

The President's Advisory Committee on a National Highway Program had an even broader goal: span the nation with concrete. And, on 29 June, 1956, the year of

Dwight D. Eisenhower's re-election, the hero president signed the greatest peacetime public works project in the history of the world. Or so Eisenhower called it when he approved the legislation establishing the Interstate Highway System. Gas tax receipts, invisible in yearly budgets – not tolls – would funnel $50 billion annually into the Highway Trust Fund to build 41,000 miles of roads. The fund would become infamous, the interstate system prodigious. No river or ravine, no gorge or gully, no urban or suburban land would stand in the way of the onrushing auto age. With Boston's Route 128 under way as the nation's first loop road, other cities followed to plunge 5,000 miles of freeways through downtowns and countryside. Before this act, less than 500 miles of urban freeways had been built. After it, no city would be untouched. Urban America would empty out on the new arteries.

The 1956 act reflected not only the urge for asphalt, the low price of oil, and the push of the auto lobbies, but also sounded the era's Red alert. Defense needs had powered road building since World War I, when military leaders advocated 'national defense roads.' In World War II the armed forces had promoted roads to reach military reservations and defense industries. Now, in the heat of the Cold War, the interstate system answered the military imperative. It was officially known as the National System of Interstate and Defense Highways, and the documents stressed 'defense.' Advocates emphasized that the roads would ease evacuation in a nuclear attack. One pamphlet offered twin images boasting of the safety of this American autobahn in the missile age. One photo showed the close-packed coziness of a Swiss village; the other depicted a sweeping vista of concrete highway, vast and empty, waiting for evacuation. The image of the village bore the warning 'unsafe' in time of nuclear attack. The highway is labeled 'safe.' For the first time, in the guise of protecting the US from Communist bombs, the federal government was ordaining roads between cities. The standards of the trucking industry – wider and pricier – would limn the route, benefiting the more than 10 million trucks registered in the mid-1950s.

While such military follies of the age of the Atomic Café ruled the road from Washington, builders and lobbyists exulted over the implications of the interstate for peacetime mobility. 'Transportation no longer will be a problem,' one enthusiast declared. 'Pedestrian and vehicle traffic ways will be separated . . . walking will once more be safe and pleasant,' the author wrote. They might be separate, but they were scarcely equal. 'The Tiger Is Through the Gates,' warned Grady Clay, the *Landscape Architecture* editor in Louisville. 'Not long ago I saw a seven-mile interstate expressway placed on a city map at the request of an anonymous official at a nearby Army post – a man never identified in public debate, never quoted except

indirectly.' And this for 'a ten- to twenty-million-dollar expressway though a crowded city,' he told his colleagues in 1958.

The US city seemed to collaborate in its own demise. When mayors and urban politicians heard that half of the initial $27 billion highway funding would pass through their hands, they became cheerleaders. In 1957, the GM president, Charles E. Wilson, proclaimed, 'What's good for General Motors is good for the country, and vice versa.' This classic phrase of the era soured many, but its message ruled the day. Eisenhower himself began to worry about the interstate's urban repercussions, noting that 'it was very wasteful to have an average of just over one man per $3,000 car driving into the central area and taking all the space required to park the car.' His misgivings did not impede its progress, however. The notion of crossing the country without a stoplight was magnetic. The 90–10 per cent split in financing – 90 from Washington, 10 from the states – both guaranteed the interstate and also stimulated local highways. The spreading network helped buses and medium-weight trucks multiply. Truck trailers, virtually nonexistent before World War II, reached more than a million before 1960, taking over the long-haul work of the freight train. And, as the cattle and hogs of the Chicago stockyards rolled off in trucks, freight trains themselves declined. 'First the freight house was closed, then the stockloading pens were abandoned, and finally the railroad station was closed,' one commentator mourned. Simultaneously, throughout the 1950s, passenger cars deteriorated, service languished, and terminals grew dank and dirty, while mass transit as a whole declined.

A 1990 cover design for Jack Kerouac's classic novel of 1957.

IN, OF, AND ON THE ROAD

In the heyday of the highway, Americans didn't fret about the outcome. They saw the romance of the getaway, not the tedium of parking. Most famously, Jack Kerouac wrote about hitting the highway in *On the Road*, heading toward the Western sun or the Arizona dawn, hitching a ride at 70 miles an hour in a Cadillac through 'Frisco,' or poking 'five miles in local buses.' Moving briskly, hitching, or sallying forth in a 'toolshack on wheels' – whatever, wherever, crossing

and recrossing America – he waved the flag of freedom in his 1955 book. In *Lolita*, Vladimir Nabokov told the erotic tale of Humbert Humbert's life on the road, too, describing the highway culture through days and nights in the roadside establishments of the auto age. There were poignant pauses at 'the lowly Eat,' visits to a log cabin 'boldly simulating the past log cabin where Lincoln was born,' or 'a winery in California, with a church built in the shape of a wine barrel.' Seedy or colorful, these were the artifacts of a motorizing landscape.

Behind the wheel of the Chevy, Ford, or Plymouth, the ordinary father who 'knew best' was using his knowledge to help Mom pile the family goods into the car and head out to the American dream home. Out along the new toll roads and turnpikes, Dad would commute by car from work. At home Mom was busy behind the wheel as well, foraging for food, chauffeuring junior, shopping daily at the supermarket, or visiting the Miracle Miles of shops that rose in sync with the vehicle miles on her odometer. Why go downtown anyhow when suburban services were a spin away, entertainment was on the TV screen, and serenity was in the green grass all around? 'Station Wagons...Ho!' columnist Erma Bombeck would later call them as Americans rolled off the exit ramps to the new suburban roads.

William Manchester used the title *The Glory and the Dream* to define the postwar exodus to the 40 million homes serviced by these multiplying supermarkets, drive-in eateries, drive-in motels – drive-in everything. Drive-in movies alone tallied 1,700 by 1950. In 1952, four years after the McDonald brothers automated their restaurant, the company recorded its first million hamburgers sold and the golden arch was born. That same year, Holiday Inn welcomed its first guests. The once-racy motel now attracted the same family customers who stopped at a Kentucky Fried Chicken or parked their cars in the wraparound lots at Sears and J. C. Penney. Bobby-soxers headed to the drive-in bowling alleys or fast-food franchises beneath the glass peaks and massive, curling steel signs. Churchgoers could even motor to Rev. Robert Schuller's drive-in church in Garden Grove, California, a 'shopping center for Jesus Christ,' opened in 1954. The auto-based suburban shopping spree swept the country. In the twenty years following 1950, the number of shopping centers grew from a hundred to some 3,000. The architecture and engineering of the motor vehicle multiplied from the four-lane roads to the eight-lane highways, cloverleaf interchanges, and toll booths on the ever smoother, straighter highway. These arrow-straight roads would send motorists to 'See America First' directly, not on scenic roads but point to point from Cape Cod to the Grand Canyon. Neither topography nor urban heritage would interfere. The roads kept city dwellers from their waterways as well. They made urban habitats less scenic by cutting communities off from the Charles, the Hudson, the Potomac, and countless other rivers.

THE GOLDEN DREAM BOAT

The children born to the baby boomers of the 'Fertility Valley' '50s would enter a golden age of consumerism which took as its axiom that 'it was human nature for all of us to want good highways,' as California Governor Earl Warren declared. And, as the postwar automobile regained its place at the head of the capitalist dream, each one of the babies would grow up to own a motor vehicle. 'U Auto BUY Now' was the creed. Incomes rose with the speed of the lengthening chassis.

The late 1950s were the time of tail fins, of fanged grilles, and of pastel paint jobs, as Americans turned in their old cars for the latest showroom models and powerhouse engines. The GM Cadillac introduced in 1948 was inspired by the Lockheed P-38, emulating the airplane by supplanting the rounded streamlined style with the tail fin mode. Harley Earl, still at the company's design helm, said that he shaped the post-war automobile for 'aerodynamic styling,' incorporating passions for motion and the spread-out shape of widening ranch houses. For 32 years GM's 'Cellini of Chrome' masterminded the design of 50 million vehicles, inspiring Ford and Chrysler as well to put an extravagant face on the country's most visible artifact. With 46 models, 32 engines, 20 transmissions, 21 colors, not to mention 9 two-tone varieties and more than 400 accessories and options, one Yale physicist estimated that 'the number of distinct cars that a Chevrolet customer could order exceeded the number of atoms in the universe!' The gadgets multiplied as well. Dials, switches, wraparound windshields, fake gun ports, tail-lights shafted like the rockets of a plane created the road warrior look of the embryonic space age in automobiles. One commentator wrote, 'Motorists were never quite sure whether they were seated in an automobile, a land-based dreamboat or an earthbound aircraft.'

Status-seeking Americans took to their rollicking, tricked-out bombers depicted in the movie *American Graffiti*. They cruised their chrome-encrusted, late-model muscle cars down Main Street. Earl's phrase 'dynamic obsolescence' would characterize this conspicuous consumption. Their increases in mileage increased fatalities, too. But that didn't dissuade contemporary Americans. From the hot rod hit at the decade's beginning, to the three-miles-a-gallon Cadillac or Thunderbird at its end, the driver's power, social standing, and spirit of adventure resided in the car. 'Drive it like you hate it . . . it's cheaper than psychiatry,' went a television commercial.

THE MAIMING OF AMERICA

The view through the rear window past the fins revealed something equally obstreperous, prompting architect Victor Gruen to denounce the automobile's environment. 'We pass through the avenues of horror, stretching for endless miles through the suburban areas, flanked by the greatest collection of vulgarity – billboards, motels, gas stations, shanties, car lots, miscellaneous industrial equipment, hot dog stands, wayside stores – ever collected by mankind,' he wrote. Gruen's answer was the shopping centre. It would 'counteract the phenomenon of alienation, isolation and loneliness,' he wrote. Ironically, his solution would become known for increasing that withdrawal.

The architect's Northland Center, built in Detroit in 1954, was an early mall. It was the first mall with an assemblage of open-air stores and walkway for shoppers. His Southdale Center near Minneapolis, which opened in 1956, proclaimed the covered, climate-controlled space that would become the automobile age's most celebrated architecture. Both were wrapped by parking lots that covered ever wider acreage. Gruen's later notions for whole cities hooded over with futuristic forms made him the king of planners in the auto-based environment of his day.

Earlier, Northgate in Seattle had established the open pedestrian shopping mall, while Shoppers World in Framingham, a half hour out of Boston, took its place as the first closed mall in 1951. Grand Rapids planner Kenneth C. Welch designed the latter as a space-age icon of architecture sheltering an

arrangement of shops so alluring, so commodious, so accessible by automobile, and – with 4,000 spaces – so parkable that his shopping 'world' would be what developers would later call a 'destination.' A highway look-alike, the mall's ramps and elevated tiers, 100 feet wide and 675 feet long, overlooked a sunken mall beneath an all-weather dome. So walkable was it in the architect's eyes that he called it 'a double-decked mainstreet.'

Arthur and Sidney Shurcliffe, landscape architects with a historic consciousness, also fancied that they were pulling a page from the past by merging the up-to-date and the antique on the mall's grounds. They spoke of re-creating the essence of the New England town common, garnishing the mall with tidy bluegrass, coiling paths, and spruce and dogwood trees. Shurcliffe took special pride in the parking lot designed by town planners Adams, Howard and Greeley, with its looping thoroughfares to make for handy parking and its fast 'ring roads' separating walkers and speeders.

But Gruen, molder of the world of concrete, had even grander visions. He would build total cities for the suburbs, with the artery as conduit and downtown as a complete, enclosed environment. 'It will be . . . possible for the young matron to assemble her spring wardrobe and arrange for her daughter's tonsillectomy without a change of parking place,' said one Westchester observer. Nothing was neglected in the pursuit of the quiet setting, the 'refined aesthetics' – nothing except the failure to mitigate the 50-acre blacktop surrounding it and the compound's role in drawing more traffic.

Together, the mall and the strip became the front guard of the automotive, suburban invasion. As 85 per cent of us housing went to bedroom dormitories and drivability became primary, Americans were yoked to their new marketplaces. No longer did commercial buildings line the boulevards with parking behind. Strip shopping backed off from the street to let the cars park on all sides, and the definition of the mall as an asphalt island spread. Supermarkets and gas stations, shopping centers and malls multiplied on a scale heretofore unknown.

ATTACKING THE ECOLOGY

As motorized America dictated this new geography and personal space, the automobile inspired the colossal environmental alteration of the new lawn culture. In the East the green front yard was paired with a backyard barbecue pit and deck. As this combination took hold, spreading over more soil, home owners turned the tap to water the power-mowered grass fed by DDT and other pesticides and herbicides. The garage was expanded and the roof of the house elongated to cover two cars plus dad's workshop. In the arid Western lands, a whole new set of environmental strains occurred as the region grabbed the waters of the Colorado and other rivers and piped them from afar to sate the thirst of new comers. The Western garden city became the enemy of the ecology of the desert landscape, a foe to the hill and valley topography chiseled into house lots. Mumford's 'town for the motor age' had become totally subservient to it. The injunction to 'come as you are in the family car' ultimately meant 300 million tons of exhaust in the 1950s, with excretions from lead and other pollutants.

Pollution had tweaked consciences throughout the early days of the automobile. As early as the 1940s, Southern Californians saw the smog. By noon the skies of Los Angeles began to look brown, unrelieved by the day's sea breezes. In the 1950s, one observer scribbled this graffiti: 'I shot an arrow into the air, and it stuck.'

Congestion came along with the dirty air. The Long Island Expressway had a traffic jam on its first day; Route 128, America's first looped parkway, would require expansion from four to eight lanes within ten years of its completion in 1949. Protesters suggested that it was not so good for the suburbs to be isolated and financially overextended. Others feared for the fate of the family farm as the lawn crop replaced the food crop on the perimeters of cities and suburbs. Already, the farm was staggered by bigness and consolidation, its fields bisected by highways, its owners reeling from the taxes required by the services for the newcomers' homes.

As the interstates swept around them, back roads and the small towns they served became backwaters. If the farmer's goods traveled further, so unfortunately must the farm family to make its rounds; if the farmer's doctor came quicker, the farmer's children got bused further away from the old one-room school. The romance of the open road, the quiet vistas of the country highway, the lyrical curve of the scenic byway began to change. So did the pragmatic and economic viability of the land's use for agriculture. 'We lost country life when we moved to tractors' was the way one farmer expressed the downside of the helpmate internal combustion machine.

'We lost city life when we moved to automobiles,' city dwellers might have chorused as manufacturers abandoned their aging urban plants and installed themselves on what were formerly the outskirts. With industry moving outward, low-skilled Mexican and African-American migrant workers could find only low-wage jobs and low-income housing in the cities. Restricted from the zoned and cordoned-off suburb by 'the Maginot Line of suburbia,' built to keep out 'undesirables,' poor and minority Americans were ghettoized. The city's vacant factories and scuttled sites, poised now beside the arteries, reflected the exodus from the Newarks, the Detroits, and the Bronxes. And the phrase 'white flight' joined the lexicon of urban necrology.

RING AROUND AMERICA

As the red, white, and blue shield of the interstate signs stamped the nation's highways, the ring road choked the heart of urban America. The freeway grid reorganized space in the name of time and safety. Benton MacKaye's vision of a ring – a road or greenbelt like a jade collar to adorn the city and keep cars out – reincarnated in Route 128 strangled the nation's cities. The concern with capacity, sight lines, grade, and continuous flow, all part of the engineers' 'high construction standards,' meant sweeping hardtop whose mission was speed and motion, not accommodating topography. The slow change of level, the long distances with unobstructed sight, the 'efficiency' of the engineer's design for speed – not the pleasure of the driver's trip or the neighbors' surroundings – mattered. Road builders fantasized savings in gas, savings in lives, savings in money. With a swipe of the pen, they inked out urban 'obstructions.' And the cloverleaf culture germinated.

The Robert Moseses of other cities had clear sailing. Public land was seen as empty and 'free.' The water's edge was cheap, and parks had no owners to do battle for them. Freeways would cleave waterfronts from cities with impunity. The Alaska Way in Seattle, the planned Embarcadero for San Francisco, New Orleans's Vieux Carré, or Hartford's riverfront looked doomed. Parkland, owned by the government, was nobody's land, 'a sitting duck,' as *Landscape Architecture* editor Grady Clay put it. 'Any attack on city park lands has the sanction of the American Association of State Highway Officials in its official bible,' he said in describing the new codes defining the nation. 'Location opportunities for arterial highways' was stamped on the landscape. 'And what do they consider a "location opportunity"?' the Louisville editor asked. 'The one and only park in the entire city.'

In 1946 only 70 cities had parking requirements in their zoning plans. A decade later, most had them plus wider roads; and one-third of America's cities were hard topped to house the car. No wonder the downtown property fell by one-quarter in the thirteen largest metropolises. Parking lots and roads made gap-toothed wastelands of historic neighborhoods. Downtown hotels were slowly edged out by motels and picture palaces by drive-in movies; historic neighborhoods succumbed to wind-whipped high-rises and cities became cadavers. Domino by domino, demolition took over the nation's cores. The urban carnage devoured America.

When downtown trembled, its institutions fell. Once retailers were no longer fed by food traffic, they moved out. Advertising dropped, and big city newspapers shuddered. Medical, social, and other services also abandoned downtown. The cure of urban renewal was worse than the disease of decline as city mayors struggled to clear and rebuild with big projects and vast parking linked to major arteries. In Pittsburgh it was David Lawrence and the Mellons and the 'Pittsburgh Renaissance' of a 'gateway center.' In New Haven it was Mayor Richard Lee, who took his success at the polls as a 'popular plebiscite' and proceeded to turn downtown into a 'Model City' by leveling the center and letting the Oak Street Connector wipe out an urban neighborhood. In San Francisco the impoverished Buena Vista community looked like fodder for a convention center. Urban, USA, seemed a graveyard of the auto age.

'This is a book for people who like cities,' sociologist William H. Whyte would write almost apologetically in 1957 in the introduction to *The Exploding Metropolis*, derived from a *Fortune* magazine report on urban America. 'Are Cities Un-American?' Whyte, an urban advocate, titled his introduction. He scored the extremes brought about by urban renewal's devastation of downtowns and by the deference to the automobile. 'They [Americans] dislike the city's variety and concentration, its tension, its hustle and bustle.' The retail core was eviscerated.

Could nothing stop the roadmongers' attack? Was there no Consciousness III on the horizon? No sense that the automobile was undermining America?

Some saw signs of opposition to its attack on the landscape. As the mechanical scythe of the highway maimed whatever it touched, sociologist Jean Gottmann coined the word 'megalopolis' to describe how the car had coagulated the Northeast into an amorphous blur. The open space marred by random development marked the demise of the bucolic landscape along with the city. 'Trees that President Roosevelt planted as a reforestation project have been removed for subdivision developments – yet they were 80 miles from New York City. Hay and trees can never pay as well per acre as motels, split-levels, or apartment houses.' Gottmann wrote.

Older suburbs suffered along with the countryside. Rather than build or retain the close, neighborly dwellings, the garden apartments, the two-, three-, four-, and multi-family dwellings, the rental units, the boarding-house spaces, the single-room occupancy buildings – the myriad hives called home – the single-family house was all. Atomized, unwalkable, unneighborly, such developments supported few stores or services. In the 1950s, courtyard architecture largely ended, dissolving shared space. Row houses and three-deckers tumbled, junked into weedy lots or high-rise wastelands by urban renewal. Main Street suffered the incursions of faceless, car-contourned, homogeneous design.

Traversing space now mattered more than creating place. Subsidized home owners had taken their subsidized cars from their subsidized homes on their subsidized roads to their malls. The middle-class home owners had fled the inner city. And, city space, public space had eroded in the flight to a rural dream. As John Kenneth Galbraith pointed out in *The Affluent Society*, the nation of consumers of private goods was not affluent in public ways. The publicly funded private car had established the auto age. As post-war Americans bought a million or more new houses a year and 2 million cars a year in the late '50s, their driving mileages soared. Few realized what they had incinerated on the altar of mobility. The automobile had become the master of their universe, and protest would come only slowly as the servants to speed and sprawl saw what it had wrought.

FROM *Asphalt Nation* (1997)

L.A. Freeway:
An Appreciative Essay

DAVID BRODSLY

The freeway system supplies Los Angeles with one of its principal metaphors. Employed to represent the totality of metropolitan Los Angeles, it is the city's great synecdoche, one of the few parts capable of standing for the whole. Freeway imagery – a graceful interchange or a bumper-to-bumper rush hour – is one of the area's principal leitmotivs. Its uses are manifold. Postcards flourish with shots of the downtown stack or a freeway set against a panoramic vista. A *National Geographic* article on the city is subtitled 'Babylon on the Freeway.'[1] As a movie or a television program opens, a shot of a freeway places the setting as precisely as any caption.

The leitmotiv is reinforced as the seemingly constant reliance on the freeway system impresses itself upon the memory of the millions who visit Los Angeles every year. Nervously clinging to the freeway for orientation, much as a visitor to Paris might rarely venture beyond walking range of the metro, the tourist or the passer-through returns home with an image of all of sprawling southern California melting into a freeway.

More often than not, the freeway as a symbol carries negative connotations. As a *New York Times* bureau chief has suggested, '"Freeway" has become an emotional word in recent years, like "hippie" or "mugger".'[2] Freeways may be associated with all the ills of a modern, and particularly automotive, metropolis: air and noise pollution, congestion, the destruction of neighborhoods, the specter of a

concrete blanket over the landscape. When country singer Jerry Jeff Walker sings of getting off the L.A. freeway, he longs to leave every perceived evil of city life behind.

By extension, the metaphor also serves for less tangible modern evils. As a product of some of the most powerful political organizations in both state and nation (particularly the California Division of Highways, the Federal Highway Administration, and various automotive and highway lobbies), the freeway can symbolize the evils of an omnipresent and insensitive bureaucracy. The testimony of a homeowner association representative seems typical, characterizing the Division of Highways as 'a colossus, a state agency which can ruthlessly roll over and through communities.'[3] Forced removals for right-of-way clearance and lightning changes in the physical landscape of local communities reveal the powerlessness of the individual. Dissenters feel like helpless victims to a conquering force of government and special interests. A frustrated resident of South Pasadena could only complain to the editor of the *Los Angeles Times* about the 'mutilation' threatened by 'the forced rape of this beautiful city by the freeway gang.'[4]

The use of the freeway as a symbol of bureaucracy is closely associated with its use as a symbol of an equally maleficent technology. The freeway serves as the latest incarnation of the machine in the pastoral garden.[5] Richard Lillard's warning is representative of

277

Left: The famed 'four-level' interchange near downtown Los Angeles, 1954.
Right: The Hollywood Freeway near downtown Los Angeles, 1953.

the genre: 'As 1970 draws near, and the Age of Super-highways is at hand, many Californians see as a new menace the white serpentine tentacles of concrete that wind around communities and smother the environ-ment. Eden has become the world's biggest concrete asphalt desert.'[6] Under the guise of the freeway, bureaucracy and technology combine to produce a modern Promethean metaphor. The concrete artifact becomes a focus for anger and frustration directed at pervasive yet intangible forces. A stanza from a folk song illustrates these sentiments:

> There's a cement octopus that sits in Sacramento, I
>   think,
> Gets red tape to eat, gasoline taxes to drink,
> And it grows by day, and it grows by night,
> And it rolls over everything in sight.
> Oh stand by me and protect that tree
> From the freeway misery.[7]

The predominance of serpentine imagery, augmented by related images such as octopus tentacles or aberra-tions of the natural world, suggests the freeway's power to represent the modern equivalent of primor-dial evil.

Just what such metaphorical references have to say about urban highways is less clear. The freeway can assume qualities in the abstract which are not necessarily associated with actual freeways in daily life. For example, studies have shown that people living near freeways like them more than people who live farther away.[8] Similarly, as late as 1973 almost 50 per cent of residents polled in southern California favored continued construction as freeways, while 38 per cent desired only limited cutbacks.[9] Since then public opinion has rapidly changed, and a poll taken only three years later found 80 per cent of its respon-dents agreeing to some extent that transit improvements were more important than new freeways.[10] But of one thing we can be certain: 80 per cent of those polled would not have preferred that existing freeways had not been built in the first place.

It is important, particularly in matters of public policy, not to confuse the different levels of the freeway's associations in people's minds. The freeway as part of a complex of social phenomena is often isolated, not for purposes of accuracy, but for purity of expression. When employed for rhetorical purposes such artistic liberties often obscure fundamental issues. Nevertheless, the symbolic uses to which the freeway is popularly put reflect real and legitimate concerns. The freeway's range as a negative symbol speaks poorly for the quality of life perceived by many in the automotive metropolis.

The American poet Hart Crane argued that literature should be able to absorb the products of the machine age 'as naturally and casually as trees, cattle, galleons, castles, and all other human associations of the past.' Yet in spite of a few noble beginnings, Los Angeles has yet to produce its own Hart Crane and the freeway has yet to find its poet. When such a poet emerges, the freeway will be seen as something more that a series of construction projects engineered by the Department of Public Works or a particular mode of transportation. The freeway will be more fully revealed as an expression of the total complex of signification that is our culture and will 'appear in its true subsidiary order in human life.'[11]

FROM *L.A. Freeway: An Appreciative Essay* (1981)

Pleasure and the Motorway

RICHARD J. WILLIAMS

On 2 November 1959, Britain's then Minister for Transport Ernest Marples officially opened Britain's first inter-urban motorway, a 72-mile stretch of the M1, linking St Albans with the West Midlands. Marples hailed the M1 as a great achievement, a turning point for British transport – but at the same time, he declared himself 'appalled' by the driving he had witnessed during the day, suggesting a slogan to encourage drivers to take care: 'If in doubt, don't.'[1] Driving behaviour had certainly been exuberant. The police estimated the *average* speed during the first few hours as 80 mph, well in excess of the capabilities of most cars of the time and, for that matter, of their drivers. And when drivers eventually stopped, they found that the hard shoulder made a fine impromptu picnic area, albeit a highly dangerous and illegal one.

Inadvertently, perhaps, Marples set the tone for the popular discourse around the British motorway. Admonition, repression and control are its watchwords, and pleasure rarely, if ever, figures. As the British motorway system was constructed, public enthusiasm was rarely shown for it. Even those magazines with a professional interest – *Car, Motor, Autocar* – wrote about the motorways in mostly negative terms, looking towards Germany with its unrestricted autobahns for a pleasurable driving experience, or to the US. Pleasure was not possible at home. The motorway was represented, and continues to be represented, as the traffic jam, the accident, the environmental disaster area – or simply as unbuilt, stalled by governmental parsimoniousness or tree-dwelling

A German autobahn in the 1930s.

protestors. The system was therefore caught between a libertarian ideal – freedom of movement – and a puritanical representation, and to this day virtually no pleasurable images of British motorways exist.

This paradox was explored by the architectural critic Reyner Banham and the circle around him in the late 1960s. Banham, possibly the only aeronautical engineer to also have been a Courtauld-trained art historian, was an unashamed enthusiast of American car culture. But car culture in its British form – compromised, ambivalent and paradoxical – was another matter. Take, for example, 'Disservice Areas', a 1968 piece on motorway service stations for the Left-leaning journal *New Society* to which Banham regularly contributed. The piece described a 'family investigation' into the quality of service areas at a moment when a rudimentary but recognizable motorway network had started to take shape. At that point, the M1 was complete as far as Leeds, and the M6 from Birmingham to Cheshire, and there were fragments of the M2, M4 and M5, clearly predicting the system's future shape. Banham, typically, visited all of it.

But the word was not good. After 700 miles, and visits to Aust, Charnock Richard, Farthing Corner, Forton, Frankley, Heston, Keele, Knutsford, Maidenhead, Strensham, Trowell and Woodall, Banham wrote that British motorway life was lacking: the service areas were tawdry and inconvenient, and the roads themselves seemed to have been built on the cheap. But it was only what could have been expected, given the 'incredible' way the system had been set up. 'Our motorways', he wrote,

The services at Charnock Richard on the M6, 1960s.

and their ancillaries are the product of the way we are now: a mixed economy; a primarily preventative body of planning law, the arable-land-is-sacred lobby, diversifying cinema companies, a belief that advertising is inherently offensive and a whole gamut of other Island Attitudes. We have got the motorways and service areas we asked for and they are very nearly what we deserve . . . We tried to get our motorways on the cheap – hence the two-lane carriageways in congested areas when four or even five lanes would have been better sense and safer. We kidded our residual puritan consciences with the myth that the function of motorways was to speed the flow of goods and boost exports – whereas they are, in Cedric Price's demythologising phrase, 'national drag strips', inadequate playways for *Minihomo Vivians Cortinensis* . . . And we also decided, for reasons which elude me, that motorway users must be some sort of social lepers whose hungers, thirsts, and overloaded bladders must be satisfied, as near as possible, right on the motorway itself for fear they might contaminate surrounding communities, or (oh horror!) lead to development pressures there.[2]

Banham's detailed objections concerned the lack of advertising on motorways – a lack which he regarded as 'inhumane' when it prevented knowledge of the operator of the next service area, or even of the exis-

The services at Forton on the M6, 1960s.

tence of a hotel bed just off the motorway – the 'inexplicable' separation of motorway life from ordinary life, so that service stations were inaccessible from the places in which they are situated; and the refusal (with the great exception of Forton, on the M6 near Lancaster) to build all but the most self-effacing ancillary buildings for fear of intruding into the 'sacred' English countryside. As he eloquently describes, the whole adds up to a paradox – a desire to have and not-to-have, to be free and yet have that freedom repressed, to travel and yet deny the essential nature of that travel.

It must be said that British motorway life has relaxed a little since Banham's time. Three rather than two carriageways are now the norm, limited roadside advertising is now possible, and lately the utilitarian service areas have developed a vaguely fantastic character. Granada's recent transformation into Moto gives the service area an agreeably southern European-retro flavour, its logo making ironic reference to the graphic style of Panini football cards, a national obsession in the 1970s.

But the rest of the experience remains much as Banham described, and his analysis – as the passage above shows – is still remarkably pertinent. However, his position, and that of sympathizers including the radical architectural practice Archigram, the architect Cedric Price and the planner Peter Hall, could not have been developed without knowledge of an alternative motorway culture, specifically that of America. Not only did the US begin building motorways long before Britain, but from the start they were conceived in pleasurable terms. The first true US motorway is generally said to have been the Long Island Motor Parkway just outside New York City, built in 1906–11; it was, as Peter Hall has written, 'deliberately landscaped to provide a recreational experience'.[3] This and other, later parkways around New York City were constructed with low bridges to exclude both commercial traffic and public transport, indicating

The Pennsylvania Turnpike.

of Four Ecologies.[4] In the chapter of the latter titled 'Autopia', Banham described the motorway in explicitly non-instrumental terms.[5] No longer was it a means to an end, a more or less tolerable way of getting from one place to another, but 'a single state of mind, a complete way of life, the fourth ecology of the Angeleno'. No doubt hoping to offend his middle-class English readers, he added that 'enlightened self-interest and public spirit' motivated lane discipline and that, as a result, commuting by freeway was a good deal less stressful than travelling by British Rail Southern Region.

The essay is full of quasi-anthropological observations of driving behaviour. In one memorable image, Banham writes of noticing, more than once, that a girl in the passenger seat of a car will adjust her hair as her car exits the motorway, in doing so unconsciously equating the exit ramp with the act of coming in from outdoors. The freeways are therefore public spaces, the exit ramps and secondary roads somehow interior or private. One does not simply use the freeway; one lives one's life on it.

Banham was not only an observer of this spectacle of pleasure, but a participant. Driving on the freeways was, he wrote in the *Listener* in 1968, 'almost unalloyed pleasure'. The intersection of the Santa Monica and San Diego freeways in particular was productive of an especially satisfying experience. Not only a convincing monument when seen from a single viewpoint, the rising, converging, separating and falling ramps – when taken at 60 mph – produced 'a spatial experience one does not normally associate

their principal role as places of leisure rather than work. Of course, later motorways, such as the first true interstate, the Pennsylvania Turnpike, did away with these restrictions, but the basic form of the American motorway has its origins in the desire to create a pleasurable kinetic experience as part of an essentially leisured situation. Significantly, the names for these forms – 'freeway', 'parkway' – have pleasurable rather than utilitarian connotations.

At the same time, Los Angeles began to develop more or less entirely motorized forms of urban association, which Banham celebrated in their mature form in a BBC film, 'Reyner Banham Loves Los Angeles', and his widely read book *Los Angeles: The Architecture* with monuments of engineering' – in fact 'the nearest thing to flight on four wheels I know'.[6]

Traditionally, Los Angeles is dangerous and aesthetically horrifying for Europeans, but in Banham's account it becomes almost utopian: a place in which desire may be freely realized, with the freeways an essential means of providing gratification. It is no accident in this connection that the Penguin edition of his LA book had David Hockney's *A Bigger Splash* on the cover, one of a series of paintings that the expatriate British artist made to illustrate the sexual freedom and hedonism then inconceivable at home. Hockney's images of naked men and swimming pools describe a relatively public and established Californian gay scene, a scene that in a wider sense was one of a range of consumer choices or lifestyles impossible – even illegal – outside LA. The city's freeways were, and are, an integral aspect of this sense of freedom, producing a landscape with more or less unlimited choices of recreation and consumption. Not only did they help to facilitate these pleasurable experiences; they were pleasurable in themselves. Whatever their environmental consequences – and whatever the actual discipline they exerted over their users in order to function – the freeways were first and foremost about fun. Drivers were 'neither retching with the smog nor stuck in a jam', wrote Banham; '. . . their white-wall tyres are singing over the diamond-cut anti-skid grooves in the concrete road surface, the selector levers of their automatic gearboxes are firmly in *Drive* and the radio is on.'[7]

Pleasure has always been a serious business, never more so than when Banham was thinking about LA. The philosopher Herbert Marcuse, then teaching at the University of California, San Diego, argued that the world would be a better place if Western societies removed their self-erected barriers against gratification. Sigmund Freud famously argued that the deferral of pleasure was essential for work to take place, that civilization was, in other words, the result of libidinal sacrifice. Marcuse turned this idea on its head in his provocative, and popular, work *Eros and Civilization: A Philosophical Inquiry into Freud*.[8] Freud's theory of pleasure, Marcuse argued, was a natural consequence of scarcity – or, to put it another way, when things are in short supply, fun is not a priority. But when scarcity no longer obtains, as for most inhabitants of late 1960s California, civilization really ought to loosen up. So from delaying gratification, one ought to be able to experience immediate, guilt-free satisfaction; from the restraint of pleasure, to have pleasure; from work, to play. Marcuse's thinking was important for the counter-cultural movements of the time, and it was widely accepted that Californian society had some genuinely 'liberated' aspects.

This was certainly the case for Banham and his circle. Los Angeles was not simply a fun place to visit, but in many ways a model of a liberated society. There were lessons for Britain. One celebrated response was the *New Society* essay 'Non-plan', which Banham wrote with Cedric Price, Peter Hall and the magazine's then editor, Paul Barker.[9] Arguing that the abolition of planning in Britain could not produce a worse result than that achieved by the existing system of repression and control, they envisaged a future society on the Southern California model: a motorized sprawl, but a democratic one, in which free movement, consumption and gratification were privileged over the protection of the past. The motorway was intrinsic, now become a way of life in true Californian terms.

I continue, however, with an earlier image of the motorway, from Hall's important and prescient

London 2000, an attempt by an unusually free-thinking planner to imagine the future form of the metropolis. For most of its 260 pages, it is a straightforward, realistic polemic in favour of considering London as a diverse, polycentric city-region of twelve million people stretching from Brighton to Cambridge, rather than as a handful of central-city monuments in need of preservation. Hall made forecasts based on then current trends and argued that the city-region should continue to grow in its current way, but with its size and dispersal recognized as facts rather than restricted by negative interventions such as the greenbelt. In the last part of the book, Hall included a short fictional account based on his predictions of what it would be like to inhabit the future city. His fictional family, the Dumills, happily commute vast distances and regard their fictional Kentish new town – 'Hamstreet', 60 miles from London – as, in effect, London: 'distance is no longer an object'. (A Channel tunnel, Hall implied, would also have brought with it the phenomenon of cross-Channel commuting.). The Dumills' commuting is facilitated by a new network of motorways. 'At 11.30', Hall wrote:

as the Dumills drive out of London by the New Kent Motorway, the expressways of London are a brilliant sight. When the first ones were built back in the sixties, the pessimists confidently predicted that they would wreck London. By 2000 most people admit that they gave it a new dimension, now trenching by the sides of railways, now flying over rooftops, now burrowing through the heart of reconstructed shopping and office centres . . .[10]

In these paragraphs, which conclude the book, Hall imagined the future in terms of pleasure rather than utility. The activities that generate travel are socializing with friends, strolling by the Thames in central London, eating in restaurants, visiting the theatre

In the 1950s the motorway offered a prospect of unrestricted freedom of movement.

and cinema; several of these things (such as dining out) would have constituted relatively luxurious experiences in 1969, and even the hour of travel – around midnight – could have appeared recklessly late for an ordinary family in 1969 (speaking against liberalization of pub opening hours in the 1970s, the former Prime Minister James Callaghan stated that no respectable person was still out by 10:00 p.m). Not only does Hall suggest new kinds of pleasures to be made available, but travel itself is envisaged in pleasurable terms – being on the motorway is not a means to an end, therefore, but another state of being embodying pleasurable visual and kinetic experience. Hall's motorway future is therefore essentially libertarian.

We are offered play, mobility and pleasure as the fundaments of a new urban Britain. Based around quasi-Marcusian principles of liberation, and informed by a deep sympathy for the built environment of the US, the motorway acts here as both a liberated mode of existence and an instrument in the process of liberation. As far as I can tell, this is more or less the last time in which British motorways were envisaged in these terms, although there are hints of it in the architectural criticism of Martin Pawley and, more nostalgically, Jonathan Glancey.[11] But these are isolated cases. And while Banham's and Hall's works on the subject are well known and have received much critical attention, at the time of their publication they did not represent a majority position, even among Left-leaning or progressive elements of the architectural profession. At the end of the 1960s, both the *Architectural Review* and *Architectural Design* published special issues on social issues, including transport, the former a series called 'Manplan'. The latter's special issue on transport, 'Mobility', contained a tribute to the Los Angeles freeway system by Warren Chalk of Archigram entitled 'Up the down ramp,' but the same issue of the magazine was framed by two profoundly negative images of motorized life: a highly compressed, cropped image of urban congestion in an unidentified American city and, on the back, a pile of crushed cars at the wreckers' yard. This was not, a caption indicated, a simple indictment of the car, but a questioning of its future role; however, the image, the black background and the letters 'RIP' suggested otherwise.[12] In this context, Chalk's piece looked curiously naïve or out of sympathy, more in tune perhaps with the earlier British enthusiasm for American pop culture. *AR*'s 'Manplan' series was less ambiguous still, articulating through photography and polemic the most apocalyptic scenario if current motor-traffic tends were to continue.[13] Both journals' use of photography resembles that found in Kevin Lynch's widely read book *The Image of the City*, which was full of grainy monotone pictures of inner-city neighbourhoods bisected by enormous motorways, overpowering traffic congestion and decay.

Certainly, there are cultural forms that have found in this relentlessly negative portrayal of the motorway what the philosopher Fredric Jameson termed a 'libidinal excitement' stemming precisely from the obliteration of the familiar or comforting – J. G. Ballard's novels, especially *Crash*, are a good example.[14] But the lack of a public language to account for the more ordinarily pleasurable aspects of the British motorway is a curious form of cultural repression, which – although relatively harmless – prevents us from fully understanding the motorway experience. It doesn't have to be like this, as the writings of Banham and his circle show. While writing this essay, I noticed a proliferation of amateur websites dedicated to motorways, which in one case rated the kinetic and spatial pleasures associated with the author's favourite parts of the M1 in a way that unconsciously recalled Banham's experience in LA. But as long as the language of enjoyment remains amateur or unofficial, the British motorway will remain a decidedly furtive pleasure.

Fade to Grey: Motorways and Monotony

MICHAEL BRACEWELL

I remember well that we played in Paris on 110 volts and all the tempos were out of tune. At 8.00 p.m. the big factories that plug into the network were making the voltage fluctuate. That's the reality. Peugeot were making our tempos change.
– Ralf Hutter of Kraftwerk, on the *Autobahn* tour of 1975

Back in 1974, when the German synthesizer group Kraftwerk released their first charting single, 'Autobahn', they not only achieved one of the signature performances in modern popular music but also updated the template for a particular sensibility. Fixated on modernity and the celebration of service technology, industry and functionalism, here was the doo-wop of the German Economic Miracle. It hymned a new landscape that was shaped by scientific efficiency but responded to the traditions of romanticism.

With its catchy robotic refrain, 'wir fahr'n fahr'n fahr'n auf der autobahn' (compared by nearly everyone to the 'fun fun fun' hook line of the Beach Boys, who shared Kraftwerk's genius for refining seemingly simple pop songs out of complex layerings of harmony) 'Autobahn', at the time, was a piece of music that was difficult to place. Was it a song, a soundtrack or both? The album version ran for a little over 22 minutes, with the bulk of the central section taken up by the sweeping of ambient traffic sounds from speaker to speaker. A few critics likened it to the novelty single by Hot Butter, 'Popcorn', simply

because of the foregrounded electronics. Others, with more acuity, described the new Kraftwerk sound as 'industrielle Volksmusik' – industrial folk music.

The French rock critic Pascal Bussy managed to prise something approaching a statement out of the famously elusive Ralf Hutter (who, along with Florian Scheider-Esleben, was the founder of Kraftwerk) with regard to his own understanding of the song: 'You can listen to "Autobahn",' said Hutter, 'and then go and drive on the motorway. Then you will discover that your car is a musical instrument. In these sorts of ideas, there are plenty of things that can be funny; it's a whole philosophy of life which comes from electronics.'

Hutter's phrase 'a whole philosophy of life' is central to the broader ramifications of 'Autobahn' as a piece of music. The idea of the car as a musical instrument relates straight back to the 'mechanical symphonies' of Italian and German Futurism. Even more important was the strand in Kraftwerk's project which espoused a nostalgia for archaic visions of the future. Rather than Futurism's fetishizing of the industrial, Kraftwerk were following a romantic road, where even the very latest developments in technology – as their stage set for the 'ComputerWorld' tour in 1981 would prove – had to be cased and presented in a style which referred to the past, to pretty much any period from 1920 to about 1955.

Rather than letting it all hang out, Kraftwerk's sound and image were to do with bringing it all back in – paring down music to bleeps and squeaks, and reverting the group's image to neat, bourgeois conservatism. With haircuts reminiscent of those favoured by bank clerks in the 1930s, and suits cut in a retro, but by no means flamboyant, style (this at a time when American and German rock style was defined by faded denim, dope and long hair – think Gregg Allman during his 'Laid Back' album period), Kraftwerk's project came across as deeply confrontational.

Lester Bangs of *Creem* magazine described Kraftwerk's intervention as 'not so much a record as an indictment'. It was also tempting to apply the French novelist Gustave Flaubert's maxim about ultra-dandyism and the reactionary mask worn by true radicals and revolutionaries: 'You must appear regular and natural in your habits like a bourgeois, in order to be violent and orginal in your work.' With this in mind, 'Autobahn' played a political card as well: here was a group whose entire premise seemed to play with cultural stereotypes – just avoiding a poised relationship with Futurism's engagement with nationalism, yet playing with the truisms of German efficiency.

In this context, what made Kraftwerk's ultra-minimalistic, robo-pop anthem in praise of driving along the motorway so extraordinary was its neat reversal of all of the prevailing trends in both pop and avant-garde rock at the time. Popular music was not supposed to address boring subjects, least of all boring subjects connected to the industrial retail complex of capitalist society. And herein lay Kraftwerk's conceptual genius, as well as the broader scheme of their particular aesthetic. The group was attempting to articulate the experience of modernity through music; their subjects – showroom dummies, motorways, radioactivity and even their very name, which meant 'Power Station' – created a mythologized landscape which was, in fact, as romantic as anything ever dreamt up by Goethe or Schiller.

This theme – the romantic experience of modernity as a kind of landscape poetry – would extend throughout the 1970s and '80s, discovering several different media for its simultaneous expression, not least the language (poeticized scientific rhetoric, positing the critic as a kind of heroic *über*-technician) and exquisitely aesthetic publishing (imprints such as 'semiotext(e)' and MIT's 'Zone' series) of critical theory itself. Other pop travellers on the Kraftwerk route – Black Box Recorder's 'Motorways of England', for instance, or Skanfrom's 'electronique supermarket' – would maintain the 'nowhere zones' of service-industry landscapes as a venue for high romanticism.

The city and its hinterlands, the service areas and retail culture, could be read as texts and explored as a landscape, for here was a new search for the Sublime, as devout as those carried out by Pantheists in Bavaria or hippies on the Magic Bus. The functional infrastructure would also provide the inspiration, and the creative chemistry, for artists working in a variety of cultural practices, through film and fine art to sociological interventions. The common denominator of these activities could be summed up in a paradox: a visceral engagement with surface – the aesthetics and conundrums of meaning within the purely functional. In 1978, Philip Oakey, the singer with the Human League, from Sheffield – at that time an 'industrial

KRAFTWERK AUTOBAHN

Emil Schult, original artwork for the cover of the Kraftwerk *Autobahn* LP, 1974, oil on canvas-board.

music' group using primitive synthesizers – would sum up this sensibility as 'the alienated synthesist' period.

But this is not to credit Kraftwerk alone with summing up in the image of the autobahn some pivotal moment in contemporary culture. If anyone did this, it was Marshall McLuhan, interviewed by Willem L. Oltmans in 1972, who first looked beyond the activity of driving and the technology of the car to what he called 'the ground' of any cultural 'figure'. Read now, McLuhan's analysis seems to fit the bill for all those modern projects which engage with the additional idea of a romantic relationship with the

landscape of service, functionalism and 'nowhere-space' hinterland. With this in mind, it is worth citing McLuhan at length:

['On ground'] is a term from Gestalt psychology. Look at the ground around the figure of the automobile or the ground around any technology, which necessarily has a large ground of services and disservices associated with it. With a motor car, most people are interested in changing designs or patterns of the car. They pay only incidental attentions to the huge service environment of roads, oil companies, filling stations and other allied services of manufacturing that are the ground of the car. It never occurred to them that this figure of the car might generate a huge ground of new services far bigger than the figure was ever thought to be. In other words, the car created a totally new environment of services . . .

By not looking at the ground around the automobile you miss the message of the car. For it is the ground of any technology that is the medium that changes everybody, and it is the medium that is the message of the technology, not the figure.

There has been a growing interest in documenting – as a sub-strand of artistic practice – what McLuhan called 'the ground' of the technology around the car. In many ways, Kraftwerk's 'Autobahn' was a precursor of these activities, deriving as it did from Hutter and Schneider driving around Düsseldorf in Hutter's Volkswagen, recording the sounds of passing traffic and the engine with a microphone hanging out of the passenger window. (Later, to 'promote' the single, they offered to drive journalists around the industrial areas of the city – like some sort of ready-made performance piece, standing in for a pop video – in just the same way that they would take journalists on a train journey to promote their 'TransEurope Express'. Here was yet another reversal of the rock and roll dynamic – no hedonistic launch party, just a drive around the boring parts of town.)

As Kraftwerk invited the listener and viewer to explore a romantic landscape of service and industry, so contemporary artists (Julian Opie's 'Imagine You Are Driving' series, for example, or Ian Davenport's 'poured paintings'), historians (David Lawrence) and curators (Jeremy Millar's 'Airport' exhibition) have continued the journey on their own slightly different terms, yet pursuing a practice that works with conceits of monotony, repetition and seemingly flat emotionlessness.

Davenport or Opie, for example, both seem to seal the art-making process within itself, creating an aesthetically perfect armour of absolute flatness around the content or 'meaning' of their painting, thus rendering them in keeping with Kraftwerk's presentation of a total world, described and defined solely on its own terms. (Hence the near-Masonic secrecy around Ralf and Florian's studio, Kling Klang, in Düsseldorf – the 'Mother Kraftwerk' of *die mensch maschine*. Florian has described himself as the Kling to Ralf's Klang.) In Martin Parr's on-going 'Boring Postcards' project, however, or David Lawrence's meticulously researched 'glove compartment history of the motorway service area', a transaction takes place between irony and nostalgia, domesticating the service landscape of functionalism by focusing on the ordinariness of daily life – in Kraftwerk's terms, admitting a human presence to disturb the efficiency of the machine. (The painter Ian Davenport also likes to see the 'human' errors – however slight a misalignment of paint – within his paintings as seeming in some way like machine errors which merely hint at human presence.)

Both Parr's 'Boring Postcards' and Lawrence's 'glove compartment history' examine McLuhan's 'ground' of the motorcar, but in a way that relates to the time-travel element in Kraftwerk's nostalgia for an archaic vision of the future. But where Kraftwerk's vision is pristine and aesthetically pitched (classically dandified, in fact), so the sheer lumpen dullness of Parr's found postcards of motorways and service stations (to say nothing of car-parks, civic centres or lobbies) triggers a comedy of recognition while also offering a debunked history of the future. They also suggest the melancholy of nostalgia – an earlier world, before the complexities of post-modern culture.

Here then, are opposed views of the same territory, one fixating on a Warholian notion of becoming a machine and achieving a kind of dehumanized immunity from stress through monotony and repetition, the other more concerned with a version of Camp – the tragically ludicrous and the ludicrously tragic, as the film director John Waters once defined the term. In Parr's postcards and Lawrence's sourced images, architectural brutalism becomes synonomous with human boredom – but not in the pro-active Warholian sense of boredom as a means of transcendence.

The point of collision between these two opposed views (the human and the robotic) of McLuhan's 'ground' of the automobile – what he describes as 'the huge service environment' – is well illustrated by Lawrence in his description of the Washington-Birtley motorway Taverna, on the A1(M) a few miles south of Newcastle:

Referred to as the country's 'first robot transport cafe' . . . all food was part cooked and then placed in vending machines. Food would be accompanied by a coloured plastic token which determined the cooking time in the microwave oven. In forty seconds a fully heated meal was ready . . . Trained in deportment, manicure and even how to deliver a baby, and wearing tailor-made uniforms, the ladies [uniformed hostesses] assisted motorists using some of the first microwaves available to the public anywhere in Britain. By all accounts the machines were temperamental. Reheated fried eggs were constantly exploding, peas jumping around on the plate, and sometimes the machines went completely wrong, reducing meals to a blackened crisp.

Here is *die mensch maschine* by way of a cartoon by Giles.

The cover of Kraftwerk's 'Autobahn' album, on the other hand, is a painting by their collaborator and associate Emil Schult, which, to quote Pascal Bussy, 'juxtaposes images of the countryside . . . against the most potent symbol of the industrial era – the motor car on the motorway'. Bussy also noted the imagery of 'the worldwide economic success of post-war Germany', symbolized by a Mercedes and 'an idealised, dream-like quality as there are no other cars to be seen, as if depicting an ideal world where there is little or no traffic and no pollution'.

Here was a prophetic notion. Kraftwerk's 'Autobahn' has proved to follow the classic romantic trajectory of passing through the stylish philosophies of High Dandyism to a version of moral or ethical conscience (from self-love to world love): Ralf and Florian's celebration of Radio-Activity and the Autobahn has been replaced by their promotion of European Green Party causes . . . and a dedication to bicycling.

Roundabouts
and Yellow Lines

MARC AUGÉ

THE REVENGE OF THE LOCAL

For the British, the roundabout is an old institution, almost historic. It is a national tradition, like driving on the left. But – unlike driving on the left - it is conquering the world, most particularly France. In France for the last ten years we have realized that the best way to prevent cars from going too fast is to stop them, and that the best way to stop them is to make them turn in an anticlockwise circle. Or, more exactly, to invite them to join the circle, only after the others have passed – well, running to its full term, a true cultural revolution, to respect priority to the left.

Cultural revolution indeed, in a country where traffic priority has always been to the right, unless a mandatory sign, usually one that's familiar to us all, indicates that one is on a main road (and does not have to worry about the right or the left) while informing others that they are on a secondary road (and *do* have to take notice of the right and left simultaneously). The French crossroads were the metaphor of a centralized and hierarchic country (all the main roads coming from the capital being, by definition, priority). This rigid rule grates against the right of free judgement from which the French driver should, in principle, benefit. He still enjoys this freedom in Paris, on squares such as L'Etoile or La Bastille. Here the roundabouts have no signs, and only the driver's skill and vigilance allow him to establish and impose his priority – plunging as close as possible towards the outside of the roundabout's circumference to keep his

pursuers and adversaries to his left. The delights of 'the regatta' that are part of the charm of driving in France and in Paris – although surprising to the foreigners eyes.

In such a context, we can conceive that the sudden appearance of roundabouts has been a shock. Indeed it was, literally, a few years ago when incredulous drivers who refused to acknowledge roundabouts, or who couldn't believe their eyes, planted their vehicles in the central floral arrangement, or crashed them against statues or other artistic constructions supposedly decorating them. The roundabout created a semantic shock in driving manuals and official instructions, which spoke in terms of 'gyratory crossroads' to avoid any Anglicism and to protect the French language. This notion seems to consider as solved the famous problem of 'squaring the circle'.

Finally, the roundabout created a psychological shock to all those, of whom I am one, who came to see it as a sign of creeping modernism and therefore proof that Great Britain was once again ahead of the game.

Today we know that communication and traffic are moving faster, we move quicker from one place to another. Information moves at the speed of light. In the world of motoring we're not there yet, although on the motorways in Europe we can drive quickly from one point to another. Motorway interchanges prevent any risk of coming together, and cars are circulating in the large European arterial roads like blood in a healthy body, without threat of cardiac arrest. The roundabout corresponds to the necessity of organising the circulation, and keeping it flowing, but at a lower level – to the driver who comes off a motorway and, impelled by his accumulated momentum, thinks he is going to reach the next town at the same speed. The roundabout imposes a check, by giving priority to the quieter stream of local traffic. It is the revenge of the local on the global.

Today in Europe each small town, each hamlet, can make drivers travel in circles, thereby obliging them to glance at the signs which indicate and promote local places of interest. The roundabout imposes the same democracy of the road on the tractor coming from a country lane as it does on the limousine exiting the motorway.

In these day of 'The Global Village', roundabouts remind us of the reality of the traditional village, and the necessity to think of global and local systems together. The roundabout's too-fast, repetitive merry-go-round momentum can tire drivers out. But it can also suggest the idea of pulling over and stopping by the side of the road.

YELLOW LINES

The yellow line guides us and orientates us, but leaves a certain number of decisions to our judgment. In this way it is sometimes formidably ambivalent. In France it guides us in two ways. It defines the route that we follow, along its straight lines and curves, to such an extent that at night drivers trust its middle line, brightened up by their headlights, more than the borders of the road which are not always marked by another yellow line. Thus getting closer to the dangerous verges of the road. At the same time, the yellow line marks the border with the 'other side', the side you can only reach by taking illicit risks. Symmetrical and inverse to the

one reserved for us. The side run by drivers who we expect to follow the same discipline as we do, and also respect the yellow line.

But there is yellow line and yellow line. Some are double, the solid line being paired on our side by a broken line, subtly imparting its message by informing us that we can overtake the vehicle that is slowing us down, by crossing the line if we judge that we have the time to do so. Sometimes extending too far towards the top of the hill, or at the beginning of a hairpin bend, this 'dotted tolerance' may go too far and present risks to the ones who blindly trust it. Although the yellow line may seem simple, it is as perverse as the cable the tightrope walker traverses. It indicates the way to follow – alongside all the dangers. But unlike the tightrope which is for solitary exploits, the yellow line is eminently social: it always presupposes, warns and organizes priorities, forbidding overtaking, imposing one way. It is the visible *alter ego* of our social existence, the representation in colour, on tarmac, of an ethic rule that we should be able to memorize without the help of yellow lines – if we were drivers who were pure in spirit. We know this is not the case and the yellow line is a timely reminder that we are not alone on this earth, that social life is a matter of compromise and that the law resulting from it affects everybody. In this respect the yellow line is the symbol of the necessities and constraints of any social life. It is therefore not surprising that the yellow line bears a metaphoric value in everyday or political language. In France today it is relatively frequent (although this metaphorical usage is only recent) for an undisciplined student, an aggressive sportsman or shameless politician to be told that they have 'gone over the yellow line'. With the help of the colour this phrase, along with sport phrases such as 'yellow card' and 'red card', indicates an ultimate warning.

From another point of view, we will distinguish the subtle and problematic yellow lines which at the same time indicate and put into order the secondary itineraries – the long and rather silly lines, without any particular message, that cut part of the motorways into parallel lanes. The yellow line on the small roads is a little like a cartoon caption (the drawing would be the road itself and its route): it tells us to keep to the right, that the bend is too close to try to overtake, that this time we can go for it, only if we get back into our lane on time – where the broken line stops – that if we have time we can turn right at the next crossroads, turn off to visit the village whose church bell-tower can be seen through the trees. It is our own journey that it is commenting upon, in a way, and we may be surprised to find that we are excusing ourselves (to it?) if we happen to clip it when we get back in lane a little late. It holds our hand (or rather our steering wheel), and is itself rather lenient as long as its designated enforcers (motor-cyclists or other officers of the law) do not decide to take issue with our interpretations and to take note of all our omissions or errors.

On the motorway, the lanes are clearly marked: they deviate little, they are writ large. The yellow line is just a marker for driving in the night or a guide towards the exit. It does not talk like the countryside yellow line; it does not tell us about the hill ahead and the bend coming up. It never make any mistakes, but it has nothing to say. And we too, silent, without regard for the impassive profiles of the drivers who pass us in the opposite lane, on the other side of the yellow line, we drive from one town to another without thinking about anything.

FROM *City A-Z* edited by Steve Pile and Nigel Thrift (2000)

Traffic

IAN PARKER

When London motorists see the state of the traffic in old black-and-white photographs of Holloway Road or High Holborn – a cart, a dog, two or three motor cars sailing through empty space like boats on the Thames – they catch a glimpse of something deep inside them: an image of their own delusion, a map of their madness. For this is the traffic we imagine we deserve. This is the traffic that we would have got this morning, when we headed off so cheerfully for Camden Town – if only things had not turned out so horribly, as they always do. Despite being the rule, bad traffic is somehow also the perpetual exception, like bad weather in winter. If only it hadn't rained, we wouldn't have got wet. If only we had set out eighty years ago, we would have been there by now.

In Cairo or Bangkok, we would live without hope. In central London – where traffic moves at an average of about ten miles per hour throughout the day, and in which a typical vehicle spends about a third of its time stationary – there is just enough slack to let us dream. There is a memory, or a false memory, of the Embankment on an autumn evening, when nothing stood in our way, or a Sunday in the City. We have driven over Tower Bridge at three in the morning. And our hopes for a rush-hour clear run – for a turn-of-the-century Pall Mall – are never quite dashed. And this guarantees constant, gnawing disappointment. Londoners arrive at each other's homes shaking their heads, surprised and aggrieved. Their cars promised them power, autonomy and control, and London traffic takes all these away – which is why people

suddenly accelerate to 60 miles per hour, if they can, even on the approach to a red light at Knightsbridge.

London is not like other cities. American cities have grids and freeways. European cities have congested centres, but their centres are smaller than London's. And in the cities of the developing world, there may be traffic turmoil, but this will not be inner turmoil. The rules are more lax. People will be driving as it makes sense to them, sounding their horns. They will be in general agreement about fairly basic driving etiquette. In London, drivers are in continuous, stressful argument with a well-mannered alter ego. There is a decent, safe, thing to do – but then there will be a BMW that needs immediate chastizing; or say, an amber light that will get you on to a green round the corner, and give you a chance of a clear run on to Vauxhall Bridge. In an interview shortly before his arrest in London last October [1998], General Augusto Pinochet praised Britain for its impeccable driving habits; his countrymen were 'rude' in comparison. But he had perhaps not experienced the anguish of driving virtue unrewarded, nor seen what happens when two conflicting London motoring philosophies decide to settle the point with baseball bats.

London's congestion and fury has a possible compensation – and this is the chance to swagger, to take credit for technique and local expertise. Because the roads are complicated and full, because 140,000 people come into the centre of London by car every morning, because accident rates are way above the national average, a journey well executed can be paraded as a kind of athletic success. London drivers prize exquisite rat-runs behind Harrods, as they do a magical Covent Garden parking space, or a neat, anticipatory lane change in the Wandsworth one-way system. If you are driving into the West End on the Westway, there comes a point where you must decide whether to stay with the flyover, or swoop down through Paddington. If you leave the road unnecessarily, you have tossed away a rare minute or two of romantic, Americanized motoring. But if you stay and hit a jam, you will be unhappy, because escape is impossible. (The police who run the traffic lights on Marylebone Road use this stretch to 'store' traffic safely when things turn ugly further on, as they also store traffic on the southbound carriageway of Park Lane. These are places where a queue will not cause other queues.) Driving in at speed, you must choose Paddington or not-Paddington. But you cannot see if there is a queue ahead until you are almost upon the slip road. You have a second, or maybe less, to react; and – if things go well – the rest of the day to feel shamefully victorious.

British culture has been slow to mythologize London traffic, to make a fuss of it in fiction. French films have lingered over congestion (*Traffic, Week-end*), and we are accustomed to New York traffic filmed from every angle – speeded up, and slowed down and forming hypnotic patterns at night, red lights ebbing and flowing like the display on a graphic equalizer. But London hides its traffic away, partly because London is a less giving place in which to shoot films (you have to steal locations; you have to organize illegal rolling roadblocks, three cars abreast with hazards lights flashing); but partly, perhaps, because London is in a kind of denial, and hopes to keep alive the fantasy that the Golden Age of London motoring is still within reach, and that our next journey will rescue us from disappointment.

Of course, like all Golden Ages, this motoring Golden Age – Mr Toad dashing up Whitehall – is a half-truth wrapped in disenchantment. While British car ownership has risen from 8,000 in 1903 to one million in 1930 and over twenty million today, average traffic speeds in the centre of London have barely changed in a hundred years, and have only dropped by about two miles per hour since the late 1960s. Long before 'jams' entered the English language from America, London was already quite familiar with 'blocks'. Gustave Doré's print *Ludgate Hill – A Block in the Street* (1872), is probably the first visual representation of London gridlock: a hearse, barrows and sheep in packed, motionless frustration below St Paul's Cathedral. In Evelyn Waugh's *Scoop* (1938), Julia Stitch's miniature black car becomes embedded in a block between Hyde Park Corner and Piccadilly Circus ('...the line of traffic was continuous and motionless, still as a photograph...'). And there are photographs that dare to argue with the photographs we remember. A set commissioned by London Transport in 1923 does include the kind of images that feed our fantasies: a single car on Fleet Street; a man dashing along a pavement, showing a flash of white sock. But this same set has a photograph of the junction of the Strand and Wellington Street. Here, in 1923, two policemen are doing their best, but horse-drawn and motor vehicles are nose-to-tail and stationary under advertisements for Oxo and government surplus underwear. A great queue stretches out on to Waterloo Bridge, and it disappears into fog halfway across the river.

In the world of London's traffic lights, seven seconds is a long time. In seven seconds, you can start a traffic jam. Or you can get about four cars past a green light – or sixteen cars, if there are four lanes. So if, at a crucial, congested junction, you find a spare seven seconds in the traffic lights sequence – seven seconds doing nothing, lying about – then you have made a discovery that can change people's lives.

Stuart Beniston is a leading traffic signal engineer. He works for a civil engineering consultancy in Derbyshire, having previously worked in the public sector. His job is to broker subtle compromises between movement and non-movement. He strives to keep our faith in a repeated little drama of responsible citizenship: After you. No, after you. And, in 1997, it was Beniston who found seven spare seconds at the Hanger Lane gyratory system. When we met there recently, on a bitterly cold afternoon at the start of the evening rush hour, he told me how it had happened. But first we went for a tour. He showed me markings in the road, and shouted over the traffic about offset timing and modelling software. As we talked, it became dark, and his fluorescent jacket began to shine in the headlights.

The Hanger Lane gyratory system – a London joke gone stale – is six miles west of Marble Arch, and is where the A40, running out of London towards Oxford, meets the A406 North Circular. To use the language of the traffic professionals, this is where a major London orbital meets a major London radial – which is a rare and significant event, because most roads in London are radial; they go in and out. Before the M25 orbital motorway was built a few miles further out, the North Circular was the only real exception to the rule that all roads in England lead to London, and in London they lead to the centre.

This used to be a humble crossroads, controlled by traffic lights. Then in 1980, concrete was poured, and 'gyratory' found an unexpected place in London's day-to-day vocabulary. You have to imagine a very large roundabout, like Marble Arch or Hyde Park Corner,

but rectangular rather than round. Traffic joins at the four corners of the rectangle, where there are traffic lights, and it moves round the system in a maximum of eight lanes, stopping now and then at other lights. In the middle of the roundabout, sunk below car level, there is room for a fairly large boating lake, or Brighton's Royal Pavilion; but instead, we find the kinds of pinched scrubby parkland that calls out for body parts in bin liners. Here, in the middle of the roundabout, there is also an overground Tube station, Hanger Lane. And underneath everything runs the A40, whose slip roads come up to join the gyratory system at two of its corners.

Stuart Beniston took me to the roof of the Amoco office building, which stands high above the north-west corner of the gyratory. From here, we could see the lights of central London. Below us, there was thick thundering traffic, and more traffic queuing to join it from the north: we could see three-quarters of a mile of slow-moving headlights. For most of the day, Beniston said, and for seven days a week, about 8,000 vehicles an hour use the gyratory, which is the kind of flow you get on a busy section of the M4 (both directions combined), where no one has to stop for traffic lights or think about bus stops and vicars on bicycles. The truth is, too many people want to use Hanger Lane - and traffic, somewhere, will have to slow down and back up. The trick, said Beniston, is to keep the slow-moving traffic off the gyratory itself, where it will block up an entrance or an exit, and cause a jam that could take hours to clear. As far as possible, you want to synchronize lights to form 'platoons' of vehicles that will pass through the roundabout in convoy, and then off, uninterrupted, to the Home Counties and Heathrow.

In 1996, when the gyratory had long since earned

a kind of macho-comic reputation for delay and grief – and when creative London drivers were making elaborate back-street diversions to avoid it – the Highways Agency asked Beniston to suggest improvements that would not involve building new roads: the improvements would have to derive from new signalling, and new lane markings. (In a country that has decided to stop building roads, it is Beniston and his colleagues – the people fine-tuning an existing network – who suddenly find themselves key players in their industry.) Beniston came down to London, he watched the traffic, he gathered data, he noted the existing traffic-light times, and – with the help of a computer modelling system called TRANSYT – he began to consider his options.

At the top of the Amoco block, in the cold, we were watching the traffic lights below. There are about 11,000 sets of lights in the country; there are 3,500 in London, and of those, about 2,000 can be influenced remotely by the Metropolitan Police: their usual sequences, which perhaps favour one direction in the morning, another at night, can be overruled by the police in response to accidents, or other oddities in traffic flow. The police choose from a number of existing sequence programmes – or 'plans', as they are known. The lights cannot be asked to flash randomly, say, or remain permanently green in one direction. Three computers survey the whole London network, and raise the possibility of *Italian Job* sabotage.

Beniston produced his digital watch. He said that a usual traffic-light cycle (that is, the time from the start of the green to the start of the next green at the same place) will be somewhere between 24 and 120 seconds. The London average is about 100 seconds. These seconds are divided up with enormous care: pedestrians may get a few seconds, traffic in every direction has to get a green phase, and between each

green phase, there must be a 'clear time' – which is the interval between the lights in one direction turning red and the lights in the other direction turning green. But, as every driver knows, not every leg of a junction gets an equal share. Traffic signal engineers are in the business of redistributing time, for the greater good of society. The shortest green times in London are about ten seconds (these are the nervy, scampering green phases where cars dash across Oxford Street, or out into Piccadilly – with the last, guilty car trying to merge with the group in front, like a faredodger shuffling behind you through an automatic Underground ticket barrier). The longest, the most leisurely green times are about 80 seconds in a 120-second sequence, for cars sailing up to Finchley Road on a sunny day, listening to Patsy Cline.

When he looked at the Hanger Lane figures, Beniston could think of ways of improving the painted lane markings (and he devised a kind of spiral arrangement that flings drivers into their exits as if by centrifugal force); and he was sure the existing, pre-programmed plans could be made more efficient. And then Beniston made a great discovery: there, in the eastern side of the gyratory, was a set of lights throwing away time. Traffic coming south, and wanting to turn west towards Oxford, had a crazily extravagant clear time. A previous programmer had needlessly lined this traffic to the movement of traffic alongside it, heading south. A stage in the sequence had been given ten seconds, when it needed just three.

Beniston pointed out the junction he meant: 'I thought, hang on. Just because *they* need the time, it doesn't mean that *they* need the time. It was a breakthrough. A bit of luck, really. A nugget of green time. Now, I had seven seconds available for the three critical movements – there, there and there. And it meant that it was a much more comfortable junction generally, and we could keep the whole side of the gyratory clear.' It would clear the south side, and free up the whole system.

Incorporating the extra seconds, Beniston devised a set of new timing plans for different parts of the day: for peak and off-peak, for clearing the gyratory after an accident, for getting rid of Wembley Stadium traffic, and so on. And one morning, in March 1997, He had a chance to test his theories. He met up with a technician at Hanger Lane, and the technician opened a roadside controller cabinet and plugged in his laptop computer and set the lights to Beniston's plan. It was eleven o'clock. 'The traffic had been a bit messy and congested when we did it. And then the plan went on. And suddenly everything started going really nicely. Straight away.' His plan left an immediate clockwise trail of clearer traffic. 'If I'd got it wrong,' he said, 'it would have been suddenly snarled up worse than normal. I'd have felt terrible. But I was looking at it, thinking yes, this is looking really good.' The technician had gone back to his office. Beniston had to celebrate on his own. He walked round Hanger Lane, very pleased.

There are junctions whose existence is known to every Londoner, but whose place on the map is known to few. Not everyone could point to Savoy Circus, Gillette Corner, The Sun in Sands Roundabout – but everyone with a radio knows the words, because they are repeated day and night, and through repetition they have gained the gravitas and the melancholy glamour of Rockall or South Utsire on the late-night shipping forecasts. These names may mean nothing to you, the traffic reports tell us, but they are dangerous places, where travellers may easily come to grief. Listen, beware.

No one says 'the Talgarth Road section of the A4'

with quite the authority of Sally Boazman who, when we spoke, was the morning traffic reporter on the BBC's Greater London Radio, but who has since joined Radio Two. She is affable and amused on air – you could not fault her DJ banter about flyovers and hangovers – but she has an edge of reporterly seriousness, a commitment to the subject, that is lacking in some of her competitors. They tend either to be younger and dizzier, trying to get a foot in radio's door; or they're giving themselves showbusiness airs. (In Boazman's stern phrase, this is 'putting yourself in front of the information'.)

It is Boazman's great professional happiness to see traffic not moving. I met her one Friday morning in her little studio in Scotland Yard, and as we spoke she was sometimes interrupted by events shown on her monitors. 'Oh!' she would say, seeing confusion at Whitechapel. 'What's going on? Can you see? Have the police got control of that?' A little later, she cried out 'Blimey!' at the sight of a broken-down van on the hard shoulder of the M25, just south of Junction 16. 'You see how my heart jumped there?'

While Capital Radio has an aeroplane, the 'Flying Eye' (which Boazman treats with half-serious disparagement: 'Can it go up in the rain? Can it go in a tunnel?'), GLR has precious access to the Metropolitan Police's network of traffic cameras. To a visitor, this is a magical toy. Three hundred cameras are fixed on posts and high buildings across London, and each has a number. On Boazman's desk was a little grey keypad. Tapping in a number, you can call up a clear, colour image of a London street; tapping in one number after another, you can skip across London at the height of a lamp-post – Bayswater, Old Kent Road, King's Cross – as if editing a rather earnest pop video for a song about urban dislocation. You can turn the camera, and you can zoom in – a fat man in a hat at Hammersmith, someone asleep in the Strand. Boazman has seen road rage on the cameras. She has tried to follow police chases, hopping from one camera to another. And at my suggestion, we tried to peer in an upstairs room in Camden High Street. 'Let's have a look,' she said. 'Hmm.' (I believed her when she said this was not normal practice.)

I watched Boazman preparing for a live broadcast, tapping her way through the camera codes, reading faxes, ringing London Transport to consult about the Circle Line. And then a red light came on, and she launched, unscripted, into: 'Euston Road eastbound . . . If you're coming up from Isleworth . . . If you're going out of town on the A3 . . . Nasty accident in Hollybush Hill.' When she finished, she waited a second to see if the disc jockey would need her for a moment's chat, and then she was off-air. I wondered if she ever used the traffic reporter's cliché, 'sheer weight of traffic' (reduced to 'SWT' in some police circles), and she said, 'No! I never use that expression. You'll never hear me say it. Sorry, I'm getting rather heated here. And I never say "an earlier accident". I hate that. I made a decision in life never to say "an earlier accident". I say, "an accident, earlier".'

I asked her, Is London traffic getting worse? 'Yes,' she said. 'It's definitely much worse than when I started doing reports in the early '80s, and a lot worse in the past four or five years. You feel there's a very fine balance; and one minor thing can start a terrible queue. But the main thing is the rush hours are getting longer. Before, you'd say the evening rush hour starts about four, goes on to about six. Now it starts about half past three and goes on till about eight in the evening. And the same in the morning, really. It used to be the rush hour started about half past seven and went through until nine, but now, if you look at the Blackwall Tunnel – one of my favourite spots – it can be stuck at half past six in the morning.'

It was midday on a Friday, just ahead of a school half-term. 'Look,' she said. 'That's the rush hour starting. That's the Westway, going out of London on the M40. The mass getaway has started. It's going to get worse and worse and worse for the rest of the day.'

It was starting to rain. 'Spray, spray!' she said. 'Good, good.'

On Tuesday 10 December 1996, Robert Thomson, then 35 years old, from Hoo, Kent – a man later described by the AA as a 'total prat' – was driving on the southbound carriageway of the A102(M) towards the Blackwall Tunnel, which is one of the crucial links in London's traffic system. He was in a large white Mercedes truck, and the truck was carrying a crane that rose high above the road. Ignoring warning signs of height restrictions ahead – or persuading himself that his load could make it, or forgetting altogether that he had a load – he approached the mouth of the tunnel without apparent anxiety. And at about two-fifteen in the afternoon, at the entrance to the tunnel, the crane on Thomson's truck hit a gantry above. A reinforced steel frame crashed down on to the truck. Thomson stopped, and so, very soon, did everyone else. Mr Thomson had set in motion one of the worst traffic jams ever seen in London.

The lorry had to be prised out of the tunnel; and the tunnel's structure had to be checked for safety. And this was on a day when the eastbound carriageway of the Limehouse Link tunnel was closed for maintenance, and the QE2 bridge at Dartford was also closed southbound. All the major routes in east London quickly filled, and then – as people struck out into the unknown – so did all the minor routes. Junctions became blocked, and queues were soon covering an area sixteen miles square, from Liverpool Street in the west to Leytonstone in the east. It was estimated that 250,000 cars were affected. One-hour journeys became six-hour journeys. People abandoned their cars. In an echo of nineteenth-century practice, fire crews had to walk in front of their vehicles, asking cars ahead to mount the pavement. Drivers stuck in the Rotherhithe Tunnel, the nearest river crossing to the Blackwall Tunnel, had to breathe through handkerchiefs as fumes from stationary cars built up. It took one woman eleven hours to get from the north of the river to the south.

The Blackwall Tunnel was reopened in the early hours of Wednesday morning. In the immediate aftermath, police did not release Mr Thomson's name. 'If we named him,' a spokesman told the London *Evening Standard*, 'half of London would want to lynch him.' But they revealed that he was feeling 'sheepish'.

The traffic police call them 'peds', but they seem to mean it kindly. I met Ben Plowden, director of the Pedestrians' Society, on the steps of the National Gallery, and we went for a walk around Trafalgar Square.

'Brixton High Street,' he said, 'which is my local shopping street, serves two mutually exclusive functions. It's a major shopping centre, where I should think 95 per cent of the people visiting are doing so on public transport or on foot, and it's also the A23, which is the major road from London to the South Coast. At any moment on a Saturday, the people on foot probably outweigh the people driving through Brixton by about twenty or thirty to one, and yet the space of Brixton High Street is designed, laid out, managed, timed, almost exclusively for the benefit of people travelling through it. And I think this raises quite

interesting philosophical questions: why is that? Why are people travelling through on four wheels, in rather small numbers, the ones who have priority at the junctions? Why is everyone else hemmed in behind a quarter-mile of continuous crash-barriers? There's a really profound implied statement underlying that, about who counts . . .'

Here, we made a dash across several lanes of traffic to reach the centre of the square. 'Go! Go!' cried Plowden. Under Sir Norman Foster's World Squares for All plans, the road we had crossed will eventually become pavement, filled with cappuccino and laughter. In the meantime, only tourists get across: Londoners resent the inconvenience and danger, and keep to the edges. A bus climbed on to the pavement in front of us.

Plowden is a man who can see transport thinking turning his way. Britain seems to be entering its second age of modern motoring, where it is agreed across a surprisingly wide spectrum that congestion cannot be defeated by road-building, and that some form of levy on driving in London (or, to put it more seductively, some sort of 'congestion charging') is inevitable, and will be a good thing, for it will free up the roads for bus lanes and bicycles, will reduce pollution, and provide revenue for grand public transport projects. (The new mayor of London will have congestion-charging powers; the government is giving other local authorities the right to set up pilot schemes.) In this new motoring age, a key text will be *Traffic Impact of Highway Capacity Reductions* (1998), by Phil Goodwin and others, which Plowden describes as the 'final piece in the jigsaw' for much progressive transport analysis. Goodwin studied 100 instances of planned or emergency road closure – Oxford Street in 1972, Interstate 10 after the Los Angeles earthquake in 1994, Hammersmith Bridge in 1997 – and saw how car drivers adapt their behaviour; they take other routes, they travel at other times, they catch the bus. They are not all so foolish as to sit in queues in the surrounding streets, shouting obscenities at one another. For people claiming extra space for bikes and for peds (and 40 per cent of journeys made in inner London are made exclusively on foot), Goodwin's work makes a handsome academic chaperone.

We walked back towards the National Gallery. It was the evening rush hour. Everywhere, pedestrians were overriding the provisions made for them; slipping through gaps, dashing between buses. A mother with a pushchair and bright bleached hair became stuck on the wrong side of a barrier, and a taxi grudgingly agreed not to run her over.

Among the officers in the Central Command Complex of the Metropolitan Police, there is resistance to the word gridlock. 'Don't ever mention that filthy disgusting word in here,' I was told. 'Gridlock is an American word. It's a traffic condition that only occurs in a grid system of roads, which you're only likely to get in America or Canada or – all right, fair enough – Stevenage New Town, but in principle you can't get gridlock in London.' He took out a piece of paper, and drew a grid, and then described the police's preferred language for London traffic. 'Green is light traffic flowing freely, amber is medium traffic flowing freely, blue is heavy traffic flowing freely, red is heavy traffic stationary for less than three minutes, and black is bus driver, feet up on the dash, reading the newspaper. And you don't get black traffic in London very often.'

We were standing in front of monitors in a very long and windowless room in the middle of Scotland Yard. From here, the police can overrule the usual traffic-light 'plans' in central London. As I watched, they were trying to favour Northumberland Avenue at the expense of Victoria Embankment. It was clearly a subtle art: a new plan goes on, but is taken off after a few minutes, then put on again. (A plan applied cack-handedly can create surrounding queues that take hours to disperse.) As they worked, the police seemed serene and upbeat. They were accentuating the positive. They had the air of group leaders in a therapeutic workshop for neurotically impatient London drivers. Where an ordinary driver would see a queue, the police tend to see a moving queue. 'That's running quite well,' they said of traffic crawling along Trafalgar Square.

It was tempting to hope for worse. Gridlock, or something similar, is an oddly seductive fantasy – spectacular and decisive, but safer than an earthquake, at least for those with strong lungs. Looking at the monitors, it was hard not to hope for a lorry to lose its load of ball-bearings at Paddington, or for a fuse to go at Parliament Square, and then a bomb scare at Waterloo and a burst water main at Euston – or any combination of four crises at four key junctions, which is what experts (and Ben Elton's novel *Gridlock*) think would bring London into a 'superjam' state. (For best results, these crises would occur in the morning, when people would be more impatient to get on their way, and be more likely to make the fatal move of abandoning their vehicles.)

But traffic was moving quite freely. The police made bantering conversation about idiot commuters. There were further thoughts about American grids. And then we caught sight of something on Piccadilly eastbound. A parked van had blocked a side junction, and a lorry unable to turn left had stopped. Nothing could move. A bus conductor had left his bus to investigate. When the camera swung round, we could see that Park Lane was already filling up southbound. And as we watched, it was becoming difficult for traffic on Hyde Park Corner to get past Piccadilly, down towards

Victoria. 'That's going to get blocked off completely. Once that happens, I'll lose Park Lane, and then the queue will go back right round, and eventually the whole thing will stop.'

They called for a police motorbike, and we saw it arrive two minutes later. The van was asked to move. The bus conductor got back on his bus. 'See. Moving nicely now.' There would be no gridlock, no breakdown of civil government, and no looting.

A few weeks ago, in a building that has the best views of central London, two rather grand, youngish people were sitting opposite each other with a desk and a computer between them. The woman wore a vivid pink suit. The man wore cuff links and red braces. He leaned way back in his chair, hands behind his head, and laughed an Alan Clark laugh: 'Yha yha yha yha!'

Although it would not have been clear to a passerby, this was a court, of sorts, and the woman in pink, Verity Jones, was a kind of judge. In the decriminalized world of London parking offences, the Parking Appeals Service is the last port of call for a person not happy with a parking ticket. It processes 35,000 appeals a year, which is about 1 per cent of all London tickets issued. This is an office that knows the difference between a parking space and a parking place, and whether a car park counts as a road and whether a tuna-fish sandwich counts as a load. This office hears the phrase 'It's not the money, it's the principle' more than most. And it has an enviable high-rise home in New Zealand House, on the corner of Haymarket and Pall Mall. It's an oddity of London local government – where people grow old waiting to hear news of their council house repairs – that a charming former champagne dealer, contesting a penalty stuck to an MG parked near his Kensington home, should find

himself in this haven of computerized efficiency, where people answer the telephone almost before it has begun ringing.

Stephen Cleeve looked supremely confident, which may be how he always looks. The Royal Borough of Kensington and Chelsea (which was not represented at the adjudication) had accused him of having illegally parked his MG on a pavement – on a 'crossover', which is the place where a car crosses a pavement to reach a front drive. But it was Mr Cleeve's contention that he had parked on a stretch of actual street – street that happened to lead to a set of iron gates, giving it the air, as it were, of a crossover. He suspected the traffic warden of having a vendetta against him: 'Always the same chap,' he said.

Verity Jones, who is a barrister, read the evidence on her computer screen. She then looked at Cleeve's photographs of the crime scene. Some questions were asked and answered – with both appellant and adjudicator using amused inverted commas round phrases like 'vehicular access'. Cleeve laughed a lot, and toyed with a Rumpolian persona. 'Flimsy evidence!' he cried out at one point.

It was over in ten minutes. On this occasion, yellow lines had served as Cleeve's great friend. He had parked on a single yellow line, and where there is a yellow line, there must surely be a street. 'I don't think the council can have their cake and eat it,' said Jones. She would allow his appeal. Cleeve said, 'Oh, very good. Thanks very much, Verity. The best man won.' In the waiting area outside, while his paperwork was being processed, Cleeve told me about his parking history. He said he gets 'hundreds' of tickets. Half of them he accepts in good grace – 'Sometimes, you've got to park, you just chuck the car down and go' – but he resents the others: 'Yesterday, I was at London Bridge, I put in one hour twenty minutes on the parking meter.

That was all the change I had. And someone I went to see was late, so they made me late, and I had a long walk back. I was eight minutes late, and I got a ticket. He said he'd just given it to me. And I asked him if he enjoyed his job. He said, Not really. I said, Give it up then, and smiled and got in the car and drove off.'

We talked about public transport. 'I've been on the Tube twice in my life,' he said. 'I just find it always breaks down. It's just so much aggro.' He recently decided to wait for a bus, but then hailed a taxi instead.

Seen at the wheel of his or her car, a typical American has the air of someone with various projects underway, just one of which happens to be driving a car. He or she will also be involved it the solemn business of, say, sitting comfortably. A London driver – even a London driver on the telephone – always looks more fully consumed by the act of driving, and rarely achieves the state of blissful, armchair disengagement allowed by automatic gears and carefully engineered holders for cans of soft drinks. It does happen: a few years ago, a very relaxed London taxi driver picked up a Japanese visitor at Heathrow, who asked for Knightsbridge. The driver meant no harm, but at some point on the journey into town, the tourist slipped his mind. The driver made a long journey to Herne Hill, parked in a front drive, turned off the engine, and went into his house, closing the door behind him. The Japanese tourist was left in the taxi, wondering.

More often, London drivers are in the grip of fear. And they fear many things: they fear arriving in London, and they fear leaving it. (London hates to let you go: it's not like *Withnail and I*. If you drive out of London towards Brighton, there are 75 sets of traffic lights before you reach the motorway, and a dozen false dawns.) London drivers fear the morning peak, and the evening peak,

and the school run rush hour, and the West End theatre rush hour. They fear Saturday afternoon traffic and Sunday night traffic. And they fear the prospect of leaving a good London parking spot: when a car fills the space they have left, they feel troubled and adrift, regretting their recklessness. There are Londoners – they are real and many – who will take a taxi from home, rather than risk giving up a resident's parking space, a lovely space, right in front of the house.

London drivers fear routes that are off their private mental map of London, and will go miles to 'get their bearings' by a landmark that is in the wrong place. They fear being a passenger in a car driven by someone with a preposterous mental map of London, but to which it would seem impolite and neurotic to draw attention. They fear violence (61 per cent of London drivers, compared to 43 per cent nationally, lock their cars from the inside when driving at night). They fear streets that once let them down badly, and can never again be fully trusted; they fear wildly revving Post Office vans; they fear the thousands of streets whose parked cars make it just too narrow for two cars to pass, and where they must play complex, draining games of oscillating generosity and aggression. They fear losing face by slowing down more than absolutely necessary when passing between width-restriction posts. And although they do not exactly fear being late – London drivers are usually in a place beyond that – they have a great fear that they are losing a race. The race is with an imaginary car that set off from the same place at the same time, but then did not get stuck behind the 31 bus, did not miss the lights, did not make that unforgivable lane error on Commercial Road. This car is way ahead.

FROM *London: The Lives of the City, Granta*, 65 (Spring, 1999)

Come Together

SANDY McCREERY

Since nineteenth-century commentators devised body metaphors that described primary city routes as arteries, traffic congestion has been seen as an urban disease. It is a condition that planners, architects and governments have consistently sought to overcome, and that still taxes the ingenuity of city administrators. In cities of the Far Eastern 'tiger economies', they have banned non-motorized vehicles, while in various European cities they have selectively banned motorized ones. In London, the new mayor is committed to introducing congestion charging.

These are all policies that should prove popular; no-one, it seems, has a good word to say for congestion. It brings delays, frustration, pollution and financial costs. For many, it epitomizes all that is wrong with unregulated, unplanned, privatized, free-market economies – they never had congestion in the Soviet Union. It has to be sorted. British vox pop TV documentaries feature tradesmen in white vans cursing the congestion caused by the school run, while well-spoken mothers complain of intimidation by an aggressive new breed of driver: so-called 'white-van man'. None of those interviewed, they admit, know the answer, but somehow it just has to be sorted. In Joel Schumacher's 1992 film *Falling Down*, a demented Michael Douglas finally cracks under the stresses of modern American life – in a traffic jam. The heat, the fumes, the flies and the sweat all accentuate the fact that he is suffocating. He has to get away, breathe again, decongest his tubes, empty his barrels. And in a similar vein, Jean Luc Godard's 1967 critique of

consumerism run wild, *Week-end*, consistently repeats one particularly telling scenario: life (and death) in a traffic jam. Following one gruesome pile-up, an hysterical woman runs back to the carnage, not to help the dying, but to rescue her beloved Hermés handbag. Congestion – it's the bane of modern life, yet no more than we apparently deserve. The manifestation of our self-obsessed, commodity-obsessed stupidity. Radical action is required.

The scenes of rage regularly witnessed by city dwellers indicate that all is not well on the roads. To describe congestion as a disease is not entirely metaphorical – we seem to be surrounded by an advancing social psychosis. And if congestion is making many of us demented, to suggest that nothing should be done to cure it is surely the opinion of a bad casualty. Certainly not of the voice of reason. Yet could it be that the conventional diagnoses are wrong? Might it be that traffic congestion is not a symptom of urban disease, even less a sign of social meltdown, but rather a mark of robust urban health? Just as physicians no longer advocate bleeding, nor seek to stimulate the flow of the humours, perhaps traffic congestion is another aspect of circulation that is best left well alone. Before dismissing this possibility, just try thinking of a decent world city that is not regularly gripped by gridlock. We might find it instructive to consider the alternatives.

Let's state it plainly: congestion is slow-moving traffic, nothing more complicated than that, although it is worth noting the discriminatory definition of 'traffic' which is generally applied only to motor traffic (twenty cars waiting at traffic lights are apparently an indication of traffic congestion, whereas twenty pedestrians waiting to cross the same road are not). So *in extremis*, we are left with two alternatives: either fast-moving motor traffic or no motor traffic. In practice, of course, these are often two sides of the same coin, as fewer vehicles have the room in which to travel faster. But is either situation actually any better than congestion? We can consider each in turn.

The speeding up of urban traffic dominated the minds of planners and city administrators throughout most of the last century. The visions of Le Corbusier and the brutal realities of Robert Moses's New York highways are only the two most widely known cases in point. When Frederick Etchells translated Le Corbusier's assertion as 'A city made for speed is made for success,'[1] he was probably unaware of the tautology. The etymological route of 'speed' is from the Old English *spówan* (Old High German *spuon*): to succeed or prosper.[2] And the intimate connection between the two notions still appears logical in many circles – on the whole, a successful economy or business is one in which money circulates, and profits accrue, rapidly. However, whereas money is an abstract, and increasingly amorphous, concept, cars unfortunately are not. Allowing hard, heavy, speeding vehicles to come into contact with fleshy mortals is a recipe for disaster, and limiting the death toll has consistently dominated the minds of planners. The approach of Modernists such as Le Corbusier and Moses was to engineer new types of urban road on which only motor vehicles would be permitted, but there are obvious limits to how far this process can proceed. Not only is the cost prohibitive, both in terms of money and destruction, but there are people inside those vehicles, heading to a place where they will want to get out, walk about, stay alive. Thus

the structures and experiences of a full-blown Modernist approach, although undeniably exhilarating, were only ever likely to occur intermittently.

Instead, in cities around the world, ways were sought to enable speeding motorists and vulnerable non-motorists to co-exist largely on existing street patterns. It has proved a tortuous exercise, and one predicated on a notion of 'reasonable' compromise: that it must surely be possible to allow motorists to enjoy reasonable speed while affording pedestrians a reasonable chance of survival. The facts are that following 20-mph impacts, roughly 95 per cent of pedestrians survive, while at 40 mph, only 15 per cent survive.[3] As you might expect, since 1934 Britain has had a speed limit in built-up areas of 30 mph.[4] Most countries around the world have a similar limit. It is, apparently, reasonable.[5] And in this mood of give-and-take, pedestrians have been contained and controlled, apparently for their own good. Trying to walk through many urban areas has become a pinball experience of pedestrian barriers, bollards, street signage, constricted pavements, walk-don't-walk signs, pedestrian underpasses, overpasses and jaywalking restrictions. This is the price extracted from pedestrians, and in return, motorists kill and seriously injure fewer people – only 6,273 in London in a typical year, for example.[6] In almost every city in the world, the violence inflicted on human beings by motor vehicles far outstrips that of crime. Not much of a deal.

And then there have been the other costs associated with trying to manage the competing claims of speed and safety, in particular those of the 'experts' – the arbitrators, designers and engineers of the so-called solutions – the countless research institutions, university departments, engineers, planners, systems analysts etc., all apparently dedicated to finding better means for managing motor traffic. Plus the costs of installing and operating their solutions; the one-way systems, tidal-flow roads, urban clearways, gyratories, underpasses, overpasses, eyes-in-the-sky, traffic lights, parking restrictions, speed cameras and so on. Few would deny that somewhere in their heads was the kernel of that Modernist vision, flashing tail-lights on elevated freeways, but the *tabula rasa* was mythical. These were real cities and real people's lives that had to be devastated before they could be rebuilt. And despite all of this physical and mental exertion, average road-journey times in London have famously remained unchanged for a century. Oh no, could it be that traffic flow is largely a self-regulating system, that these interventions are pointless? Engineer larger roads for higher speeds and in no time you will find them choked with new cars, making new journeys. Speeds return to previous levels. Congestion is no pushover. Perhaps the pinnacle of underachievement has been the one-way systems. These have achieved the holy grail of a sustainable increase in vehicle speed, an increase almost precisely matched by the increased distance that has to be travelled to get through the system. Brilliant. Those academicians of road science resembled bleeding eighteenth-century physicians!

In fairness, many traffic engineers now accept that you will never sustainably speed up urban traffic flow by expanding road capacity, and in many quarters the approach has shifted from accommodating speeding motor vehicles to discouraging them. Yet had it proved feasible to speed up vehicles in cities, would it even have been desirable? Presumably, we've all come across those isolated urban roads on which the traffic flows rapidly (often stretches beyond the last hold-up, behind which the traffic crowd remains stuck) and experienced the uniform desolation of

such areas. The noise, the threat, the filth, the absence of street life, the human and commercial casualties. J. G. Ballard's *Concrete Island* [7] depicts life in such an environment taken to its extreme; cowering, non-motorized individuals scratch a primitive survival among the ruins left by highway engineers while oblivious drivers continue by. There's nowhere to stop. This is non-place, transit space. And if we want to see a real-world example of the free-flowing built-up area, we can look to the new American sprawls such as Dallas-Fort Worth. There no-one in their right mind would think of venturing anywhere except by motor vehicle. Cars can speed along without killing too many people because there are next to no people, no street life. This is not a city in any meaningful sense. If you really wish to tackle congestion by getting urban traffic flowing rapidly, and you don't want carnage on the street, then you must kill the street. Not a great option.

The other approach, the one currently finding more favour in most European cities, is to restrict motor vehicles entering city centres. Without parallel measures to slow down the remaining vehicles, speeds will increase, and indeed this is the main intention of many restriction policies. The congestion charging about to be introduced in London is a misnomer; it is speed that drivers will be paying for, and with it will come increased danger, severance and blight. [8] If urban traffic speeds increase, and other conditions remain unchanged, more people die, simple as that. Thus the sophisticated approach is to restrict both the number of motor vehicles and their potential speed. This is the approach found in cities such as Amsterdam and in many smaller towns throughout northern Europe, including Cambridge, Bath and York in the UK. It is eminently sensible, and disturbingly dull. It produces cities that are pretty and precious. Tidy, prescriptive, vegetarian cities devoid of the glamour, excess and public egos that make major cities exciting. That make them, and consequently us, feel big. These tend to be sanctimonious, self-denying and painfully polite tourist cities which, perhaps unsurprisingly, are often associated with places of learning and 'culture'. They have all the guts and sincerity of *The Truman Show*. There's less accidental death in such places, but then there's less life. Clearly, removing congestion removes something more from the city than just a few delays.

It is time to reassess congestion in a rather more positive light. Congestion is slow-moving traffic. In cities, it is good because slow-moving motor traffic is better than fast-moving motor traffic. It is also good because living with cars is more fun than living without them. Cars are big toys, and they should make us happy. This is worth repeating only because many people appear to have lost sight of it. When those auto-pioneers were seeking to spark life into their machines, they were not feverishly imagining their creations carrying frustrated commuters from a boring job to some bland home. There were no advertisements that claimed 'Buy this, it'll make your life really dull.' Cars are dream machines, always have been, that allow us to transcend our everyday lives and surroundings. And just like their narcotic equivalents, it is when we let them become part of our everyday lives that problems begin. Congestion is the great moderator. It forces us to confront the consequences of dependency. Sure there are those too weak, foolish or emotionally insecure to do anything about it, but most take control and moderate the auto habit. Enjoy a drive, enjoy the enjoyment, and make sure it stays that way.

And when indulging in the pleasures of motoring, we would do well to remember the madness of it all. A car is not primarily a tool. It is not for undertaking tasks. Almost all motoring journeys were simply not made before the inception of the car. They were not originally undertaken in response to some pre-existing need, but in order to explore the possibilities; playful possibilities. And consider the manner in which they are made. Driving is not dissimilar to watching TV from a comfortable seat at home. There is the screen, a controlled environment, personal audio, interactive technology, soft upholstery and that comforting sense of privacy. Indeed, an average sofa is of similar width to a car. In our motorized world, we effectively roll our sofas out into the street (together with the all of the other home entertainment paraphernalia) and propel them forwards at 30 mph.[9] Picture that – is it reasonable to expect that no-one should get in our way (not that there is anything reasonable about the whole surreal business – just what planet were those planners on?)? And why, in the midst of such excessive indulgence, would anyone want to rush? This is surely a transport of delights.

By its very nature, congestion is a shared experience, the urban crowd of the automotive era. Its etymology is from the Latin *congero*, 'to bring together'. This is not an urban disease, but what cities are all about, their very essence. And just as the crowd was celebrated as the apogee of the urban condition (while simultaneously feared by the powerful), so it could be with congestion. It exists because there is somewhere worth going to, or being in, together – the city. And that somewhere ceases to exist if congestion is ever eradicated. In Tom Wolfe's *A Man in Full*,[10] there is a scene in which the Black youth of Atlanta create gridlock on their way to Freak-nic. Yet this is not a cause for frustration, but part of their celebration. They climb out of their cars, pump up the volume and flaunt themselves – their Blackness, sexiness, togetherness

– in the faces of the horrified White patricians staring down from one of their privileged private clubs. The kids' dancing challenges the most basic social and mental categories through which power operates: reason, separation, circulation and progress. This is not rational, not in the right place, not going anywhere, and things don't come much better. It is a very literal return of the repressed. A triumph of the human over the system. Then again, congestion *is* the triumph of the human over the system.

And perhaps the most human attribute that congestion encourages is thought. Even snarl-ups themselves raise philosophical questions – it is surely a willed downfall of Nietzschean proportions to have humans imprisoned in their escape machines. But, thinking less introspectively, it is clear that the very slowness of congestion affords us time to contemplate our surroundings – to dwell upon them in a way that is impossible when speeding through them. City-centre congestion is seldom dull. The comings and goings, repulsions, attractions, emotions, expressions, fashions and bodies offer *flânerie* of the highest calibre. And it is worth remembering that this is only feasible because of congestion – such street life would not exist, does not exist, in situations where motor traffic is racing by. Sat in your car, you really are part and parcel of the pageant. That again is worth thinking about. And if you're sat in an appealing car, chances are everyone else will be taking notice of you too. It is a similar kind of mutual consideration, a taking notice, that is acted out in slow-moving funeral processions. Slowness allows the world to dwell upon the deceased, while the mourners can contemplate an emptier world. And it is thoughtful communication, born out of slowness, that features in a closing scene of the 1953 film *Genevieve*.[11] Two veteran cars have been cynically raced from Brighton to London. They

are side by side at a red traffic light, moments from the finish line, when an elderly gentleman strikes up a conversation with one of the drivers. He has recognized the model of car, it was his first, the one in which he courted his future wife, and his memories are flooding back. As the lights go green, the driver must either continue with the race or with his new acquaintance. Momentarily, he is torn, until with gallant resignation, with an emphatic adherence to human values, he steps out of the race to embrace his new friendship. He would be glad to take the elderly couple out for a spin. The shared joy is palpable.

Congestion. It takes us out of the race. Allows thoughtful communication. It can be a beautiful thing.

Squealing Wheels and
Flying Fists

JACK SARGEANT

'Let's break out of the horrible shell of wisdom and throw ourselves like pride-ripened fruit into the wide, contorted mouth of the wind! Let's give ourselves utterly to the Unknown, not in desperation but only to replenish the deep wells of the Absurd!'

The words were scarcely out of my mouth when I spun my car around with the frenzy of a dog trying to bite its tail, and there, suddenly, were two cyclists coming towards me, shaking their fists, wobbling like two equally convincing but nevertheless contradictory arguments. Their stupid dilemma was blocking my way – Damn! Ouch! . . . I stopped short and to my disgust rolled over into a ditch with my wheels in the air . . .

– F. T. Marinetti, *The Founding and Manifesto of Futurism*

The roar of the engine, the smell of rubber, the shine of chrome . . .

Cars remain the ultimate realization of individual affirmation. The possibility of climbing behind the wheel and just driving, following the contours of the road and tracing the landscape. Cars are the great enablers of freedom; to drive is to engage in the promise of the open road. Except that such visions are not – and never have been – true. In the end, the freedom promised in songs, films, books, advertisements and even in dreams has never been realized. As Marinetti discovered while skidding into a shit-filled ditch nearly a century ago, other people always get in the way.

Automotive transport was in part responsible for the growth of cities – and the ability to transverse the increasing distances between them – but even as the journey itself became possible, it became a pressure. If mass car ownership heralded the beginning of consumer capitalism – of the ability to purchase and pay by instalments – then it also announced the need for the employment necessary to make payments punctually.

Climbing into cars in order to get to work, the morning rush hour, the evening rush hour. The weekend leisure drive. Even as driving emerged as a possibility of the taste of freedom, its potentialities were chocked in slow-moving maximum-stress fender-to-fender jams.

New York's bridges and tunnels, London's M25, Birmingham's Spaghetti Junction and all of Los Angeles' expressways – all of these crucial highways, freeways and motorways that allow rapid access to strategic locations in cities become clogged with traffic at rush hour. Helicopters buzz endlessly overhead, radio reports confirm the worst: 'slow moving . . . delays . . . road works . . .' From scalding California sun to freezing London rain, tensions mount, tired hands lean on horns, frustrated feet hover suspended between brake and accelerator, work or home calls, you're tired, stresses increase.

Coined in 1994, the term 'road rage' (and its subsequent bastard spawn, the banal pop-psychology buzz terms such as 'air rage', 'desk rage' and '[shopping] trolley rage') covers a wide range of infractions – from shouting abuse at a driver for taking a parking space, tailgating another car or aggressively cutting in front of another road user, to more serious confrontations involving slamming on the brakes, leaping from the car and attacking another driver – with occasionally fatal results. Cases range from the quasi-Dada absurdity of the death of Leo, the pet dog snatched from a car during an altercation in San Jose, California, and thrown into oncoming traffic, to the driver who pursued a car for 5 miles through Bristol, England, and onto a dual carriageway in his double-decker bus while passengers were flung from their seats in a journey recalling the Keystone Cops. And the dreaded fear invoked by the handful of notorious cases in which confrontations have led to manslaughter and even homicide.[1] Road rage has emerged in the last decade as both a diagnosed symptom and a cause of angry driving; the popular media are rich with details of confrontations between aggressive drivers.

Psychologists have suggested that violation of an individual's personal space – ostensibly an imaginary bubble around the physical self – could create an aggressive response. Notably, for those readily disposed to violence, it is hypothesized, this zone is larger and more easily penetrated. Behind the wheel of a car, the bubble expands, surrounding the entire automobile; thus any driving infraction, whether actual or imagined, is perceived as a territorial invasion, even as an attempted assault. In part, road rage emerges as the atavistic response to this penetration of personal space. But while this transgression may be seen as the trigger of a road-rage event, in an increasingly stressful culture other forms of pressure may additionally find their release within bad or aggressive driving and auto-violence. Put simply: while driving in our cars, we have the freedom, power and anonymity with which to express extreme and violent emotions we may suppress in the rest of our lives.

A further factor considered to be a contributor to road rage is the sheer volume of traffic. Car ownership has boomed, and the road infrastructure has become increasingly burdened with a massive increase in traffic that has not been matched by a growth in the number of roads. In America, the number of licensed drivers has increased by 60 per cent since 1970, while the number of roads increased by only 6 per cent over the same period.[2] This glut of road users has been increased further due to people driving their cars more often, no longer feeling safe as pedestrians on city streets erroneously perceived by many as crime-ridden, and unwilling to risk the haphazard vestiges of under-funded public transport. Cars are now used under the most dubious pretexts for even the shortest journeys.

Road rage has become a regular fixture on TV, manifested in skids, crashes and physical violence, in programmes such as 'Cops', 'Police Stop!', 'Police Camera Action' and 'The World's Wildest Police Videos'. These cheap 'quasi-mondo' documentaries (occasionally referred to as edu-tainment) string together endless moments of newsreel and CCTV surveillance footage, footage that almost invariably includes aggressive driving, crashes and – very occasionally – actual deaths, fulfilling a multitude of social functions and audience desires. At their most socially acceptable level, these programmes are intended to be educational, consciously entertaining updates on the Driver's Educational films of the '50s and '60s, blurting simplistic driver-awareness messages that can largely be reduced to the predictably stupefying maxims 'Be careful' and 'Obey the rules.' But behind such platitudes, these programmes also offer gleefully salacious images of the chaos that is auto-mayhem. Their message may be intended as broadly social, but their visual pleasures are associated with humanity's most atavistic traits and rudimentary instincts. They reveal the intrinsic nature of our relationship with violence and road rage: we fetishize it as much as we fear it; we dread personal involvement in violent confrontation even as we enjoy its televisual representation. These programmes – and media reports of such crimes – construct our experience of road rage.

Conceptually, road rage may only be seven years old, but suddenly it is everywhere, a new term for an old psychosis. In a Gallop International Survey carried out in 2000, 80 per cent of UK drivers claimed to have experienced – or been victims of – road rage,[3] while the American Automobile Association has suggested that incidents of violent driving have increased by 7 per cent per year since 1990.[4] These statistics betray two truths. Certainly, violence on the road has increased, but what has increased far more dramatically is the interpretation of any confrontation as an example of some indefinable yet knowable rage. Where once people were merely tailgated, they are now encouraged to self-identify and speak as victims of a new socio-cultural phenomenon, a new crisis. Moreover, in an increasingly neurotic culture of confession, drivers admit to committing acts of road rage, by which they almost invariably mean they drove aggressively, hardly a new phenomenon, just a new manifestation of guilt and, almost invariably, cringing self-pity.

It has been estimated that the chance of being killed in a road-rage confrontation in the UK is one in 9.5 million, while the chance of dying in a car crash is one in 15,686,[5] but car crashes are not an easily read symptom of either an imagined or an actual cultural decline and social malaise. Road rage will remain as an attempt to explain the ultimately unknowable reasons for the fears, frustrations and helplessness that are replacing the promise of freedom once offered by the mythology of the car and the empty road.

Motopia: Cities, Cars and Architecture

MURRAY FRASER & JOE KERR

In the early evening twilight on the Champs-Élysées, it was if the world had suddenly gone mad. After the emptiness of the summer, the traffic was more furious than ever. Day by day the fury of the traffic grew. To leave your house meant that once you had crossed your threshold you were a possible sacrifice to death in the shape of innumerable motors... Motors in all directions, going at all speeds. I was overwhelmed, an enthusiastic rapture filled me. Not the rapture of the shining coachwork under the gleaming lights, but the rapture of power. The simple and ingenious pleasure of being in the centre of so much power. We are a part of it. We are part of that race whose dawn is just awakening. We have confidence in this new society, which will in the end arrive at a magnificent expression of its power. We believe in it.
– Le Corbusier, *The City of Tomorrow*[1]

The relationship between cars and architecture is a long and complex one, as long indeed as the history of the car itself. From the very moment that self-powered vehicles took to the city streets of Europe and America in the last decade of the nineteenth century, architects and planners have been forced to confront the challenge of accommodating the car within the built environment. The car provided the provocation for architects who were seeking to explode pre-existing urban forms and diagrams, and to articulate the new order of the modern industrial city. Le Corbusier's account of his Damascene conversion to the cult of the automobile, in terms that were reminiscent of the purple prose of the Italian Futurists prior to World War I, captured the fervour with which modernist visionaries dreamt of a new epoch for architecture and urbanism.

It is these proselytizing plans and manifestos of polemical modernists that have tended to dominate the historical discourse about cars and architecture, but there is another, less acknowledged, dimension to the subject that merits an equal measure of attention. For the car industry itself proved one of the most significant patrons of the new approach to architecture, from the design of the first purpose-built factories in the early years of the twentieth century, to the decline of the established manufacturing system some 60 years later. This essay will link these two related but distinct narratives together in tracing, by way of a few key examples, the dialogue between automobiles and architecture over the last century.

In any account of architectural responses to modernity, Le Corbusier is rightly accorded a special status. In his work, the need to define an appropriate relationship between humans and their machines – most particularly the motorcar – was investigated at many different scales: from the private family dwelling up to the idealized city for three million people. However, it is important to recognize that this relationship between man and machine was predominantly expressed by Le Corbusier in a symbolic or theoretical form, whether in terms of design, or the representation and dissemination of that design. His belief in the symbolic power of the car was felt on several different levels. At its most abstract, the car represented the purest and most dynamic expression of the epoch, and as such was an object lesson for architecture, which in Le Corbusier's view had clearly failed to respond to modern conditions: 'If the problem of the dwelling or the flat were studied in the same way that a chassis is, a speedy transformation and improvement would be seen in our houses.'[2] But how could architectural 'problems' possibly be solved through the emulation of the car? Le Corbusier continued: 'If houses were constructed by industrial mass-production, like chassis, unexpected but sane and defensible forms would soon appear, and a new aesthetic would be formulated with astonishing precision.'[3]

Thus if Taylorist principles and systems of managing production, as implemented by Henry Ford

with such spectacular success just a decade earlier, could be applied to the production of houses, then not only could they be produced more cheaply and in greater numbers, but also their form would more correctly express the spirit of the industrial age. In the early 1920s Le Corbusier evolved a prototypical expression of this idea in his 'Citrohan' house, a simple concrete-framed design that was suitable for industrialized production. With its name deliberately

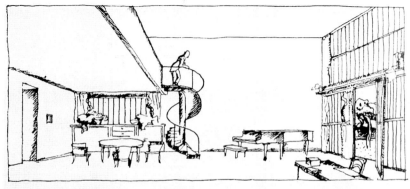

LE CORBUSIER, 1921. MASS-PRODUCTION HOUSE

'A house like a motor-car': Le Corbusier's Citrohan House.

evocative of the French manufacturer Citroën, this was intended to be a 'house like a car', not only in its method of production but more literally in its box-like simplified form. However, the problem for architects attempting to express such a relationship was that cars were self-evidently more exciting and dynamic than static buildings could ever hope to be. In what appeared to be an acknowledgement of this irreconcilable difference, Le Corbusier often carefully arranged a car in the foreground of images of his new buildings, as if somehow the architecture could assume the car's qualities by close association. Nor, incidentally, did it prove possible for architecture to adapt easily to the demands of Fordist industrialized production, despite

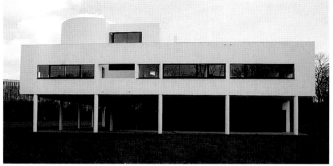

Above: A machine for living in: Le Corbusier's Villa Savoye, 1930.

Left: Fast living: Le Corbusier's double house, Weissenhof Siedlung, Stuttgart, 1927.

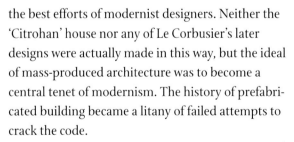

the best efforts of modernist designers. Neither the 'Citrohan' house nor any of Le Corbusier's later designs were actually made in this way, but the ideal of mass-produced architecture was to become a central tenet of modernism. The history of prefabricated building became a litany of failed attempts to crack the code.

It proved far more possible for the motorcar to provide a direct influence on the design process. The dimensions of Le Corbusier's iconic Villa Savoye of 1930 were determined by the turning circle of the motorcar in which the inhabitants would arrive at this weekend house, a gesture that was analogous to the way in which classical architects had derived their system of proportion from the human body in the

pre-industrial era. As historian Tim Benton observed: 'As a sequel to Vitruvian Man (the measure of humanist classical architecture), can we talk here of the Vitruvian Car (the measure of machine-age man)?'[4] But it was at the urban scale that the car became the principal determinant of the human environment. In terms of Le Corbusier's theoretical city plans of the 1920s, he argued that most historic cities had grown up in the haphazard 'way of the donkey', but that under industrialization such cities had become unmanageable; so now the 'way of man' demanded an urbanism of rigid geometry planned on Taylorist lines. In the 'Ville Contemporaine' the lofty glass towers of the technocratic rulers, the high-density apartments of the citizens, and the dynamic industrial suburbs were demarcated and linked by broad, straight highways on which vehicles would speed through the city, in a dramatic diagram of the reified life of a car-based society. In his subsequent 'Plan Obus' for Algiers, Le Corbusier strove for the absolute integration of human and machine within modern life, by designing a sinuous motorway viaduct that was simultaneously an apartment building beneath. Here, once again, Le Corbusier's plans could only be

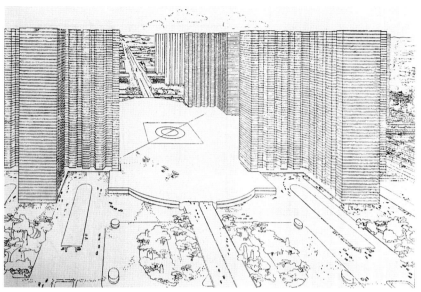

Cities for speed: Le Corbusier's Ville Contemporaine, 1923.

life in suburban Chicago. Indeed, the client, Frederick C. Robie, was actually a pioneering automobile maker.[5] The Robie House was hence one of the first house designs of the twentieth century to openly and unambiguously make provision for an integral garage and an associated parking area. This was clearly the route by which the owners and their guests expected to arrive and depart, and the ostensible 'front door' became little more than a hidden service entrance around the far side of the house.

However, it was not the design of private houses for the wealthy elite, but the production of buildings for the car industry itself that proved to be America's most significant contribution to the architecture of the automobile. In the key text of early modernism, Le Corbusier's *Vers Une Architecture* of 1923, there appears an uncaptioned photograph of a large factory, intended to represent 'the reassuring first fruits of the new age'. The lack of attribution is clearly meant to imply that this building was somehow an unconscious expression of the new zeitgeist that Le Corbusier was intent on articulating himself. The building was in fact Albert Kahn's Highland Park factory in Detroit, built for Henry Ford in 1910, a structure that was significant not only as the site of the first use of the continuous moving assembly line, but also because of the frank architectural expression of the industrial materials from which it was constructed. Kahn went on to design factories and office buildings for most of the major car makers in the USA, the majority of whom were of course concentrated in Detroit, and for many other industrialists as well; by the start of the World War II it was

conceived of, at best, as theoretical diagrams, yet they were later to provide a blueprint for the reconstruction of many western cities following the destruction of the World War II.

For the European modern movement in the 1920s, the inspiration of the car could only ever be a theoretical one, given that vehicle ownership at that time was still so low. But in America, substantial numbers of private vehicles – 50 per cent of them Model T Fords – were already to be found on a fast-growing road network in the inter-war period. American architectural responses to the car were therefore always more likely to be rooted in practical considerations of how to accommodate it than in theoretical concerns about the future it might produce. For example, Frank Lloyd Wright's Robie House of 1909 is famous for articulating a symbolic relationship between the dwelling and the landscape of the American prairie, but it is equally relevant in this context for its adaptation to the new realities of

A house for a motorist: Frank Lloyd Wright's Robie House, 1909.

Assembling modernity: Albert Kahn's Highland Park plant, 1910.

reckoned that Kahn's office was responsible for nearly 20 per cent of all architect-designed industrial building in America. His influence abroad was immediate and widespread. When Fiat boss Agnelli came to Detroit in the 1920s to meet Henry Ford, he was so struck by Ford's Kahn-designed River Rouge plant, that on his return to Italy he commissioned the Lingotto Factory in Turin. This building, with its ascending production line leading up to the much-photographed banked test track on the roof, captured the drama and dynamism of the car like no other building, by seemingly combining the rational

The dynamism of speed: the roof-top test-track at Giacomo Matté-Trucco's Fiat Lingotto factory, Turin, 1923.

systems of Ford with the lyrical and emotional celebration of speed proclaimed by the Futurists.

The enthusiasm with which Albert Kahn's factories were received by progressive artists and architects both in America and Europe is described elsewhere in this book, but here a telling irony needs to be pointed out. For it was the case that the adulatory response to Kahn's industrial architecture by Le Corbusier, and by other modernists such as Erich Mendelsohn, who were more willing than Corb to acknowledge Kahn's achievement, was never reciprocated. Indeed, Kahn remained deeply suspicious of contemporary trends in European modern architecture, writing that:

The attempt to continue a vital architecture and one related to and enriching our own time instead of merely repeating old forms is, of course, proper. What is wrong with the movement today is the throwing to the winds all precedent, the idea that new style may be created by an abandonment of all old.[6]

Indeed, Kahn's affinity with the older Beaux-Arts tradition from Europe allowed him to practice in a variety of historicist architectural styles, in response to the nature of the individual commission. Thus

A house for an industrialist: Albert Kahn, Edsel and Eleanor Ford House, Grosse Pointe, Michigan, 1925.

Corporate architecture:
Above: William van Allen's Chrysler Building, New York, 1928–30.
Right: Eero Saarinen's General Motors Technical Center, Flint, Michigan, 1955–6.

while his factory buildings achieved a degree of frank industrial expression that was the envy of his European admirers, the houses he designed for the new barons of the automotive industry, were not likely to impress the same exponents of architectural modernism. When Edsel Ford commissioned Kahn to design his house in the mid-1920s, he and his father, Henry Ford, took the architect to the Cotswolds area of England, 'to survey various styles of residential architecture'. The younger Ford was rewarded with an 'authentic' English manor house, full of genuine imported historical plasterwork and fittings, but

designed on a truly grand American scale.[7] Other American architects also showed that the symbolic response to automobile production need not emphasize efficiency or speed, as was demonstrated by William Van Alen's dreamy evocation of gargantuan radiator hoods in the crown of the Art-Deco Chrysler Building in midtown Manhattan (1928–30).

The fundamental contradiction that modernist architects, whether they were European or American, faced in their attempt to make connections with the automobile came from their continuing belief, entrenched in discourse since the Italian Renaissance, that the resolution of ideas had to come through architectural form. The limitations of this approach, and the means of escaping such limitations, is best seen in another building for an American car producer, this time the General Motors Technical Center in Warren, Michigan (1950–56).[8] The dramatic expansion of the post-war US economy was driven by the aggressive empire-building activities of huge corporations, and none was more mind-bogglingly successful than the largest car company in the world, General Motors: by the mid-1960s it was to grow to such an extent that it employed 730,000 workers, and enjoyed an annual profit that was equal to the *combined* profits of the 40 leading companies in Britain, Germany and France.

The project for the GM Technical Center was designed by Eero Saarinen, the son of a renowned immigrant Finnish architect, Eliel Saarinen, himself the founding head of the influential Cranbrook Institute of Design outside Detroit. The young Eero Saarinen sought a tougher and more modernist approach to design, and soon built up close ties with Charles Eames, a brilliant tutor at Cranbrook. Together they formulated a new method of design that looked explicitly to the *systems approach* to production that was becoming the orthodoxy within American corporate thinking. At heart, the systems approach rejected the idea that a predetermined solution, or indeed any kind of fixed end-product, should be the goal of design or manufacture. More important was, first, an exhaustive and rigorous definition and analysis of the problem in hand; and, second, the creation of a flexible and innovative atmosphere in which any possible solution could be researched and developed. The emphasis was now on the open nature of the research process, rather than on any image or notion of the resulting product.

General Motors had started to realize not just the full extent of the post-war consumer boom, but also the key role that the research and development (R&D) of new car models would play in fuelling demand. The historical mistakes of Henry Ford, who had clung on for too long to his costly and fixed assembly line systems, and had hence over-produced his Model-T and Model-A cars, were not lost on his greatest rivals. Research and innovation were, from now on, the kings at General Motors, resulting in the famous new models designed by Harley Earl and his team. Therefore GM decided to escalate dramatically the scope of their proposed research institute. The budget rose to a truly staggering sum of $100,000,000. This was corporate patronage on the grandest scale ever, more akin to the aspirations of Louis XIV than anything industrial architecture had seen before.

For the General Motors Technical Center, built on a massive 900-acre site in Warren, Saarinen borrowed quite blatantly from the minimalist design method and the rational, modular constructional techniques then being used by Mies van der Rohe in Chicago for the Illinois Institute of Technology (1940 onwards). This Miesian approach was relatively easy for other architects to replicate, as the homages that became *de rigueur* across the USA in the 1950s amply showed. In contrast, the brilliance of Saarinen's design for the GM Technical Center was that it proposed two genuine innovations.

The first lay in the introduction of cutting-edge technology from the automobile industry itself. Here the aim was to create a sleek, high-precision form of architecture that had all the shiny allure of the latest big and brazen American cars. The most copied, but far from only, technological innovation by Saarinen at General Motors was the use of neoprene gaskets to

hold in place the infill elements in the curtain walls, handled in the same manner as car windscreens in the nearby automotive factories. It was an early example of direct technology transfer, with the architects designing the details in conjunction with GM's own technical staff. And it worked; the principles of Saarinen's gasket technology were those adopted by starry-eyed High Tech architects like Norman Foster and Richard Rogers in 1960s Britain, and are still broadly the same today.

The problem, however, with the High Tech technology-transfer approach was that yet again it located the influence of automobiles in terms of built elements, and taken on this level, it could never compete. Hence the second, and more important, feature of the GM Technical Center was its conscious attempt to use the huge site to develop an architectural aesthetic that could only be comprehended when travelling around the site in an automobile. A scale appropriate for a car-based society was Saarinen's stated goal. This explains why the layout appears now to be excessively fragmented, and why an immense, 22-acre ornamental lake was used as the centrepiece of the composition. It also explains the bold formal gestures in the scheme. But even more striking is the use of colour. Whereas Mies van der Rohe relied on a restrained palette in his campus, Saarinen introduced vivid end walls of glazed brickwork in blue, red, and yellow. When experienced as an environment, the play of grid and colour reads as a three-dimensional analogy of an abstract painting by Piet Mondrian.

The design for the GM Technical Center implied a large-scale, punchy aesthetic that could never be

Learning from Las Vegas: Sands Hotel, Las Vegas strip, and classic American neon.

appreciated by the static critic, but only by someone who was travelling at speed in a motor car. What it meant was that two decades before Robert Venturi and Denise Scott Brown's celebrated polemic for a car-based aesthetic system, *Learning from Las Vegas*, Saarinen had suggested the possibility of a mobile design approach.[9] And this connection was no coincidence, for the fresh-faced Robert Venturi was one of the many ambitious and talented architects who eagerly came to work in Eero Saarinen's office in the mid-1950s. Venturi stayed for two-and-a-half years, during which time the GM Technical Center was the main project on the drawing board. Later, he and Scott Brown went on to become the champions of the most ubiquitous and despised manifestations of American car culture, the roadside architecture of signs, sheds, motels and diners. In *Learning From Las Vegas*, and in projects such as Fire Station No. 4 in Columbus, Indiana (1967), they explicitly sought to draw lessons from an urbanism that was designed to be consumed from inside a moving car. Largely under their influence, the 'kitsch trash' of the American roadside has gained widespread acceptance within the high culture of architecture, and subsequently certain architects have revelled in highly self-conscious displays of affection for this 'modern vernacular'. The emphasis on this semiological analysis of architecture-as-a-sign-system was helped unwittingly in the USA by a ruthless approach to new motor-based planning goals. Not only did this facilitate the rise of the tract suburbs and the 'edge-city' phenomenon, it simultaneously decimated post-war American cities. Modern road planning meant elevated urban freeways smashing through the existing fabric in order to recast the city for the car. At least Robert Moses, the planning supremo of New York City, was brutally honest when he observed: 'When you operate in an overbuilt

metropolis, you have to hack your way with a meat axe.'[10] The results of Moses's approach, as Marshall Berman has pointed out, was the rapid decline of subjugated areas such as the Bronx into poor African–American ghettos. Disillusion with this reckless treatment of cities crept in at exactly the same time in the 1960s that the first alarm bells were ringing about the car itself. In 1961, Jane Jacobs's *The Death and Life of Great American Cities* exposed the effects of car-based suburbanization on traditional inner-city communities, providing a warning that was listened to but not acted on in America, where continued 'white flight' led to massive depopulation and decline from which many industrial cities are still struggling to recover.[11]

In Europe, the attitude towards car-based planning and car-based architectural aesthetics has always been more circumspect. There was no doubt that the car needed to be accommodated. Le Corbusier's English translator, Frederick Etchells, noted, in his introduction to *The City of Tomorrow*, of 1927 that 'the problem of transit and transportation alone is quite enough to demand the reconstruction of the modern city!'[12] In the depression-hit decade of the 1930s, such ideas lay dormant until post-war reconstruction provided the opportunity for modern architects to implement their carefully nurtured theoretical ideas. With Le Corbusier's emphasis on the arterial traffic route firmly in their minds, architects across Europe began the task of recasting their cities in a modern idiom. The County of London Plan, produced in 1943, is archetypal of clumsy attempts to reconcile Le Corbusier's *tabula rasa* approach to the urban plan with the battered remnants of an existing city. Despite the ponderous official language, the dissatisfaction with the old, haphazard fabric of the city is clear, and the message is ominous when the report calls for:

Cities for cars: Abercrombie and Forshaw's 1943 *County of London Plan*.

the imposition, on the present network of thoroughfares, of a properly co-ordinated system of road communications, in the form of a ring-radial-cross system, incorporating a ring-road for fast traffic and facilities for quick egress from the congested centre.[13]

    This somewhat deadpan sentence embraces the now all too familiar blueprint for the modern city, in which a 'properly co-ordinated system of road communications' actually means a US-style infrastructure. A little of this was built in European cities, though nothing on the same scale, and instead car-use was heavily conditioned through official reports such as the *Buchanan Report on Traffic in Cities and Towns* (1963) in Britain, and by a whole raft of transport-control policies across Europe.

    As an ideological struggle, the question of whether architecture and urbanism should welcome or reject the motorcar continues, even if the debate has lost much of its urgency. Today, the widespread acceptance is that conventional architecture and urbanism are incompatible with the demands of a car-based society, and the landscape needs to be transformed on a scale comparable with the Industrial Revolution of two centuries ago. Out-of-town shopping malls, office complexes and low density residential suburbs have effectively created a new pattern of urban life across America, and increasingly the rest of the world as well. Yet, some of the road-signs seem to be pointing in the other direction. Venturi and Scott Brown admit that they are horrified by the fact that their beloved Las Vegas, which they once praised for its fast car-based Strip and casinos that were nothing more than huge 'decorated sheds'

Return to a simpler age: Andres Duany and Elizabeth Plater-Zyberk, estate in Seaside, Florida, 1980s.

with fancy billboard signs outside, has now turned into a pedestrianized, Disneyfied theme park where, horror of horrors, people elect to walk![14] This trend is reinforced by the so-called 'new urbanism' in the United States, typified by the planned communities of Seaside and Celebration in Florida (and taken up in Britain by Prince Charles and his acolytes in developments such as Poundbury near Dorchester), which sees resistance to the impact of the motorcar as a definite goal. A recent text in support of 'new urbanism' noted pointedly that 'there is a significant difference between running into someone while strolling down a street and running into someone while driving'.[15]

But there is now a further twist in the tale of the relationship between architecture and urbanism, one where the initial reliance on formal analogies is rejected along with the subsequent and equally redundant approach based on attempting to design for a car-based aesthetic. The issue is no longer whether to search for any forms or symbolic values from the automobile, positive or negative. The approach of Rem Koolhaas, in his writings on the 'generic city' and the rapidly growing cities of the Pearl River Delta in China, seems to offer another, and far more audacious, approach.[16] Here the talk of cars and their infrastructure is fully subsumed into the discussion of

Generic city: Shanghai, 2001.

architecture and urbanism. The car is no longer something 'other' that is to be emulated, symbolized, liked or disliked. It is simply there within the maelstrom of consumerist capitalism. So perhaps the final act in the relationship of the automobile to architecture / urbanism is for them simply to dissolve into each other, thereby pushing things far further than Le Corbusier or Eero Saarinen or Venturi and Scott Brown would ever have dared. In turn, maybe Koolhaas has simply transferred the architectural fascination with cars and roads into one with planes and airports, but that is the subject of another essay.

MYTHS AND MOTORS

Love at first sight?
Has the car taken up the burden of sex in an increasingly neuter world?
Have we been rushed into some sort of polygamy by the car?

MARSHALL McLUHAN[1]

It was not long after Harley J. Earl had placed his first trademark tail fins on the 1949 Cadillac that McLuhan's groundbreaking assault on the 'collective dream' of American mass culture first appeared. It is one of the great ironies in the history of the automobile that at the very moment when the culture of the car seemed at its apogee, its debunking as the epitome of Modern progress was already under way.

Yet the golden age of car design was only just in full swing, as affluent American consumers fell in love with the motorcar, and the design studios of Detroit abandoned any pretext of functionalism to indulge in an exuberant, extravagant excess of styling that was to last for a further decade. When Le Corbusier dreamed in the 1920s of the car evolving towards an ideal form, he clearly didn't have the 1957 Chevrolet Bel Air in mind, and when he wrote that competition would force manufacturers 'to prosecute the search for a perfection and a harmony beyond the mere practical side, a manifestation not only of perfection and harmony, but of beauty',[2] he had obviously failed to imagine the effect a full-scale consumer boom would have on corporate car design. Yet nearer home, Corb's faith in the car as the cultural icon of the age was echoed in responses to France's own dream car, the Citroën DS. To Roland Barthes in the mid-1950s, the DS appeared as 'a superlative *object*' that appeared to have fallen from the sky.[3]

In the 1960s, however, the myth of the motorcar itself fell to earth with devastating consequences, as the price to be paid for this orgy of excess was slowly revealed. The first portent of trouble ahead came with the spectacular failure of the extravagantly over-styled Ford Edsel, launched in 1957 after ten years and $250 million worth of development, and promptly scrapped after only two years of poor sales. In 1965, Ralph Nader's *Unsafe at Any Speed* [4] revealed how Detroit was happy to produce and market cars that it knew to be unsafe. Nader's prime targets were two of America's most popular 'muscle' cars, the Mustang and the Corvair; sales of the latter subsequently dropped by 93 per cent. By the early 1970s, the oil crisis was spelling the end for the great American gas guzzlers, and economy and efficiency were becoming the mantras of the late twentieth-century, Japanese-inspired auto industry.

In a post-McLuhan world, it is hard to imagine that there was ever a time when cars could have been hailed as the 'exact equivalent of the great Gothic cathedrals'.[5] Yet it seems that the desire to endorse the mythic properties of the motorcar remains undiminished. Speed, sex and power are still the predominant sales pitches for most models, and the gender symbolism of body styles is no less apparent than it was; it has simply become more ambiguous. Post-industrial man, it seems, still desires his mechanical bride.

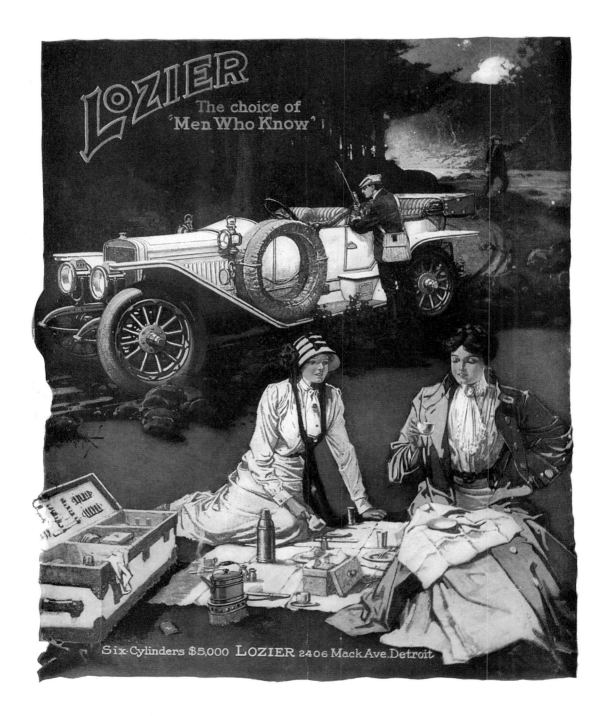

An advertisement for Lozier cars, Detroit, 1910s.

Nature...

IT'LL GROW BACK

DAMAGE
POISON FOR THE ROAD

Top: Promotional diorama in the 'Ford Rotunda' at the River
Rouge plant, Detroit, c. 1958.
Right: An 'adbusting' image of the 1990s.

Top: Depression-era Packard ad outside the Packard plant.
Above: Post-war Packard ad by the Packard plant.

Ad for a 1957 Dodge Custom Royal.

The 1958 Ford Edsel Citation.

WHEN BETTER AUTOMOBILES ARE BUILT BUICK WILL BUILD THEM

Hundreds of thousands of families have already made the magnificent change to the

MOST TALKED-ABOUT STYLE OF TODAY

Right from the start there was talk about this '59 Buick's style. Clean, fresh, totally new, designed to stay new for years to come . . . and as the year rolls on, more and more we hear enthusiasm from owners for the pleasures beneath the eye-stopping style.

Owners tell of 15 to 18 miles per gallon from

the ablest engines and transmissions Buick ever built. They talk of the amazing quietness of these cars and of their superb riding comfort and roadability. They like the extra safety of brakes found only on Buick in America today . . . big, fast-acting, sure-feeling brakes with aluminum front drums, fin-cooled both front and rear. Take

it from these hundreds of thousands of owners . . . more that's new will happen to you in Buick '59 than in any other car. Let your Quality Buick Dealer show you The Car . . . today!

LeSABRE · INVICTA · ELECTRA

BUICK MOTOR DIVISION, GENERAL MOTORS CORPORATION

THE CAR: BUICK '59

An ad for the 1959 Buick.

Shooting ads: top, 1940s; bottom, 1990s.

Top: Hisham Abdel Hadi, photo taken on the road to the Dead Sea, Palestine, 1955.
Right: Trabant with a Rolls-Royce badge, Prague, 1990.

The Birth of the Automobile

ILYA EHRENBURG

Charles Bernard at first dealt in cigarette paper. Then he sold the paper depot and simply began living. He lived slow and wise, like a turtle. He read the *Almanac of Nature Lovers*. The almanac explained which clouds were a sign of rain and which of wind. It also explained when the swallows and linnets came back, and how to raise rabbits, and where to pick fragrant lavender. Bernard didn't have rabbits. He had never seen a linnet. He lived in Paris, on narrow Rue Estrapade. Under his windows, the day smelled of red cheeses in the dairy, and the night of garbage cans.

Bernard read the almanac, for he had a great deal of time. In addition, he had a dreamy heart and a small private income. After breakfast, he usually went to the Botanical Garden. There he fed the sparrows crumbs of yesterday's bread and smiled at the drooling babies who were squeaking in their carriages.

He could have lived quietly to a ripe, old age: turtles are famous for their longevity.

Bernard's younger sister, who lived in Perigueux, often invited Bernard to visit her. But he pleaded business or illness. He was afraid of the trip: stations, hurly-burly, whistles. After all, it was twelve hours to Perigeux! Bernard preferred the *Almanac of Nature Lovers*.

Little by little, though, disquiet started oozing into Bernard's life. It began with some stupid movie. Earlier, Bernard had only gone to the circus with the concièrge's children. Friends dragged him to a film. Bernard liked everything: a galloping horse, an Apache on the roof of a very tall house, the life of underwater reptiles. He took to going to the movies every Friday. A harmless entertainment: The movie house was on the next block, and it showed poignant melodramas. But it was there that the bad thing happened. In the dark theater, amid the smooching couples and the comforting rattle of the projector, Bernard unexpectedly started trembling: A car raced across the screen. The entire audience was racing in that car. Bernard suddenly felt that he too was racing somewhere. Everything else was quickly forgotten. Did it matter that the car belonged to a young soccer-player, that his lovely fiancée was waiting for him in a cottage, and that they both feared her father's curse? Bernard only saw the flashing bushes and dust. Even though the theater was very stuffy, his face felt a sharp wind. His skin contracted and burned. Bernard forgot himself to such an extent that he stood up. Behind him, people yelled: 'Hey you! Sit down!. . .' Without waiting for the picture to end, he ran out into the street. Let them marry or not marry! It was all the same to him! He had come to realize a great deal. Bernard did not go home. He walked swiftly through the deserted streets. He wished that the houses could always flash by like the bushes. He was far away, perhaps in Granada or at the North Pole.

As of that day, he neglected the almanac. He bought an old guide to the Pyrenees, some maps, and a compass. Only he didn't travel anywhere. He journeyed, while sitting in his home on Rue Estrapade. He could still fight temptation.

Then a new serpent moved into his home. It

hissed sweetly. It was the radio. Bernard's day still had an appearance of well-being. But at night he went crazy. He wore warm slippers with pompons. But he wasn't sitting at his fireplace; no, he was whizzing through the world. His lips moved suspiciously. He was looking for waves. Here was Barcelona . . . Here was Karlsruhe . . . The German word 'bitte.' Bach. Spaniards. A charleston. The winner of the race at Oxford. The Royal Dutch rates. An Italian lesson: forte, morte, cannelloni. The victory of the Conservatives in Sweden. The bells of the Kremlin: The *Internationale*. Another charleston. The world moohed, bleated, meowed. Charles Bernard whizzed through the world, in soft slippers with pompons, that same Charles Bernard who had once dealt in cigarette-paper. His thinny-thin moustache wriggled convulsively, his face turned lilac. He really looked fearful in the silence of his musty room. No one saw him, however. He was still at home, on Rue Estrapade.

Then? Then the inevitable happened. It was not for nothing that tens of thousands of people bent their backs; it was not for nothing that the conveyor belt screeched; it was not for nothing that the fateful letters blazed night after night on the Eiffel Tower. The streets of Paris, swarming with automobiles, were covered with posters as cajoling and coddling as the hiss of the nocturnal serpent. Charles Bernard remembered the almanac and his sister in Perigueux. He would be able to admire the clouds, the various clouds from the *Almanac of Nature Lovers*: cumuli, cirri, strati. At last he would get to see those unknown linnets! And the lavender! . . . What a fine fragrance it must have!

The car wasn't cheap, however, and Bernard still vacillated. But then he recalled the evening at the movies. He ran to one of the dealers. The man received him, calm, friendly, as though he had known

for a long time that Bernard, modest Bernard, the turtle-man, would come to him sooner or later.

Bernard purchased a marvellous car: ten H.P., eighteen monthly instalments, a smooth drive, steel body, and last, last but not least, an electric lighter and a luxurious vase. That night he didn't even listen to the meowing of Barcelona. Nor did he sleep. He sat silent in the dusty armchair, throwing his arms up from time to time. He was probably flying. His eyes were moist like the green earth after the fall of man.

Every morning he went to driving-school. He learned quickly. Two weeks later he went to take the test. He was so careful that ex-dealer in cigarette-paper! Long before reaching a crossing he would slow down and honk menacingly. He never tried to pass another car. He drove slowly and wisely, like a turtle, and naturally he passed all the tests.

Then he began preparing for his trip. He bought a knitted jacket, a first-aid kit, and a strategic map. He went to the Botanical Garden for one last time to feed his sparrows. Tomorrow he was driving to Perigueux. He was driving, more precisely, to his sister Louise. But he admitted to the sparrows: 'Messieurs, I am driving to the linnets. Those are remarkable birds! . . .' There was only one thing he didn't admit to them. And he was afraid to admit it even to himself. His face was already burning, it was singed by the extraordinary wind.

And thus Charles Bernard, a man of private means, drove off to his sister in Perigueux.

At first, Bernard drove slowly and sedately. He knew that you mustn't drive a car fast for the first 500 miles. That was what they had taught him at school, that was what the dealer had told him, that was what it said in the instruction booklet. Still, 30 kilometers an hour seemed like a furious flight to Bernard. He couldn't distinguish hills, trees, or people. Everything flashed by as in the movie-theater. He halted. He almost wanted to see if there were any linnets about. After all, he was already far away from Paris. But instead, he looked at the bolts in the wheels. Then he drove on. Forgetting himself, he increased the speed somewhat. The needle shot forward, and the wind suddenly became as huge as the world.

Aha, so they were all lying: the dealer and the instruction-booklet. You can drive a new car a lot faster than they said. Well, all the better! He hadn't bought a car just to creep along. He wasn't a turtle. Away with the Botanical Garden! But wait, Charles! What's the hurry? Louise had already waited eight years. She'd wait another day. Why, supposedly, you were driving off to see the lavender. Stop the car! Have a rest! Lie down on the grass! The grass must be downy here, like the fleecy cirri. That was Charles Bernard, the former cigarette-paper dealer, speaking. But Charles the second didn't reply. Charles the second knew only one thing: surge and wind. He squinted. He was drunk, as though he had polished off a bottle of cognac. He grinned. He was zooming faster and faster.

A train is faster than an eagle. But a fly, a teeny fly, can outspeed an express train. A swallow flies faster than a fly. But any swallow is outstripped by a car. Bernard had once read about that in the Sunday papers. But now he wasn't thinking about the swallow. He wasn't even looking at the needle: What did he need numbers for? The car raced for dear life. A long, straight highway. Perhaps he should slow down? . . . It was a new car, after all . . . The first 500 kilometers . . . The man who had once dealt in paper muttered dolefully: Perhaps? . . . However, the car ought to know itself. After all, it was the car that was zooming. Bernard had nothing to do with it. He had merely bought it on the installment plan. . . . Besides, he was insured. . . . And his life? The sparrows? Too late to think. He had already stopped smiling. The wind struck his face painfully. His eyes stuck together. Bernard couldn't see anything. He turned off to the right. Perhaps it wasn't Bernard turning. Some people hollered: Yes! He didn't hear. Then – only one thought: What had happened to the car? . . . Oh well, it was quite obvious! Bernard opened his eyes for a moment. Quite obvious: The car had gone crazy. Things like that happen. A chapter in the manual: 'Illnesses of the Engine.' Addendum: Mental Illnesses. White, incredible sun and wind. Better close your eyes. Here comes the end. The highways ended. The long, straight highway came to an end. School, cigarette paper, Estrapade, sparrows. Everything ended. Faster! Faster, faster!

Then a soft shriek. That's how children's balloons perish. Emerald-green or light raspberry-pink. The crazy car raced toward a slope. It was dreadful and simple. It no longer had a thousand parts, it only had one cruel will. It was ancient and human now. With the lofty joy of self-oblivion it flew downward, into a pitiful dale filled with dry juniper.

The linnets warbled, and the lavender was sweet and fragrant. Car No 180A-74 – iron splinter, glass shards, a lump of warm flesh – lay unstirring beneath the solemn midday sun.

FROM *The Life of the Automobile* (1929)

The New Citroën

ROLAND BARTHES

I think that cars today are almost the exact equivalent of the great Gothic cathedrals: I mean the supreme creation of an era, conceived with passion by unknown artists, and consumed in image if not in usage by a whole population which appropriates them as a purely magical object.

It is obvious that the new Citroën has fallen from the sky inasmuch as it appears at first sight as a superlative *object*. We must not forget that an object is the best messenger of a world above that of nature: one can easily see in an object at once a perfection and an absence of origin, a closure and a brilliance, a transformation of life into matter (matter is much more magical than life), and in a word a *silence* which belongs to the realm of fairy-tales. The *D.S.* – the 'Goddess' – has all the features (or at least the public is unanimous in attributing them to it at first sight) of one of those objects from another universe which have supplied fuel for the neomania of the eighteenth century and that of our own science-fiction: the *Déesse* is *first and foremost* a new *Nautilus*.

This is why it excites interest less by its substance than by the junction of its components. It is well known that smoothness is always an attribute of perfection because its opposite reveals a technical and typically human operation of assembling: Christ's robe was seamless, just as the airships of science-fiction are made of unbroken metal. The *D.S. 19* has no pretensions about being as smooth as cake-icing, although its general shape is very rounded; yet it is the dove-tailing of its sections which interest the public

most: one keenly fingers the edges of the windows, one feels along the wide rubber grooves which link the back window to its metal surround. There are in the *D.S.* the beginnings of a new phenomenology of assembling, as if one progressed from a world where elements are welded to a world where they are juxta-posed and hold together by sole virtue of their wondrous shape, which of course is meant to prepare one for the idea of a more benign Nature.

As for the material itself, it is certain that it promotes a taste for lightness in its magical sense. There is a return to a certain degree of streamlining, new, however, since it is less bulky, less incisive, more relaxed than that which one found in the first period of this fashion. Speed here is expressed by less aggres-sive, less athletic signs, as if it were evolving from a

primitive to a classical form. This spiritualization can be seen in the extent, the quality and the material of the glass-work. The *Déesse* is obviously the exaltation of glass, and pressed metal is only a support for it. Here, the glass surfaces are not windows, openings pierced in a dark shell; they are vast walls of air and space, with the curvature, the spread and the brilliance of soap-bubbles, the hard thinness of a substance more entomological than mineral (the Citroën emblem, with its arrows, has in fact become a winged emblem, as if one was proceeding from the category of propulsion to that of spontaneous motion, from that of the engine to that of the organism).

We are therefore dealing here with a humanized art, and it is possible that the *Déesse* marks a change in the mythology of cars. Until now, the ultimate in cars belonged rather to the bestiary of power; here it becomes at once more spiritual and more object-like, and despite some concessions to neomania (such as the empty steering wheel), it is now more *homely*, more attuned to this sublimation of the utensil which one also finds in the design of contemporary household equipment. The dashboard looks more like the working surface of a modern kitchen than the control-room of a factory: the slim panes of matt fluted metal, the small levers topped by a white ball, the very simple dials, the very discreteness of the nickel-work, all this signifies a kind of control exercised over motion, which is henceforth conceived as comfort rather than performance. One is obviously turning from an alchemy of speed to a relish in driving.

The public, it seems, has admirably divined the novelty of the themes which are suggested to it. Responding at first to the neologism (a whole publicity campaign had kept it on the alert for years), it tries very quickly to fall back on a behaviour which indicates adjustment and a readiness to use ('*You've got to get used to it*'). In the exhibition halls, the car on show is explored with an intense, amorous studiousness: it is the great tactile phase of discovery, the moment when visual wonder is about to receive the reasoned assault of touch (for touch is the most demystifying of all senses, unlike sight, which is the most magical). The bodywork, the lines of union are touched, the upholstery palpated, the seats tried, the doors caressed, the cushion fondled; before the wheel, one pretends to drive with one's whole body. The object here is totally prostituted, appropriated: originating from the heaven of *Metropolis*, the Goddess is in a quarter of an hour mediatized, actualizing through this exorcism the very essence of petit-bourgeois advancement.

FROM *Mythologies* (1957)

Sexual Ambiguity and Automotive Engineering

PATRICK KEILLER

After a hundred years or so, the political and environmental legacy of the car is sufficiently problematic that it seems almost beside the point to suggest that, within an overview of general irredeemability, there is difference. One suspects that even Amory Lovins's Hypercar concept, with its promise of lightweight, super-efficient, hydrogen-powered vehicles that emit only water vapour, may, in the end, offer little compensation for the anti-urban, socially atomistic, death-dealing, child-killing propensities of the car. One wonders if there have ever been 'good' cars, and, if so, what they were, and what happened to them?

In his essay 'The New Citroën', Roland Barthes wrote, of the DS19:

We are . . . dealing here with a humanized art, and it is possible that the *Déesse* marks a change in the mythology of cars. Until now, the ultimate in cars belonged rather to the bestiary of power; here, it becomes at once more spiritual and . . . it is now more *homely* . . . One is obviously turning from an alchemy of speed to a relish in driving.[1]

On the other hand, in his remarkable and prophetic 'non-fiction' novel of 1929 *The Life of the Automobile*, Ilya Ehrenburg wrote, of André Citroën:

He was figuring out how to combine American know-how with European poverty. He had to make low-priced cars. These cars had to consume very little fuel. These low-priced cars had to look very smart. The European was poor, but vainglorious, he was so proud of his thousand years of culture! He would put up with a feeble engine, but not ugly proportions.[2]

For much of the twentieth century, the majority of cars adopted a layout in which the engine was placed at the front, aligned with the length of the car, driving the rear wheels through a clutch, a gearbox and a drive shaft. This arrangement tended to result in various formal characteristics: a relatively long bonnet; a housing for the gearbox between the driver's and the front-seat passenger's legs, from which projected a gear stick; and a tunnel along the centre of the floor of the passenger compartment. The front wheels were often at the very front of the car, so that, in order to minimize the wheelbase and the length of the drive shaft, the rear wheels were also placed as far forward as possible, with wheel arches that protruded into the passenger compartment, diminishing both the width of the rear seat and the comfort of any passengers who sat on it.

The HRG, a 'standard layout' sports car produced in the UK between 1939 and 1953, as illustrated in the 1963 *I Spy a Sports Car* book.

Some cars still adopt this layout, though since the 1970s, in Europe and Japan at least, front-engine, front-wheel drive has become the norm, and cars look slightly different. In cars that retain rear-wheel drive, such as all BMW and most Mercedes-Benz models, some of the formal characteristics listed above seem to have become more pronounced in recent years, as if in a conscious effort to evoke the designs of the 1930s. Curiously, many present-day front-wheel drive designs adopt an arrangement in which the gear stick is positioned on top of a volume that resembles the gearbox housing of a rear-wheel drive car, but does not contain the gearbox, or very much else.

The front-engine, rear-wheel drive arrangement evolved quite quickly:

The French company of Panhard et Levassor acquired the French rights to the Daimler engine in 1889. They originally made woodworking machinery in Paris and then diversified into motor cars. After experimenting with putting the engine in the centre or the rear of the vehicle they produced a car with a front-mounted, vertical, two-cylinder engine driving the rear wheels through a clutch and three-speed gearbox. This was to be the basis of the standard layout for cars for [most of] the next hundred years.[3]

In France, however, both front-engine, front-wheel drive and rear-engine, rear-wheel drive arrangements were already common by the 1950s, and since the mid-1930s the most innovative and arguably most impressive (most 'spiritual', in Barthes' terms) cars have avoided the 'standard layout' in favour of one or the other of these configurations. It is probably a mistake to think of the development of artefacts and technologies in quasi-Darwinian terms: the sexuality involved in car design is not the sexuality of cars, but the sexuality of people. Cars did not evolve tail fins to attract other cars. Nevertheless, the dominance of the 'standard layout' was probably initially practical, despite its rather obvious phallic symbolism. For a long time, the obstacle to front-engine, front-wheel drive was the more ambitious technology required to enable the steered wheels to be driven.

In any consideration about the design of a car, were it not for the desire to carry passengers, the best arrangement would presumably be to put the engine in the middle, which is more or less where it is placed in a modern racing car. A passenger car, however, consists of two or three volumes placed in line – the engine, the passenger compartment and, usually, a space for luggage. With a few exceptions such as Buckminster Fuller's Dymaxion car of 1933, the Fiat Multipla of the 1950s or the Volkswagen camper van, the people have not been placed at the front, and since the earliest years of the automobile, in only a few sports cars has the engine been placed in the middle. In the Dymaxion car, the engine was at the back and drove the front wheels, with the steered wheel at the rear, a feature that probably, more than anything else, led to its demise (in other respects, the Dymaxion was not so unlike a present-day 'people-carrier'). In practice, the alternatives to the 'standard layout' have been either rear-engine, rear-wheel drive, as in the original Volkswagen and its predecessors, or front-engine, front-wheel drive, as in the pre-war Citroën *Traction Avant* and its successors, the Saab 92, the Mini, and the majority of small and medium-sized cars produced today that are descended from these and other prototypes.

The front-engine, rear-wheel drive layout has the advantage of robust simplicity. Apart from the bestiary of power, its imagery might evoke the agricultural sturdiness of the tractor, the heroism of the truck – as driven by Yves Montand in *The Wages of Fear*, perhaps – or the civility of the Routemaster bus. Echoes of all of these might be found in, say, the Volvo Amazon, the Peugeot 403, the Morris Minor or any number of similarly 'decent', well-designed cars of the 1950s and '60s. Just when it was becoming less common in Europe, however, the 'standard layout' was also the common characteristic of a variety of cars associated with a rather disreputable, mostly heterosexual masculinity – American 'muscle' cars of the 1970s; their European poor relations like the Ford Capri; even, in certain contexts, BMW's. As far as I know, James Bond has never driven a front-wheel drive car. In this context, phrases such as 'hot rod' and 'straight six' clarify the symbolism of the 'standard layout', though it readily permits homo-erotic interpretation – as in, for instance, Kenneth Anger's *Kustom Kar Kommandos*. In the end, it's not so much that the layout's phallic symbolism suggests heterosexuality or problematic masculinity, but rather, perhaps, that non-'standard layout' cars – the *Déesse*, for instance – can be more readily interpreted in terms of sexual ambiguity. A modernist enthusiasm for aerodynamics and innovative engineering has never been a reliable indicator of radicalism in either political or sexual matters,[4] but it's intriguing that front-wheel drive began to dominate in the 1970s and '80s, at a time when the questioning of gender stereotypes began to be admitted to the mainstream media.

Generally, 'standard-layout' cars are often good at going fast on straight roads ('the alchemy of speed'), but even BMW's are often said to be not particularly good at going round corners, and the company's advertising seems increasingly concerned to justify its adherence to 'traditional' rear-wheel drive. Front-wheel drive cars do tend to handle better ('the relish of driving'). Rear-engine cars were often less predictable, especially at speed, but their design-

ers generally pursued similar goals of lightness, agility and aerodynamic efficiency. The most outstanding front-wheel drive cars have rarely been particularly powerful, succeeding rather through sophisticated design: 'One is obviously turning from an alchemy of speed to a relish in driving.' They have often evoked flight in various ways – in their handling, their lightness, their advanced suspension technologies (such as the self-levelling hydro-pneumatic suspension pioneered by Citroën), their aerodynamic shape and even, as in the case of Saab, by their being manufactured by an aircraft company. In this context, flight might be invoked as an enlightened, or even an ecstatic, state of mind. There is a utopian aspect to these aeronautical cars, as if their existence confirms the possibility of a world in which material well-being is more the result of creativity than of mere increased consumption.

With the globalization of car production, the homogeneity in design that has developed with it, and growing opposition to the car *per se*, this aspiration is increasingly difficult to credit. Cars in general have become more energy efficient, more reliable, safer, faster, more comfortable and cheaper, but they are, above all, much, much more numerous. At the same time, truly breathtaking cars, comparable with those in which the concepts of present-day designs were first developed, have disappeared.

In retrospect, Ehrenburg's dismissal of Citroën and his priorities seems somewhat premature, arrived at prior to the technological initiatives pioneered in Europe in the 1930s. These included the series of aerodynamic, rear-engine cars produced by Tatra in Czechoslovakia, and Citroën's *Traction Avant*, introduced in 1934 in France. Intriguingly, both of these extraordinary cars were the product of cultures in which Surrealism developed.

KNEE ACTION CARS

INDEPENDENT STEERING

CENTRAL TUBE CHASSIS

ENTIRELY JOINTLESS DRIVE

AIR COOLING

SELF CARRYING MOTOR

Engineering details of the Tatra T77.

One wonders what, if anything, this might indicate, as there seem to have been no direct connections. Although Surrealism was at least as much a programme for revolution in life as it was for one in art, the original movement involved no designers or architects. One might infer something of the Surrealists' attitude to design from some of their enthusiasms – their admiration, for instance, for the natural-history films of Jean Painlevé: *The Seahorse* and so on. Even as late as 1935, André Breton was denouncing the rationalism of International-Style modern architecture and endorsing Art Nouveau. The Surrealists were certainly involved with artefacts, with architecture and with spatial experience generally, but their architecture, for instance, was all borrowed – from Gaudí, from the *facteur* Cheval and so on – at least until Frederick Kiesler's magic architecture of the 1940s.

On the other hand, one can probably say that the mere fact of Surrealism and its enthusiasms encouraged, or perhaps merely paralleled, various tendencies in modern design in France and pre-war Czechoslovakia – the biomorphic, the ready-made, the improvisatory, the curvilinear, the poetic, the erotic – as opposed to the rationalist, classicizing,

repressing tendencies (illustrated perhaps, in terms of car design, by Walter Gropius's designs for Adler). One might see the work of Jean Prouvé, for example, in quasi-surrealist terms, or the organic, 'extended' functionalism of Hugo Häring and Hans Scharoun, who was influential in Czechoslovakia in the '30s. There is a good deal of both Art Nouveau and marine biomorphism in Citroën's cars of the 1940s, '50s and '60s – the 2CV, the DS and the Ami 6 – and one wonders if perhaps this would have been the case without the diffused influence of Surrealism and its precursors. In the 1950s and '60s, looking across the Channel from the UK, these and various other French cars certainly looked like a serious attempt to poeticize the everyday.

In Czechoslovakia, the influence was more explicit. By 1919, Czech architects had already built a good deal of the Cubist architecture that remained largely hypothetical elsewhere, and had evolved their own 'national' version of Art Nouveau. With independence, these regional styles in architecture, together with parallel movements in art and literature, gave way to a wholehearted embrace of avant-garde influences from all over Europe. By the

The Tatra T77A.

mid-1930s, many Czechoslovakian artists had aligned themselves with international Surrealism, and Czech architecture had evolved an organic, aeronautical strand of International-Style modernism in which curved surfaces and non-rectilinear forms were becoming common.[5] Breton's critique of International-Style rationalism and his endorsement of Art Nouveau were delivered in a lecture, 'Surrealist Situation of the Object', given in Prague in 1935.[6] During the '20s, poets, artists and architects had shared the common platform of the Devĕtsil group, with Karel Teige's two-track ideology of poetism in art and literature, and functionalism in architecture and design. In theory, these distinct positions reflected the different roles of artists and designers, but in practice there was a good deal of crossover between the poetic, surrealist tendency and the functionalist. There was also contact with Hans Scharoun.[7] Aeronautical associations were particularly marked in, for example, Bohuslav Fuchs's 1928 Hotel Avion in Brno, or Ladislav Žák's 1933 Villa Hain in Prague, built for a prominent aircraft designer.[8] Between 1918 and 1939, modernism permeated Czech society, probably more, and for longer, than in any other country in Europe.

The aerodynamic Tatras were conceived in this context.[9] They were developed by a team directed by the Austrian engineer Hans Ledwinka (1878–1967).[10] Ledwinka had been a nineteen-year-old engineering student when Nesseldorfer Wagenbau – since 1850 a successful producer of carriages and railway wagons – had built its first car, the Präsident, in 1897. By 1901, he was jointly managing NW's car production. In 1921, having twice left and rejoined the company – now renamed Tatra – he directed the design of a small, fuel-efficient car suitable for the poor roads of Eastern Europe. The car was introduced in 1923 as the Tatra T11 and became very popular all over Europe. It had a central tubular spine, which housed the drive shaft, and independent, swinging half-axle rear suspension, an arrangement which became known as 'the Tatra chassis'. The T11 concept was developed in a range of successful designs, culminating in the popular T57, of which 22,000 were produced in a variety of versions between 1931 and 1949.

In the early 1930s, Ledwinka initiated the development of a small streamlined car with an air-cooled engine at the rear, adopting the streamlining patents of Paul Jaray, who had designed and tested cars in the wind tunnel of the Zeppelin works at Friedrichshafen. A prototype was produced in 1931, and in 1933, Tatra

The Tatra T87, side view.

presented the V570 'People's Car'. This design, which anticipated the later Volkswagen, never reached production, but was the basis of the larger production cars of the following two decades. The rear-engine layout eliminated the drive shaft, which increased efficiency, reduced noise and vibration, and made possible a lower, flat floor. It was easier to achieve an aerodynamic form, and engine noise was largely left behind, especially at speed. Air-cooling avoided the risks of freezing in winter and boiling over in summer.

The production cars were designed by Erich Übelacker (1899–1977) and a team of young engineering graduates, under Ledwinka's supervision.[11] Like other Czech modernists of the period, they sought to demonstrate the latest ideas in design and engineering, and when the first production model – the T77 – was presented to the press in March 1934, it was like nothing seen before. The body was a monocoque construction; the wings and headlamps were integral with the body; there were no running boards; and the underbody was as smooth as possible. A large tail fin decreased the effect of side winds and improved road-holding. The 3-litre 60-bhp V8 engine formed a monobloc assembly with the gearbox and rear axle, mounted in the forked rear of the central box-frame

chassis and removable for maintenance and repair. In some cars, the steering wheel was placed in the centre of the dashboard, with front passenger seats on either side of, and slightly behind, the driver, a feature also adopted for the contemporary Panhard Dynamic. The design was revised in 1935 as the T77A, with an even bigger 75-bhp engine and a central third headlamp, which on some cars moved with the steering, like the headlamps of the revised Citroën DS over 30 years later. Between 1933 and 1938, only 255 of both models were built. They were extremely expensive: in the UK, the T77 was offered at £990 – a very high price, especially when even cars that claimed a degree of sophistication were becoming cheaper.[12] Weighing 1,700 kilos, the car was also rather heavy, especially at the back, and Ledwinka instigated work on a successor.

This was the T87, the best known and most successful of the aerodynamic Tatras, also designed by Übelacker, of which 3,023 were produced between 1936 and 1950. It had a shorter, all-steel monocoque body with a fully integral frame and a light alloy 3-litre 75-bhp V8 engine, which together reduced the weight by 330 kilos. It had a top speed of 160 kph, cruised at 130 kph and was one of the fastest production cars of

The Tatra T87.

the period. It too was extremely expensive, offered in Germany in the late '30s for 8,450RM.[13]

The T87's basic concept endured, in a succession of increasingly bureaucratic post-war metamorphoses, for over 60 years, but Tatra never attained Ledwinka's goal of an energy-efficient, affordable, technologically advanced 'people's car'. Instead, he had produced an exclusive car of such unorthodox technological superiority that it could hardly fail to attract the interest of the *luftbegeistert* Nazis. Dr Fritz Todt, the inspector-general of the autobahn network, owned one, and production was permitted to continue during World War II, so that Tatra were the only company in Europe to produce cars for civilian use throughout the war. It is said that a number of German military personnel lost their lives in T87's, the weight of the V8 engine behind the rear wheels causing sudden loss of control if the car was driven too fast into bends.

In 1936, Tatra had also developed the T97, a smaller, less expensive car designed by Ledwinka's son Erich, who succeeded Übelacker as chief car designer, but production ceased after the Nazi occupation in 1939, when only 508 cars had been built. Apparently, although the T97 was larger (and a great

deal more expensive), its resemblance to Ferdinand Porsche's KdF-Wagen – which was to become the Volkswagen – embarrassed Hitler. Porsche, who had been in regular contact with Hans Ledwinka since 1933, was under pressure from Hitler to get the KdF-Wagen into production. Hitler admired Ledwinka's cars, having been driven thousands of kilometres in a T11 during the 1920s. When the KdF-Wagen appeared, its design infringed several patents held by Tatra, and the company initiated ten legal actions. Porsche was about to settle with Tatra when Hitler stopped him, shortly afterwards invading Czechoslovakia. The legal actions were resumed after the war, and in 1961 VW paid Tatra 3,000,000DM. Ledwinka, meanwhile, had been accused of collaboration and was imprisoned between 1945 and 1951. On his release, he was offered the opportunity to run the Tatra factory, but left for Austria, having retained his Austrian citizenship, and later moved to Munich. He kept his own T87 until 1965, when he donated it to the Deutsches Museum there.

Apart from a five-year period in the 1950s, Tatra continued to produce cars until 1998, though never in large numbers. After the war, the T97 was developed as the T600 Tatraplan, first produced in 1947. In 1952,

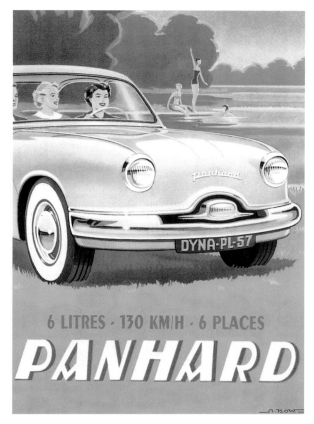

Poster for the Panhard Dyna 57.

Tatra's car production ceased until the Czechoslovakian government discovered the need for an indigenously produced limousine, which emerged as the Tatra T603, not so much a development as a *metamorphosis* of the T87, first exhibited in 1955 and produced between 1957 and 1975. It was updated as the T613, produced until 1996, and as the T700 until 1998. In the last year of production, only two T700's were built. Tatra continues to produce trucks, still built on Ledwinka's Tatra chassis. Apart from these vehicles, and a number of surviving pre-1950 Tatras, Ledwinka's legacy survives through his influence on Ferdinand Porsche, in the thousands of Volkswagens still running throughout the world, and in the Porsche 911 sports car, which is still produced.

After the war, similarly poetic strands of innovative car design and engineering were more often

found in France. André Citroën (1878–1935) had become a successful industrialist mass-producing munitions during World War I, and in 1919 converted his factory to car production. By the 1930s, front-wheel-drive cars were not unprecedented – in the UK, for example, the Alvis (*aluminium* + *avis*, Latin for 'bird') company had manufactured one in 1928 -- but when the *Traction Avant* was launched in 1934, it was the first front-wheel-drive car to enter mass production. The new Citroën adopted other innovations: it had independent front suspension, and its low, more than usually aerodynamic body was a monocoque shell, like the T87's, without a separate chassis. With exemplary handling and road-holding, the car was years ahead of its time. The *Traction Avant* was produced in a variety of versions until 1956, by which time it had been superseded by the DS19.

Unlike the Tatra, both the *Traction Avant* and the DS were successful in a growing mass market, but they were still fairly large, expensive cars for relatively well-off people. The Citroën 2CV, introduced in 1949, was a triumph of material economy and design, but no matter how endearing, it was a car conceived – explicitly – for peasants and did not really offer the high-speed, long-distance travel possibilities that came to be expected of the car in the post-war era. In the increasingly competitive market for medium-sized cars, until 1965, the cars with a standard of design and engineering comparable with that of Citroën were those produced by Panhard.

Panhard et Levassor survives as a part of PSA Peugeot Citroën, though the last Panhard car was produced in 1967, and since then the name has only been given to armoured cars. It might seem ironic that the name of such a beautiful car should only survive in a military context, but this is not such an unusual fate for an innovative motor manufacturer,

A Panhard PL17, side view.

shared in the UK by Alvis.

In 1876, Panhard et Levassor had been the first company in France to manufacture internal-combustion engines, producing the first 'standard-layout' car in 1891. By 1939, Panhard had a well-established reputation for big, luxurious, somewhat innovative cars, like the 1936 Dynamic, but under the post-war French government's Pons Plan, manufacturers received materials only if they concentrated on commercial vehicles and small or medium-sized cars. The Citroën 2CV, Renault 4CV, Peugeot 202, Simca 8 and Panhard Dyna were all produced in this context. During the war, Panhard had developed a largely aluminium 250-cc air-cooled engine for a project called the Voiture Petite. Encouraged by another experimental design – the Aluminium Français-Grégoire – demonstrating the potential of aluminium for car bodies, Panhard began work on a four-door front-wheel drive design for aluminium construction which was

launched as the Dyna in 1947 and put into production the following year.

The Dyna Z was introduced in 1953, with a much more aerodynamic body and its predecessor's 42-bhp engine. With a low centre of gravity and independent front suspension, it handled very well and was light, fast and fuel-efficient, carrying six passengers in comfort. The entire car weighed only 650 kg (with a full tank), a mere 108 kg per passenger. Aluminium construction was expensive and was gradually abandoned – by 1957, the body was built entirely of steel, but the cars still performed impressively. In 1959, a Tigre version with a 50-bhp engine was introduced, developed from a car built for the Le Mans 24-hour road race.

In 1955, Panhard had temporarily resolved its financial problems by selling a 25-per-cent stake to Citroën and assembling 2CV vans. When the subsequent model – the PL17 – was introduced in 1960, it

A Panhard PL17, front view.

was distributed by Citroën dealers. The PL17 was essentially the Dyna Z with a redesigned front and rear. The engine's power output was increased to 50 bhp (60 bhp for the Tigre) in 1962.

In the history of alternatives to the 'bestiary of power', one might see the Dyna Z as a high point. Beneath the car's aerodynamic, dolphin-like exterior is an organization of almost biomorphic functional clarity. The entire front section of the body lifts, hinged at the rear, to reveal the car's engine, transmission, steering and suspension, so that its mechanics are uniquely accessible. The two-cylinder aluminium engine – its horizontally opposed cylinders projecting on either side – the clutch and the gearbox form a monobloc from which the drive shafts connect to the front wheels. This, the front wheels and the suspension are mounted in a tubular steel frame bolted to the front of the passenger compartment, so that the entire front end of the car is removable for mainte-nance. The detailing of door handles, lamps and the openings of doors and boot is also quite unlike that of other cars. The front and rear ends of the car are rather similar, suggesting a curious ambiguity of orientation. The Panhard is perhaps even more 'spiri-tual' and 'homely' (in Barthes' terms) than the Citroën. Apart from the first car of 1891, Panhard do not feature much in English-language automotive crit-icism, but Dorling Kindersley's *Ultimate Classic Car Book*[14] states that Panhard claimed the lowest drag coefficient of any car in 1956, and describes the PL17 as 'light, quick, miserly on fuel and years ahead of its time', adding that it won the Monte Carlo rally, aver-aged 38 mpg and could accelerate from 0 to 60 mph in 23.1 seconds. A photograph shows factory-original tiger-skin pattern inserts in the door interiors.

The PL17 was produced until 1965, when Citroën finally bought out Panhard completely. In an inter-view, Jean Panhard recalled that 'when the [Citroën]

The Panhard Dyna 54, from a feature in *Autocar,* August 1953.

Ami 6 was launched, it became clear that the PL17 was in the way. Citroën then deliberately smothered Panhard. I'm not bitter, I drive a Citroën XM 2.5L turbo.'[15] The last Panhard was the 24CT sports car, which was produced from 1963 until 1967.

In retrospect, the post-war Panhard concept of a lightweight, spacious, aerodynamic car with a small, energy-efficient engine seems very modern. While it might also recall Ehrenburg's caricature of Citroën – the idea that Europeans 'would put up with a feeble engine, but not ugly proportions' – even the 22-bhp Dyna was no less powerful than its contemporaries, and the PL17's engine, which produced 50 bhp (60 bhp in the Tigre) was not at all feeble. In the mid-'60s, 50 bhp was a typical power output for much heavier cars with much larger engines.[16] Nevertheless, the Panhard probably did not suit a certain sort of driver. It travelled fast, but its competitive successes were achieved perhaps partly because a car that handles unusually well does not need to slow down as often as its competitors. Its attraction lies in the idea that, while it was both fast and elegant, it was a non-aggressive car.

Forty years later, car designers no longer have to choose between a light, energy-efficient engine and a high power output. Even small, economical cars are now surprisingly, unnecessarily powerful and can be, and often are, driven just as aggressively as other cars, so that although the Panhard's concept has aged well,

perhaps its most intriguing quality – what might be described as a combination of effectiveness and sensitivity – has not survived.

The design of most present-day cars, and the past successes of the Tatra and Volkswagen,[17] may appear to confirm the modernist idea that there was something inherently progressive about alternatives to the 'standard layout', but the wider ideological and other implications of these alternatives seem to have proved rather ambiguous. Ledwinka's initiative at Tatra was directed into expensive, low-volume production (presumably underwritten by the much larger turnover of the company's railway-wagon undertaking) and then co-opted by the Nazis. While fascist ideologies are sometimes accompanied by a degree of homo-eroticism, so that 'non-standard' engineering might, at least in this context, be read as queer, this hardly confirms the suggestion that the Tatra offered an emancipatory, non-violent alternative to the 'bestiary of power'.

On the other hand, while the Panhard's demise might confirm one's fear of there being no future for a non-aggressive car, and though it seems to have been the result of some kind of quasi-Darwinian market imperative, the Panhard was actually extinguished to make way for the Ami 6, a fascinating and even less aggressive (and much slower) car, the first of a series of designs that evolved until the late 1980s, when the

Citroën Visa was discontinued. Since it amalgamated with Peugeot, however, Citroën's designs have become increasingly difficult to differentiate from the European mainstream.

While the majority of modern cars are more economical, more efficient and better designed than they were, say, 30 years ago, car manufacturers still appear to pander largely to some of the least attractive insecurities of masculinity, perhaps even more than they used to. Not only that, but many of the ways in which they do this – by promoting huge, supposedly off-road vehicles for urban use, for example – seem equally attractive to some women. Like the artefacts of some extinct, utopian (and perhaps more feminine) culture, surviving examples of the Citroëns and Panhards of the 1950s and '60s appear as evidence that things do not always have to be they way they are. Perhaps they also offer models for more benign cars in the future. It might be difficult to claim a particular approach to car design as representative of some quasi-utopian sexual ambiguity, and in any case, all such considerations are completely relative – in the us, for example, perhaps any European car might be read as evidence of its driver's 'sophistication', snobbery, effeminacy etc. – but the demeanour of these 'lost' French cars at least suggests that, despite all the evidence to the contrary, there is nothing inescapably brutal about technology or, by implication, sexuality, even masculine sexuality. With cars, as in so many other areas of life, the possibility of lasting, achievable improvement seems to depend on a willingness to rethink questions of eroticism and sexuality, in particular conventional, reactionary assumptions about the nature of masculinity.

America's Love Affair with the Automobile in the Television Age

KARAL ANN MARLING

There's something wonderful, disquieting, and, in the end, embarrassing about America's cars of the 1950s: the lunkers, the dreamboats, the befinned, bechromed behemoths that lurked in the driveways of our brand new ranch houses in the suburbs (because they wouldn't fit in the garage!). They were the kinds of cars – those bloated GMs, Fords, and Chryslers – that Danny Thomas and Ozzie and Harriet drove; the kinds that Jim taught Margaret how to drive, thus precipating the only spat ever to mar the Quaaluded domesticity of *Father Knows Best;* the kind of car that Ward parked at the curb in front of 211 Pine Street, Mayfield, USA (a suburb of Utopia).[1]

They were the kinds of cars that drove foreigners to unseemly outbursts of envy, so extravagant and wasteful, so baroque and, well, so American did they seem in their excesses of horsepower and gadgetry. There are those, for example, who claim that the Englishmen Maclean and Burgess were driven mad by Detroit, that they were propelled into the arms of Mother Russia by the sheer garishness of the two-tone family cruiser with 285 horses under the hood. As Europe lay in ruins, the Yanks (who owned three-fourths of all the cars in the world) indulged themselves in a veritable orgy of Naugahyde and power steering. Quite right, what? Any decent chap might turn to espionage. 'Whilst the Russians had been developing "Sputnik,"' wrote a disgusted Reyner Banham before his epochal meeting with Los Angeles

and heavy-duty glitz, 'the Americans had been debauching themselves with tailfins.'[2]

But there's a greedy innocence about the pleasure such autos brought to the post-war United States, an innocence wasted on the jaded Brits. Chuck Berry said it all in a clean, simple lyric that would shame a T. S. Eliot:

> As I was motoring over the hill
> I saw Maybelline in a Coupe de Ville.
> Cadillac rollin' down the open road,
> But nothin' outrun my V-8 Ford . . .[3]

If the cars were complex beyond all telling, with their Dynaflow pushbutton transmissions, their power brakes, automatic windows, vacuum ashtrays, retractable roods, and wraparound windshields, the feelings they aroused in their owners were straightforward: after the privations of the Great Depression, after the hardships and shortages of the war, victorious Americans deserved nothing but the best. Within a year of the surrender of Japan, twelve million GIs had been sent home, every last one of them in search of a girl, a car, a new house, and – although they didn't know it just then – a television set: the American Dream. In 1945, 200,000 new houses had been built nationwide; in 1950, 1,154,000. In 1945, outside a few labs, there were no television sets in private hands; in 1950 alone 7,500,000 were sold. In 1945, 70,000 cars rolled off the assembly line; 6,665,000 in

1950.[4] The good life rolled by on big, soft Goodyear tires: it was the car that fuelled the new industrial prosperity, created the suburbs where new houses sprouted like dandelions after rain, and shaped the suburban lifestyles whose mores and manners were codified on the TV sitcoms of the 1950s.[5] The car was the new Conestoga wagon on the frontier of consumerism, a powerful instrument of change, a chariot of fiery desire.

Never one to avoid looking squarely at the human emotions invested in the detritus of popular culture, Stephen King turned his attention to the big, American car in *Christine*, a 1983 novel. King's hero, a nerdy tract-house teenager of the 1980s, quite literally falls in love with a car – specifically, a red and white 1958 Plymouth Fury ('The new shape of motion! The forward look! Suddenly, it's 1960!' hooted that year's TV ads.)[6] The bonds of affection possible between man and machine had been noted earlier, of course. During the 1965–66 season on NBC, the haplessly oedipal Jerry Van Dyke found himself the owner of a 1928 auto that harbored the ghost of his late mom, a feminized, gas-powered version of Mr Ed.[7]

My Mother the Car was comedy (or so the network claimed) whereas *Christine* has sinister and, ultimately, tragic overtones. So many human feelings have been grounded in the crimson fastness of Christine that she becomes an animated being, a humanoid capable of growing a new bumper at will, or sprouting a shiny new grille. But she is also capable of rage and murder and, in a perversion of the symbiotic relationship between car and driver that inspired the designers of the 1950s, the emotions of the machine become those of Arnie, her ostensible owner. The possessor is seduced, beguiled, and possessed by the aptly named blood-red Plymouth Fury.

Christine is fiction but the facts of the car business in 1950s America more than justify the premise. In the 1920s, the auto industry had been faced with a crisis: by 1926, according to market research, everyone who could afford a car already had one and, in 1927, production and sales plummeted for the first time. The answer was not Fordism: the durable, dependable, unchanging Tin Lizzie.[8] The solution was Sloanism or the annual style change, named for Alfred P. Sloan, president of General Motors. The object of such superficial changes, Sloan said, was 'to create demand for the new value and, so to speak, create a certain amount of dissatisfaction with past models as compared with the new one'.[9]

In practice, then, a business once ruled by engineering took on the trapping of the dressmaker's salon; the notion of the obsolescence of a serviceable product was transferred from the clothing of the upper class to the single most important industrial product made in America. With the help of the copywriter, status and symbolism became compelling reasons for buying a brand new car, even though the old, back Model T out in the yard still ran like a top. The purchaser of an auto was no longer paying for a piece of machinery: 'He, or she, was buying a new life.'[10]

Some old-fashioned ad men of the 1920s, according to the social critic Roland Marchand, balked at selling products on the basis of color and design. Was the old washing machine no good simply because it wasn't 'Karnak Green'? Was last year's kitchen range beyond the pale because it lacked the fashionable applied tracery of the 1927 edition?[11] But ethical objections faded beside the demonstrable results achieved by Sloan. General Motors adopted the annual overhaul in 1927 and the Chevrolet promptly overtook the Ford for the first time. The advertising that moved the new models was evocative and suggestive: it catered to dreams. GM, for example, conjured up the two-car family: the man who could present the little woman with her own runabout clearly stood to gain a stature unattainable by those déclassé types with one all-purpose buggy. Even Henry Ford joined the parade with the Model A and a new publicity campaign full of Fords in which the driver might speed over class barriers. As the author E. B. White later noted in the pages of *The New Yorker*, 'From reading the auto ads you would think that the primary function of the motor car in America was to carry its owner to a higher social stratum, and then into an exquisite delirium of high adventure.'[12]

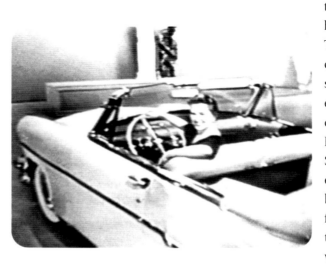

A miasma of adventure, sexual and otherwise, hung over the salesroom of the late 1920s like a cloud of high-octane fumes. There were the opulent settings, the bon-ton hauteur, but there were also the legendary Jordan ads in which the roadster became a wild horse, the parkway the prairies of the untamed West, and the new woman in the driver's seat a girl who was – ahem – just rarin' to go.[13] Romance, speed, freedom, high fantasy: they all came with the easy-payment coupon book.

And the car was always a 'she,' even after the old Tin Lizzie gave way to her more glamorous competitors. As William Faulkner once observed (and George Babbitt proved), 'The American really loves nothing but his automobile.'[14] In the 1940s industrial psychologist Ernest Dichter decided that the typical American male looked upon the convertible as his mistress and the saloon model as his wife.

Forerunners of the Las Vegas-style 'Motoramas' of the 1950s, the World's Fair auto show of the 1930s had spotlighted 'dream cars,' models that offered more or less realistic glimpses of future improvements – all in the spirit of making the customer anticipate trading in the model he was still paying for. The streamlined dream car was, by today's standards, a dignified exercise in modernist design principles, à la Frank Lloyd Wright. Speed was discreetly expressed by thin bands of horizontal fluting applied in triadic clusters. Air was invited to flow smoothly over fluid surfaces that eddied and bulged like the derrière of a Vargas pin-up painted on the nose of streamlined B-24 bomber.[15] If form could not be said to follow vehicular function with any real accuracy, the former did help to define the latter: the car, said bodies styled by Raymond Loewy, Buckminster Fuller, and the rest, was a machine for zooming along toward a crisp, efficient and thoroughly modern tomorrow.

Many of the theoretical considerations that went into the design of automobiles also determined the shapes of trains, submarines, airplanes.[16] Thus it happened that Harley Earl, head of the Styling Section at General Motors, a former Hollywood customizer to the stars (he did the bodywork on one-of-a-kind jobs for Fatty Arbuckle and Tom Mix), made friends with an Air Force designer who was testing new fighter planes at Selfridge Field, near Detroit. Shortly before the end of the war, Earl and his styling team (Bill Mitchell, Frank Hershey, Art Ross) were allowed – from a distance of 30 feet, under tight security – to examine the twin-tailed Lockheed P-38 Lightning pursuit plane, with its paired Allison engines, fuselages, and tail-fins. According to Earl, who recalled the event in a first-person article for *The Saturday Evening Post* in 1954, automotive history was made that day. 'That viewing,' he wrote, 'after the war ended, blossomed out in the Cadillac fishtail fenders which subsequently spread through our cars and over much of the industry as well.'[17]

Although aviation imagery had appeared on cars before – the 1940 Ford and the Studebaker had propellerlike gizmos in front, revived in the grillwork of the 1950s – the pleasing little winglet or hump mounted on the rear fender of the 1948 Cadillac revolutionized the auto business. A housing for the stoplights, it was the first, embryonic tail fin, and it was applied to a body that had been roughed out before Pearl Harbor, under the old dispensation of rational, form-follows-function thinking. But subsequent Harley Earl models took their cue directly from the fin. The car became the armature on which to mount a whole panoply of expressive shapes. In time, the car transcended its prosaic function altogether and became a piece of figurative sculpture, a powerful work of art.

By 1959, the Cadillac tail fin had acquired a life of its own: it towered three and one-half feet above the pavement. And as the back end rose, the front end strained forward: in 1953, Cadillac bumpers were finished off with new, factory-fresh 'gorp' in the form of 'bombs' or 'Dagmars' (named for the late-night TV bombshell of the moment) – protruding breasts that were utterly devoid of utility and impossible to repair after the most minor of collisions.[18] Chrysler, which had shamefacedly entered the tail-fin derby later than the other automakers, tried to justify the more excessive of its three-dimensional embellishments as being 'based on aerodynamic principles [that] make a real contribution to the remarkable stability' of the 1959 models.[19] The competition made no such apologies for art. Lacking any pretense of functional justification, their added hunks of rubber and chrome existed simply to communicate. They were metaphors, analogs. And sold by analogy, the car of the 1950s – a chorus girl coming, a fighter plane going – was a semiotic anagram of considerable interest.

As the design historian Thomas Hine and others have suggested, the doctrine of luxury for all, the postwar American Dream, helped to load down the car with an average of 44 pounds of surplus chrome for the mid-line Detroit product of the late 1950s. Whereas Harley Earl's finny 1948 Cadillac was considered a bit much for the average Joe, by 1955 all of its most gratuitous features were also available on the humble Chevy. The 1957 Cadillac Eldorado Brougham, at $13,074 uninflated bucks, was a mobile seraglio hitched to a dashboard with a built-in tissue box, a vanity case, a lipstick that harmonized with the paint job, and a set of four gold-finished drinking cups.[20] Along with the usual power accessories, deep-pile upholstery, padded interiors, coil springs, and bargelike proportions, the car offered the trappings of kingly ease to a culture that also gave the world the mink-handled beer can-opener, the gold-plated charge-a-plate, whiskey-flavored toothpaste, radar-equipped fishing rods, and hair colors with such names as Golden Apricot Delight and Champagne Beige.

According to Harley Earl, fins and Dagmars caught on because they gave customers 'an extra receipt for their money in the form of a visible prestige marking for an expensive car.'[21] In other words, the fin bespoke luxury, too-muchness, no-expense-spared largesse.

The combination of sex (the bumpers and radiators: one Chrysler exec. said he wanted the front of the dowdy Dodge to project the image of 'Marilyn Monroe as a housewife')[22] and aggressive, militaristic violence (those fins) hints at certain repellent aspects of the American psyche that neither the women's movement nor recent outpourings of national repentance for Vietnam have done much to alter. Sex and violence for all, served up in a flashy chrome package: the Ward Cleavers and Jim Andersons of the 1950s led secret lives, infinitely richer and more disturbing than anything Walter Mitty might have imagined. And their cars, the ones with the rocket launchers and the 44-D cups, were first and foremost family cars: the nuclear family of the Eisenhower years, it would seem, came by that title honestly.

But for a decade or so – the flourishing of the two-and-a-half ton salmon pink steel space rocket with sexual appendages – Hayakawa and his fellow scoffers were wrong. Americans were willing, indeed eager, to spend huge amounts of money on objects that were symbols of their desires, reflections of themselves, expressions of their fantasies; on artifacts that succeeded or failed on the basis of appearance; on wheeled sculpture; on what can only be described as works of popular art in which the nation freely invested a fifth of the GNP. There is, in fact, in much of the story of Detroit in the 1950s an element of aesthetic self-consciousness, a tacit challenge to the self-righteous rigidity of modernist dogma, and what can only be described as the first stirrings of a post-modern sensibility.

Consider, for example, the GM Motorama. An offshoot of the old World's Fair car exhibits and the annual luncheons Sloan held for friends at New York's Waldorf-Astoria during National Auto Show week, Earl held the first Motorama in the hotel ballroom there in 1949.[23] Entitled 'Transportation Unlimited,' the event set off the most evocative of the 'dream cars' with a 35-minute musical extravaganza. Dancers pranced; singers warbled; an MC extolled the virtues of the GM line. Showgirls pointed at the new Cadillac fin. Mounted on turntables, the autos pirouetted beneath colored spotlights. Until 1961, the Motorama (there were eight of them) served as GM's most effective marketing tool and the scourge of the competition: as Autorama, it travelled from New York to the hinterlands, always greeted by enormous crowds and breathless excitement. In 1949, a Buick Le Sabre XF-8 with sensors that raised the convertible hood in case of rain and the world's first wraparound windshield was the big attraction. In 1954, Motorama introduced Earl's never-to-be-built Firebird, a literal translation of a new fighter jet. But performance and plausibility were not the issues that kept the crowds coming.

The Motorama was a show, an exhibition, a flashier version of a New York opening on Madison Avenue, the first of the multi-media happenings.[24] As for the cars, people came to look at them in a museumlike environment, not to drive them or to see them being driven (many of the non-production models didn't have motors). They were displayed on revolving pedestals which moved not to suggest the open road but to facilitate a minute inspection of a three-dimensional form from every angle. If the critics Clement Greenberg and Harold Rosenberg had their Jackson Pollocks to look at – frozen action, paintings rich in dark, personal meaning – the rest of America (the two million who attended every GM show, at any rate) had Motorama, the art of Neal Cassidy and Jack

Kerouac – cars that never moved, chromium statuary larded with primal emblems of war and lust. A parody on the pretensions of American high culture, Motorama answered extravagant claims for art with outright extravagance, claims for hidden meaning with overt nods to jets and Jane Russell.

The notion of the car as work of art was reinforced in other subtle ways. In television ads – and the automakers were that new medium's biggest clients – integrated into variety shows (remember Dinah Shore? 'Drive your Chev-ro-lay, through the USA! America's the greatest land of all!') it was often practical to represent an on-stage Motorama in miniature, with gesticulating models and revolving pedestals: Julia Mead, Lincoln's elegant, upwardly-mobile spokeswoman of the period, used this format in spots on the Ed Sullivan show, for instance, and Pat Boone's Chevy commercials also opened with a studio shot.[25] Bevis Hillier, reviewing the common decorative motifs of the 1950s, notes the use of a picture frame to transfer the importance and prestige attached to a work of art to whatever turned up within its perimeters.[26] The Motorama shot – the car as sculpture on exhibit – served much the same function, I think, on television. An establishing shot, it was usually followed by film footage displaying the car in motion, almost as an afterthought, a guilty admission that the work of art was also a means of taking Junior to the orthodontist.

It is noteworthy too that the footage of cars

rolling down the new Hollywood freeway or a suburban cul-de-sac succeeds in making motion virtually
motionless. Cars never bob or weave; they never start
or stop with visible effort. Only the changing landscape convinces the viewer that Julia and her mink
stole are actually coursing toward the Beverly Hills
Hotel. In part, this technique appeals to a strong
customer preference for
the heavy, 'mushy' car
that denies any kinship
with the surface beneath
it; in part, the gliding
motion refers to aerody-
namics – the car seems to
be a plane, liberated
from earthly potholes
and sharp corners; but
the motionless motion
demonstrated was also
the aesthetic ideal
embraced by the stylists
who created the American car.

There were several kinds of TV car commercials:
the Motorama, the mini-drama, the pseudo-docu-
mentary, the ersatz 'lecture' by an expert (often
Truman Bradley, the man who passed out checks for
The Millionaire and hosted *Science Fiction Theater*).
What all these types have in common is an obsession
with design, and specifically with a set of artistic principles that it is presumed the audience understands
and appreciates. One of Truman Bradley's outings – a
long ad for the 1956 Chrysler line – contains a
sequence in which the driver stops at a suburban golf
course and a supermarket. In both venues, ordinary
citizens burst into spontaneous tributes to Chrysler
styling. It has 'the forward look of motion – even
when it's stopped!' exclaim the duffers, while the bag

boy notices that the shape of the rear end derives from
that of a jet plane.

But even more to the point is the illustrated
lecture by Professor Tom Foldes, 'artist, author,
educator,' which sold the 1955 Ford. Foldes shows
precisely how draftmanship – design – can make a
static form move: speed lines (the old technique of
streamlining) are addi-
tive and superficial, he
insists, whereas good
contemporary design
bends the form as a
whole toward the image
the stylist wishes to
create. 'The expression of
motion through design is
the goal of all modern
automotive styling,' he
says: this means visor
headlights surging
forward, a rakedback tail
assembly, and a highlight running from bumper to
bumper in a smooth, unbroken arc. 'When the design
of a car expresses its function forcefully and imagina-
tively, we derive more pleasure from owning and
driving it,' Professor Foldes concludes.

The Ford commercial is a stunning piece of television for several reasons. Its length seems excessive
by today's standards: network time was cheaper in
1955 and the audience still had a reasonable attention
span. Even given the willingness to stay on the couch,
however, Foldes's chalk-talk is a remarkably sophisticated slice of Art Appreciation 101, with its
distinction between superficial embellishment and
form, and its assumption that genuine aesthetic
pleasure is accessible to everyone and available in the
form of mass-market, manufactured goods. Detroit

knew that it was selling sculpture but what is more important, Detroit knew that we knew it too and hired experts, like Professor Foldes, to distinguish good art from bad.

This kind of pop-culture artiness infuriated sophisticates. While the Abstract Expressionists, by and large, ignored the whole vulgar spectacle (and bought foreign cars), pioneers of industrial art, like Raymond Loewy, fulminated against the so-called stylists and their 'forward looks.' In 1955, Loewy (recently fired by Studebaker, where he had been head designer since 1938), blasted the industry in an address to the Society of Automotive Engineers; that speech, printed in the *Atlantic Monthly*, details the case against Detroit, whose latest models Loewy called 'jukeboxes on wheels' – aesthetic aberrations that masked the workings of the machine beneath layers of tawdry 'flash.'[27] Much of what Loewy had to say made ethical sense: the weight of increased ornament and big, smooth autobodies had led to over-horsed engines, rising costs, ruined roadways, and huge fuel bills (although the critic failed to ask why Americans loved their big cars despite these drawbacks). But Loewy's real objection to the 1955 model was its shape. 'Is it responsible,' he asked, 'to camouflage one of America's most remarkable machines as a piece of gaudy merchandise? Form, which should be the clean-cut expression of mechanical excellence has become sensuous and organic.'[28]

In that one phrase – 'sensuous and organic' – Loewy reveals himself as the puritan, morally superior to the herd; the monklike disciple of a modern movement which had tried, albeit without much success, to convince people to live in pure white cubes and commune with pure geometry. Although corporate America occasionally succumbed to modernist auster-

ity in the interests of economy and an efficient image, Americans resisted the incursions of modernism into their private lives, the place where their hopes, desires, and fantasies grew lush, convoluted, profoundly sensuous. They liked the new, efficient, rectangular dinnerware best when it was enlivened with boomerangs of turquoise and gold; the squared-off ranch house on a slab when it was warmed up with Early American accessories (remember the eagle emblazoned on Ozzie and Harriet's impeccably geometric fireplace); a car when it came with a built-in vanity, a matching lipstick, Dagmars, and fins. They liked complexity, lots of stuff, scale, everything but the kitchen sink: in an odd way, their taste was closer to Jackson Pollock's than to Raymond Loewy's. And the car was its most public expression.

But what, in the end, does the family car have to tell us about America in the Eisenhower years? That it was a more communal, a less privatized, a less pluralistic time? That emotions and aspirations were closer to the surface? That women, thanks to Maidenform, looked a lot like the cars they tooled around suburbia in, as did the rockets being tested by Chuck Yeager and the macho, *Right Stuff* crew? That male and female, sexuality and violence, domesticity and high adventure, entertainment and economics, waste and technological efficiency came together in blatant, unprecedented, unparalleled, and highly original configurations? That the average American has probably never taken a greater interest in how things look, and why, and how they make him – or her – feel?

Well, that's all true. But the most interesting thing about those old Fords, Chevies, and Chryslers is the hold they still have on the American imagination

30 years later. They beckon us to a long, smooth ride to foreverland in luxury fit for the gods themselves. Bruce Springsteen says it best:

Eldorado fins, whitewalls and skirts
Rides just like a little bit of heaven here on earth,
Well buddy when I die throw my body in the back
And drive me to the junkyard in my Cadillac.[29]

And now that I think of it, that's probably where Elvis is. The first thing he bought with his newfound wealth in 1956 – the year Tupelo gave him a welcome-home parade – was a candy-pink Fleetwood sedan for his mom. Gladys Presley didn't drive. So the car sat in the driveway outside Graceland, a two-ton love trinket, a symbol of love, money, and home, a statue, a monument to the tragedy of dreams come true. It sits there still.[30]

FROM *Design Quarterly,* 146, 'Autoeroticism' (1989)

Men, Motors, Markets and Women

GRACE LEES-MAFFEI

'See 500 sexy models reveal all.' This motor-show slogan provides a graphic reminder of the traditional role of women in car culture – as adjuncts rather than drivers. Stephen Bayley's 1986 essay 'Sex, Drink and Fast Cars' typifies 'man's relationship' with his car as being all about power, as it is articulated by designers, stylists, advertising creatives and marketing professionals. For Bayley, a woman in a powerful car is 'at once titillating and de-masculating' and represents 'an overt sexual statement'.[1] The fact that this feeling seems to be mutual is suggested by the female journalist who admitted: '. . . men who are ambivalent about driving are not attractive to me. And it's not just me.'[2] The masculine dominance of car culture is sustained even though an increasing number of women drive and work as car journalists.

Where women have not been used to eroticize cars as objects of desire, they have been cast by the producers of car culture as figures of influence on purchases by men. In the inter-war period, concern about the corrupting influence of women on design pointed to an increasing emphasis on comfort and aesthetics. Manufacturers excused model changes through reference to the influence of women on the market. During the late '20s and early '30s, Harley Earl's Art and Color department at General Motors was viewed as excelling at such feminized features as style, colour and comfort even while Earl himself was concerned to recruit only male employees in case 'any hint of femininity would handicap his struggle in the

rough-and-tumble, masculine world of the automobile industry'.[3] The 1920s US car producer Ned Jordan was acutely aware of the influence of women on car purchase and, consequently, the necessity of comfort, beauty and style in car design. However, Jordan also stands out as having been thoroughly seduced by the ideal of an independent woman driver, as most famously exemplified in his 1920s fantasy 'Somewhere West of Laramie', a eulogy to women drivers.

What is the reality of the role of women in car culture? Women have been driving in large numbers from the inception of widespread car use, as is exemplified by the setting up of the Ladies Automobile Club of Great Britain in 1903. In 1933, women held 12 per cent of driving licences. In 1964, 13 per cent of women held driving licences, compared with 56 per cent of men. By the late 1970s, 30 per cent of women and 68 per cent of men were licensed to drive.[4] By 1993, nearly half of all driving licences, more than fourteen million in total, were held by women and more than a third of women drivers owned their own cars.[5] In the UK, the proportion of men passing their driving tests has been higher each year since 1988. The number of women passing their tests has also been higher each year in this period. Therefore, significantly, more driving tests have been taken by women than men in the last twelve years, and the number of licensed women drivers is increasing more quickly than that of men.[6]

In the early decades of private car use, in cases of joint ownership of a single family car, it was assumed that the male partner usually had the primary claim on it. Since then, however, the average number of cars owned by a household has increased. In 1951, 13 per cent of households owned one car, and 1 per cent owned two. By 1986, 17 per cent of households owned two cars, whereas by 1996 this figure had increased to 23 per cent. Households with three or more cars increased from 3 per cent in 1986 to 5 per cent in 1996.[7] Today, 42 per cent of cars are bought by women, and 80 per cent of car purchases involve a woman's input.[8]

Car advertisers have assumed that while men use their cars for work activities, women drive for leisure. Once again there is a fault line between representation and present reality. For the period 1996–8, British men made more journeys for the purposes of commuting, business, education and leisure than women, who made more school runs and shopping journeys. But approximately 20 per cent of school runs are followed by a journey to work;[9] it is clear that women use cars to help them combine work and childcare.[10] So the assumption that cars are leisure objects for women is erroneous and trivializes the empowerment women have experienced, both personally and professionally, behind the wheel.

Women are not only influential on car purchases made by men, we have been driving in increasing numbers, buying more cars – to the extent that we represent nearly half of all car purchasers – and relying on cars to perform our various work roles. Little of this has altered the representation of women in car culture. Sean O'Connell has pointed out that, 'Despite growing evidence of female competence at the wheel, the myth of greater masculine ability was not allowed to die.'[11] In May 1987, *Your Car*'s regular day-in-the-life column featured a driving instructor whose tutees were exclusively women described as

lacking in confidence and competence.[12] This isolated example is not drawn from a rich variety of representations of women in *Your Car*: we are absent to an astonishing extent. Two years later, *Your Car* offered a 'Reader's Lives' account of a mother's mismanagement of her car illustrated with a cartoon captioned 'Honest Mum – I was laughing with you, not at you.'[13] The popularity of this strain of humour has led Roy Bolitho, for example, to write *Woman at the Wheel*, a compendium of jokes about women's driving incompetence.

A recent study conducted in Northern Ireland provides interesting evidence of the mythical nature of man's greater driving competence. The 1999 Road Survey Monitor for Northern Ireland reported that of the 75 per cent of men and 55 per cent of women who drove, 53 per cent of men and 37 per cent of women described themselves as 'well above' or 'above' average in their driving skills.[14] However, the greater confidence of male drivers in Northern Ireland is not explained by their success in driving tests. 61 per cent of men passed their driving tests in the fourth quarter of 1996, as compared with 52 per cent of women. However, in the same period, 72 per cent of women passed the driving theory tests as opposed to 63 per cent of men.[15]

A debate continues nonetheless about whether women or men are better drivers. The Transport Research Institute, the Automobile Association and the Royal Automobile Club have publicized reports confirming that women drivers are 'safer and more skilful than their male counterparts'. Such statistics are countered by critics who claim that men do more driving and are therefore more likely to become involved in accidents.[16] Elsewhere, biological explanations have been offered to 'prove' women's lesser competence, such as the fact that the part of the brain used for visualizing objects in three dimensions, estimating time and judging speed is smaller in women than in men.[17] Women's lack of confidence as drivers is exemplified by road-user support projects such as the one set up by Devon County Council, which was attended almost entirely by women.[18] Such a lack of confidence is unfounded, however, so much so that insurance companies have routinely offered advantageous deals for women.

One explanation for the lack of confidence felt by women in the driving seat might have to do with the sort of seat it is. Both men and women may experience discomfort from car design geared towards the 'international standards' of body shape and size formed by the Society of Automotive Engineers.[19] Seat design has traditionally been aesthetically rather than ergonomically oriented, compounded by the fact that more than a third of men drive with their legs extended and almost a third of women sit too close to their steering wheels.[20] But women experience additional, specific problems with car design. A recent article on women's seatbelt discomfort noted that while women buy around half of cars sold, their needs remain neglected in automotive design as shown by a seatbelt manufacturer's admission that the company's research and development have never entailed asking women about their experiences of car design.[21]

Japanese manufacturers have been quicker than US or UK car manufacturers to provide the compact cars women desired. Recent cars targeted at women drivers include the Honda Logo, Nissan's Micra, the Seat Leon, the Twingo, Ford's Ka, the Yaris, the Matiz and the VW Lupo.[22] Journalist Lesley Hazleton has described Detroit designers working with 'paper clips taped to their fingers so that they'd know how it feels to open a car door when you have long nails.'[23] Penny Wark, the motoring editor of *Women's Journal*, was

incensed by the way 'a report which purports to represent women's views manages to leave the impression that women . . . seek safety, comfort, economy – and a place to put their handbag'.[24] Wark went on to complain that the fact 'that women, unlike men, react emotionally to cars' is ignored.

Part of the problem might be the lack of women involved in automotive design and engineering. In 1999, of the 8,500 members of Retail Motor Industry Training, only 5 per cent were women, and this was an improvement on previous years.[25] Ford has recently set up a 'women's marketing panel' comprising female employees who have suggested larger and simpler dashboard controls and tailgate handles. Ford is apparently recruiting more women into its design and engineering departments.[26] This activity is a necessary corrective to the association of men with technological know-how.[27] However, it is not only in design that issues particular to women must be taken on board if manufacturers are to fully realize that sector of the market:

It is true that there are now several cars on the market that are designed specifically and accurately for women. But many men in the industry have yet to work our how to pitch them without resorting to 'nippy runaround' and 'women's car' cliches, which they whisper but never include in brochures or press releases because they are terrified of being politically incorrect.[28]

As an extension of the consultation groups mentioned above, guidebooks published to support and advise car owners address the experience of women in a variety of ways. The first example, Dorothy Levitt's *The Woman and the Car* (1909), advises on suitable dress and the need to carry a gun, the latter indicative of the North American provenance. More recently, Longman's *Cars: A Consumer's*

Renault's 'Nicole-Papa' campaign for the *Clio* ran for seven years from 1991.

Guide (1987) discusses all aspects of car ownership and maintenance, including the experiences of readers who feel marginal to car culture: 'Many people "switch off" when technical terminology is used – especially if they are unable to visualise "big ends" or "crankshafts" and understand their functions.'[29] The book is trenchantly gender-neutral however, and replicates the male-oriented nature of much car culture in that of nine case studies of purchase and repair problems, only one mentions a woman (in a discussion of the legal intricacies of joint ownership). However, by 1993 Judith Jackson's *Every Woman's Guide to the Car* (published by the pioneering UK feminist imprint Virago) dared to discuss issues particular to woman drivers: 'Although the market recognises the rapidly growing numbers of female buyers, sadly, there are still dealers who regard solo woman customers as insignificant.'[30] The same bias has been noted by women seeking car maintenance who are seen as sufficiently incompetent technically to be overcharged by mechanics in 80 per cent of cases.[31] By 2000, the situation was only marginally improved. Only 30 per cent of car sales staff were female, and 80 per cent of women took a male companion with them when buying a car for a confidence boost, even though women bought almost half of the cars sold.[32] One solution that has been suggested is to buy on-line.[33]

The advertising of cars has been as important to the continuation of the industry as stylistic and technical innovations. Cars are durable, and purchasing one is therefore postponable.[34] By the early 1970s, the world market for cars had reached saturation point.[35] Advertisers have employed a range of co-existent approaches in order to stimulate the market. In the early twentieth century, car advertising was dominated by technical information; it was only in the 1920s that a shift towards 'evocations of consumer desires for modernity, status, and autonomy' was recognized.[36] Subsequently, the history of car advertising ranged 'from plutocratic to sexual display, through environmental concern to latter-day technophilia'.[37] More recently, advertisements aimed at women as drivers have featured aspirational figures such as powerful career women, efficient mothers, women with desirable lovers and so on, all of which appeal to men and women simultaneously. One such example is Renault's 'Nicole-Papa' campaign, which boosted sales to women to the extent that the Renault Clio was bought by men and women in equal numbers.[38]

One significant recent trend in advertising has been the promotion of cars as fashionable accessories. Such an association is not exclusive to cars, of course. Other technological products have been presented as fashion accessories, including the Nokia mobile phone, which has been presented as the contents of a fragrance bottle, as jewellery and as a pair of expensive sunglasses. This approach may be seen as an attempt to make technology accessible and appealing through recourse to familiar forms. In addition, it implies the extent to which one's technological choices enhance personal identity and become, in a necessary corruption of McLuhan's dictum, an 'extension of woman'.[39] This approach is not new. In 1961, Volkswagen used miniaturization to advertise the Beetle. An image of a woman holding a toy model of a car had the strap-line 'Your Car Madam'; the same copy accompanied an ad showing a VW seen through the frame of a handbag handle and a gloved hand.[40] Scale here was manipulated to connect the car with the woman's glove and handbag, thereby presenting the automobile as another of her personal accessories.

In 1993, Volkswagen ran a print advertisement with the strapline 'Discover the fragrance of Umwelt. By Volkswagen.' The closing line of text 'For man. For woman.' recalled the slogans of Calvin Klein's fragrance advertising such as 'Escape. For Men.' It offered a minimalist aesthetic at odds with the rococo extravagance depicted in this image of a man and woman in evening dress kissing on the bonnet of a car against a night-time cityscape. So while the text connected the ad to a particular fragrance campaign, the image and text combined to refer in a general way to the genre of fragrance advertising. The extended metaphor of this ad continued in the provision of folded piece of paper with the instruction 'open fold to experience Umwelt', which copied the perfume samples offered in women's magazines. This ad appeared in such periodicals alongside actual examples of the perfume advertisements it was imitating. The intention was that no scent would be discerned because, as the copy informed us, the Umwelt featured a 'turbo charger for less smoke' and a 'catalytic converter for less toxic gases', thus creating 'A

Discover the fragrance of Umwelt. By Volkswagen.

Fragrance-free motoring: Volkswagen campaign for the environmentally-friendly Umwelt, 1993.

fragrance so subtle you'd wonder if it was there at all'. So while this ad aimed to communicate technical information, it did so through the language and imagery of fragrance advertising, an essentially feminized sphere of visual culture. The fact that no fragrance was available presented a humorous critique of the hype of fragrance advertising. But this ad has another more insidious function: it offers technical information in the romantic disguise of fragrance advertising, albeit humorously overstated.

Peugeot has exploited the association of sex and cars more recently in a bid to meet and enhance the already buoyant female market for their cars. By 1995, women were buying 60 per cent of Peugeot's new cars.[41] The company's TV campaign for the 106 featured a pastiche of the ultimate scene from Ridley Scott's 1991 road movie, *Thelma and Louise*, itself a corruption of cinematic conventions of gender and genre. The 1997 print campaign for the 106 Independence also worked with gender subversion to achieve its aim.

The illustration (see over) showed an image of the Peugeot 106 car transfer-tattooed onto a woman's hip under the words 'Declare your independence.' The

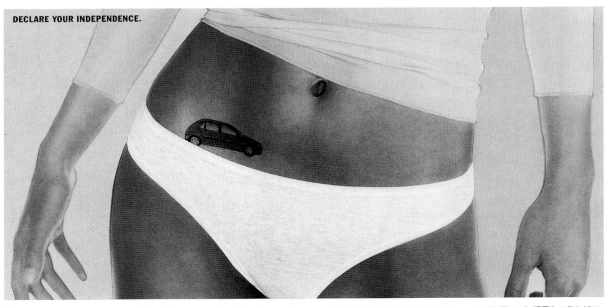

DECLARE YOUR INDEPENDENCE.

1 YEAR'S **FREE** INSURANCE

Conformists won't like the new Peugeot 106 Independence. With the XL model they'll find its range of metallic and pearlescent vibrant colours disturbingly different.

On the outside, the special

badging, characteristic tilting glass sunroof, individual body coloured bumper skirts and unique tinted glass will do little to appease them.

The five speed gearbox will be considered altogether too racy.

As will the special cloth trim, the stereo radio

cassette, the engine immobiliser and plip central locking. Not to mention the power assisted steering.

Furthermore, the freedom to choose between 3 or 5 doors, 1.1 litre petrol engine or a 1.5 litre diesel 5 door will flummox even the most broad-minded of them.

And at the **drive away price of £8,895** they will doubtless suspect a catch. But enough about conformists. If you would like more information call 0345 106 106* or visit your local Peugeot dealer.

THE NEW SPECIAL EDITION PEUGEOT 106 INDEPENDENCE.

106 PEUGEOT
THE DRIVE OF YOUR LIFE

Peugeot 106 Independence centrefold, part of a campaign for the 106, 206 and 306 initiated in 1993 to target women.

imperative language is a call to arms that recalls discussions of the importance of cars to a sense of personal freedom, whether one is male or female. Judy Wajcman has asserted that women's relations to cars depend on practical issues such as safety, mobility and independence.[42] Penny Sparke is just one design historian to have noted the 'desire, narcissism, envy and a quest for self-identification' mobilized by cars for men and women alike.[43] Recently, Stephen Bayley has rephrased his understanding of the meaning of cars to echo Wajcman's feminist analysis: 'The real emotional pull of the car is not sex, or social status, or all those things that we associate with car lovers – it is that the motor car gives you the sense that you are a free person.'[44]

The woman in the Peugeot tattoo ad is depicted without legs, in the manner of voyeuristic imagery from the world of Classical Greek art and – particularly as the image is spread across two pages in close-up – pornography. Stripped down to her under-

wear, she displays to the viewer a personal physical feature in a manner suggestive of sexual proffering and intimacy. She remains anonymous in that we cannot see her face. Her mobility comes, it is implied, from the car she drives, but she has no car, only the image of one in the form of bodily ornament. She declares her independence by wearing a tattoo. While tattoos are intricately bound up with the expression of personal identity, historically of a tribal or sub-cultural nature, in the West they are increasingly employed as just another kind of adornment.

The Peugeot woman is not decorated with jewellery or (as far as we can see) with make-up, but with a tattoo, thus suggesting a permanent commitment to the car. In his study *The Car Culture*, James Flink points out that the cosmetics and car industries are united by the fact that both insist on achieving unusually high profits.[45] The conservatism of the Peugeot ad is reflected in its text, which, while it begins with the words 'Conformists won't like the new

Peugeot 106 Independence,' continues in a manner conforming to gender stereotypes by referring to the 'range of metallic and pearlescent colours', 'special badging', 'body coloured bumper skirts' and 'cloth trim'. Technical aspects mentioned include a 'racy' gearbox, stereo radio, central locking and power-assisted steering. This image, then, while superficially offering something of a challenge to the traditionally masculine emphasis of car culture, is found on closer inspection to echo the imagery and assumptions of traditional male-stream car culture.

Another attempt at a car ad that communicates female power is the Peugeot image of the 106 logotype shaved into a woman's hair. Like the tattoo ad, this example straddles both stereotypical and subversive approaches to the business of advertising cars to women. It carries identical copy to the tattoo image. Again, the shaved motif functions as a decorative expression of the woman's identity through the act of label-display and its associations of brand allegiance, in the manner of branded sportswear. However, for a woman to shave her head remains an act of visible rejection of the normative ideal of femininity. Both the haircut and the motif shaved into it associate the product with the masculine imagery of sub-cultural street style, behind which lies a raft of subtler contra-dictory references with pop cultural, racist, homo-erotic and military nuances. All of these associ-ations garner masculine power for the woman who presents herself in this manner.

These two advertisements are interesting for the way in which they negotiate feminine stereotypes. On the one hand, the ads offer a new visual language that places women in a position of power, as exemplified by the name '106 Independence'. On the other hand, the name evokes the timeworn association of women with an ideal of femininity reminiscent of the sexual-

THE NEW PEUGEOT 106 INDEPENDENCE

This 1997 poster for the 106 Independence also appeared in a two-page format in magazines and newspapers.

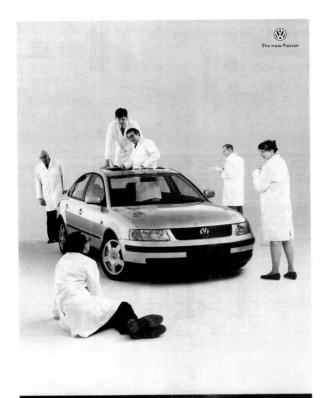

The print ad for the 1997 VW Passat mixes references to fragrance and shampoo with stereotypes of German technical excellence.

ized women of extant car culture who exist to titillate male viewers. These advertisements exemplify the traditional association of women with fashionableness, vanity and a concern for aesthetics – in this case, the emphasis on automotive aesthetics subsumes a concern for technical specification.

In 1997, Volkswagen advertised its new Passat with the line 'Obsession from Laboratoires Volkswagen.' The text continued: 'The look of it. The feel of it. The fully galvanised body of it.' The word *obsession*, the typeface and the washed-out, monochromatic image again recall advertisements for Calvin Klein. But another reference is made this time, to the hair and beauty products company Laboratoires Garnier. Obsession, unlike the unisex CK1, is sold separately

for men and for women. This advertisement featured five men and one woman in white coats attending to the car, suggesting that the ad was intended to target a mixed audience, an assumption supported by its appearance in a national daily newspaper rather than a women's magazine. This advertisement reveals the narcissistic relationship some consumers have with their cars, and the borrowed imagery, recalling a leading fashion company, suggests an emphasis on the Volkswagen's design values. This text references two distinctly recognizably beauty products, but the image, by mainly featuring males, appeals to a mixed audience.

In sum, these ads represent a concerted effort on the part of car producers, via advertising and marketing professionals, to address the female sector of the car market. This is achieved through recourse to the language and imagery of fashion and beauty, realms associated with women. These advertisements subvert conventions of both gender and genre, thereby appealing to a knowing awareness in the target audience. However, such advertisements are only partly progressive. It appears that we are in a transitional stage in the history of advertising cars to women, one reflective of an ambiguous relation to stereotypes. References in car ads to unrelated women-centred areas of consumption such as fashion, fragrance and cosmetics are specific to a stage in which traditional, sexualized car culture has not yet thoroughly incorporated female consumers, referring instead to another feminized market sector. It is worth remembering that while advertisements are key tools for the enforcement of stereotype, they can also be a route to the dissolution of those very stereotypes.

The Downfall of the Dymaxion Car

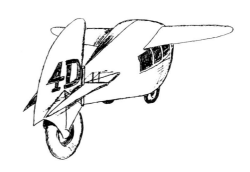

MARTIN PAWLEY

In the long history of the motorcar, there have been many attempts to set its development on an entirely new course, with inventors and engineers striving to achieve radical breakthroughs in performance to match the eclipse of the airship, the birth of the helicopter or the replacement of the propeller by the gas turbine. But unlike the dramatic conquest of the air – and despite the sometimes Herculean efforts of individual inventors and designers – the evolution of the motorcar has been almost totally incremental. From the earliest hand-crafted horse-less carriage to the latest digitally controlled, lights-out assembly line, it has been the means of producing the motorcar that has undergone the most radical change, not the motorcar itself. As a result, the greater part of the progression from the primitive Benz three-wheeler of 1886 to the sophisticated sports utility vehicle of 2002 has been linear. The smaller, more volatile part – which involved such fundamental matters as the eclipse of steam and electricity by petroleum, the decisive shift from three wheels to four and from tiller to steering wheel, the relocation of the engine from back to front, and so on – was effectively over by the beginning of the twentieth century.

From 1914 on, the invention of the production line set a seal on this new orthodoxy. Henry Ford's mass-produced one-colour Model T wrought a revolution by doubling and redoubling automobile output, but it also raised an insuperable barrier to the old pattern of haphazard mutation. Except for special-purpose machines, it became fruitless to try to build or sell motorcars unless they resembled other motorcars that were produced in volume and value engineered down to a comparable cost. The effect of this change was dramatic. Between 1914 and 1926, the number of motor manufacturers in the US (where at the time three-quarters of the world's motorcars were to be found) fell from 125 to eight, and the price of the

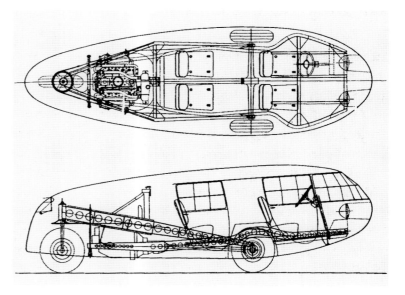

Top: Buckminster Fuller's first sketch for his '4-D Auto Airplane', the genesis of the Dymaxion car.
Above: General arrangement drawing of the Dymaxion car, 1933.

cheapest vehicle, the Model T Ford, dropped by 50 per cent.[1]

This massive shakeout meant that by 1929, when the Wall Street Crash triggered the Great Depression, the American motorcar had become a practical utensil, rather than an object of display or an experiment in leading-edge technology, to a greater extent than at any time before or since. Throughout the 1920s, product development in the motor industry was considerably retarded as competitive pricing forced manufacturers into the predicament defined by the then president of Continental Airlines: 'By focusing on cost you end up with a product that nobody wants to buy.'[2]

It was in the early 1930s, at the beginning of the Great Depression, that the idea of re-launching the motorcar as an exciting transport form of the future was born. Instead of becoming more and more utilitarian, cars would recapture their lost spirit of pioneering excitement by becoming distinctive objects of desire, boasting revolutionary new features. Demand for these revolutionary new transport forms would galvanize the automobile industry into action and reinvigorate the entire economy.

This idea was seized upon in more than one country, but in the US the standard-bearer was a celebrated aircraft engineer named William Stout, designer of the Ford Trimotor, the first genuinely successful passenger airliner. Stout berated the motor industry for its failure to produce better and more elaborate cars. In 1932, he issued his own specification for a car of the future in a lecture to the Society of Automotive Engineers of America.[3] Entitled 'What Aviation Can Do for Motor Cars', Stout's prescription was for more of everything. More streamlining, more internal space within the same track and wheel base; greater luxury, better suspension, road-holding and

quietness; more powerful engines to permit acceleration from a standing start to 60 mph in a few seconds; power steering, automatic transmission and fuel consumption better than 30 mpg.

This remarkably accurate prediction of the car of 50 years in the future received much publicity at the time. After the newspapers had finished with it, the trade and technical press took it up, and in November 1932 a transcript of Stout's lecture was published in a magazine called *Shelter*, an avant-garde architectural monthly published in Philadelphia and edited by a 37-year-old designer and entrepreneur named Richard Buckminster Fuller.

Fuller had a keen interest in visionary projects. He already had a reputation as a result of the publicity attending his published designs for a house of the future called the Dymaxion house,[4] a project for a lightweight dwelling suspended from a tubular mast that would make use of many new materials and methods – up to and including the possibility of aerial delivery by Zeppelin. To Fuller, Stout's vision was interesting but too incremental. His own thinking about visionary cars, like his answer to the housing problem, called for a clean break with the past. He wanted to transform the motorcar into a multifunctional machine. The true car of the future, he believed, would not only be able to drive nimbly in traffic and cruise on the open road, but fly like an aircraft and skim over water like a speedboat.

ENTER THE INVENTOR

Despite the frequent use of the terms in connection with his work, Richard Buckminster Fuller was neither a scientist nor an engineer. His untrammelled innovative thinking, which over his long life was to express itself in mathematics and geometry, mechanical engineering, product design, architecture, cosmology, sculpture and poetry, was not of academic origin. It came from an inborn childhood curiosity, a brief experience of university and two years as a junior officer in the US Navy during World War I. 'Every sailor knows what it means to shunt winds, tides, tension and compression to human advantage,' he said when asked to account for his intuitive grasp of structures. But apart from his brief attendance at Harvard University (he was sent down twice and never took a degree), seamanship, navigation, the study of industrial production and omnivorous reading constituted the sum of his education.

After demobilization from the Navy in 1919 at the age of 23, Fuller took a series of jobs before ending up as sales director of Stockade Building Systems, a company formed jointly with his architect father-in-law to market a new kind of building block made from cement and wood shavings. It was the unsuccessful battle to get this product accepted by the building-control bureaucracies of municipalities in the north-eastern and mid-western states that gave Fuller the low opinion of regulatory bodies and conventional wisdom that was to last for the rest of his life. As he told his biographer Robert Marks years later,

The failure of Stockade showed me that craft building – in which each house is a pilot model for a design that never has a production run – is an art that belongs in the middle ages. I have known ever since that all the decisions in craft-built undertakings are based on methodical ignorance.

Rendered jobless by the failure of Stockade in 1927, Fuller withdrew into himself and began designing an entire world of the future – houses, tower blocks, commercial buildings and flying cars. The design of his proposed factory-made Dymaxion house was the most detailed of these projects. It was to have featured the first domestic use of revolving doors, plastics, pneumatics, built-in furniture, automatic environmental controls and advanced electronics, but no full-size version was ever built. Fuller said the houses could sell for $1,500 each, but that it would cost a hundred million dollars to tool up for assembly-line production. With his strictures on 'methodical ignorance' in mind, he refused to allow a hand-made prototype be built for the 1933 World's Fair in Chicago.

THE CAR OF THE FUTURE TAKES SHAPE

The Dymaxion car project began life in the same series of sketches as the Dymaxion house. At first, Fuller called it an 'Auto-Airplane', because of its intended ability to fly. He also talked of having it powered by 'liquid air turbines' instead of conventional petrol engines, but – like the wings – these power plants never materialized. What did emerge in the spring of 1933 was a three-wheeled rolling chassis, no longer intended to fly or skate over water, but confined to the motorway. This was the real, as opposed to the ideal, Dymaxion car, and three examples of it were to be built by Fuller in partnership with the successful America's Cup yacht designer Starling Burgess. Unlike Fuller, Burgess is today a forgotten man, but he may well have had a great deal to do with the magnificent streamlining of this otherwise anti-climactic vehicle. Even in its simplified form, the first Dymaxion car was radical enough in appearance to show how far into the untried Fuller was prepared to take his partner in the rejection of the motor industry's 'methodical ignorance'.

To build the Dymaxion cars, Buckminster Fuller and Starling Burgess leased a former dynamometer factory in Bridgeport, Connecticut, from the bankrupt

The wooden framing of Dymaxion No. 1 awaiting its aluminium skin at the 4-D Car Company plant in 1933.

Locomobile Car Company and renamed it the 4-D Dymaxion Car Manufacturing Company. Funding came from a Philadelphia stockbroker named Philip Pearson who had allegedly been convinced by the project after seeing a model of Fuller's Dymaxion house in a bookshop window. The fact that the new car company opened for business in 1933, the worst year of the Great Depression for bank and savings-and-loan failures, discouraged none of the protagonists. They believed that if the miracle car caught on, it could kick-start the economy into prosperity in much the same way as Henry Ford's Model T had done twenty years before.

Their euphoria did not last long. Within weeks,

it became clear that to make a flying car would be a long and complicated business best left to a later stage of development. Instead, the first car was to become what would today be called a 'concept car' – a streamlined machine that only *looked* as though it might hurtle along a turnpike at 100 mph driven by 'liquid air turbines'.

PROBLEMS OF DIRECTIONAL STABILITY

Surviving photographs of the three cars that were manufactured by the 4-D Dymaxion Car Manufacturing Company between the summer of 1933 and the spring of 1934 show that there was steady progress in

Dymaxion No. 1 at rollout on 12 July 1933. Note the absence of doors on this side of the car.

the direction of increased weight and Stoutian 'luxury' with each chassis completed. For this reason, the first car is the most dramatic and shows more evidence of its origins in the flying, turbine-powered, tri-modal machine of Fuller's early sketches than either of the other two. When it was first rolled out in July 1933, this car revealed itself as an aluminium-clad, three-wheeled, lozenge-shaped vehicle nearly 18 feet long – longer than a full-size Chevrolet Suburban is today. Although it was not fitted with a propeller or the pump-up inflatable wings of Fuller's original design, its cabin roof was fabric-covered where the wings would have been attached had the prospect of flight not been set so far in the future. Also, under the nose was a large air scoop similar to that shown in the early sketches as a duct intended to direct air into the inflatable wings by ram effect – now blanked off and adapted to serve as a housing for the car's single headlight. In subsequent cars, scoop and duct alike were deleted. In addition to these traces, the first Dymaxion also lacked certain accessories. It had no opening windows, and doors only on one side; it had no provision for windscreen wipers; and sections of its Perspex windscreen had to be removed for ventilation. Finally, just as the inflatable wings were never designed or fitted, nor were the tail plane, fin and rudder, which were to have provided the steering control necessary for the '4-D Auto-Airplane' at high speed on the ground or in flight. Now, despite its purposeful appearance, the first Dymaxion car was little more than a wingless, tail-less aircraft.

Perhaps the phrase 'little more than' is inappropriate here, for even the process of turning the rump of a taxiing aircraft into a road-going vehicle is not as easy as it sounds. Needing power following the abandonment of the mythical 'liquid air turbines', Fuller and Burgess had stepped down considerably to a side valve Ford V8 car engine. This was mounted in the rear of the body facing forward, with its drive shaft connected to a transverse beam axle still further forward, making it the only rear-engine front-wheel-drive car in the world. But even more remarkable than its configuration was its steering gear, which, like the location of the engine, was the same for all three cars. In place of the intended aerodynamic fin and rudder, there was a single pivoting road wheel in the tail which was moved by long cables from a yacht-size steering wheel in the nose and would turn through 360 degrees.

Although it no longer even hoped to be an aircraft, like all of the aircraft of the early 1930s, the Dymaxion car had a tail-wheel-tail undercarriage and a nose-up posture on the ground. Had it also been fitted with a tractor air screw and a tail assembly – fin, rudder, tail plane and elevators, set in the slipstream of the air screw – it would have been possible to steer it on the ground like a taxiing aircraft. 'Tail-draggers' of that period were generally steered on the ground by means of a castoring tail wheel and individually cable-braked forward wheels or by means of a tail wheel that moved with the aerodynamic rudder to produce a steering movement – the very arrangement shown in detail in the original '4-D Auto-Airplane' sketch. Unhappily, the Dymaxion car was equipped with neither of these systems. It had no air screw and no tail surfaces and only looked like a taxiing aircraft because of the location of its wheels and its nose-up posture.

The most serious, not to say terminal, fault in the design of the Dymaxion car can be traced to its steering gear and the distinction between *drawn* and *driven* that first came to light with the introduction of powered road transport in the nineteenth century. At that time, carriages were *drawn* by horses, whose task was eased by the free rotation of the vehicles' wheels. The new horse-less carriages, on the other hand, were *driven* along by the forced rotation of their powered wheels. This distinction had many effects on steering and braking, as well as on road design and mainte-

nance, some of which cars and aircraft, roads and runways, perpetuate to this day. Propeller-driven aircraft on the ground, for instance, are still *drawn* by their engines, like horse-drawn carriages, and even jet airliners are either pulled by a tractor or pushed by the thrust of their engines. Uniquely, and almost certainly unknowingly, the Dymaxion car combined the powered wheels of a *driven* vehicle with the steering system of a *drawn* one – a combination of different technologies that created control problems its designers were never able to solve.[5]

This did not prevent Fuller, with his contempt for 'methodical ignorance', from trying to solve them. Even if the Dymaxion car would no longer fly, it was still going to be steered from the stern, like a fish, a bird, a ship or an aircraft – all possessed of the highly desirable ability to make high-speed turns under power. To achieve this capability, Fuller and Burgess had come up with a steering system containing all of the elements of the undercarriage of a tail-wheel aircraft, but used in a different way. The tail wheel was key. Instead of merely castoring after the vehicle, it was promoted to steering it.

This brilliant piece of lateral thinking led directly to disaster. The convention that a car should stand level on the road had been an early casualty of the Dymaxion design. When it was abandoned in favour of the aggressive nose-up stance of a 1930s aircraft, it became a positive inconvenience to its passengers. Why was this permitted? Because the real design objective was not to keep the nose high, but to keep the tail low! – so that the engine could be mounted as far below the centre of gravity as possible to prevent the tail wheel from lifting under braking and causing the loss of steering control.

In Fuller and Burgess's design, so much stress and weight was concentrated at the rear of the vehicle

Seated, middle and right. Starling Burgess and Buckminster Fuller in
front of Dymaxion No. 1, 11 August 1933.

A 'Taildragger' amphibian Republic Seabee next to Dymaxion No. 3
at Wichita in 1945, showing similarity of stance.

– with only the single steerable wheel to resolve it – that the threat of tyre failure alone should have been enough to make them think again. In the event, even the nimble turning circle made possible by rear-wheel steering could only be demonstrated at the slowest of speeds. If the driver of a Dymaxion turned sharply enough, or went fast enough to swing the pendulum-like weight of the rear-mounted engine outside the track of the front driving wheels, the car would begin to over-steer. In the case of the first Dymaxion car, this is exactly what did happen when the car rolled over and collided with another vehicle, killing its driver and seriously injuring its passenger. This event, more than anything else, demonstrated why the Dymaxion failed to set the development of the motorcar off in a new direction when it was demonstrated to admiring crowds[6] in the summer of 1933.

REAR-WHEEL STEERING

In over a century of road-going passenger-car development, exclusively rear-wheel steering has only ever been marketed twice. First on the four-wheeled French Leyat of 1923, and last on the three-wheeled Dymaxion of 1933. Since then, rear-wheel steering has remained stubbornly confined to the realm of combine harvesters, fork-lift trucks, low-profile airport tractors and Thrust SSC, the world's only supersonic car, which jet-powered itself into the record books at 771 mph in October 1997 at Black Rock, Nevada. Thrust SSC was of course no more a passenger car than is a combine harvester; nonetheless, it is worth noting that after his hair-raising record run, driver Andy Green commented: 'Rear-wheel steering should be limited to forklift trucks in future.'

Not since 1934, when Dymaxion car number three left the soon-to-be-bankrupt 4-D Dymaxion Car Company with its purchaser, the famous orchestra conductor Leopold Stokowski, white-knuckled at the wheel, has another exclusively rear-wheel-steered passenger car been built.

References

'Cars in Culture', introduced by Joe Kerr

1 Filippo Tommaso Marinetti, 'The Founding and Manifesto of Futurism', in R. W.Flint, ed., *Marinetti: Selected Writings* (New York, 1972), p. 42. Quoted in Roland Schaer, Gregory Claeys and Lyman Tower Sargent, eds, *Utopia: The Search for the Ideal Society in the Western World* (New York, 2000), p. 279.
2 Le Corbusier, *Towards a New Architecture*, trans. Frederick Etchells (London, 1946), pp. 130–31.
3 Diego Rivera, *My Art, My Life: An Autobiography* (New York, 1991), pp. 111–12.

PETER WOLLEN, 'AUTOMOBILES AND ART'

1 John Willett, *The New Sobriety 1917–33: Art and Politics in the Weimar Period* (London, 1987).
2 Gerald Silk, *Automobile and Culture* (New York, 1984), p. 77.
3 *Creative Art*, XII/4 (April 1933).
4 Stephen Bayley, *Design Heroes: Harley Earl* (Grafton, 1992), p. 41.
5 *Ibid.*, p. 45.
6 Robert Lacey, *Ford: The Men and the Machine* (New York, 1986), p. 274.
7 Ann Hindry, ed., *Renault as Art: A Modern Adventure* (Paris, 1991).
8 Silk, *Automobile and Culture*, p. 157.
9 *Ibid.*, p. 125.
10 *Ibid.*, p. 126.
11 *Art Cars: Bringing Together Artist and Automobile* (BMW AG Public Relations, n.d.).
12 *Kustom Kulture*, exh. cat., Laguna Art Museum (Laguna Beach, 1993).
13 *Ibid.*
14 Judy Chicago, *Through the Flower* (Garden City, 1977), p. 36.
15 Krysztov Wodicko, *Critical Vehicles* (Cambridge, MA, 1998).

ALLEN SAMUELS, 'ACCIDENTS: THE CAR AND LITERATURE'

1 Comparison with the glory of the Gothic cathedral was a favourite Ruskinian device which others have followed and which, as here, nearly always serves to show modern decline.
2 Marshall Berman has argued that 'serious thinking about modern life has polarised itself into the sterile antithesis . . . "modernolatry" and "cultural despair"' – in other words, the modernizers, those who embrace change, speed and power, versus those who hold to the decline theory of the quality of life. But this is not new or particularly modern. The nineteenth century witnessed the same debate, admittedly in terms that had nothing to do with cars and without using the word *modernism*. What distinguished the twentieth-century debate was the sheer power and, above all, the rate of change in advances in the sciences and technology.
3 We know that cars bring about death and cause disabling accidents. To take two representative dates, there were, in the UK in 1986, 300,000 road accidents of which more than 5,000 were fatal. Each major accident, it is estimated, costs the welfare services (police, ambulance, fire service) more than £10,000. In 1931, there were 5,746 deaths and 129,756 non-fatal road accidents. but with far fewer cars on the roads. Driving was more dangerous. In the US, it is estimated that someone is involved in an auto accident every three seconds.
4 The first 'closed car', metaphorically speaking, was the Wooden Horse. The notion of the car as an enclosed space in which the hidden-from-view takes place merely took over a long history of what had gone on in coaches. The carriage circumambulating Rouen with Randolph and Emma Bovary in it is the prime example of this and a forerunner of car romances. Sex *in* the car is a story unto itself.

E. L. WIDMER, 'CROSSROADS: THE AUTOMOBILE, ROCK AND ROLL AND DEMOCRACY'

1 Cynthia Golomb Dettelbach, *In the Driver's Seat: The Automobile in American Literature and Popular Culture* (Westport, CT, 1976), p. 58; Stephen W. Sears, *The Automobile in America* (New York, 1977), p. 82; and David L. Lewis,

'Sex and the Automobile', in David L. Lewis and Lawrence Goldstein, eds., *The Automobile in American Culture* (Ann Arbor, MI, 1983), p. 125.

2   Leroi Jones, *Blues People* (New York, 1963), pp. 97–8.

3   'Notes on the State of Virginia', in Merrill Petersen, ed., *The Portable Thomas Jefferson*, (New York, 1975), p. 93.

4   Paul Oliver, *Aspects of the Blues Tradition* (New York, 1970), pp. 213–15.

5   Richard M. Longworth, ed., *Encyclopedia of American Cars, 1940–1970* (New York, 1980), pp. 47, 48, 102; Jerry Flint, *The Dream Machine* (New York, 1976), pp. 9, 156. For the car-radio information, I am indebted to General Motors and their helpful information staff.

6   Ed Ward et al., *Rock of Ages* (New York, 1986), pp. 31, 123; *Encyclopedia Americana* (Danbury, CT, 1988) on 'Sound Recording and Reproduction'; Oliver Read, *From Tin Foil to Stereo*; and Joseph N. Kane, ed. *Famous First Facts* (New York, 1981).

7   Gilbert Seldes, *The Great Audience* (Westport, CT, 1970), p. 109.

8   Lawrence W. Lichty and Malachi C. Topping, *American Broadcasting* (New York, 1975), p. 400.

9   See especially the title essay and 'The Last American Hero' in Tom Wolfe, *The Kandy-Kolored Tangerine-Flake Streamline Baby* (New York, 1963).

10 Earlier uses include the Boswell Sisters' 'Rock and Roll' (1934), Buddy Jones's 'Rockin' Rollin' Mama' (1939), and Bill Moore's 'We're Gonna Rock, We're Gonna Roll' (1947). See Dave Marsh and Kevin Stein, eds., *The Book of Rock Lists* (New York, 1981), p. 186.

11 Robert Palmer, *Deep Blues* (New York, 1981), pp. 223–4.

12 Albert Goldman, *Elvis* (New York, 1981), pp. 99, 112.

13 Unless we consider Webb Pierce's 1963 Bonneville, with 1,000 silver dollars in the upholstery, ornamental rifles, and carpet made from foetal calfskin (currently on display in the Car Collector's Hall of Fame in Nashville). For the details about the Gold Car, I am indebted to Marge Crumbaker and Gabe Tucker, *Up and Down with Elvis Presley* (New York, 1981), pp. 95–99.

14 Goldman, *Elvis*, pp. 641, 162.

15 Chuck Berry, *Chuck Berry: the Autobiography* (New York, 1987), p. 144. For an entertaining and provocative reading of Berry's 'Maybellene', see Warren Belasco's 'Motivatin' with Chuck Berry and Frederick Jackson Turner', in Lewis and Goldstein, pp. 262–79.

16 Berry, *Autobiography*, pp. 143, 195, 257.

17 Stephen Bayley, *Sex, Drink and Fast Cars* (London, 1986), p. 45.

18 Ralph Waldo Emerson, 'The Poet', in *The Complete Essays and Other Writings*, ed. Brooks Atkinson (New York, 1950), p. 336.

DAVID PASCOE, 'VANISHING POINTS'

2   See Jack Sargeant, 'Vanishing Point', in Jack Sargeant and Stephanie Watson, eds, *Lost Highways: An Illustrated History of Road Movies* (London, 1999), pp. 89–98.

2   Jean Baudrillard, *America*, trans. Chris Turner (London, 1988) p. 5.

3   *Ibid.*, p. 5.

4   *Ibid.*, p. 9.

5   *Ibid.*, p. 10.

6   *Ibid.*

ERIC MOTTRAM, 'BLOOD ON THE NASH AMBASSADOR: CARS IN AMERICAN FILMS'

1   Marshal McLuhan, *Understanding Media* (London, 1964), p. 18; Victor Turner, 'Themes in the Symbolism of Ndembu Hunting Ritual,' in John Middleton, ed., *Myth and Cosmos* (New York, 1967), p. 269; Hans Selye, *Stress Without Distress* (London, 1977), p. 18.

2   Stanley Milgram, *Obedience to Authority* (New York, 1974).

3   William Gaddis, *The Recognitions* (New York, 1955), p. 844.

4   Lawrence Alloway, *Violent America: The Movies 1946–1964* (New York, 1971), p. 7.

5   Michel Carrouges, *Les Machines célibataires* (Paris, 1954).

6   Stan Brakhage, *Film Biographies* (Berkeley, CA, 1977), p. 175.

7   *Ibid.*, pp. 155–6.

8   François Truffaut, *Hitchcock*, (London, 1969), p. 324.

9   Pier Paolo Pasolini, 'The Cinema of Poetry,' in *Movies and Methods*, ed. , Bill Nichols (Berkeley, CA, 1976), pp. 544–5.

10 Peter Gidal, 'Theory and Definition of Structural/Materialist Film', in Peter Gidal, ed., *Structual Film Anthology* (London, 1976), p. 3.

11 Christian Metz, *Film Language* (New York, 1974).

12 Charles Olson, 'An Ode on Nativity', in *Archeologist of Morning* (London, 1970), n.p.

13 Cahiers du Cinéma, 'John Ford's Young Mr Lincoln', in Nichols, ed., pp. 493–529; Posolini in Nichols, ed., p. 545; Umberto Eco, 'Articulations of the Cinematic Code', in Nichols, ed., pp. 593ff. See also Umberto Eco, *A Theory of Semiotics* (London, 1977), pp. 191ff.

14 Raymond Lee, *Fit for the Chase* (New York and London, 1969). For the car industry see, for example, James J. Flink, *America Adopts the Automobile, 1895–1910* (Cambridge, MA, 1970); Joseph J. Schroeder, *The Wonderful World of Automobiles, 1895–1930* (Northfield, IL, 1971).

15 Nicholas Ray, 'Story into Script,' in *Hollywood Directors, 1941–1976*, ed., Richard Koszarski (Oxford and New York, 1977), pp. 244–56 (quotation from p. 253).

16 cf. Michael Balint, *Thrills and Regressions* (New York, 1959).

17 David Dalton, *James Dean: the Mutant King* (New York, 1975), pp. 290, 301, 358.

18 Donald Allen, ed. , *The Collected Poems of Frank O'Hara* (New York, 1972), pp. 228–31; Kenneth Anger, *Hollywood Babylon* (Phoenix, ARIZ., 1965), p. 181; John Dos Passos, *Mid Century* (New York, 1961), pp. 468–75.

19 Malachy McCoy, *Steve McQueen* (London, 1974), from which the following information and quotations are derived.

20 James Goode, *The Story of the Misfits* (New York, 1963).

21 William Friedkin, 'Anatomy of a Chase,' in Koszarski, pp. 392–403.

22 McLuhan, *Understanding Media*, pp. 42, 220.

23 Gilles Deleuze and Felix Guattari, *Anti-Oedipus*, trans. Robert Hurley, Mark Seem, and Helen Lane (New York, 1977), p. 18.

24 Leonard Berkowitz, 'The Effects of Observing Violence,' *Scientific American* (February, 1964), p. 35.

25 Arthur Penn, 'Bonnie and Clyde: Private Morality and Public Violence,' in Koszarski, pp. 360–4 (quotation from p. 360).

26 Cited in Michael Pye and Linda Myles, *The Movie Brats* (London, 1979), p. 120.

27 Tuffaut, *Hitchcock*, p. 331; Alloway, *Violent America*, p. 25.

28 Jay Berman, *The Fifties Book* (New York, 1974), pp. 76–7.

29 Colin McArthur, *Underworld USA* (London, 1972), pp. 23–24.

30 Metz, *Film Language*, p. 47; James Monaco, *How to Read a Film* (New York, 1977), pp. 150–1.

31 McArthur, *Underworld*, pp. 30, 32.

32 Deleuze and Guattari, *Anti-Oedipus*, p. 235.

33 Alloway, *Violent America*, p. 15.

34 Antonio Gramsci, 'Americanism and Fordism,' in *Selections from the Prison Notebooks*, ed. Quentin Hoare and Geoffrey Nowell-Smith (London, 1971), pp. 279–322.

35 Ivan Illich, *Tools for Conviviality* (London, 1973), p. 2.

'Cars and Capital', introduced by Joe Kerr

1 Antony Beevor, *Stalingrad* (London, 1999), pp. 392–3.

2 Gillian Darley, *Factories* (London, forthcoming).

3 W. Hawkins Ferry, *The Legacy of Albert Kahn* (Detroit, 1987), p. 24. Between 1928 and 1932, a Kahn office in Russia trained thousands of architects, engineers and technicians, and built 521 factories across the country.

4 Peter Gavrilovich and Bill McGraw, eds, *The Detroit Almanac: 300 Years of Life in the Motor City* (Detroit, 2001), p. 208.

JOE KERR, 'TROUBLE IN MOTOR CITY'

1 Gavrilovich and McGraw, *The Detroit Almanac: 300 Years of Life in the Motor City* (Detroit, 2001) p. 3.

2 Kenneth Gilpin, 'G.M. Registers 73% Decline in Net Income for Quarter', *New York Times*, 12 August 2001.

3 Detroit Historical Museum Website: www.detroithistorical.org.

4 Quoted in Suzanne E. Smith, *Dancing in the Street: Motown and the Cultural Politics of Detroit* (Cambridge, 1999), p. 12.

5 General Motors Corporation Website: www.gmc.com.

6 A late-nineteenth-century slogan for Detroit; *The Detroit Almanac*, p. 287.

7 Quoted in Mike Smith, 'Spirit of 1937', *Detroit at 300: Michigan History Magazine*, special issue, p. 62.

8 Le Corbusier had not visited America at this time, and it is said that he took the image of Highland Park from an earlier book by Mies van der Rohe.

9 Quoted in the exhibition *Albert Kahn: Inspiration for the Modern*, University of Michigan Museum of Art, Ann Arbor, June 2001.

10 Gavrilovich and McGraw, *Detroit Almanac*, p. 168.

11 See Brian Carter, ed., *Albert Khan: Inspiration for the Modern*, exh. cat., University of Michigan Museum of Art (Ann Arbor, MI, 2001).

12 Charles A. Wills, *A Historical Album of Detroit* (Brookfield, CT, 1996), p. 42.

13 The title of a John Lee Hooker song about the 1967 Detroit riot.

14 John Schnapp, 'It's Best, Worst of Times for Carmakers', *Detroit News*, 11 September 2001.

15 Ford's World headquarters are in Dearborn, close to the Rouge, General Motors have moved their world headquarters to the Renaissance Center in downtown Detroit, and Chrysler is headquartered in Auburn Hills – although the world headquarters of Daimler Chrysler is now in Germany.

16 Gavrilovich and McGraw, *The Detroit Almanac*, p. 294.

17 Henry Ford, as quoted in the *Chicago Tribune*, 25 May 1916. From Bob Allen, 'Detroit: It Starts with a T', in *Detroit at 300 . . . Then and Now* (Detroit, 2001), p. 1.

GEREMIE R. BARMÉ, 'ENGINES OF REVOLUTION: CAR CULTURES IN CHINA'

My thanks to Sang Ye for providing me with an extraordinary range of anecdotal and historical material, as well as coming to my aid with the full version of the children's rhyme about Chairman Mao and the Red Flag when my memory failed. My gratitude also to Linda Jaivin for her inspired rendering of that rhyme, to Richard Rigby for providing me with the Sapajou cartoon, and to the Long Bow Group and Lois Conner for their generous help with other illustrative materials. My fond regards to Wu Zuguang and his late wife Xin Fengxia, who provided Linda and me with the use of a stretch limo for our Beijing nuptials on 7 July 1986.

1 'Nihongdengxiade shaobing', directed by Wang Ping and Ge Xin, Tianma Film Studios, 1964.

2 Jonathan Hutt, '*La Maison d'Or* – The Sumptuous World of Shao Xunmei', *East Asian History*, 21 (June 2001), p. 120.

3 Traditionally, a cart driver would run along with the vehicle or, if necessary, sit on the jutting axle beside the cabin.

4 Simon Leys, *Chinese Shadows* (New York, 1978), pp. 56–60.

5 See Koshizawa Akira, '"Manshuukoku" no shuto keikaku to kenchiku yōshiki – sono senshinsei to seijisei,', in Andō Hikotarō, ed., *Kindai Nihon to Chuugoku: Nitchuu kankeishi ronshuu* (1989), pp. 314, 322, 325. My thanks to Gavan McCormack for bringing this material to my attention.

6 Again, as Simon Leys described the urban-scape of Beijing in the early 1970s, 'The vast boulevards call to mind the false airports which cargo-cult devotees in New Guinea hack out of the jungle in the hope that this will persuade their gods to send planes full of treasure: one is sometimes tempted to believe that the building of the Autobahns, now used only by a few dismal cyclists or donkey carts, might similarly be part of a magic ritual, as if miles of macadam might generate the sudden appearance of hordes of hooting, stinking, triumphant cars – simultaneously the nightmare of the consumer society and dream of the socialist one.'

7 Because of the famine conditions created by the disastrous Great Leap Forward of the late 1950s, the provision of basic foodstuffs was strictly controlled. Cadres were given special rations during what were euphemistically called the 'three difficult years' (1959–62): officials of the thirteenth to fifteenth ranks were allowed supplies of cigarettes and edible oils – therefore they were known as 'cigarette-oil cadres' (*yanyou ganbu*); sixteenth- to nineteenth-level bureaucrats had extra rations of sugar and soybeans, and were accordingly dubbed 'sugar-bean cadres' (*tangdou ganbu*).

8 *Xiao qiche, di-di-di,*
shangmian zuozhe Mao zhuxi.
Mao zhuxi, zuo Hongqi,
qisi Meidi Kennidi.
Kennidi, gan zhaoji,
caizhe yikuai xiguapi.
yi shuai shuai ge zui ken ni,
ge'rpi zhaoliang Dalaxi.

9 This quotation is taken from Sang Ye, *1949, 1989, 1999* (Hong Kong, 1999), pp. 273–4; an English-language version edited by Geremie Barmé with Miriam Lang will appear under the title *Chairman Mao's Ark: The People on the People's Republic* (Boulder, CO, 2003).

10 The year Deng Xiaoping announced a radical new phase of the market-oriented economic reforms during a 'tour of the South' (*nanxun*), in the course of which he visited Shanghai and Special Economic Zones in Guangdong province.

11 *che dao shanqian bi you lu, you lu bi you Fengtian che*. The advertisement for Toyotas appeared on a hoarding on Airport Road which had originally carried the exhortation 'People of the world unite to overthrow American Imperialism and all its running dogs!' Today, a sign with the more anodyne message 'Beijing Welcomes You!' occupies this site.

12 Su Xiaokang, 'Longniande beichang – guanyu Heshang de zhaji', in Su, *Ziyou beiwanglu* (Hong Kong, 1989), p. 267, trans. in Geremie Barmé and Linda Jaivin, eds, *New Ghosts, Old Dreams: Chinese Rebel Voices* (New York, 1992), p. 274.

13 The names of mainland and Hong Kong pop singers.

14 Quotations from Barmé and Jaivin, *New Ghosts, Old Dreams*, pp. 275–6.

15 Also called the *Haidi lake* in contrast to the Cadillac (*Kadilaike*), and a callous reference to the famous handicapped intellectual Zhang Haidi, who was promoted in the early 1980s as a model citizen by party propagandists.

16 See Zhongguo diyi qiche jituan gongsi, 'Hongqi – hecai! jiayou!!!', *Beijing qingnianbao*, 31 January 1997. Prizes offered for winning slogans ranged from 10,000 *yuan* in cash to scale models of the new Red Flag. See G. Barmé, *In the Red: On Contemporary Chinese Culture* (New York, 1999), pp. 239–40.

17 Personal communication, 28 August 2001, quoted with permission. Lynne O'Donnell was the Beijing-based correspondent for *The Australian* newspaper. For details on both the Red Flag and the Audi, see the manufacturer's website at www.faw.com.cn.

18 *Zanmen liuxie you liuhan, gongchang zhengle jishiwan. Tamen maige wuguike, limian zuoge wangbadan* and *Bie kan yamen xiao, cunzhang zuo Lanniao; buguan shenme ji, dou lai zuo Aodi. Qiye kuile qian, zhaoyang wan Bentian; gongsi mei qian fa, mai liang Sangtana.*

19 *Mei che, keshi wo you ben'r* and *Wanquan jiaxiao, song nin shixiang mingtian.*

20 These statistics are from John Schauble, 'Private Cars Deliver New Audience', *Sydney Morning Herald*, 21 May 2001.

21 See G. Barmé with Sang Ye, 'The Great Firewall of China', *Wired*, 5/6 (June 1997), pp. 138–50, 174–8.

CHRISTOPHER PINNEY, 'AUTOMONSTER'

1 The term is taken from Nicholas Thomas, *Entangled Objects: Exchange. Material Culture, and Colonialism in the Pacific* (Cambridge, MA, 1991). Thomas has significantly modified his position in 'The Case of the Misplaced Poncho: Speculations Concerning the History of Cloth in Polynesia', *Journal of Material Culture*, vol. IV. No. 1, 1999, pp. 5–20.

2 The summary is Daniel Miller's in his introductory discussion of Diana Young's chapter in his edited collection *Car Cultures* (Oxford, 2001), p. 3.

3 *Ibid.*, p. 30.

4 This analogy was first raised by Mihaly Csikszentmihalyi and Eugene Rochberg-Halton in *The Meaning of Things: Domestic Symbols and the Self* (Cambridge, 1981), p. 16 and

has subsequently been discussed by Bruno Latour in *Pandora's Hope: Essays on the Reality of Science Studies* (Cambridge, MA, 1999), pp. 176–77. See Mike Michael, 'The Invisible Car: The Cultural Purification of Road Rage' in Daniel Miller, ed., *Car Cultures* (Oxford, 2001), p. 75 for further discussion.

5 Although as Auden proposed, with regard to another catastrophe, 'Accurate scholarship can/Unearth the Whole Offence' (September 1, 1939).

6 Bruno Latour, *Pandora's Hope*, p. 190.

7 Martin Heidegger, 'The Age of the World Picture', in *The Question Concerning Technology and Other Essays* (New York, 1977), p. 133.

8 'Which driver is not tempted, merely by the power of his engine, to wipe out the vermin of the streets, pedestrians, children and cyclists? The movement machines demand of their users already have the violent, hard-hitting, unresting jerkiness of Fascist maltreatment.' Theodore W. Adorno, *Minima Moralia: Reflections from Damaged Life* (London, 1978), p. 19.

9 Bruno Latour, *We Have Never Been Modern* (Hemel Hempstead, 1993), p. x.

10 Latour, *Pandora's Hope*, p. 176.

11 Roland Barthes, 'The Metaphor of the Eye' reprinted as a supplement to Georges Bataille, *Story of the Eye* (Harmondsworth, 1982), p. 119.

12 For a brilliant discussion which takes these as its starting point see Jonathan Lamb, 'Modern Metamorphoses and Disgraceful Tales', in *Critical Inquiry*, 2001.

13 Barthes, 'The Metaphor', p. 120.

14 *Ibid.*, p. 121.

15 Similarly, Christopher Tilley has recently written about the terms 'solid metaphor' in relation to material culture in *Metaphor and Material Culture* (Oxford, 1999).

16 Barthes, 'The Metaphor', p. 123.

17 *Ibid.*, p. 125.

18 *Ibid.*, p. 122.

19 Lewis Mumford, *Technics and Civilisation* (New York, 1934), p. 163.

20 Alan Brownjohn, 'For a Journey', in Edward Lucie-Smith, ed., *British Poetry since 1945* (Harmondsworth, 1970), p. 266.

21 Philip Larkin, 'The Whitsun Wedding' in A. Alvarez, ed., *The New Poetry* (Harmondsworth, 1962), p. 81.

22 'Drought-hit states facing famine', *Guardian*, 30 October 2001, p. 9.

23 *Time*, vol. 157, No. 14, 9 April 2001, pp. 22–36. The sugges-
    tion is that man-made emissions (in which the car is a
    major contributor) trigger climate changes which will lead
    to further, more dramatic changes.
24 Paul Virilio, 'The Last Vehicle' in Dietmar Kamper and
    Christoph Wuld, eds, *Looking Back on the End of the World*
    (New York and Los Angeles, 1989).
25 Sven Lindqvist, *Exterminate all the Brutes* (London, 1997),
    p. 48.
26 *Ibid.*, p. 68.
27 Barthes, 'The Metaphor', p. 125.

'Motor Spaces', introduced by Joe Kerr

1 J. B. Priestley, *English Journey* (London, 1934), p. 73.
2 E. H. Fryer of the Automobile Association, quoted in
   David Matless, *Landscape and Englishness* (London, 1998),
   pp. 54–5.
3 John Kenneth Galbraith, 'To My New Friends in the Affluent Society – Greetings', *Life*, 27 March 1970, p. 20.
   Quoted in Robert Venturi, Denise Scott Brown and Steven
   Izenour, *Learning from Las Vegas: The Forgotten Symbolism of
   Architectural Form*, rev. edn (Cambridge, MA, 1977), p. 78.
4 Venturi, Scott Brown and Izenour, *Learning from Las Vegas*,
   p. 3.

MARSHALL BERMAN, 'ROBERT MOSES: THE EXPRESSWAY WORLD'

1 These statements are quoted by Robert Caro in his monu-
   mental study, *The Power Broker: Robert Moses and the Fall of
   New York* (New York, 1974), pp. 849, 876. The 'meat ax'
   passage is from Moses's memoir, *Public Works : A Dangerous Trade* (New York, 1970). Moses's appraisal of the
   Cross-Bronx Expressway occurs in an interview with Caro.
   The Power Broker is the main source for my narrative of
   Moses's career. See also my article on Caro and Moses,
   'Buildings Are Judgment: Robert Moses and the Romance
   of Construction', *Ramparts*, March 1975, and a further
   symposium in the June issue.
2 Speech to the Long Island Real Estate Board, 1927, quoted
   in Caro, *The Power Broker*, p. 275.

DAVID BRODSLY, 'L.A. FREEWAY: AN APPRECIATIVE ESSAY'

1   Robert de Roos, 'Los Angeles', *National Geographic* 122
    (October 1962), pp. 451–501.
2   Steven V. Roberts, 'Ode to a Freeway', *New York Times
    Magazine*, 15 April 1973, p. 30.
3   California Assembly Interim Committee on Natural
    Resources, Planning and Public Works, *Highway and Free-
    way Planning* (Sacramento, CA, 1965), p. 23.
4   Owen B. Shoemaker, letter to the editor, *Los Angeles Times*,
    21 March 1972.
5   See Leo Marx, *The Machine in the Garden* (New York, 1964).
6   Richard Lillard, *Eden in Jeopardy: The Southern California
    Experience* (New York, 1966), p. 204.
7   From 'The Cement Octopus,' Words and music by Malvina
    Reynolds, copyright 1964, Schroeder Music Co. (ASCAP).
8   'Freeways Called Good Neighbors', *Los Angeles Times*, 27
    January 1974; Goodwin, 'Growing Freeway System', p. 576.
9   Ted Thackery Jr., 'Californians Still Like Freeways – with
    Restraints', *Los Angeles Times*, 11 April 1973, I, p. 15.
10 California Department of Transportation and Southern
    California Association of Governments, *1976 Urban and
    Rural Travel Survey, vol. II: Summary of Findings: Attitudinal
    Data* (Los Angeles, 1978), p. 50.
11 Hart Crane, 'Modern Poetry', in *The Complete Poems and
    Selected Letters and Prose of Hart Crane*, ed. Brom Weber
    (Garden City, NY, 1966), p. 262.

RICHARD J. WILLIAMS, 'PLEASURE AND THE MOTORWAY'

1 *The Times*, 3 November 1959.
2 Reyner Banham, 'Disservice Areas', *New Society*, 23 May
   1968, pp. 762–3.
3 Peter Hall, *Cities of Tomorrow* (Oxford, 1996), p. 110.
4 'Reyner Banham Loves Los Angeles', BBC (1972).
5 Reyner Banham, *Los Angeles: The Architecture of Four Ecologies* (London, 1971), pp. 213–22.
6 Reyner Banham, 'Roadscape with Rusting Nails', *Listener*,
   80 (29 August 1968), p. 268.
7 Banham, *Los Angeles*, p. 216.
8 Herbert Marcuse, *Eros and Civilisation: A Philosophical
   Inquiry into Freud* (London, 1956).
9 Peter Hall, *London 2000*, 2nd edn (London, 1969); Reyner
   Banham et al., 'Non-Plan: An Experiment in Freedom',

New Society, 20 March 1969, pp. 435–43.

10 Hall, *London 2000*, pp. 271–2.

11 See for example, Martin Pawley, *Terminal Architecture* (London, 1998). Jonathan Glancey's criticism for the *Guardian* has often referred to motorway architecture, although more often as a phenomenon of the past rather than of the present.

12 'Mobility', *Architectural Design*, special issue (September 1968).

13 'Manplan 2', *Architectural Review*, special issue (October 1969).

14 Fredric Jameson, 'The Antinomies of Postmodernism' [1989], in *The Cultural Turn: Selected Writings on the Post-modern 1983–1998* (London, 1998), p. 38.

SANDY McCREERY, 'COME TOGETHER'

1 Le Corbusier, *The City of Tomorrow and Its Planning* (originally published in French in 1924 as *Urbanisme*), trans. Frederick Etchells (London, 1929) p. 179.

2 *Oxford English Dictionary Online*: 'speed, n'.

3 'Killing Speed and Saving Lives', Slower Speeds Initiative report, 2001. The 1998 UK Government (Department of Transport) report 'New Directions in Speed Management: A Review of Policy' found that 'about 40 per cent of pedestrians who are struck at speeds below 20 mph sustain non-minor injuries however, this rises to 90 per cent at speeds up to 30 mph.'

4 From 1903, Britain had a 20-mph speed limit until it was removed altogether in 1930. Motorists' organizations had actively campaigned against the speed limit; indeed, the Automobile Association was originally a radical direct-action organization set up to frustrate police speed traps by positioning scouts to warn oncoming motorists. Members received free legal representation to fight speeding prosecutions. The 30-mph limit was introduced in 1934 following concern about the rising death toll.

5 At 30-mph impacts, 55 per cent of pedestrians usually survive ('Killing Speed and Saving Lives'); however, this fact must be balanced with the fact that only a small proportion of drivers comply with 30-mph limits. According to an NOP Solutions poll for London's *Evening Standard* newspaper (23 March 2001), only 19 per cent of drivers in London and the south-east of England claim not to regularly exceed 30-mph limits.

6 In 1998; source: Metropolitan Police website: http://www.met.police.uk/about/fact5.htm

7 J. G. Ballard, *Concrete Island* (London, 1974).

8 Another uncertain consequence will be the effects on the economic geography of London – whether, for example, businesses will relocate to outside the charging zone.

9 There is a man in South London who is regularly seen driving his home-made motorized couch.

10 Tom Wolfe, *A Man in Full* (London, 1998).

11 *Genevieve*, directed and produced by Henry Cornelius, UK, 1953 © Sirius Production Ltd.

JACK SARGEANT, 'SQUEALING WHEELS AND FLYING FISTS'

1 In Britain, the most infamous case of road-rage homicide is possibly that of Kenneth Noye, who was found guilty in April 2000 of murdering Stephen Cameron during an altercation at the M25 Swanley interchange on the afternoon of 19 May 1996. Although Noye stated that he stabbed Cameron in self-defence, he was found guilty and jailed for life. In April 2001, he began appeal proceedings. Source: Nick Hopkins, 'M25 Road-rage Murderer Jailed for Life', *Guardian*, 20 April 2000.

2 See www.CarAccident.com.

3 Mark Rowe and Nicholas Pyke, 'Britain Is Road Rage Capital of Europe', *Independent on Sunday*, 14 May 2000.

4 See: www.CarAccident.com and www.drivers.com.

5 Dominic Connell and Mathew Joint, *Driver Aggression*, Road Safety Unit, Group Public Policy, 1996, AAA Foundation for Traffic Safety, www.aaafts.org.

MURRAY FRASER AND JOE KERR, 'MOTOPIA: CITIES, CARS AND ARCHITECTURE'

1. Le Corbusier, *The City of Tomorrow* (London, 1987), p xxiii.

2 Le Corbusier, *Towards a New Architecture*, trans. Frederick Etchells (London, 1946), p. 123.

3 *Ibid.*

4 Tim Benton, 'Villa Savoye', in *Le Corbusier: Architect of the Century*, exh. cat. (London, 1987), p. 64.

5 Joseph Connors, *The Robie House of Frank Lloyd Wright* (Chicago, 1984), pp. 5–6.

6 Kahn, quoted in W. Hawkins Ferry, *The Legacy of Albert Kahn* (Detroit, 1987), p. 21.

7 James A. Bridenstine, *Edsel & Eleanor Ford House* (Detroit, 1988).

8   This account of the General Motors Technical Center is taken from Murray Fraser, 'Eero Saarinen and the Boundaries of Technology', in Murray Fraser, ed., *The Oxford Review of Architecture*, vol. I: *Culture and Technology* (Oxford, 1996), pp. 58–67.

9   Robert Venturi, Denise Scott Brown and Steven Izenour, *Learning from Las Vegas: The Forgotten Symbolism of Architectural Form*, rev. edn (Cambridge, MA, 1997).

10 Quoted in Marshall Berman, *All That Is Solid Melts Into Air* (New York and London, 1982/83), pp. 290–312.

11 Jane Jacobs, *The Life and Death of Great American Cities* (New York, 1961).

12 Le Corbusier, *The City of Tomorrow*, p. xiv.

13 J. H. Forshaw and Patrick Abercrombie, *County of London Plan* (London, 1943), p. 50.

14 'Relearning from Las Vegas: An Interview with Robert Venturi and Denis Scott Brown', in Rem Koolhaas/Harvard Project on the City 2, *Harvard Design School Guide to Shopping* (Cologne, 2001), pp. 590–617.

15 Jonathan Rose, 'Violence, Materialism and Ritual: Shopping for a Center', *Modulus 23: Towards a Civil Architecture in America* (August 1994), pp. 137–51, quoted in Andres Duany, Elizabeth Plater-Zyberk, and Jeff Speck, *Suburban Nation: The Rise of Sprawl and the Decline of the American Dream* (New York, 2000), p. 62.

16 Rem Koolhaas, 'The Generic City', in Rem Koolhaas/Bruce Mau, *S,M,L,XL* (Rotterdam: 010 Publishers; 1995), pp. 1238–1264; Rem Koolhaas/Harvard Project on the City 1, *Great Leap Forward* (Cologne, 2001).

'Myths and Motors', introduced by Joe Kerr

1   Marshall McLuhan, *The Mechanical Bride: Folklore of Industrial Man* (New York, 1967), p. 82.

2   Le Corbusier, *Towards a New Architecture*, trans. Frederick Etchells (London, 1946), pp. 127–8.

3   Roland Barthes, 'The New Citroën', in *Mythologies*, trans. Annette Lavers (London, 1972), p. 88.

4   Ralph Nader, *Unsafe at Any Speed: The Designed-in Dangers of the American Automobile* (New York, 1965).

5   Barthes, 'The New Citroën', p. 88.

PATRICK KEILLER, 'SEXUAL AMBIGUITY AND AUTOMOTIVE ENGINEERING'

1   In Roland Barthes, *Mythologies*, selected and trans. Annette Lavers (London, 1972), p. 89.

2   Ilya Ehrenburg, *The Life of the Automobile*, trans. Joachim Neugroschel (London, 1985), p. 27.

3   From a website of the Science Museum, London, documenting the restoration of an early Panhard et Levassor car.

4   The late Alan Clark MP, for example, was a great admirer of the DS.

5   See, for instance, Lubomír Šlapeta's Villa Kremer of 1934, Jaromír Krejcar's Czechoslovakian Pavilion for the 1936–7 World Exhibition in Paris, or Bohuslav Fuchs's work in the late '30s.

6   See, André Breton, *Manifestoes of Surrealism*, trans. Richard Seaver and Helen R. Lane (Ann Arbor, MI, 1969), p. 155.

7   Lubomír and Cestmír Šlapeta worked for Scharoun in Breslau in the late '20s.

8   For these and other examples, see Vladimír Šlapeta and Jan Kaplicky, *Czech Functionalism 1918–1938* (London, 1987), and Vladimír Šlapeta, *Die Brünner Funktionalisten* (Innsbruck, 1985).

9   Tatra also had some more direct contact with the architectural culture of the period. In 1931, Lubomír Slapeta designed a version of the Tatra T57, and in 1932 Jaroslav Fragner built a Tatra showroom in Kolín.

10 For a comprehensive account, see Ivan Margolius and John G Henry, *Tatra: The Legacy of Hans Ledwinka* (London, 1990).

11 Übelacker seems to have had the central role. According to Margolius and Henry, the cars were designated T77, T87, T97 etc. because seven was Übelacker's lucky number. He was working on the engine for the next series of the T57, with so little success that he was threatened with the sack, when he suddenly produced a design for a new car with an aerodynamic body.

12 When the SS Jaguar 2.5-litre saloon was unveiled in 1935 and those present were invited to guess its price, the average guess was £632, but the actual price was £395. In 1933, the T57's UK price was £260.

13 At around 12.25RM to the pound in 1938, this was equivalent to £690.

14 Quentin Willson, *The Ultimate Classic Car Book* (London, 1995).

15 Jean Panhard ran the company from 1944 until 1966. The interview, for *Le Figaro*, is reprinted on various websites.

16 The Porsche 356's 1086-cc engine produced 44 bhp. In the UK, the 1959 Morris Oxford's 1500-cc engine produced 55 bhp, and the 1969 Ford Capri's 1300-cc engine 52 bhp. Many American cars of the period had engines of 5 litres or more with outputs of 150–300 bhp. The 1962 Ford Falcon, the first US 'compact' car, was available with a 2.4-litre engine of 85 bhp.

17 Other rear-engine cars were the Fiat 500, Renault's Dauphine, pre-1989 Skodas and the unfortunate Chevrolet Corvair (of Ralph Nader's *Unsafe at Any Speed*). Apart from the Porsche, few rear-engine cars are still produced.

KARAL ANN MARLING, 'AMERICA'S LOVE AFFAIR WITH THE AUTOMOBILE IN THE TELEVISION AGE'

1 For family drama of the period, see Rick Mitz, *The Great TV Sitcom Book* (New York, 1988).

2 Quoted by Bevis Hillier, *The Style of the Century, 1900–1980* (New York, 1983), p. 147.

3 The number five hit in the Top Fifty for 1955, Chuck Berry's song was recorded on the Chess label (Arc, BMI). See H. Kandy Rohde, ed., *The Gold of Rock and Roll, 1955–1967* (New York, 1970), pp. 30–35.

4 Arthur J. Pulos, *American Design Ethic* (Cambridge, MA, 1983), pp. 422–423.

5 John R. Stilgoe, *Borderland: Origins of the American Suburb, 1920–1939* (New Haven, CT, 1988), p. 301, and Clifford Edward Clark Jr., *The American Family Home, 1800–1960* (Chapel Hill, NC, 1986), pp. 217–236

6 Stephen King, *Christine* (New York, 1983).

7 See Kevin Allman, *TV Turkeys* (New York, 1987), pp. 68–75.

8 Roland Marchand, *Advertising the American Dream* (Berkeley, CA, 1985), pp. 156–157. See also Jeffrey L, Meikle, *Twentieth Century Limited* (Philadelphia, 1979), pp. 12–13, 106.

9 Quoted in Julian Pettifer and Nigel Turner, *Automania* (Boston, MA, 1984), p. 131.

10 Jane and Michael Stern, *Auto Ads* (New York, 1984), p. 40.

11 Marchand, *Advertising the American Dream*, p. 159.

12 Quoted by Paul Rambali, *Car Culture* (New York, 1984), p. 40.

13 Paul A. Carter, *Another Part of the Twenties* (New York, 1977), p. 134.

14 Quoted by Cynthia Golomb Dettelbach, *In the Driver's Seat: The Automobile in American Literature and Popular Culture* (Westport, CT, 1976), p. 97.

15 See Ian Logan and Henry Nield, *Classy Chassy* (New York, 1977).

16 See, e.g. Donald J. Bush, *The Streamlined Decade* (New York, 1975).

17 Harley Earl (with Arthur W. Baum), 'I Dream Automobiles,' *The Saturday Evening Post*, 227 (7 August 1954), p. 82.

18 These terms were used by designers themselves; see Thomas Hine, *Populuxe* (New York, 1986), p. 94.

19 As quoted in Pettifer and Turner, *Automania*, p. 137.

20 See Hillier, *The Style of the Century*, p. 147.

21 Earl, 'I Dream Automobiles', p. 82.

22 Hine, *Populuxe*, p. 101.

23 Alfred P. Sloan, *My Years with General Motors* (Garden City, NY, 1963), esp. Ch. 15, and Gerald Silk et al., *Automobile and Culture* (New York, 1984), pp. 237–239.

24 A Motorama-like unveiling of a new model is the centre-piece of the 1988 film, *Tucker: A Man and His Dream*, directed by Francis Ford Coppola.

25 TV commercials of the period have been collected and preserved in several video versions. See e.g., *Cars of the Fabulous Fifties* (Union, NJ, 1987).

26 Hillier, *The Style of the Century*, p. 118.

27 Raymond Loewy, 'Jukebox on Wheels,' *Atlantic Monthly*, 195 (April 1955), pp. 36, 38.

28 *Ibid.*, p. 37.

29 Quoted by King, *Christine*, p. 87.

30 See entry for 'Pink Cadillac' in Fred L. Worth and Steve D. Tamerius, *Elvis: His Life from A to Z* (Chicago, 1988), p. 154.

GRACE LEES-MAFFEI, 'MEN, MOTORS, MARKETS AND WOMEN'

1 Stephen Bayley, *Sex, Drink and Fast Cars: The Creation and Consumption of Images* (London, 1986), pp. 32–3.

2 L. Cross, 'Driving Miss Crazy', *Guardian*, 28 February 2000.

3 D. Gartman, *Auto Opium: A Social History of American Automobile Design* (London and New York, 1994), p. 87.

4 S. O'Connell, *The Car in British Society: Class, Gender and Motoring, 1896–1939* (Manchester, 1998), pp. 43–8.

5 J. Jackson, *Every Woman's Guide to the Car* (London, 1993), p. vii.

6 'Private Motoring: Driving Tests, 1988–1998', Table 3.16, *Transport Statistics Great Britain: 1999 Edition* (Department of Environment, Transport and the Regions, Stationery Office, 1999).

7 'Households with regular use of car(s): 1951–1998', Table 9.2; 'Private Motoring: households with regular use of cars', Table 3.14, *Transport Statistics Great Britain: 1999 Edition*.

8 Mintel report, 'Car Retailing', March 2000; S. Hacker and S. Cutler, 'The Price for You Madam', *Guardian*, 3 April 2000; R. Coward, 'Into the Driving Seat', *Guardian*, 16 November 1999.

9 'Number of Journeys by Purpose and Sex, 1996/98', Table 1.7. Escort-education journeys have increased from 3.2 per cent of all journeys in 1985/6 to 4.8 per cent in 1996/8, accounting for 3 per cent of journeys made by men and 7 per cent made by women. M. Dickson, 'Characteristics of the Escort Education Journey', *Transport Trends 2000* (London, 2000), p. 47.

10 J. Moorhead, 'Take a Walk on the Wild Side', *Guardian*, 30 June 1999.

11 O'Connell, *The Car In British Society*, p. 59.

12 'An L of a Living', *Your Car* (May 1987), pp. 66–7.

13 'Reader's Lives', *Your Car* (September 1989), p. 11.

14 Northern Ireland Road Safety Monitor, Department of the Environment Central Statistics and Research Branch, 1999.

15 'Women Drivers are Better than Men – In Theory', Northern Ireland Information Service, 10 April 1997, Road Transport Statistics Bulletin, Department of the Environment (NI).

16 L. Spinney, 'Once a Boy Racer . . .', *Guardian*, 14 February 2000.

17 N. Hawkes, 'Size Matters with Male Brain Lobe', *The Times*, 11 December 1999.

18 C. Dodd, 'Wheel Thing: New Research Reveals Why Some Women Become Wimps in the Driving Seat – and Men Are to Blame', *Guardian*, 25 May 2000.

19 S. Birch, 'Are You the Wrong Shape for Your Car?', *The Times*, 12 February 2000.

20 S. Birch, 'Why Car Seats Can Be Such a Pain in the Back', *The Times*, 6 May 2000.

21 S. Langley, 'Designers Don't Care that Seatbelts Can Be a Sore Point for Women', *The Times*, 12 February 2000.

22 S. Hacker, 'Road Test Honda Logo and HR-V', *Guardian*, 1 May 2000; M. Sawyer, 'Spanish Flyer', *Observer*, 11 June 2000; P. Wark, 'Why Women Want Something Different', *The Times*, 22 October 1999.

23 L. Hazleton, 'Sex Drive', *Guardian*, 20 September 1999.

24 Wark, 'Why Women Want'.

25 'Have You the Drive to Be an Engineer?', *Guardian*, 16 October 1999.

26 Coward, 'Into the Driving Seat'.

27 R. Oldenziel, *Making Technology Masculine: Men, Women and Modern Machines in America 1870–1945* (Amsterdam, 1999).

28 Wark, 'Why Women Want'.

29 J. King, *Cars: A Consumer's Guide* (Harlow, 1987), p. 1.

30 Jackson, *Every Woman's Guide*, p. 9.

31 M. Agace, 'Not Just a Pretty Bonnet', *Vogue* (UK edn) (November 1995), pp. 51–2.

32 Hacker and Cutler, 'The Price'.

33 V. Freeman, 'Buy a New Car with Your Baked Beans and Bleach', *The Times*, 2 September 2000.

34 D. Jones and S. Prais, 'Plant Size and Productivity in the Motor Industry: Some International Comparisons', *Oxford Bulletin of Economics and Statistics*, 40 (1978), pp. 131–52, quoted in J. Tomlinson, 'The Government and the Car Industry 1945–1970', *The Journal of Transport History*, XX/1 (March 1999), p. 24.

35 J. Flink, *The Car Culture* (Cambridge, MA, 1975), p. 211.

36 Gartman, *Auto Opium*, pp. 23, 42.

37 Bayley, *Sex, Drink*, p. 101.

38 Agace, 'Not Just a Pretty Bonnet', p. 51.

39 M. McLuhan, *Understanding Media: The Extensions of Man* (Cambridge, MA, and London, 1994).

40 D. Young, *Advertising the Beetle 1953–1978* (London, 1993), pp. 44, 32.

41 Agace, 'Not Just a Pretty Bonnet', p. 51.

42 J. Wajcman, *Feminism Confronts Technology* (Cambridge, 1991), p. 135.

43 Coward, 'Into the Driving Seat'.

44 'A Classic of Modern Design', *Guardian*, 17 July 1999.

45 Flink, *The Car Culture*, p. 201.

MARTIN PAWLEY, 'THE DOWNFALL OF THE DYMAXION CAR'

1 The architect Walter Gropius found these trends 'most illuminating' and used them to justify his own contention that houses should be standardized and made on production lines. See 'Toward a Living Architecture', *American Architect and Architecture* (February 1938).

2 See, for example, the delayed introduction of independent front suspension, hydraulic brakes and coil ignition. Alan Baker, in *The Component Contribution* (London, 1979), refers to the 1930s as 'a period of consolidation' and gives

many examples of the delayed introduction of engine improvements.

3 Herbert Austin in England, for example, followed the same path. As, in his way, did Adolf Hitler with his strong support for the KdF project, later to become the Volkswagen Beetle. Stout himself went on to build several examples of his own car of the future called the Scarab, chiefly remembered today for having independent oleo aircraft suspension and movable furniture inside instead of fixed seats.

4 The word *Dymaxion* was coined by a Marshall Fields publicity man who while listening to Fuller speaking in 1928, noted the three words he used most often: *DYnamic*, *MAXimum* and *tensION*.

5 Nor even to recognize, for Fuller toyed with drawings pointing out the similarity between the outline of a horse-drawn carriage and a conventional front-engine saloon, contrasting both with the streamlined outline of the 'teardrop' Dymaxion.

6 For example, on 11 August 1933 Dymaxion 1 put in an appearance at the Roosevelt Raceway on Long Island before a capacity crowd. It was announced that the car was capable of 120 mph, but it did not race and no timed runs were made.

Bibliography

Lawrence Alloway, *Violent America: The Movies 1946–1964* (New York, 1971)

Martin Anderson, *The Federal Bulldozer* (Cambridge, MA, 1964)

Umbro Apollonio, *Futurist Manifestos* (New York, 1973)

Neal Ascherson, *Black Sea* (London, 1995)

John Baeder, *Gas, Food and Lodging: A Postcard Odyssey* (New York, 1982)

J. G. Ballard, *A User's Guide to the Millennium* (New York, 1966)

—, *Concrete Island*, (London, 1973)

—, *Crash*, London (New York, 1973)

Michael Balint, *Thrills and Regression* (London, 1959, reprinted 1987)

Reyner Banham, *Los Angeles: The Architecture of Four Ecologies* (New York, 1971)

—, 'Industrial Design and Popular Art', *Civilta delle Macchine*, 6 (August 1955)

—, *Theory and Design in the First Machine Age* (New York, 1967)

Reyner Banham, Peter Hall, Cedric Price and Paul Barker, 'Non-Plan: An Experiment in Freedom', *New Society* (20 March 1969)

Deanne Barkley, *Freeway* (New York, 1978)

George Barris and David Fetherston, *Barris TV and Movie Cars* (Osceola, WI, 1996)

Roland Barthes, *Mythologies* (London, 1972)

Jean Baudrillard, *America* (London, 1988)

Stephen Bayley, *Sex, Drink and Fast Cars: The Creation and Consumption of Images* (London, 1986)

James Belasco, *Americans on the Road: From Autocamp to Motel 1910–1945* (Cambridge, MA, 1979)

John Bentley, *Great American Automobiles: A Dramatic Account of Their Achievements in Competition* (Englewoods Cliffs, NJ, 1957)

Marshall Berman, *All That Is Solid Melts Into Air: The Experience of Modernity* (London, 1999)

Peter Blake, *Form Follows Fiasco* (Boston, MA, 1974)

—, *God's Own Junkyard* (New York, 1964)

Harold Blank, *Wild Wheels* (San Francisco, 1993)

Scott L. Bottles, *Los Angeles and the Automobile: The Making of the Modern City* (Berkeley, CA, 1987)

Stan Brakhage, *Film Biographies* (Berkeley, CA, 1977)

Matthew Cullerne Bown, *Art under Stalin* (New York, 1991)

—, *Socialist Realist Painting* (New Haven and London, 1998)

Svetlana Boym, *The Future of Nostalgia* (New York, 2001)

David Brodsly, *L.A. Freeway: An Appreciative Essay* (Berkeley, CA, 1981)

John Burby, *The Great American Motion Sickness* (Boston, MA, 1971)

D. Burgess, *Automobile Archaeology* (Cambridge, 1981)

Virginia Button and Charles Esche, *Intelligence: New British Art 2000* (London, 2000)

Cars of the Fabulous Fifties (Union, NJ, 1987)

Brian Carter, ed., *Albert Khan: Inspiration for the Modern* (Ann Arbor, MI, 2001)

Charles Chaplin, *My Autobiography* (New York, 1964)

Dominic Connell and Mathew Joint, *Driver Aggression* (Road Safety Unit, Group Public Policy, 1996)

Richard A. Crabb, *Birth of a Giant: The Men and Incidents that Gave America the Motorcar* (Philadelphia, 1969)

Philip Davies and Brian Neve, eds, *Cinema, Politics and Society in America* (Manchester, 1981)

Richard O. Davis, *The Age of Asphalt: The Automobile, the Freeway, and the Condition of Metropolitan America* (Philadelphia, 1975)

Detroit Institute of Arts, *The Rouge: The Image of Industry in the Art of Charles Sheeler and Diego Rivera* (Detroit, 1978)

Cynthia Golomb Dettelbach, *In the Driver's Seat: The Automobile in American Literature and Popular Culture* (Westport, CT, 1976)

Nora Donnelly, ed., *Customized: Art Inspired by Hot Rods, Low Riders and American Car Culture* (New York, 2000)

Andres Duany, Elizabeth Plater-Zyberk and Jeff Speck, *Suburban Nation: The Rise of Sprawl and the Decline of the American Dream* (New York, 2000)

Ilya Ehrenburg, *The Life of the Automobile* (London, 1985)

David Evans, *Big Road Blues* (Berkeley, CA, 1982)

W. Hawkins Ferry, *The Legacy of Albert Kahn* (Detroit, 1987)

Christopher Finch, *Highways to Heaven* (New York, 1992)

'Five Cars – Five Artists', *Art in America*, 56 (May–June 1968)

James J. Flink, *America Adopts the Automobile 1895–1910* (Cambridge, MA, 1970)

—, *The Automobile Age*, (Cambridge, MA, 1988)

—, *The Car Culture* (Cambridge, MA, 1975)

R. W. Flint, ed., *Marinetti: Selected Writings* (New York, 1971)

Flint Institute of Arts, *Art and the Automobile* (Flint, MI, 1978)

Robert M. Fogelson, *The Fragmented Metropolis: Los Angeles 1850–1930* (Berkeley, CA, 1993)

Henry Ford, *My Life and Work* (Salem, NH, 1987)

Mark Foster, 'The Motel-T, the Hard Sell and Los Angeles' Urban Growth: The Decentralization of Los Angeles during the 1920s', *Pacific Historical Review*, 44 (November, 1975)

—, *From Streetcar to Superhighway: American City Planners and Urban Transportation 1900–1940* (Philadelphia, 1981)

Peter Freund and George Martin, *The Ecology of the Automobile* (Montreal, 1993)

Michael Frostick, *Advertising and the Motor-Car* (London, 1970)

Peter Gabrilovich and Bill McGraw, eds, *The Detroit Almanac: 300 Years of Life in the Motor City* (Detroit, 2001)

Francesco Gallo and Angelo Mistrangelo, *Sironi* (Sonzogno, 1989)

Joel Garreau, *Edge City: Life on the New Frontier* (New York, 1991)

D. Gartman, *Auto Opium: a Social History of Automobile Design* (London, 1994)

Norman Bel Geddes, *Magic Motorways* (New York, 1940)

Nick Georgano, ed., *The Beaulieu Encyclopedia of the Automobile*, 2 vols (Chicago and London, 2000)

Juri Ginsburg, et al., *Odessa Die Stadt und Ihr Traum* (Berlin, 1999)

Stephen B. Goddard, *Getting There: The Epic Struggle Between Road and Rail in the Twentieth Century* (New York, 1994)

John D. Graham, *Auto Safety: Assessing America's Performance* (Dover, MA, 1989)

Antonio Gramsci, 'Americanism and Fordism' in *Selections from the Prison Notebooks*, ed. Quentin Hare and Geoffrey Nowell-Smith (London, 1971)

John A. Gunnell, ed., *Standard Catalogue of American Cars 1946–1975* (Iola, WI, 1982)

Peter Hall, *Cities of Tomorrow* (Oxford, 1996)

Lawrence Halprin, *Freeways* (New York, 1966)

Anne Coffin Hanson, ed., *The Futurist Imagination* (New Haven, 1983)

Jim Heimann, *Car Hops and Curb Service: A History of American Drive-In Restaurants 1920–1960* (San Francisco, 1996)

Maurice D. Hendry, *Cadillac, Standard of the World: The Complete Seventy-Year History* (New York, 1973)

Ann Hindry, ed., *Renault as Art: A Modern Adventure* (Paris, 1991)

D. B. Inbles, *Art and the Automobile* (New York, 1978)

John A. Jackle and Keith A. Sculle, *The Gas Station in America* (Baltimore, 1994)

J. Jackson, *Every Woman's Guide to the Car* (London, 1993)

Kenneth T. Jackson, *The Crabgrass Frontier: The Suburbanization of the United States* (New York, 1985)

Jane Jacobs, *The Death and Life of Great American Cities* (New York, 1961)

Jan Jennings, ed., *Roadside America: The Automobile in Design and Culture* (Ames, IA, 1990)

Paul J. Karlstrom, 'Reflections on the Automobile in American Art', *Archives of American Art Journal*, 20, no. 2 (1980)

Jane Holtz Kay, *Asphalt Nation* (Berkeley, CA, 1997)

Ulrich Keller, *The Highway as Habitat: A Roy Stryker Documentation 1943–1955* (Santa Barbara, CA, 1986)

Ben Kelley, *The Pavers and the Paved* (New York, 1971)

Marla Hamburg Kennedy ed., *Car Culture* (Salt Lake City, UT, 1998)

Walter C. Kidney, *The Architecture of Choice: Eclecticism in America 1880–1930* (New York, 1974)

Killing Speed and Saving Lives, Slower Speeds Initiative Report, 2001 (UK Government, Department of Transport)

Stephen King, *Christine* (New York, 1983)

Max Kozloff, 'The Rivera Frescoes of Modern Industry at the Detroit Institute of Arts: Proletarian Art under Capitalist Patronage', *Artforum*, 12 (November 1973)

Kustom Kulture, exh. cat. Laguna Art Museum (Laguna Beach, CA, 1993)

Robert Lacey, *Ford: The Men and the Machine* (New York, 1986)

Philip Langdon, *Orange Roofs, Golden Arches: The Architecture of American Chain Restaurants* (New York, 1986)

William Lass, ed., *Freedom of the American Road* (Dearborn, MI, 1956)

Dirk Leach, *Technik* (Montpellier, 1986)

Helen Leavitt, *Superhighway-Superhoax* (New York, 1970)

Le Corbusier, *The City of Tomorrow and Its Planning* (London, 1987)

Le Corbusier, *Towards a New Architecture*, trans. Frederick Etchells (London, 1946)

David L. Lewis, ed., 'The Automobile and American Culture', *Michigan Quarterly Review* (Fall 1980, Winter 1981)

David L. Lewis and Laurence Goldstein, eds, *The Automobile and American Culture* (Ann Arbor, MI, 1991)

Chester H. Liebs, *Main Street to Miracle Mile: American Roadside Architecture* (Boston, MA, 1984)

Richard M. Longworth, ed., *Encyclopedia of American Cars 1940–1970* (New York, 1980)

Chip Lord, *Ant Farm: Automerica* (New York, 1976)

Emily Lowe Gallery, *Art Around the Automobile* (Hempstead, NY, 1971)

Ulrich Luckhardt, *Art Car David Hockney* (Munich, 1995)

Robert S. Lynd and Helen M. Lynd, *Middletown: A Study in Modern American Culture* (New York, 1925)

Roland Marchand, *Advertising the American Dream* (Berkeley, CA, 1985)

Ivan Margolius, *Automobiles by Architects* (Chichester, 2000)

Ivan Margolius and John G. Henry, *Tatra: The Legacy of Hans Ledwinka* (London, 1990)

Karal Ann Marling, *The Colossus of Roads: Myth and Symbol along the American Highway* (Minneapolis, 1984)

Peter Marsh and Peter Collett, *Driving Passion: The Psychology of the Car* (London, 1986)

Philip P. Mason, *A History of American Roads* (Chicago, 1967)

Marshall McLuhan, *The Mechanical Bride: Folklore of Industrial Man* (New York, 1967)

Leo Marx, *The Machine in the Garden* (New York, 1964)

Clay McShane, *Down the Asphalt Path: the Automobile and the American City* (New York, 1994)

Daniel Miller, ed., *Car Cultures* (Oxford, 2001)

H. Moorehouse, *Driving Ambition: An Analysis of the American Hot Rod Enthusiasm* (Manchester, 1991)

Eric Mottram, *Blood on the Nash Ambassador* (London, 1983)

Lewis Mumford, *The Highway and the City* (New York, 1963)

Ralph Nader, *Unsafe at Any Speed: The Designed-in Dangers of the American Automobile* (New York, 1965)

Julian Nowill, *East European Cars* (Stroud, 2000)

S. O'Connell, *The Car in British Society: Class, Gender and Motoring 1896–1939* (Manchester, 1998)

R. Oldenziel, *Making Technology Masculine: Men, Women and Modern Machines in America 1870–1945* (Amsterdam, 1999)

Tod Papageorge, *Walker Evans and Robert Frank: A Study of Experience* (New Haven, CT, 1981)

Ian Parker, 'Traffic', *London: The Lives of the City, Granta*, no. 65 (London, Spring 1999)

Martin Pawley, *Terminal Architecture* (London, 1998)

H. Perkin, *The Age of the Automobile* (London, 1976)

J. Pettifer and N. Turner, *Automania: Man and the Motor Car* (London, 1984)

Bernd Polster, *Tankstellen, die Benzingeschichte* (Berlin, 1982)

R. Porter, *Economics at the Wheel; The Costs of Cars and Drivers* (San Diego, 1999)

J. B. Priestley, *English Journey* (London, 1934)

John B. Rae, *The American Automobile: A Brief History* (Chicago, 1965)

—, *The Road and the Car in American Life* (Cambridge, MA, 1971)

S. Rajan, *The Enigma of Automobility* (Pittsburgh, 1996)

Paul Rambali, *Car Culture* (New York, 1984)

Burkhard Riemenschneider and Uta Grosenick, *Art Now* (Cologne, 2001)

Diego Rivera, *My Art, My Life: An Autobiography* (New York, 1991)

Peter Roberts, *A Picture History of the Automobile* (London, 1973)

Mark H. Rose, *Interstate Expressway Highway Politics 1941–1956* (Lawrence, KS, 1979)

Emma Rothschild, *Paradise Lost: The Decline of the Auto-Industrial Age* (New York, 1973)

W. Sachs, *For Love of the Automobile: Looking Back into the History of our Desires* (Berkeley, CA, 1984)

Jack Sargeant and Stephanie Watson, eds, *Lost Highways: An Illustrated History of Road Movies* (London, 1999)

V. Scharff, *Taking the Wheel: Women and the Coming of the Motor Age* (New York, 1991)

Kenneth R. Schneider, *Autokind vs. Mankind* (New York, 1971)

Joseph J. Schroeder, *The Wonderful World of the Automobile 1895–1930* (Northfield, IL, 1971)

Stephen W. Sears, *The Automobile in America* (New York, 1977)

Bruce E. Seely, *Building the American Highway System: Engineers as Policy Makers* (Philadelphia, 1987)

Lev Shugurov, *Avtomobile strany sovietov* (Moscow, 1983)

Gerald Silk et al., *Automobile and Culture* (New York, 1984)

Upton Sinclair, *The Flivver King: A Story of Ford-America* (Chicago, IL, 1984)

Vladimír Šlapeta and Jan Kaplicky, *Czech Functionalism 1918–1838* (London, 1987)

Alfred P. Sloan, *My Years with General Motors* (Garden City, NY, 1963)

Suzanne E. Smith, *Dancing in the Street: Motown and the Cultural Politics of Detroit* (Cambridge, 1999)

David J. St Clair, *The Motorization of American Cities* (New York, 1986)

Spessi, *Spessi-Bensin* (Brooklyn, NY, 2000)

Jane and Michael Stern, *Auto Ads* (New York, 1978)

R. Vahlefeld and F. Jacques, *Garagen und Tankstellen* (Munich, 1956)

Robert Venturi, Denise Scott Brown and Steven Izenour, *Learning from Las Vegas: The Forgotten Symbolism of Architectural Form* (Cambridge, MA, 1977)

Daniel Vieyra, *Fill'er up! An Architectural History of America's Gas Stations* (New York, 1979)

Martin Wachs and Margaret Crawford, eds, *The Car and the City: The Automobile, the Built Environment and Daily Urban Life* (Ann Arbor, MI, 1992)

Michael Wallis, *Route 66: The Mother Road* (New York, 1990)

Lawrence J. White, *The Automobile Industry since 1945* (Cambridge, NJ, 1971)

Whitney Museum of American Art, *Auto-Icons* (New York, 1979)

William H. Whyte, *The Exploding Metropolis* (Berkeley, CA, 1993)

Quentin Willson, *The Ultimate Classic Car Book* (London, 1995)

Andrew Wilson, *The Ukrainians: Unexpected Nations* (New Haven, CT, and London, 2000)

Paul C. Wilson, *Chrome Dreams: Automobile Styling Since 1893* (Radnor, PA, 1976)

Michael Karl Witzel, *The American Gas Station* (Osceola, WI, 1993)

Krysztov Wodicko, *Critical Vehicles* (Cambridge, MA, 1998)

W. Wolf, *Car Mania* (London, 1996)

Tom Wolfe, *The Kandy-Kolored Tangerine-Flake Streamline Baby* (New York, 1965)

Charles L. Wright, *Fast Wheels: Slow Traffic* (Philadelphia, 1992)

D. Young, *Advertising the Beetle 1953–1978* (London, 1993)

Reimar Zeller, ed., *Das Automobil in der Kunst* (Munich, 1986), *Sense of the Other* (1998), *An Anthropology of Contemporaneous Worlds* (1999), *The War of Dreams* (1999) and *Fictions fin de siècle* (2000).

Contributors

CATHERINE ADDISON is an Associate Professor of English at the University of Zululand, South Africa.

MARC AUGÉ is Director of Studies at the Ecole des Hautes Etudes en Sciences Sociales, Paris. Known and respected as an Africanist, he is perhaps the most important French anthropologist active today. Of his many books the most recent are *Non-Places* (1995), *An Anthropology of Contemporaneous Worlds* (1999), *The War of Dreams* (1999) and *Fictions fin de siécle* (2000).

GEREMIE R. BARMÉ is a professor in the Research School of Pacific and Asian Studies, Australian National University, Canberra, specializing in twentieth-century Chinese intellectual and cultural history. He is also a prominent and well-regarded media commentator on contemporary Chinese affairs. His recent books include *In the Red: On Contemporary Chinese Culture* (1999) and *An Artistic Exile: A Life of Feng Zikai 1898–1975* (2002).

ROLAND BARTHES (1915–1980) was a French social and literary critic whose writings on semiotics caused structuralism to become one of the leading intellectual movements of the twentieth century. Barthes' writings, including *Writing Degree Zero* (1953) and *Le Plaisir du texte* (1973), have had a considerable following both in and beyond France.

MARSHALL BERMAN has been described as the 'distinguished voice of modernity'. He has written several books, the most famous of which is *All That Is Solid Melts Into Air* (1982), the sequel to his first book, *Politics of Authority*.

MICHAEL BRACEWELL is the author of six novels, the most recent of which is *Perfect Tense* (2001). His selected essays and journalism, *When Surface Was Depth: The 1990s*, is published in 2002. He contributes to several magazines and newspapers, including *The Financial Times* and *Frieze*.

DAVID BRODSLY is the author of *L.A. Freeway: An Appreciative Essay* (1981). He subsequently went into finance, primarily the financing of public infrastructure and now works as a financial consultant to local government in California.

ANDREW CROSS is a photographer and curator. His book *Some Trains in America* was published in 2002.

ILYA EHRENBURG (1891–1967) was a prolific journalist and writer. He was the author of *The Life of the Automobile*, first published in Russian in 1929.

PATRICK FIELD writes on travel and technology and founded the London School of Cycling, which provides training and consultancy to a range of private, corporate and municipal clients. His career as an actor includes credits in film, TV, theatre, radio and opera.

MURRAY FRASER is an architect and historian who is Professor of Architecture at Oxford Brookes University. The author of *John Bull's Other Homes: State Housing and British Policy in Ireland 1883–1922* (1996), he is currently co-authoring a book on the influence of America on post-war British architecture with Joe Kerr.

PETER HAMILTON trained as a professional photographer and is now a lecturer in sociology for the Open University. His main research interest is the sociology of visual culture, with particular emphasis on photography. He is currently writing a book on panoramic photography to be published by Reaktion.

JANE JACOBS is an urban theorist and author. As Associate Editor of *Architectural Forum* (from 1952 to 1968) she earned a reputation for attacking urban planners for destroying diverse older neighbourhoods with expressways and housing projects. Her most influential work is *The Death and Life of Great American Cities* (1961). She has just published her sixth book, *The Nature of Economies* (2001).

JANE HOLTZ KAY is architecture and planning critic for *The Nation*. Her books include *Asphalt Nation* (1997) and *Lost Boston* (1982). She has written for *Architecture, Landscape Architecture, Planning, The Boston Globe, The New York Times, Preservation* and *Sierra*. She is currently writing a new book, *Last Chance Landscape: Taking the Earth in for Repairs*.

PATRICK KEILLER is an architect and film-maker, best known for his features *London* (1994) and *Robinson in Space* (1997), the latter extended as a book in 1999. *The Dilapidated Dwelling*, a feature-length documentary made for Channel 4 television, was completed in 2000.

JOE KERR is an architectural historian and critic. He is Head of Department of Critical and Historical Studies at the Royal College of Art, London, and Commissioning Editor for architecture and design at Reaktion Books. Co-editor of *Strangely Familiar: Narratives of Architecture and the City* (1996) and *The Unknown City: Contesting Architecture and Social Space* (2000), he is currently writing a book with Murray Fraser.

DIRK LEACH has written *Technik* (1986), *Propaganda*, the sequel to *Technik*, excerpted in the German journal *West & Ost* (1995), *Punk in Germany*, a memoir of 'die Bleierne Zeit' (1981), and is currently working on a journal about teaching at the worst high school in New York.

MICHAEL R. LEAMAN is the Publisher and Editorial Director of Reaktion Books. His essay is based on recent travels in Russia and Ukraine.

GRACE LEES-MAFFEI is Senior Lecturer in the History and Theory of Design and Applied Arts at the University of Hertfordshire. Her research interests centre around the mediation and reception of design.

KARAL ANN MARLING teaches American Culture at the University of Minnesota and is pop-culture commentator for Station KNOW, Minnesota Public Radio. Her books include *The Colossus of Roads: Myth and Symbol along the American Highway* (1984).

SANDY MCCREERY lectures at Middlesex University. His recent publications include an essay in *The Unknown City* (2000) and *New Babylonians* (2001).

ERIC MOTTRAM (1924–95) was Professor of American Literature at King's College, London. A poet and critic, he was the author of fifteen books of poetry and of studies of Faulkner and Ginsberg.

VIVIANA NAROTZKY is Senior Lecturer in Design and Architectural History at Kingston University. Her recent exhibition 'Architectures of Discourse' at the Antoni Tàpies Foundation explored the retailing of designer goods in Spain and the new social discourses emerging from the Barcelona model of urban regeneration.

ADRIAN OŢOIU is a Romanian novelist and essayist. His novel *The Skin of the Matter* (1996), which won three national awards, was followed by two collections of short stories, a cultural travel guide to Maramures and a two-volume critical study of Romanian post-modern fiction. He currently teaches English and American Literature in Romania.

IAN PARKER is the television critic of the *Observer*.

DAVID PASCOE is Reader in English Literature at the University of Glasgow. His most recent publications are *Peter Greenaway: Museums and Moving Images* (Reaktion, 1997) and *Airspaces* (Reaktion, 2001).

MARTIN PAWLEY is an architectural writer and critic. Among his publications are *Design in Exile: The Architecture of Eva Jiricna* (1991), *Buckminster Fuller: A Biography* (1992), *Future Systems: The Story of Tomorrow* (1993) and *Tokyo* (1994) and *Terminal Architecture* (Reaktion, 1998).

CHRISTOPHER PINNEY is Reader in Visual Culture at the Department of Anthropology, University College London. His interests include visual practices in India and the history of exotic material culture in Europe. His publications include *Camera Indica* (Reaktion, 1997) and several edited collections.

A. L. REES is Senior Research Fellow in Film at the Royal College of Art, London and author of *A History of Experimental Film and Video* (1999). He teaches and writes about artists' film and video.

DONALD RICHIE is well known as the foremost Western expert on the Japanese film. He has also written books about many other aspects of Japan, among them the travel classic *The Inland Sea* (1972), as well as *Tokyo: A View of the City* (Reaktion, 1999) and *Public People, Private People* (1972).

ALLEN SAMUELS is Tinsley Honorary Visiting Professor at Georgian Court College, New Jersey, and Honorary Research Fellow at the University of Cardiff. He is the author of *Hard Times: The Critics Debate* (1992) and of articles on eighteenth-century art bibliography. He is currently completing a book on Thomas Rowlandson.

ZIAUDDIN SARDAR, writer and cultural critic, is Visiting Professor of Postcolonial Studies, Department of Arts Policy and Management, City University, London. His recent books include *Postmodernism and the Other* (1997), *Orientalism* (2000), *The Consumption of Kuala Lumpur* (Reaktion, 2000) and *The A to Z of Postmodern Life* (2002).

JACK SARGEANT teaches Cultural and Cinematic Theory at the London College of Printing. He is the author of numerous books on cinema and culture, including *Deathtripping: The*

Cinema of Transgression (1995) and, with Stephanie Watson, is the editor of *Lost Highways: An Illustrated History of Road Movies* (1999).

E. L. WIDMER is Director of the C. V. Starr Center for the Study of the American Experience at Washington College in Chestertown, MD, and an Associate Professor of History at Washington College. He is also the author of *Young America: The Flowering of Democracy in New York City* (1998) and is currently working on a book about early African-American music.

RICHARD J. WILLIAMS is a lecturer in History of Art at the University of Edinburgh. His publications include *After Modern Sculpture* (2000). He is currently writing a book on contemporary British urbanism.

PETER WOLLEN is a film scholar, film teacher and film-maker who has written widely about the visual arts and curated internation exhibitions in Europe and North America. He has taught film at many universities in the US, including Vassar College. His recent books include *Riding the Icebox* (1993) and *Singin' in the Rain* (1992). He is currently working on a book about the 60 things that have most influenced him.

Acknowledgements

The editors and publishers gratefully acknowledge permission to reprint copyright material in this book as follows:

MARC AUGÉ: from *City A-Z*, edited by Steve Pile and Nigel Thrift, published by Routledge, 2000, reprinted by permission of the publisher and the author. ROLAND BARTHES: 'The New Citroën' from *Mythologies*, first published in French by du Seuil in 1957, reprinted by permission of the Estate of Roland Barthes, the translator, Jonathan Cape as publisher and The Random House Group Ltd. MARSHALL BERMAN: from *All That Is Solid Melts Into Air: The Experience of Modernity* first published by Simon and Schuster, New York, 1982, copyright © 1982 by Marshall Berman, reprinted by permission of Verso, London. DAVID BRODSLY: from *L.A. Freeway: An Appreciative Essay*, published by University of California Press, 1981, copyright © 1981 by The Regents of the University of California, reprinted by permission of the publisher. ILYA EHRENBURG: from *The Life of the Automobile*, copyright © 1929 by Petropolis Verlag, translation © 1976 by Urizen Books, reprinted by permission of Serpent's Tail, London. JANE HOLTZ KAY: from *Asphalt Nation*, first published by University of California Press, 1997, copyright © 1997 by Jane Holtz Kay, reprinted by permission of Crown Publishers, a division of Random House Inc. JANE JACOBS: from *The Death and Life of Great American Cities*, published by Jonathan Cape, 1962, copyright © 1961 by Jane Jacobs, reprinted by permission of The Random House Group Ltd. DIRK LEACH: from *Technik*, published by Editions Gris Banal, 1986, copyright © 1986 by Gris Banal, Editeur/Dirk Leach, reprinted by permission of the author. KARAL ANN MARLING: from *Design Quarterly*, No. 146, 'Auto-eroticism', copyright © 1989 by the Walker Art Center, reprinted by permission of the author. ERIC MOTTRAM: from *Blood on the Nash Ambassador*, published by Hutchinson, 1981, reprinted by permission of The Random House Group Ltd. IAN PARKER: from *London: The Lives of the City*, Granta, 65, Spring 1999, copyright © 1999 by Ian Parker, reprinted by permission of Peters, Fraser and Dunlop Ltd on behalf of the author. E. L. WIDMER: from *Roadside America: The Automobile in Design and Culture* edited by Jan Jennings, published by Iowa State University Press, 1990, reprinted by permission of the publisher.

Photographic Acknowledgements

The editors, essayists and publishers wish to express their thanks to the following sources of illustrative material and/or permission to reproduce it. While every effort has been made to identify and credit copyright holders, we would like to apologize to anyone who has not been formally acknowledged.

Reproduction © ADAGP, Paris: pp. 27, 31, 42; reproduction courtesy of Elsa Flores Almaraz: p. 47 (foot); photo © Arab Image Foundation, Beirut (Coll. H. Abdel Hadi/FAI): p. 336 (top); reproduction © ARS, New York, 2002: p. 33 (foot); photos from the Collections of the Archive of Labor and Urban Affairs, University Archives, Wayne State University, Detroit: p. 119 (top), 120, 128 (middle); photo Marc Atkins/panoptika: p. 296; photos courtesy BMW AG Public Relations: p.36; photo courtesy Galerie Christine & Isy Brachot: p. 46; photo Sydney Byrne: p. 219; photos courtesy of Caltrans Transportation Library: pp. 278, 279; photo Leo Castelli Photo Archives/© James Rosenquist/VAGA, New York, 2002: p. 34; Art Institute of Chicago (Julian Levy collection, gift of Jean and Julian Levy) - photo © 2002 Art Institute of Chicago, All Rights Reserved: p. 129 (top left); photos Lois Conner: pp. 188, 189; courtesy of Matthew Connolly: p. 269; photos Andrew Cross: pp. 250, 251, 252, 253, 254, 255, 256, 257; photos Culver Pictures: pp. 236, 330; reproduction © DACS, London, 2002: pp. 24, 26 (foot), 27, 31, 33, 34, 36 (top), 42; Detroit Institute of Arts (photos © Detroit Institute of Arts): pp. 30 (bequest of Eleanor Clay Ford), 34; photos courtesy of the Detroit Public Library, National Automotive History Collection: pp. 115, 118 (top), 119 (bottom), 131 (foot), 133, 332, 335 (top); Detroit Public Library, National Automotive History Collection (Northmore-McGuire Photographic Archive): pp. 132, 327, 333 (top); photo Archives Denyse Durand-Ruel: p. 31 (foot); photo Art & Public: p. 38; photos courtesy of Helen Evenden: pp. 237, 238 (top right), 240; photos from the Collections of Henry Ford Museum & Greenfield Village: pp. 29 [P.833.99907.1], 118 (bottom left) [P.833.917], 120 (foot) [P.O.5827], 128 (top) [P.833.682], 129 (top right) [P.833.107856.14], 319 (foot) [P.O.3139], 331 (top) [P.833.115609.3], 333 (foot) [P.833.110207.771]; photo Murray Fraser: p. 326 (middle); photos Roy Garner: pp. 141, 144; photo Alan Gignoux: p. 220 (bottom right); photo courtesy of Mr Johan Grootveld: p. 238 (foot); Solomon R. Guggenheim Museum, New York (photo © David Heald/The Solomon R. Guggenheim Foundation, New York, 2002): p. 42; photo Kenneth Hamm/Photo Japan: p. 143; photos Shaun Harris: pp. 223, 224; photos Michael Herrmann: pp. 170 (top), 172; photo Ken Heyman Woodfin-Camp Agency: p. 21; Hood Museum of Art, Dartmouth College, Hanover, NH (gift of James. J. Meeker, in memory of Lee English, Class of 1958): p. 45 (foot); photo Nadine Hutton: p. 220 (bottom left); book cover © 1955, 1957 by Jack Kerouac, renewed © 1983 by Stella Kerouac, renewed © 1985 by Stella Kerouac and Jan Kerouac – used by permission of Viking Penguin, a division of Penguin Putnam Inc.: p. 271; photos Joe Kerr: pp. 5, 122, 124, 135, 136, 137, 138, 190, 239 (top), 239 (bottom right), 241 (left), 317 (right), 320 (foot), 321, 323, 326 (top), 336 (foot); photo Kleinefenn, courtesy Marian Goodman Gallery, New York: p. 40; photos Balthazar Korab: pp. 8-9, 49 (foot), 239 (bottom left), 241 (right), 242; photos Dirk Leach: pp. 147, 148, 149, 150, 151, 152; photos M. Leaman/Reaktion Books: pp. 153, 155, 156, 157, 158, 159, 161, 163, 164, 165, 166, 199; photos T.J. Lemon: p. 220 (top), 222; © The Estate of Roy Lichtenstein: p.36 (top); photo courtesy of the Long Bow Group: p. 7 (foot), 187; Los Angeles County Museum of Art (Art Museum Council Fund - photo © 2001 LACMA - All rights reserved): p. 49 (top); photo T.C. Malhotra: p. 210; photos courtesy of Ivan Margolius: pp. 345, 347; photo courtesy George Merritt & Colin Escott: p. 61; photo courtesy of Metro Pictures: p. 48; photos Jason Morris 2001: pp. 168-9, 171 (top), 173; photo Jason Murgatroyd: p. 205 (middle); Musée Nationale d'Art Moderne, Paris: p. 24 (top); photo Museo Vostell-Malpartida de Cáceres: p. 33 (top); Museum of Contemporary Art, Gent (on permanent loan from a private collection): p. 46; The Museum of Modern Art, New York (photos © The Museum of Modern Art, New York/Scala, Florence): pp. 43, 45 (top); photos Viviana Narotzky: pp. 7 (top), 170 (foot), 171 (foot), 174, 175, 176; photos Ken Oosterbroek: pp. 221, 225; photos courtesy of Peugeot/Euro RSCG Wnek Gosper: pp. 368, 369; PictureNET Africa: pp. 210, 219, 220, 221, 222, 223, 224, 225; photos Chris Pinney: pp. 208, 211, 212, 213, 215; photo Jean-Claude Planchet/CNAC/ MNAM Dist. RMN/© Estate Russolo: p. 26 (top); photo from the photography archive of Elvis Presley Enterprises, Inc. (used by permission, Elvis Presley Enterprises, Inc.): p. 69; photo courtesy of Publicis and Renault PLC, © Publicis and Renault PLC: p. 366; photo Bill Rauhauser: p. 335 (foot); photos Walter P. Reuther Library, Wayne State University, Detroit: pp. 118 (bottom right), 130, 134 (top) - Walter P. Reuther Library (Detroit News Collection): p. 128 (foot), 129 (middle right), p. 131 (top) - Walter P. Reuther Library (Tony Spina Collection): p. 134 (middle); photo Jeff Saltzman, © 1999: p. 245; photo Emil Schult: p. 290; photo Sloan: p. 229; photos Mike Slocombe/urban75.com: pp. 123 (foot), 233; photo Tony Spina: p. 134 (middle); photo US National Archives - Records of the Soil Conservation Service (114-SD-5089): p. 229; photo Sacha Vitorovich: p. 218; photo © The Andy Warhol Foundation for the Visual Arts, Inc., 2002: p. 33 (foot); photos courtesy of the artist (Rubén Ortiz Torres): p. 39; photos courtesy of the authors: Peter Hamilton, pp. 191, 193, 194, 195, 196, 197; Patrick Keiller, pp. 346, 348, 350, 351; Adrian Oţoiu, pp. 201, 203, 205 (top).

Index

Adams, Henry 50
Ajantrik 214–15
Alloway, Lawrence 106–7
Almaraz, Carlos: *Beach Crash 47*
Ambassador 208, 209–18
American Graffiti 13, *14*, 34, 105–6, 272
Anderson, Martin 268
Anger, Kenneth 34, 88, 99, 101, 344
Ant Farm Collective: *Cadillac Ranch* 34–5, *35*
Antonioni, Michelangelo 84, 85, 91, 105
Archigram 283, 287
Arlen, Michael 50
Arman 32, 33, 34; *Long Term Parking 31*
ARO 203, 204
Assault on Precinct 13 107, 108
Aston Martin 84
Auden, W. H. 50
Audi A6 188
Austin Apache 223

Balint, Michael 14–16
Balla, Giacomo 25, 27; *Abstract Speed 26*
Ballard, J. G. 10, 16, 89; *Concrete Island* 17, 309; *Crash* 14, 17, 18, 58, 287
Bangs, Lester 289
Banham, Reyner 281–3, 284–5, 287, 354
Barker, Paul 285
Barris, George 37, 67–8, 70–1
Barthes, Roland 40, 51, 230, 328, 342, 351
Basho 145
Bataille, George: *Story of the Eye* 230–1, 232
Baudrillard, Jean: *America* 76–8 *passim,* 249
Bayley, Stephen 16–17, 30, 3 63, 368

Beijing 212 jeep 181
Beniston, Stuart 299–301
Bentley 35, 85, 93
Benton, Tim 317
Benz, Carl 10, 25
Bergman, Ingrid 93–4
Beria, Lavrenti 167
Berkowitz, Leonard 103
Berlin, Irving 50
Berman, Jay 107
Berman, Marshall 324
Bernard, Claude 95
Berry, Chuck 63–4, 71–3, 74, 354
Big Business 97
The Big Heat 102, *102*, 107
Bill, Max 35
Black Box Recorder 289
Blade Runner 88
Blake, Blind 127
Blood Simple 84
Blowup 84–5, 93
Blume, John Morton 267
BMW (car) 12, 37, 160, 221, 343, 344
BMW (company) 32, 37
Boazman, Sally 301–2
Boccioni, Umberto 25
Bogart, Humphrey 86, 98
Bolitho, Roy 364
Bombeck, Erma 271
Bonnie and Clyde 14, 96, *96*, 103, 114, 14
Boulevard Nights 106
Boym, Svetlana 160
Bradley, Truman 360
Brakhage, Stan 91, 97
Brando, Marlon 100
Breathless 85, 91
Brecht, George: *Motor Vehicle Sundown* 91
Brenston, Jackie 68, 72
Breton, André 345, 346
Brown, James 73
Brownjohn, Alan 231
Bugatti 35

Buick 72, 86, 171, *334*; GLX 188; Le Sabre XF-8 359; Sable 41; Super *172*
Bullitt 101
Burden, Chris 35
Burgess, Starling 373–4, 375, 376–8
Burra, Edward 89
Bussy, Pascal 288, 292

Cadillac *61*, 66, *166*, 173, *175*, 272, 272–3, 328, 357; Eldorado 69, 132, 176, 357, 362; Elvis's passion for 62, 63, 69, 70–1; in Chuck Berry songs 64, 71–3, 354; in films 98, 99; Sedan de Ville *132*
Cage, John 86, 91
Cagney, James 98, 99, 100, 114
Calder, Alexander 37
Calle, Sophie 93
Carpentier, Alejo 175
Castle Keep 105
Céline, Louis Ferdinand 52
César 32; 'Helsinki' Compression *31*
Chalk, Warren 287
Challenger 75–6, 77–8
Chamberlain, John 34, 89
Chaplin, Charlie 19, 99
Charley Varrick 108
Chéret, Jules 25
Chevrolet 99, 111, 173, 214–15, 223, 355, 357, 359; Bel Air 132, 170, *170*, 328; Styleline 176
Chicago, Judy 39–40
Chinatown 86–8, 103
Christie, Ian 88
Chrysler, Building 321, *321*; company 135, 136, 137, 272, 357; commercials 88, 360
Citroën, André 342, 344, 349, 352
Citroën (car) 223, 345, 353; 2CV 349, 350; Ami 6 351–2, *352*; Axel 204; BX 81–2; DS (*Déesse*) 40, 51, 328, 340–1, 342, 344,

347, 349; *Traction Avant 343*, 344, 349; XM 352
Citroën (company) 316, 344, 351–2, 353
Cixi, Empress Dowager 178
Clay, Grady 270, 275
Cleeve, Stephen 305–6
Cochran, Eddie 60, 73
Cocteau, Jean 85
Connor, Bruce 91
Conrad, Joseph: *An Outcast of the Islands* 232
Convoy 108, *109*, 110, 111–13
Coogan, Jackie 98
Corvair 40, 135, 329
Corvette 33
Crane, Hart 280
Crash (film) 18, 86
The Crowd Roars 106

Dacia *201*, 202–3, 205, 207
Daimler, Gottlieb 10
Davenport, Ian 291
Davis, Stuart 29
Dean, James *11*, 12, 37, 86, *87*, 100–1; crash 12, 17, 37, 51, 73, 86, 99, *see also Giant; Rebel Without a Cause*
Delaunay, Sonia 28–9, *28*
Delillo, Don 254
Demand, Thomas 91
Deng Xiaoping 181, 183, 185
Derain, André 35
The Detective 103–5
Le Diable probablement 105
Diana, Princess 12, 51
Dichter, Ernest 356
Diddley, Bo 73
Dine, Jim 18, 34
Dinning, Mark 73
Dodge 176, 358; Challenger 110; Coronet *174*; Custom Royal *333*
Doré, Gustave 298
Dos Passos, John 101
Dreyfus, Pierre 32

Driver 84, *85*, 108
Dubuffet, Jean 32
Duchamp, Marcel 27, 28, 30
Duel 103, *104*, 109–10
Duesenberg 99
Dymaxion 29, 343, 371–8

Each Dawn I Die 99
Eames, Charles 322
Earl, Harley 10–11, 31, 37, 132,
174, 272, 322, 328, 356–7, *358*,
359, 363
Eco, Umberto 98
Ehrenburg, Ilya 50, 53–4, 342,
344, 352
8 1/2 105
Eisenhower, Dwight D. 62, 269,
270
Eisenstein, Sergei: *The Old and
the New* 88
Eliot, T. S. 50, 52, 53, 54, 56–7
Ellard, Graham 91
Elton, Ben: *Gridlock* 304
Emerson, Ralph Waldo 74, 101
Emigholz, Heinz 92
Erro 32
Estes, Sleepy John 66
Etchells, Frederick 308, 324

Falling Down 307
The Family Jewels 97
Faulkner, William 356
Fernadez, Pablo Armando 171
Fiat (car) 172, 173, 207, 223; *124*
164; *127* 176; Bianchina 17;
Multipla 343
Fiat (company) 32, 164, 192
Fields, W. C. 97, 98, 99, 114
Fit for the Chase 98
Fitzgerald, F. Scott 50, 56, 57
Flaubert, Gustave 289
Fleury, Sylvie 40; *Skin Crime 3 38*
Flink, James J. 10, 12–13, 368
Foldes, Professor Tom 360–1
Ford, Edsel 31, 137, 321
Ford, Henry 18, 25, 60, 64, 66,
116, 117, 129, 138, 146, 322
Ford cars: advertising 356, 360–1;
in art 41, 91; Edsel 328–9, *333*;
in films 86, 97, 99, 103; Model
T 66, *118*, 127, *128*, 140, 318,

322, 371–2, 374; Mustang 135,
329; Packard *131*, 137, *332*; road-
ster 18; Rotunda *331*; Taunus
222, 223; Thunderbird 33, 99,
272–3
Ford (company) 30, 31–2, 126–7,
135, 137, 140, 166, 272, 365;
plants *118*, *119*, *121*, *128*, 129–31,
129, 132, *135*, 319
Forster, E. M. 50, 55–6
Fourie, Charl 219, 220
The French Connection 101–2, 105
Freud, Sigmund 14, 51, 285
Fried, Michael 91
Friedberg, Anne 88
Fuchs, Bohuslav 346
Fuller, Richard Buckminster 29,
343, 356, 372–6
Funahashi, Atsushi: *Echoes* 84
The Fury 102

Gaddis, William 96
Galbraith, John Kenneth 234, 276
Gaz 166, 167, 181
Geddes, Norman Bel 29, 255
General Motors 30–1, 125, 135,
136–7, 140, 188, 267, 270, 363;
advertising 355–6; Building
137; Technical Center 132, *321*,
322–3
Genevieve 311
Gervais, Paul 25
The Getaway 95, 108
Giant 99, 101
Gibson, Cleo 66
Gim 180
Ginsberg, Allen 244
Ginzburg, Carlo 232
Glancey, Jonathan 287
Godard, Jean-Luc 76, 91, 102, *see
also Week-end*
Goddard, Judith 92–3
Goodwin, Doris Kearns 266
Goodwin, Phil 303–4
Gordy, Berry 134
Gottmann, Jean 276
Graham (car) 103
Grahame, Kenneth 50; *The Wind
in the Willows* 54–5, *55*
Grand Prix 101, 102–3
The Grapes of Wrath 86, 97, 114

The Great Race 99, 103
Green, Andy 378
Gropius, Walter 345
Gruen, Victor 133, 260, 261–3,
273
Guns of Darkness 97
Gunter, Arthur 'Hardrock' 70
Guyton, Tyree: street art *49*

Hail, Hail, Rock and Roll 73
Haley, Bill 68
Hall, Peter 283, 285–7
Hamilton, Richard 34, 89
Häring, Hugo 345
Harlow, Jean 98
Hatari 98, 99
Hawks, Howard 17, 86, 99, 108
Hazleton, Lesley 365
Heidegger, Martin 19, 147–8, 149,
150, 228, 230
Hein, Birgit and Wilhelm 92
Hemingway, Ernest 50
Hepworth, Cecil 83
Hickey, Dave 89
Hill, Bertha Chippie 66
Hill, Walter 106, *see also Driver*
Hillier, Bevis 359
Hine, Thomas 357
History Lessons 92
Hitchcock, Alfred 84, 91, 97–8,
106, 109
Hitler, Adolf 117, 266, 267, 348
Hockney, David 37, 285; *BMW
850C5I 'Art Car'* 36
Holly, Buddy 60, 61, 62–3, 73
Hopper, Edward 173; *Gas 45*
How to Read a Film 107
Howard, John T. 268
HRG 342
Huston, John 88, 101, 102
Hutter, Ralf 288, 291, 292
Huxley, Aldous 50–1

Illich, Ivan 114
Independent Group (Institute of
Contemporary Arts) 89
Irwin, Robert 39
Isherwood, Christopher 50
Isotta Fraschini 84, 98
It's a Gift 97

Jack, Wolfman 13, 105
Jackson, J. B. 256–7
Jackson, Judith: *Every Woman's
Guide to the Car* 366
Jacobs, Jane 12, 324
Jaguar 35, 84
James, Henry 50, 254
Jameson, Fredric 287
Jan and Dean 73
Jaray, Paul 346
Jefferson, Blind Lemon 66
Johns, Jasper 91
Johnson, Robert 66–7
Johnstone, Steve 91
Jones, George 59, 64
Jones, Jesse 267
Jones, Verity 305
Jordan, Ned 363
Joyce, James 54
Jünger, Ernst 147–8
Junior Bonner 101
J. W. Coop 110–11

Kahlo, Frida 130
Kahn, Albert 116, 129, 132
Keaton, Buster 96–7
Kennedy, John F. 51, 176
Kerouac, Jack 255, 359; *On the
Road* 250, 258, 271, *271*
Kerr, Joe 12
Keystone Kops 99, 101, 113, 114,
313
Khan, Albert 318–21
Kienholz, Edward 91; *The Back
Seat Dodge 49*
King, Charles Brady 126
King, Martin Luther 134
King, Stephen: *Christine* 58, 355
Kings of the Road 77, 79
Kipling, Rudyard 50
Knudsen, William 131, 267
Koichi, Shimakawa 141
Komanosuke, Uchiyama 139
Koolhaas, Rem 326
Kraftwerk: and *Autobahn* 288–9,
290, *290*, 291, 292
Kubelka, Peter 91
Kustom Kar Kommandos 34, 88,
99, 344
Kwei, Kane 38

La Salle 31

Lada 155: *156*; 158, 162, 164–6, *164*, 172, 176, 191–8, 204

Lanyon, Peter 91

Larkin, Philip 231

Lartigue, Henri 34

The Last Picture Show 105

Lăstun 202, *203*, 204

Latour, Bruno 228, 228–9

Laurel and Hardy 97, 99

Lawrence, D. H. 51, 54

Lawrence, David 291, 291–2

Lawrence of Arabia 93

Le Corbusier 29, 31, 260, 262, 308, 315–18 *passim* 22, 23, 320, 324, 326, 328

Le Parc, Julio 32

Leach, Dirk 19–20

Leavis, F.R. 50

Ledwinka, Hans 346, 347, 348, 349, 352

Lee, Raymond 98, 99

Lei Feng 181–2, *182*

Lenin, Vladimir Ilyich: car *121*

Lenoir, Etienne 10

Leone, Mario 17–18

Lepape, Georges: *Vogue* cover design *28*

Levitt, Dorothy: *The Woman and the Car* 365

Leys, Simon 180

Lichtenstein, Roy 34, 37; *BMW 3201* 'Art Car' *36*

Lillard, Richard 277–8

Lincoln 99; Cosmopolitan 62; Zephyr Coupe 70

Lindqvist, Sven 232

The Line Up 105

Liston, Virginia 66

Liu Xinwu 184–5

Loewy, Raymond 356, 361

Longo, Robert: *Love Police 48*

Loos, Adolf 29

Lowell, Robert 57

Lozier: advertisement *330*

Lu Xun 177

Lucas, F.L. 50

Lucas, George 17; *American Graffiti* 13, 105–6; *THX 1138* 106

Lucas, Sarah 41, 91

Lumière brothers 83

Lye, Len: *Rhythm* 88

Lynch, Kevin: *The Image of the City* 287

Lynd, Helen and Robert 12, 13

McArthur, Colin 107

McFadyen, Jock: *Horse Lamenting the Invention of the Motor Car* 90, 91

MacKaye, Benton 255, 275

McLuhan, Marshall 102, 290–1, 292, 367

MacNeice, Louis 50

McQueen, Steve 95, 101

Les Machines célibataires 102

The Magnificent Ambersons 83–4, *83*, 88, 107

Malcolm X 134

The Man on the Flying Trapeze 107

Manchester, William 271

Mandela, Nelson 221, *222*

Mao Zedong 181, *181*, 182, 186–7

Marchand, Roland 355

Marcuse, Herbert 285

Marinetti, F. T. 22, 25, 27, 34, 51, 52, 312

Marples, Ernest 281

Maruti 218

Matisse, Henri 28, 89, 91

Maybach, Wilhelm 10

Mead, Julia 359

Mendelsohn, Erich 320

Mercedes Benz 84, 99, 152, 160, 183, 343; Gull-wing *37*; in South Africa 221, *222*

Metropolis 88, 106, 341

Metz, Christian 98, 107

Michaux, Henri 33

Mies van der Rohe, Ludwig 322, 323

Milgram, Stanley: *Obedience to Authority* 95

Millar, Jeremy 192

The Misfits 101, 110

Mitsubishi 140, 176

Moholy Nagy, László 29

Moore, Henry 35

Morris: Cowley 222; Marina 192; Mini 92, 222, 343; Minor 344; Oxford 209

Moses, Robert 244–8, 268, 308, 324

Moskvich 155, *155*, *157*, 158, 158–60, 162–4, 191–2, *193*–4

Mulvey, Laura 94

Mumford, Lewis 231, 274

Nabokov, Vladimir: *Lolita* 271

Nader, Ralph 135, 329

Nash: Ambassador 99; family sedan 267

Nekes, Werner 92

Nelson, Michael Jagamara 37

Nervous Norvus 73

The New Centurions 107, 114

Nicholson, Ben 89, 91

Nissan: Bluebird 41

North by Northwest 84, 109

Oakey, Philip 289–90

Ochoa, Eliades 176

O'Connell, Sean 364

O'Donnell ,Lynn 188

O'Hara, Frank 51, 101

Olds, Ransom E. 126

Oldsmobile 17, 68

Oliver, Eli 128

Oltcit 202–3, *202*, 204

Opel Kadett 191, 200, *207*

Opie, Julian 291

Orozco, Gabriel: *La DS 40*, *40*

Ortiz Torres, Rubén: *Alien Toy 39*, *40*

Orwell, George 50

Otomogo 139–40

Otto, Nicolaus 10

Ozenfant, Amédée 31

Painlevé, Jean 345

Panamarenko: *Prova Car 46*

Panhard et Levassor 343, 349–52

Panhard (car) 349–53; Dynamic 347, *349*, 350, 351, 352, *352*; PL17 350–1, *350*, *351*, 352

Parr, Martin 231, 291–2

Pasolini, Pier Paolo 98

Paul, Les 67

Pawley, Martin 287

Penn, Arthur 95–6, 103

Performance 84–5

Perry, Stuart 10

Peterson, Ray 73

Peugeot (car) 81, 176, 344, 350; advertising campaign for 106 367–70

Phillips, Sam 68, 70

Picabia, Francis 27–8, 30, 89; *The Child Carburetor 42*

Pimenov, Yuri: *New Moscow* 162, *163*

Pla, Josep 171

Play Time 85, 88

Plowden, Ben 303

Plymouth (car) 103; Belvedere V-8 169; Fury 355

Pobeda 155

Pollock, Jackson 17, 30, 51, 86, 111, 359, 361

Pontiac 111, 171, *172*

Porsche, Ferdinand 348, 349

Porsche (car): 911 sports car 349; Dean's 550 Spyder *11*, 17, 37, 86, 99, 101; KdF-Wagen 348

Potts, Don 35

Presley, Elvis 63, *63*–4, 64, 74; Cadillacs 60, *61*–2, 69, 70–1, 72, 362

Price, Cedric 282, *283*, 285

Priestley, J. B. 51, 52, 234

Prouvé, Jean 345

Psycho 91, 97–8, 106

Rauschenberg, Robert 32–3, 34, 37

Ray, Man 92

Ray, Satyajit 214

Rebel Without a Cause 33–4, 37, 86, *87*, 100, 103, 105

Red Flag limousine 180, 182, *186*, 187–8

The Reivers 101

Renard, Claude-Louis 32

Renault Clio 366, *366*

Renault (company) 32–3, 37, 51, 200, 203

Reuther, Walter P. 116

Richard, Little 68, 70, 73, 74

Rio, Dolores del 98–9

Rist, Pippilotti 41

Rivera, Diego 22–3, 30, 31–2, 130; *Detroit Industry 44*; *Edsel B. Ford 30*

Rivers, Larry 34

Roberts, Henry Flood 18
Robie, Frederick C. 318
Rockwell, Norman: *The Farmer Takes a Ride* 29
Roja 214
Rolls-Royce 57, 84–5, 98, 99
Rosenberg, Harold 247, 359
Rosenquist, James 34; *Ultra-Violet Cars 34*
Rossellini, Roberto: *Viaggio in Italia* 85, *92*, 93–4
Ruscha, Ed 91; *Standard Station 45*
Russell, Ken: *Aria* 88
Russolo, Luigi: *Dynamism of an Automobile* 25, *26*

Saarinen, Eero 132, 322–3, 326
Sarafian, Richard *see Vanishing Point*
Scarface 114
Scarpitta, Salvatore 35
Scharoun, Hans 345
Schlemmer, Oskar 27
Schneider-Esleben, Florian 288, 291, 292
Schoffer, Nicolas 32
Schrader, Paul: *Blue Collar* 88
Schult, Emil: artwork for Kraftwerk's *Autobahn* 290, 292
Scorpio Rising 88, 101
Scott Brown, Denise 324, 325–6, 326
Segal, George 34
Seisakusho, Tokyo Jodosha 139
Self, Colin 89
Selye, Hans 95
Sennett, Mack 19, 97, 99
Sentries under the Neon 177
Severini, Gino 35
Shao Xunmei 177
Sheeler, Charles 130; *American Landscape 43*; *Industry 129*
Shintaro, Yoshida 139
Shri 227
Shuler, Dustin: *Spindle 241*
Shurcliffe, Arthur and Sidney 273
Siegel, Don 95, 105, 108
Silk, Gerald 27
Sinclair, Andrew 107
Siquieros, Alfaro 30, 39

Sironi, Mario 32; *Fiat 1900 24*
SITE: *The Ghost Parking Lot Project 47*
Skanfrom 289
Skateboard Kings 106
Skoda (car) 204; (company) 198
Sleeper 105
Slither 108–9
Sloan, Alfred P. 355, 358
Smith, Bessie 60
Smith, Tony 91
Snow, Edgar 186
Snow, Michael: *Seated Figures* 91
Soto, Jesús Rafael 32
Sparke, Penny 368
Springsteen, Bruce 362
Stagecoach 256
Starr, Georgina 91
Steel Cowboy 111, 113–14
Stein, Gertrude 50
Stella, Frank 35, 37
Stella, Joseph 27
Stokowski, Leopold 378
Stout, William 372
Stovall, Vern *63*
The Street-fighter 106
Studebaker (car) 85, 357
Su Xiaokang 184
Sugarland Express 111
Sunset Boulevard 84, *84*
SUV (Sports Utility Vehicle) 20

Takis 32
Talbot 28, 200
Targets 108
Tati, Jacques 85
Tatra 344, *345*, 346–9, *346*, *347*, *348*, 352
Taxi Driver 99, 100
Teige, Karel 346
Thelma and Louise 14, *15*, 367
They Came to a Ferry 105
Thieves Like Us 13, 14
Thomas, Hugh 170
Thomas, Ramblin' 66
Thomson, Robert 302–3
The 300 Yard Drive 98
THX 1138 106
Tico 204–5, *205*
Tinguely, Jean 33

Togliatti, Palmiero 192
Torao, Yamaha 139
Total Recall 89, *89*
Toulouse-Lautrec, Henri de 25
Toyota (corporation) 136, 140, 183, 222
Toyota Landcruiser 227
Trabant 117, *122*, 174–5, 204, *205*, 336
Train Entering a Station 83
Two Lane Blacktop 110, *111*

Übelacker, Erich 347

Valentino, Rudolf 98
Van Allen, William 321
The Vanishing 78, *79*, 81–2
Vanishing Point 75–8, 103, *104*, 110, 112
Vasarely, Victor 32
Venturi, Robert 324, 325–6, 326
Vertigo 84, 91
Viaggio in Italia 92, 93–4
Virilio, Paul 88, 91, 232
Voisin 28, 98
Volga 155, *157*, 162, 166, 180
Volkswagen (car) 84, 105, 291, 348, 349, 352; Beetle 367; camper van 343; Citigolf 222; Passat 370, *370*; Umwelt 367, *367*; Variant 223
Volkswagen (company) 19, 188, 198, 222
Von Dutch 37, *37*, 38, 38–9
Vostell, Wolf 33; *V.O.A.E.X. 33*

Wajcman, Judy 368
Walker, George 10–11
Warhol, Andy 18, 33, 34, 37, 89; *Green Disaster 33*
Wark, Penny 365
Warsaw (car) 180
Wartburg 204
Washboard Sam 66
Waters, John 292
Waugh, Evelyn 50; *Scoop* 298
Wayne, John 98, 99, 108, 112
Week-end 18, *19*, 58, *77*, 78–81, *80*, 85–6, 103, 307
Welch, Kenneth C. 273
Welles, Orson *see The Magnificent*

Ambersons
Wenders, Wim 92, *see also Kings of the Road*
Wharton, Edith 50
White, E. B. 356
Who'll Stop the Rain 107–8, 112
Whyte, William H. 276
The Wild Bunch 83–4
Williams, Hank 59–60, *60–1*, *61*, 62, 63, 64
Williams, Tennessee 75, 110
Wilson, Charles E. 131, 132, 270
Wilson, Edmund 50
Wines, James: *The Ghost Parking Lot Project 47*
Winning 100
Winston Flier 101
Wodicko, Krzystov 41
Wolfe, Ernie 38
Wolfe, Tom 67; *A Man in Full* 310–11
Wood, Robert E. 13
Woolf, Virginia 50
Wright, Frank Lloyd 29, 356; Robie House 318, *319*

Yeager, Chuck 18, 361
Yengeni, Tony 221
Young, Filson 25

Zabriskie Point 105
Žák, Ladislav 346
Zaporozhets 157–8, 192
Zil 162, 167